D1807488

Civil Procedure Used for Enforcement of EC Competition Law by the English, French and German Civil Courts

International Competition Law Series

Volume 24.

The titles published in this series are listed at the end of this Volume

Civil Procedure Used for Enforcement of EC Competition Law by the English, French and German Civil Courts

By

George Cumming, Brad Spitz and Ruth Janal

KLUWER LAW
INTERNATIONAL

Published by:
Kluwer Law International
P.O. Box 316
2400 AH Alphen aan den Rijn
The Netherlands
E-mail: sales@kluwerlaw.com
Website: http://www.kluwerlaw.com

Sold and distributed in North, Central and South America by:
Aspen Publishers, Inc.,
7201 McKinney Circle
Frederick, MD 21704
United States of America

Sold and distributed in all other countries by:
Turpin Distribution Services Ltd.
Stratton Business Park
Pegasus Drive
Biggleswade
Bedfordshire SG18 8TQ
United Kingdom

A CIP catalogue record for this book is available from the Library of Congress.

ISBN 978-90-411-2471-5

© 2007, Kluwer Law International BV, The Netherlands

All rights reserved. No part of this publication may be reproduced, stored in a retrieval system, or transmitted in any form or by any means, electronic, mechanical, photocopying, recording or otherwise, without prior written permission of the publishers.

Permission to use this content must be obtained from the copyright owner. Please apply to: Permissions Department, Wolters Kluwer Legal, 76 Ninth Avenue, 7th Floor, New York, NY 10011, United States of America. E-mail: permissions@kluwerlaw.com

Printed in the Netherlands.

Table of Contents

Chapter 13
German Procedure Costs and Limitation Periods 273

Chapter 14
Conclusion 279

Preface

The reform of European Competition Law resulting from the Regulation EC 1/ 2003 entered into force on 1 May 2004, placed undertakings as well as competition law practitioners, economists, arbitrators and judges, before unprecedented challenges. Decentralization of the application of the European competition law, primacy of this law when intra-community trade is affected, creation of a system of parallel competences; national courts now have, more or less, powers and obligations comparable to those of national competition authorities when they deal with damages claims on the grounds of Articles 81 and 82 EC.

However, the principle of procedural autonomy has not been put into question. Today as yesterday, Community competition law refers to the national laws the rules that apply to sanctions against anticompetitive practises taken on the basis of the European competition law.

Significant steps have been made towards harmonization of the procedural rules in Europe, which cover the allocation of the competent court (Reg. 44/ 2001), the cooperation between Member-States courts for the obtaining of evidence (Reg. 1206/2001), *res judicata* applying to judgments made by courts of Member States provided the parties and the object of the litigation are the same (Reg. 44/2001). And last but not least, the enactment of a common set of rules governing the fairness of the trial, the adversarial principle and the rights of the defence, provided for in the ECHR.

But diversity remains: this concerns the rules governing the bringing of the claim, those applicable to the principles which underlie the trial, to the function of the judge, to the collecting and use of evidence, as well as the assessment and compensation of prejudice.

Here lies the primary interest of the novel presentation proposed by George Cumming, Brad Spitz and Ruth Janal of procedural rules used by English, French and German civil and commercial courts in civil litigation involving articles EC 81 and 82.

This remarkable work offers an excellent tool for enlightening the procedural organization and the balance which has been sought between the different actors of the procedure in each of the systems they study. It also constitutes, for practitioners, a particularly useful guide by reason of its clear presentation, its exposes of doctrine and of national and European case-law as well as its bibliographical references.

In an era of increasing internationalization of economic disputes, no doubt this book will contribute to a better harmonization of the national rules of procedure in Europe, which is a factor of legal certainty for the economic actors and a guarantee for building a legal space which is truly European.

Jacqueline Riffault-Silk
President at the Court of Appeal of Paris

Introduction

This study of the enforcement of EC Articles 81 and 82 by the English, French and German courts in terms of their respective rules of civil procedure will focus on the following: first, on certain of the areas of procedure as opposed to substantive law which the European Commission identified in two documents, the Green Paper[1] and the Commission Staff Working Paper,[2] as constituting impediments to the enforcement of the Community competition rules by means of actions for damages; and second, on certain aspects of the rules of the respective national procedures which although not identified in the aforementioned documents arguably operate to impede in varying degrees the effective enforcement of EC Articles 81 and/or 82. Further, it is submitted that both the specific areas of enforcement identified in the two aforementioned Commission documents as impeding the enforcement of the EC competition rules by means of damages actions as well as those procedural aspects which are not identified therein may well vary in form and nature according to each of the three national systems of procedure examined herein. Once the particular enforcement difficulty is identified within the national system of procedure in relation to the enforcement of EC Articles 81 and 82 the analysis will then proceed to the next stage: namely, the application of the doctrine of effectiveness and in some

1. Green Paper 'Damages Actions for Breach of the EC Anti -Trust Rules' COM (2005) 672 (19.12.2005) FINAL; *see generally* for a presentation of EU legislation and projects in procedural harmonization not pertaining to the enforcement of EC Art. 81 and 82 by the national courts M. Freudenthal, 'The Future of European Civil Procedure' *Electronic Journal of Comparative Law* (EJCL) Vol 7.5; <www.ejcl.org/ejcl/75/art75-6.html>; Communication form the Commission to the European Parliament and the Council: A More Coherent European Contract Law: An Action Plan: COM (2003) 68 FINAL; C. Cifro, 'First Steps Towards the Harmonisation of Civil Procedure: The Regulation Creating a European Enforcement Order for Uncontested Claims' (2005) 24 CJQ 200-25.
2. Commission Staff Working Paper: Annex to the Green Paper: 'Damages Actions for Breach of the EC Anti-Trust Rules SEC (2005) 1732 (19.12.2005).

cases the doctrine of non-discrimination in order to provide a possible procedural solution in terms of the national rules of procedure. However, the application of the doctrine of effectiveness will require consideration of the fundamental principles which underlie the respective English, French and Germans systems of civil procedure.

The next stage will consist of an analysis of certain aspects of the English French and German systems of civil procedure which constitute enforcement difficulties for EC competition damages actions. Subsequent to that analysis, it will then be necessary to consider whether the doctrine of effectiveness and or non-discrimination may intervene so as to require changes in the form of the national procedural rules. In the event that the doctrine of effectiveness does require certain modifications of the national procedure an attempt will then be made to propose the possible form that these modifications may take: it is submitted that the procedural modifications which will be proposed, in turn, may be justified according to the doctrine of effectiveness in terms of their being necessary in order to ensure adequately effective enforcement of EC Articles 81 and 82.

A.   DOCTRINE OF EFFECTIVENESS

Before first analysing the procedural aspects identified by the Commission in the Green Paper and the Commission Staff Working Paper and second, those procedural aspects which are not considered therein, it is appropriate to consider the nature of the EC doctrine of effective enforcement.[3] Arguably, there are two basic principles which are involved in the enforcement by the national courts of EC law generally and in particular EC competition law in terms of the use of the national rules of procedure: the first principle is that of primacy or supremacy of EC law in relation to national law. This principle establishes that where a conflict exists between a provision of national law and EC law, the EC law provision must

---

3. *See generally* M. Struys, 'Le Droit communautaire et l'application des règles procédurales
    nationales' (2000) J.T.D.E 49; S. Prechal' Community Law in National Courts: the Lessons
    from van Schiyndel' (1998) C.M.L.R. 681; S. Perchal, *Directives in EC Law*, (2nd ed (Oxford
    University Press 2005) *see* ch 7 generally; P. Girerd, 'Les principes d'équivalence et d'effecti-
    vité: encadrement ou désencadrement de l'autonomie procédurale des Etats membres?' (2002)
    RTDE (38) 75–102; Himsworth, 'Things Fall Apart: The Harmonisation of Community Judicial
    Procedural Protection Revisited' (1997) ELRev 291; W. van Gerven 'Of Rights, Remedies and
    Procedures '(2000) C.M.L.R. 501, P. Oliver 'Le Règlement 1/2003 et les Principes d'Efficacité et
    d'Equivalence' (2005) CDE 352 at 354 describes the doctrine of effectiveness and equivalence as
    exceptions to the rule of procedural autonomy which in turn he relates to the principle of sub-
    sidarity: 'Il ne faut pas perdre de vue le fait que ces deux principes constituent des exceptions au
    principe que l'on pourrait appeler le principe de l'autonomie procédurale des ordres juridiques
    nationaux. L'ensemble de ces principes remontent aux arrâts Comet et Rewe et ont été confirmés
    à de nombreuses reprises depuis lors. Le principe de l' 'autonomie procédurale' qui relève du
    principe de subsidiarité veut qu'il appartienne aux Etat membres de prévoir leurs propres pro-
    cédures et voies de droit pour la mise en œuvre du droit communautaire par leurs juridictions'.

prevail. However, the principle of primacy does not necessarily require that in terms of the rules of civil procedure a provision of EC law must always be enforced by means of specific changes to the national system of procedure. Advocate General Jacobs observes: 'the principle of primacy does not prevent a Member State from extending to EC claims limits or conditions applicable to national claims merely because the claims are based upon EC law'.[4]

The second principle establishes that enforcement of EC law by the national courts must be effective and non discriminatory. However, arguably this principle or doctrine has some restrictions on the scope of its application: Advocate General Jacobs observes that:

The principle of effectiveness of EC law requires no more than proper application of EC law and adequate remedies for the breach of EC rights. Proper application of the law does not necessarily mean that there can be no limits on its application. The interest in full application must be balanced against considerations such as legal certainty, sound administration and the orderly conduct of proceedings by the Court . . . I should like to suggest that the European Court's case law can be assessed in terms of the need to achieve the appropriate balance between on the one hand the need for national courts to provide protection for Community rights involved in the national courts and on the other, the importance of respecting within appropriate limits the procedural and indeed organizational autonomy of the Member States' legal system.[5]

---

4. F. Jacobs QC, 'Enforcing Community Rights and Obligations in National Courts and Striking the Balance' in J. Lonbay, & A Biondi, *Remedies for Breach of EC Law* (London, Wiley, 1997) at p 25.
5. F. Jacobs QC, 'Enforcing Community Rights and Obligations in National Courts and Striking the Balance' *ibid.* in J. Lonbay & A. Biondi, *Remedies for Breach of EC Law* (Wiley, London, 1997) at p. 27; G. de Burca, 'National Procedural Rules and Remedies: the Changing Approach of the Court of Justice' in Remedies for Breach of EC Law, J. Lonbay & A Biondi, *Remedies for Breach of EC Law* (London, Wiley, 1997) *ibid.*, 37 at 45 observes: 'It would however appear that the approach adopted by the Court in van Schijndel and Peterbroeck is one which attempts to steer somewhere between the strong principle of supremacy and effectiveness outlined in Simmenthal and the ready deference to national rules seen in Johnson. The two most recent rulings despite the fact that their reasoning is far from satisfactory seem to take the view that in order to determine whether a given national rules renders the exercise of a community right excessively difficult, the reasons for the application of that general rule in the context of the case should be examined to see whether it is justified. Thus the question of excessive restrictiveness would seem to depend upon the precise details and circumstances of the individual case. This suggests more of a balanced and reasoned approach than has been seen in many earlier cases but it obviously makes predictions difficult and complicates the role of the national court'. De Burca is no doubt accurate in stating that the determination of excessive restrictiveness depends upon the details of the case. Notwithstanding, it still remains possible to consider the rules of civil procedure in abstracto, that is, independent of their application to facts. The analysis in abstracto of national rules is the basis of both the Commission Green Paper (Dec 2005) on damages actions op.cit., and the Commission Staff Working Paper (2005) op.cit. and that of the instant analysis.

In applying what might be termed the doctrine of effectiveness and non-discrimination the ECJ however established in cases such as San Giorgio[6] the general limits to the scope of the application thereof in the following terms:

> In the absence of Community rules on the subject, it is for the domestic legal system of each Member State to determine the procedural conditions governing actions at law intended to ensure the protection of the rights which individual derive from the direct of effect of Community law, provided. However, this is provided that such conditions of enforcement are not less favourable than those relating to similar actions of a domestic nature nor framed so as to render virtually impossible or excessively difficult the exercise of rights conferred by EC law.

1.   Balancing of National Principles and the Application
      of the Doctrine of Effectiveness

This relatively straight forward approach to the matter of enforcement based upon the application of the doctrine of effectiveness and non-discrimination and, implicitly, the doctrine of supremacy, may gradually lead, however, to the development of a series of additional principles: in essence, by taking into consideration the notion of the autonomy of the national courts the ECJ has arguably come to restrict, somewhat, the application of the doctrine of effectiveness and non-discrimination in the following manner: the doctrine is to be applied to national substantive law and procedure by taking into account their position within the national legal system in order to ascertain whether or not the national restriction on the enforcement of EC Law and in particular EC competition law can be said to be reasonable or not. Arguably, it is only if the restriction on the enforcement is unreasonable in the sense that there is no justification in the principles underlying the national system of civil procedure that the doctrine of effectiveness and non-discrimination would apply to as to effect a change in the national system of procedure or substantive law.[7] Perchal[8] describes this process as the application of the test of reasonableness in the following terms:

---

6. *Amministrazione delle Finanze dello Stato v. SpA San Giorgio* Case 199/82 [1983] ECR 3595; *see also*, *Comet Case* 45/76, [1976] ECR 2043; *Rewe Case* 33/76 [1976] ECR 1989; and *V. Manfredi v. Lloyd Adriatico Assicurazioni*: joined cases C-295/04 – C 289/04, Date of judgment: 13 July 06: <www. curia.europa.eu>.
7. M. Struys 'Le Droit communautaire et l'application des règles procédurales nationales' (2000) J.T.D.E. 67 March: quaere whether a national rule of procedure, which although rendering the application of EC Art. 81 and 82 impossible or very difficult, could nevertheless be justified in terms of the national principles.
8. S. Perchal, 'Community Law in National Courts: the Lessons from van Schijndel' (1998) 35 CMLR 681, *op.cit.* at 687.

Time limits, standing rules, rules about evidence, rules limiting the submissions of new arguments, restriction son raising new pleas, restriction on damages, rules about the payment of interest, concepts as abuse of rights, etc. have usually been introduced into the national legal system for certain valid reasons. Therefore, they should not be dismissed for the simple reason that they serious hamper the application of Community law provisions. The conflict should be resolved through a balancing exercise between the interests which are served by the national rules at issue and the effectiveness of Community law. Obviously, the principles or aims underlying these rules must as such be compatible with the Community legal order. Moreover, the Court seems to find it important that the principle at issue is part of the legal heritage common to the Member States.

Perhaps the two cases of *Van Schijndel*[9] and *Peterbroeck*[10] are the most striking examples of this recent development of the ECJ's approach to procedural enforcement by the national courts. In *van Schijndel*, a reference from the Netherland's Supreme Court, the applicant challenged compulsory membership in an occupational health arrangement for physiotherapists. In challenging this compulsory scheme the applicant sought to rely on EC competition law for the time in the Supreme Court whose jurisdiction was limited to the Netherlands law to correcting errors of law made by the Court below within the framework of the dispute as defined by the parties in their pleadings. The ECJ held that EC law and in particular the doctrine of effectiveness and non-discrimination did not require the creation of a national law in order to permit a court to raise a point of EC law of its own motion in the following circumstances: namely, where that obligation would oblige the court to go beyond the ambit of the dispute defined by the parties and to rely upon facts not pleaded by them.

In *Peterbroeck*, the issue was a procedural rule preventing litigants from raising new pleas before the Belgian Court of Appeal after the expiry of a 60 day period from the lodging by the administration of a copy of the contested administrative decision. This rule also prevented the Court of Appeal from raising new pleas of its own motion. The tax payer, Peterbroeck, sought to challenge a decision of the tax authorities on the basis of Art. 52 of the EC Treaty. The ECJ held however, that on the facts of the case, unlike in *van Schijndel*, the national rule of procedure was inconsistent with EC law. In developing the principle that a rule of national procedure must not make reliance on EC law 'virtually impossible or 'excessively difficult' the ECJ observed:

For the purposes of applying these principles, each case which raises the question whether a national procedural provision renders application of the Community law impossible or excessively difficulty must be analysed by

---

9. *Van Schijndel v. Stichting Pensioenfonds voor Fysiotherapeuten*, Case C-430, 431/93 (1995) ECR I 4705.
10. *Peterbroeck v. Belgian State* Case C-312/93 [1995] ECR I 4599.

reference to the role of that provision in the procedure, its progress and its special features viewed as a whole before the various national instances. In the light of that analysis the basic principles of the domestic judicial system such as the protection of the rights of the defence, the principle of legal certainty and the proper conduct of t he procedure must where appropriate be taken into consideration.[11]

The ECJ concluded that while such a 60 day period was not objectionable in itself, nevertheless the rule was unjustifiable given the following situation: the Court of Appeal was the first court able to make a reference for advice to the ECJ. This national rule prevented the Court of Appeal from raising its own motion at the hearing the question of compatibility of the contested measure since the 60 day period had already elapsed. No other court or tribunal could consider that question. This national rule which prevented issues being raised by a court of law of its own motion was not, therefore, reasonably justifiable by principles such as legal certainty or the proper conduct of procedure. It may be that the ECJ also considered the nature of the proceedings to be of determinative nature:[12] namely, that in *van Schijndel*, the proceedings were party to party and that normally, it is for the parties to define their interests without the intervention of the Court. In contrast, the proceedings in *Peterbroeck* were effectively administrative in nature: while it is clear that normally challenges to administrative acts should be brought quickly, it would appear that a 60 day period was in the circumstances unjustifiably short in relation to what existed in other administrations. The result of this rule was that the rights of the defence were unreasonably restricted in favour of rapid resolution of eventual administrative disputes.

An additional example of the application of the doctrine of effectiveness and non-discrimination is to be found in the ECJ judgment in *Crehan*[13] at paragraph 29 therein:

> However in the absence of Community rules governing the matter, it is for the domestic legal system of each Member State to designate the courts and tribunals having jurisdiction and to lay down the detailed procedural rules governing actions for safeguarding rights which individuals derive directly from Community law provided that such rules are not less favourable than those governing similarly actions (principle of equivalence) and that they do not render practically impossible or excessively difficult the exercise of rights

---

11. *van Schinjndel v. Stichting Pensionenfonds voor Fysiotherapeuten*, Case C-430, 431/93 [1995] ECR I 4705 *op. cit.* at para. 19 and *Peterbroeck v. Belgian* State Case C-312/93 [1995] ECR I 4599 *ibid.* at para. 20.
12. G. de Burca, 'National Procedural Rules and Remedies: The Changing Approach of the Court of Justice' in J. Lonbay, & A. Biondi *Remedies for Breach of EC Law* (London, Wiley, 1997), *op.cit.*
13. *Courage Ltd. v. Bernard Crehan*, Case C 435/99 [2001]ECR I-6297.

conferred by Community law (principle of effectiveness) *see* Case C-261/95 Palmisini (1997) ECR I-4025 at para. 27).

2.   DOCTRINE OF NON-DISCRIMINATION (EQUIVALENCE)

As noted above, the second doctrine developed by the ECJ in order to ensure the effective application of EC law by the national courts in terms of their rules of procedure is that of non-discrimination or equivalence. Indeed, in Pasquini[14] the ECJ observed that the doctrine of non-discrimination was simply the expression of the principle of fundamental equality of treatment:[15]

> Paragraph 70: The principle of equivalence which requires that two comparable situations, one of Community origin and the other purely internal, should be subject to the same rules, is in fact simply an expression of the principle of equal treatment which is one of the fundamental principles of Community law.

Perchal[16] observes with respect to the doctrine of equivalence which he describes as 'non-discrimination':

> The principle of non-discrimination, which requires that the relevant rules cannot be less favourable than those relating to similar actions of domestic nature, has not generated many spectacular results. Only in a few case has the Court made plain that special (less favourable) rules introduced by the Member States for certain Community law claims could not be upheld.

---

14. *Pasquini v. INPS* Case C 34/02 at point 70.
15. P. Oliver, 'Les Principles d'Efficacité et d'Equivalence', (2004) CDE 351 *op.cit.* at 359 observes that it necessary to distinguish this principle of non discrimination from EC Art. 12 which prohibits discrimination on the basis of nationality. "Le principe d'équivalence n'est pas à confondre avec l'article 12 CE qui interdit la discrimination en raison de la nationalité" It is clearly unrelated to EC Art. 12. In *EDIS v. Ministero delle Finanze*, Case C-231/96 at paragraphs 36 the ECJ held: 'Observance of the principle of equivalence implies for its part, that the procedural rule applies without distinction to actions alleging infringements of Community law and to those alleging infringements of national law to the same kind of charges or dues. That principle cannot however be interpreted as obliging a Member State to extend its most favourable rules governing recovery under national law to all action for payment or dues levied in breach of Community law' *See also*: M. Struys, 'Le droit communautaire et l'application des règles procédurales nationales' (2000) J.T.D.E. No. 67, *op.cit.*, argues that the primary difficulty in applying the principle of equivalence is the comparability of situations: 'Cette seconde condition peut, au niveau de son application, engendrer certaines difficultés en termes de comparabilité des situations'. This in contrast to the case of *Kraaijeveld*, Case C-72/95 ECR I 5431; W. van Gerven, 'Of Rights, Remedies and Procedures' (2000) CMLR 501 at 534 feels that if the doctrine of effectiveness is raised to the level of adequate as opposed to minimal effectiveness the reliance upon the doctrine of non-discrimination will be reduced.
16. S. Prechal 'Community law in the National Court: the Lessons from *van Schijndel*' (1998) 35 CMLR 681 *op.cit.* at 687.

Interestingly, more recent case law illustrates the potential possessed by the principle of non-discrimination. A good example is the *Draehmphael* case (C-180/95). In this case the Court found, inter alia, that a ceiling on the possible amount of compensation payable for discrimination was unacceptable because there was no equivalent in other rules of German labour law. Although it has been observed that the decision as to what is a 'similar action of domestic nature' is sometimes far from clear (*Jacobs,* Opinion in Case C 312/93 *Peterbroeck* paras 20–27) the application of the non-discrimination principle has only been addressed by the ECJ very recently. In *Palmisani*, at least the Court indicates the two elements to be taken into account: the objective pursued by the relevant rules and the essential characteristics of the rules at issue.

It is submitted, however, that the doctrine of equivalence operates in a manner which is not entirely dissimilar to that of effectiveness. There are two steps in its application: first, it is necessary to establish whether the procedural restriction is reasonable. Arguably, the test of reasonableness is established in terms of the principle of effectiveness which implicitly by reason of cases such as *Peterbroek and van Schyndel* requires that the principles of national procedure be considered. For example, in *EDIS*[17] which involved the limitation period for recovery of money wrongly paid to fiscal authorities under EC legislation, there were effectively two limitation periods: one which applied to recovery of overpayment in fiscal or tax matters and one which applied to recovery of overpayment in non-fiscal matters, clearly a much larger category: the limitation period for recovery in fiscal matters was three years whereas as that for non-fiscal recovery was ten years. The ECJ summarized the position of the parties as follows:

> Paragraph 32: According to the three governments which have submitted observations a Member State is entitled in fiscal matters to impose a time bar different from that applicable under the ordinary law provided that it applies in the same way to claims for repayment under Community as to claims under national law that being he position in this case.

At Paragraph 35 the ECJ assesses the reasonableness of the time limit for the recovery of fiscal overpayment as reasonable:

> As regards the latter principle, the Court, as point out in paragraph 20 of this judgment has held that it is compatible with Community law to lay down reasonable limitation periods for bringing proceedings in the interest of legal certainty which protects both the taxpayer and the administration concerned. Such time limits are not liable to render virtually impossible or excessively difficult the exercise of rights conferred by Community law. In that regard, a time limit of three years under national law reckoned from the date of the contested payments appears reasonable.

---

17. *Edis v. Ministero delle Finanze*, Case C-231/96 [1998] ECR I 7141.

At Paragraph 37, the ECJ notes that the limitation periods, although reasonable, appear in different recovery regimes, one for fiscal matters and one for general matters. There is no restriction on the ability of a Member State to establish different limitation periods for different systems of recovery provided that within the same recovery system, the limitation period, established as reasonable, applies without distinction to both national and EC fiscal matters. It is only in that sense that a comparison is possible:

> Thus, Community law does not preclude the legislation of a Member State from laying down along side a limitation period applicable under the ordinary law to action between private individuals for the recovery of sums paid but not due special detailed rules which are less favourable governing claims and legal proceedings to challenge the imposition of charges and other levies. The position would be different only if those detailed rules applied solely to action based on Community law for the repayment of such charges.

In *Palisami*,[18] the ECJ also analysed the reasonableness of the limitation periods at issue before proceeding to consider the difference of the legal categories involved. This case involved a difference in limitation periods between actions for State liability in general which apparently was ten years and that established for State liability arising from non-implementation of EC legislation which was one year: there was an identical period of one year dealing with applications for compensation once the EC legislation had been implemented by the Italian government. With respect to reasonableness the ECJ observed at paragraph 29:

> Furthermore a time limit of one year commencing from the date of entry into force of the measure transposing the Directive into national law which not only enables the beneficiaries to ascertain the full extent of their rights but also specifies the conditions under which loss or damage sustained as a result of the belated transposition will be made good cannot be regarded as making it excessively difficult or a fortiori virtually impossible to lodge a claim for reparation.

The second step in the application of the doctrine of equivalence is as follows: it is necessary to ascertain either simultaneously to the analysis under the reasonableness test or subsequent thereto, whether the category or type of law in which the element of procedure involving EC law is situated comes within the same category of law in which the more favourable national procedure is located. In order to ascertain whether or not the categories are identical it is appropriate to consider their teleological function: in short, their legal purpose. It would seem that it is only if the restriction is unreasonable and if the more favourable procedural device is located in the identical category of national law that the

---

18. *Palmisani v. INPS*, Case C-261/95 [1997] ECR I-4025.

principle of non-discrimination will apply so to impose the more favourable national method of procedure on that of the EC enforcement. Accordingly, the ECJ observes in this regard in *EDIS*[19] at paragraph 36:

> That principle cannot however be interpreted as obliging a Member State to extend its most favourable rules governing recovery under national law to all action for repayment of charges and dues levied in breach of Community law.

In *Palmisani*,[20] the ECJ emphasizes the necessity of identifying the categories of law in the following manner:

> Paragraph 36: 'Since applications made in connection with the implementation of the Directive and those made under the compensation scheme laid down by it differ as to their objective there is no need to undertake a comparison of the procedural rules which govern them'.

The ECJ stated that, effectively, it was impossible to compare the ten-year limitation available for general actions involving State liability as it did not possess sufficient information in order to ascertain whether or not that system could be used in EC actions. Accordingly, if only one of these two conditions is fulfilled, as for example, the procedural restriction on the EC enforcement is reasonable but the more favourable procedural disposition applicable to national law involves a different category of law from the one in which the EC procedural disposition is found then the following situation would prevail as noted in *Palmisani* the doctrine of non discrimination does not apply. In short, it is sufficient that one of these conditions is absent in order for the doctrine of non-discrimination to not apply.

3.   CONCEPT OF ADEQUATELY EFFECTIVE ENFORCEMENT

Following *van Gerven*,[21] it would seem, however, that the application of the doctrine of effectiveness and non-discrimination appears to establish what might be termed a minimum level of procedural enforcement by national rules of EC law. Accordingly, an attempt will be made to apply the doctrine of effectiveness and non-discrimination so as to permit where possible a higher standard of enforcement of EC law by national law which might be termed 'adequate' enforcement. It is submitted that it is possible to attain such a standard particularly in those instances where the national procedure provides various procedural alternatives: one of these procedural alternatives can be said to provide more effective enforcement of EC Articles 81 and 82 in terms of

---

19. *EDIS v. Ministero delle Finanze*, Case C-231/96 (1998) ECR I 7141 *op.cit.*
20. *Palmisani v. INPS*, Case C-261/95 (1997) ECR I- 4025.
21. W. van Gerven 'Of Rights, Remedies and Procedures' (2000) CMLR 501.

implementing more fully the national principles of procedure. Indeed, it is only if the doctrine of effectiveness and non-discrimination is applied in order to achieve what might be termed 'adequate' as opposed to minimum enforcement that it is possible to make a principled decision in such cases; that is, a choice between competing solutions in national procedure for more effective enforcement of EC Articles 81 and 82 on a particular procedural matter. Accordingly, it is submitted that the doctrine of effectiveness particularly if interpreted restrictively in the literal sense of permitting procedural changes only where a national procedural rule either prevents or makes enforcement of EC law exceedingly impossible leads to the following consequence: it excludes the possibility of choosing between what might be termed more effective as opposed to less effective enforcement of EC law by national procedure. Indeed, this is particularly the case with certain of the English rules of civil procedure which will be examined herein. Therefore, it is necessary to interpret the doctrine of effectiveness and non discrimination as having as their objective the achievement of an adequate as opposed to a minimum standard for the enforcement of EC law in the manner suggested by van Gerven as follows:

> In all of these cases the real issue is whether national remedial rules are such as to ensure that individuals can obtain sufficient protection in national courts for the rights which they derive from Community law. This requires the Court to strike the correct balance between the Community law aim of protecting Community rights of individuals at a level sufficiently uniform in all of the Member States and the specific aim which the domestic remedial rule pursues in the context of the Member States' legal order. To strike such a balance, different elements must be weighed against each other, such as, on the one hand the nature of the Community right and of the Community rule from which it is derived the nature and the gravity of the breach and the seriousness of the injury cased and on the other, the nature and aim of the domestic law provision under scrutiny in light of basic principles of due process and of the defence as well as of legal certainty and good administration which part of the Member State as well as the Community's legal order. Especially because of the need to take account of the interference with the individual claimant's right, adequate protection appears to be a more appropriate yardstick than minimum protection. The true significance of this balancing approach came to the fore in the Court's judgments in *Peterbroeck* and *van Schijndel* unfortunately within the framework of minimum protection rather than of adequate protection. The 'balancing' approach as applied in *Peterbroeck* and *van Schijndel*, where the impact of a national procedural rule or principle on the effectiveness of a Community law remedy i.e., the preliminary ruling procedure was examined should as indicated above be con-sidered within the framework of the adequacy test – i.e., not preventing the remedy from being sufficiently adequate rather than as the Court did within the framework of the minimum effectiveness test i.e., not rendering the remedy virtually impossible or excessively difficult. That is so, because the latter involves too cursory a reading of national rules by looking at whether the

enforcement of Community rights are not entirely or almost entirely precluded instead of adopting the more demanding approach contained in the adequacy test which looks more positively and constructively to the level of enforcement of Community rights. In other words, it requires the (national or Community) judge to include in his balancing approach all circumstances enabling him or her to assess the role and importance of the national provision concerned including those which are intended to ensure the quality of protection which individuals can obtain for their Community rights. In particular whether the interference with and injury caused to such rights can be made good sufficiently well and whether the relief granted under a particular national legal system does not put the complainant at too large a competitive disadvantage as compared with complainant looking for similar relief in other Member States.[22]

Overall, the major thrust of van Gerven's analysis and his justification for seeking to introduce the concept of adequate national procedural enforcement, which does not exclude in certain instances the achievement of a minimum standard of enforcement, arises from the necessity of ensuring adequate as opposed to minimal protection of EU rights:[23]

The main point in the preceding analysis is the submission that the principle of adequate judicial protection of Community rights through national law

---

22.   W. van Gerven, 'Of Rights, Remedies and Procedures' (2002) CMLR 501 ibid. at 525-6. Further, it might possibly be argued that Peterbroeck is in itself an example of what may be termed more adequate as opposed to minimal enforcement: minimal enforcement was, arguably, the situation in which the litigant was able to amend his pleadings to include a point of EC law up to 60 days after the close of pleadings which period of time the ECJ considered acceptable. However, it would seem that the ECJ's decision to require modification of the Belgian legal restriction of the possibility for the court to introduce an EC point of law ex officio after the 60 day period was based on the conclusion that such a provision when coupled with the normal 60 day limitation on party amendment of pleadings provided a more effective method of enforcement as opposed to one based exclusively on the party based amendment during the 60 day period. However van Gerven observes at p. 531 as quoted above: 'The true significance of this balancing approach came to fore in the Court's judgment in Peterbroeck and van Schijndel unfortunately with the framework of "minimal protection" rather than "adequate protection" '.

23.   W. van Gerven, 'Of Rights, Remedies and Procedures' (2000) CMLR 501 at 536 seems to feel that although the distinction between rights and remedies (quaere the definition of rights as opposed to remedies in relation to procedure and procedural rights stricto senso: *see*, C.M.G Himsworth, 'Things Fall Apart' (1997) ELRev 22 291 at 308–9 in which he advances a clear case for harmonization on the basis of 'fairness' at p. 310; S. Prechal, *Directives in EC Law*, (2nd ed, Oxford, Oxford University Press, 2005) p. 134) which he has used in order to try to justify the concept of adequate enforcement may not in itself be absolutely tenable nevertheless the following is the case: namely, that overall this distinction is useful in seeking to justify the use of the concept of adequately as opposed to minimally effective enforcement with respect to the national rules of procedure used to enforce EC rights: he observes: 'Whilst the proposition that the (dogmatic) distinction between rights and remedies may be useful in reconciling the principles of effectiveness and the requirement of uniform interpretation of Community law may remain doubtful'.

remedies, rather than the principle of minimum effectiveness provides the proper test for assessing the consistency of domestic rules with Community law (in combination with the test of equivalence), the scope of application of which, will have be less than when it is used in combination with the effectiveness test and that such a test must be applied with the help of a fully fledge balancing approach in the same vein as the proportionality principle.[24]

Accordingly, in order to apply the doctrine of effectiveness in a manner which will ensure adequate enforcement of EC Articles 81 and 82 by domestic procedure it is necessary as noted earlier, to consider the fundamental principles of English, French and German civil procedure. These principles will then be taken into account in order to carry out a balancing operation in order to assist in establishing the most adequately effective method of enforcement provided by the English, French and German systems of civil procedure of EC Articles 81 and 82. It is of use, however, to bear in mind the following observations: first, the application of the doctrine of effectiveness and non-discrimination, arguably, is case sensitive: in order to obtain legal certainty, its application can be sustained and verified by a reference emanating from the national court to the ECJ pursuant to EC Art. 234; second, and perhaps, felicitously, the application of the doctrine of effectiveness in addition to producing adequately effective enforcement of EC Articles 81 and 82 may also have an unsuspected consequence; namely, the advancement of procedural reform within the context of the domestic systems of national procedure. In this regard it is perhaps useful to consider the observation made by Professor Otto Freund-Kahn:[25] 'one may say that procedural law is tough law. All that concerns the technique of legal practise is likely to resist change'. This is particularly so in so far as the doctrine of effectiveness is applied in the sense of producing not a minimum but rather an adequately or most adequately effective enforcement of EC Articles 81 and 82. It is in this context that certain of the elements of English civil procedure which will be examined herein are to be considered and evaluated.

---

24. W. van Gerven 'Of Rights, Remedies and Procedures' (2000) CMLR 501 *op.cit.* at 536. Argu-ably, by reason of the fact that van Gerven incorporates the higher level of adequate enforce-ment within the process of balancing which involves consideration of the relationship of the procedural rule to the principles within the national system of procedural the following will occur: the balancing process should serve to uphold the principle of national autonomy: see footnote 6 *supra* and in particular of Sir Francis Jacobs QC in relation to the effect of the balancing principle in upholding national procedural autonomy.
25. O. Freund-Kahn, 'On Uses and Misuses of Comparative Law', (1974) MLR 1 at p. 20 and S. Perchal 'Community Law in the National Courts: Lessons from van Schjndel' (1998) 35 CMLR 681 *op.cit.* at p. 689.

B.   PRINCIPLES UNDERLYING THE RULES OF CIVIL
            PROCEDURE OF THE ENGLISH FRENCH AND
            GERMAN ORDINARY COURTS

Following Advocate General Jacobs and the ECJ it is clear that the application of
the doctrine of effectiveness requires consideration of the fundamental principles
of the national rules of civil procedure. The ECJ referred to principles, non-
exhaustively, such as protection of the rights of the defence, legal certainty, and
the proper conduct of procedure. The Advocate General described the latter as
sound administration and the orderly conduct of proceedings by the court. As
noted these fundamental principles of the national systems of procedure arguably
serve two functions: first they serve to explain more fully the purpose of a
specific rule of the national civil procedure and more specifically the manner in
which the rule is to be applied. Following the ECJ and Advocate General Jacobs,
it is these principles which serve to assist in determining whether impediments or
difficulties created by the rules of national procedure in enforcement of EC
Articles 81 and 82 may be justifiable at least in first instance and thereby resist
changes imposed by the doctrine of effectiveness. The second function is that the
principles of the national procedure assist in demarcating the procedural
autonomy enjoyed by the ordinary national courts in terms of using their own
civil procedure in order to apply EC Articles 81 and 82. Accordingly, the basic
underlying principles of the respective systems English, French and German rules
of civil procedure will be considered.

C.   PRINCIPLES OF ENGLISH CIVIL PROCEDURE

There exist two venues for enforcement of EC competition cases in England: on the
one hand, the ordinary English courts and, on the other, a statutory tribunal, the
Competition Appeal Tribunal (CAT). Accordingly, the fundamental principles of
both the Civil Procedure Rules (CPR) of the ordinary English courts and the Rules
of the CAT will be examined in relation to certain procedural areas identified in the
Commission Green Paper and the Commission Staff Working Paper.

1.   FUNDAMENTAL PRINCIPLES

Pursuant to S 2.1 of the European Communities Act (1972) (ECA), EC Articles
81 and 82 are enforceable by the ordinary civil courts in England by reason of the
EC doctrine of direct effects. ECA S 2 (1) provides:

> All such rights, powers liabilities, obligation and restrictions from time to time
> created or arising by or under the treaties and all such remedies and procedures
> from time to time provided for by or under the Treaties as in accordance with
> the Treaties are without further enactment to be given legal effect as without

further enactment to be given legal effect or used in the United Kingdom shall be recognized and available in law and enforced, allowed and followed accordingly,; and the expression 'enforceable Community right' and similar expressions shall be read as referring to one to which this subsection applies.

In contrast to the CAT, the ordinary English civil court is able to enforce EC Articles 81 and or 82 either by means of a free standing action for damages or by means of a follow on action based upon an infringement decision rendered by the Office of Fair Trading. As noted, the ordinary civil court obtains its competence to enforce EC Articles 81 and or 82 by means of a free standing action for damages from the doctrine of direct effect. On the other hand, the ability to enforce EC Articles 81 and or 82 by means of a monetary action based upon an EC Articles 81 or 82 infringement decision taken by the Office of Fair Trading (OFT) arises by virtue of S 58 A of the Competition Act (CA) (1998) as amended by S 20 of the Enterprise Act (2002). This section provides that an OFT infringement decision involving EC Articles 81 and or 82 binds the ordinary court upon the expiration of the period for appeal of the decision.

S 58 A CA (1998) provides: Findings of Infringement
    This section applies to proceedings before the court in which damages or any other sum of money is claimed in respect of an infringement of
    . . .
    (c) the prohibition in Art. 81 (1) of the Treaty
    (d) the prohibition in Art. 82 of the Treaty
    In such proceedings, the court is bound by a decision mentioned in subsection (3) once any period specified in subsection (4) which relates to the decision has elapsed.
    The decisions are:
    . . .
    b) a decision of the OFT that the prohibition is Art. 81 (1) or Art. 82 of the Treaty has been infringed.

As of June 2004 special allocation rules came into effect for cases involving EC competition cases in the ordinary English courts wherein a claimant seeks to recover damages as a remedy for a loss caused by a breach of either EC Articles 81 or 82. Henceforth, the Practise Direction: EU Competition Law,[26] contained within the CPR ensures that all EC competition cases be commenced or transferred to the Chancery Division of the High Court. Accordingly the CPR applies as the rules of civil procedure for enforcement of EC competition cases in the ordinary court in England which is the Chancery Division.

---

26. CPR: Practise Direction: Competition Law Claims Relating to the Application of Articles 81 and 82 of the EC Treaty and Chapters I and II of Part I of the Competition Act 1998: October 2005.

The CPR were created by means of delegated legislation conferred on the Civil Procedure Committee by virtue of ss 1 and 2 of the Civil Procedure Act (1997). This process of delegated legislation follows on the S 84 (1) of the Supreme Court Act (1981) which empowered the Supreme Court Rules Committee to make rules for the High Court and S 75 of the County Courts Act (1984) which delegated the responsibility for creating the rules of civil procedure used in the County Court. *Safeway Stores PLC v. Tate*[27] established that the Civil Procedure Act does not enable delegated legislation to repeal or amend primary legislation which create fundamental rights such as for example the right to a trial by jury in certain circumstances. However the Civil Procedure Act does permit amendment of matters which deal with procedure.

The CPR, arguably, deal with two types of principles: the first type consist, implicitly, in the objective of achieving what might be termed the rectitude of the decision: that is 'the principle goal of civil procedure remains that of doing substantive justice in the sense of deciding disputes in accordance with facts and the correct application of the law'.[28] This objective is in turn related to the fundamental right of procedural fairness. 'The requirements of fair trial are timeless and universal. Rules of procedural fairness such as impartiality, publicity or the right to be heard must be observed regardless of considerations of economy, efficiency or indeed of whether they help or hinder the ascertainment of truth'.[29] The second type of principles concerns efficiency, economy proportionality in the use of resources. These principles are embodied expressly in the Overriding Objective contained in CPR 1. The Overriding Objective serves

---

27. *Safeway Stores PLC v. Tate* [2001] QB 1120.
28. A.A.S. Zuckerman, *Civil Procedure* (London, Lexis Nexis, 2003) *op.cit.* at p. 2. J. Jolowicz in I.R. Scott, *International Perspectives on Civil Justice* (London, Sweet & Maxwell,1990) at 45 presents a different view of the purpose of civil procedure: 'The process of civil litigation serves purposes other than that of doing justice to those who appear before the courts and those purposes must be reflected in the procedure': this is as opposed to what Professor Jolowicz describes as a purpose which seeks to simply solve the problem between the two litigants, that is dispute resolution: 'If the decision has been in accordance with the available evidence and with the law, then justice will have been done (Air Canada, 2 AC 394 per Lord Wilberforce). Such an approach equates justice with procedural justice: it restricts the court to a decision between rival contentions of the parties and encapsulates the dispute resolution purpose of civil litigation'. Under this classification, the EC doctrine of effectiveness envisages national civil procedure in the sense of dispute resolution. Further, Professor Jolowicz seeks to distinguish the attainment of truth by the adversarial method as opposed to judge found truth in terms of the type of evidence which may used: he observes in his *On Civil Litigation*, (Cambridge, Cambridge University Press, 2000) at p. 86 'Other things being equal, an inquisitorial type of procedure is therefore, more likely to produce the correct decision than an accusatorial or adversarial procedure where the judge's role is only to decide between the rival contentions of the parties. Whatever we may mean ultimately by a "correct decision" it would be odd to describe as correct a decision that the judge himself believes to be wrong because he was deprived of information he considered he should have had or was debarred from applying the rule of law which he thought appropriate to the case'.
29. A.A.S. Zuckerman, *Civil Procedure* (London, Lexis Nexis, 2003) *ibid.*; at p. 4.

as the basis upon which the court is to interpret the rules and exercise its discretion. This is in contrast to the situation which prevailed under the Supreme Court Rules (RSC) and the County Court Rules (CCR) where the court relied upon Common Law principles as well as principles of Equity coupled with maxims and precedents. Accordingly, by reason of its importance in terms of constituting the basis upon which the courts interpret the CPR and exercise their discretion thereto, it is necessary to consider the constituent elements of the Overriding Objective contained in CPR 1.

2.   OVERRIDING OBJECTIVE AND UNDERLYING PROCEDURAL PRINCIPLES

a.   **CPR 1 Provides the Rules Which Constitute the Overriding Objective**

CPR 1 1(1). These rules are a new procedural code with the overriding objective of enabling the court to deal with cases justly.
(2). Dealing with a case justly includes, so far as practicable:
(a) ensuring that the parties are on an equal footing
(b) saving expense
(c) dealing with the case in ways which are proportionate
    (i) to the amount of money involved
    (ii) to the importance of the case
    (iii) to the complexity of the issues and
    (iv) to the financial position of each party
(d) ensuring that it is dealt with expeditiously and fairly
(e) allotting to it an appropriate share of the court's resources which taking into account the need to allot resources to other cases.
    The court must seek to give effect to the overriding objective when it –
(a) exercises any power given to it by the Rules
(b) interprets any rule subject to rule 76.2
1.3 The parties are required to help the court to further the overriding objective
    It is submitted, therefore, that the two categories of procedural principles of the CPR, namely, those which might be said to underlie the express rules contained within the CPR and the express rules themselves correspond to the principles referred to non exhaustively by Advocate General Jacobs for the following reasons:

b.   **Underlying Principles of a Fair Trial and the Rectitude of the Decision**

It is submitted that the underlying principles of a fair trial and the rectitude of the decision may indeed include the principle of 'legal certainty' and the 'protection of the rights of the defence' particularly in the sense of fairness and respect of the rights of both parties.

c.   **Explicit Principles of the Overriding Objective**

It would appear that CPR 1, the Overriding Objective, encapsulates succinctly the principles of the 'proper conduct of procedure' noted by the ECJ in *Peterbroeck* and *van Schijndel* and the 'administration of justice' and the 'orderly conduct of proceedings'. The most proximate rule is perhaps the following: CPR 1.(1) (2) (d): 'ensuring that it is dealt with expeditiously and fairly'. It may be that the requirement of ensuring that it is dealt with . . . fairly, in addition to the CPR 2. 'Dealing with the case justly: may include also "legal certainty" '. As is noted from the text of CPR 1.2, the enumeration is not exhaustive: 'Dealing with a case justly includes. . . . '

3.   COMPETITION APPEAL TRIBUNAL (CAT)

The CAT was given competence to hear with 'monetary claims' under S 47 A of the Competition Act (CA) (1998) introduce by S 18 of the Enterprise Act (EA) (2002). Monetary claims include claims in any part of the UK for damage suffered as a result of an infringement of EC Articles 81 and or 82 contained in a decision rendered either by the (OFT) or the European Commission which has not been appealed.
    S 47 A CA (1998) provides:

47 A Monetary Claims before the Tribunal
(1) This section applies to:
a) any claim for damages, or
b) any other claim for a sum of money
In this section 'relevant prohibition' means any of the following
    . . .
the prohibition of Art. 81 (1) of the Treaty
the prohibition of Art. 82 of the Treaty
The decision which may be relied on for the purpose of proceedings under this section are:
    . . .
d) a decision of the OFT that the prohibition of the Art. 81(1) or 82 has been infringed.

Further, in terms of enforcement, the CAT has its own Statutory Rules of Procedure and accordingly, it is necessary to consider the fundamental procedural principles contained therein. These rules were adopted by the Secretary of State in exercise of the powers conferred by Schedule 4 of the Enterprise Act (2002) S

15 of and Part 2 thereof respectively. The legal basis of the CAT Rules is to be found in SI 2003 NO 1372 (2003) effective as of 20 June 2003 and applicable to all proceedings before the CAT from that date. The CAT Rules apply to damages claims under S 47A and 47B CA (1998). The Guidelines[30] issued by the CAT which have the authority of a binding Practise Direction within the CPR state *inter alia* the following principles:

> 3.1 The Rules are based upon the same general philosophy as the CPR and pursue the overriding objective of enabling the Tribunal to deal with cases justly in particular by ensuring that the parties are on an equal footing, that expense is saved and that appeals are dealt with expeditiously and fairly.
>
> To achieve this objective in the particular context of the 1998 Act, the rules are partly modelled on the CPR and partly on the rules of the procedure of the Court of First Instance. A central feature of both the CPR and the Rules of Procedure of the CFI is the Case Management by the Court.
>
> However it should be borne in mind that the Tribunal's Rules are different in various respects. Parties should not assume that the CPR or the Rules of Procedure of the CFI apply to a particular procedure.

4.   DIRECTIONS: CASE MANAGEMENT (CAT)

Art. 19 (1) of the CAT Rules provides: The Tribunal may at any time on the request of a party or of its own initiative, at a case management conference, pre-hearing review or otherwise, give such directions as are provided for in paragraph (2) below and such other directions as it thinks fit to secure the just, expeditious and economical conduct of the proceedings.

Bearing in mind S 3.3 of the Guidelines, it would appear that there is a clear relationship between the fundamental principles expressed in Art. 19 (1), notably, 'to secure the just, expeditious and economical conduct of the proceedings' and those expressed in the Overriding Objective in CPR 1.1'. As such, it is useful to recall the similarity of the principles in both the CAT Rules and the CPR in deciding whether the doctrine of effectiveness may require changes in those procedural areas where enforcement problems may exist in both the CPR and the CAT Rules in the context of the Commission Green Paper and the Staff Working Paper.

D.   PRINCIPLES OF FRENCH CIVIL PROCEDURE

Both High Courts of First Instance (*'Tribunaux de Grande Instance'* – Civil Courts) and Commercial Courts (*'Tribunaux de Commerce'*) are competent to hear claims for damages based on breach of French and EC competition law. Pursuant Article L.420-7 of the French Commercial Code, litigations relating to the application of the domestic French competition rules contained in Articles L.420-1 to L.420-5

---

30. Competition Appeal Tribunal Guide to Proceedings (October 2005).

Commercial Code and the EC rules contained in Articles 81 and 82 EC Treaty may only be brought before specific Civil Courts and Commercial Courts.

Commercial Courts have jurisdiction over litigation between traders (*'commerçants'*) in the course of their business and litigation relating to commercial instruments and contracts. Where the litigation involves a trader and a non-professional claimant, the latter may bring the case before either a Civil Court or a Commercial Court. The Commercial Courts are composed of traders, with no specific training in law, elected by their peers. However, on appeal, the commercial division of the Court of Appeal, composed by professional judges, will hear the case. A majority of competition law actions are heard by the Commercial Courts, as these actions are usually brought by professionals against other professionals.

The Civil Courts have jurisdiction to hear all matters, including actions for breach of competition law, where a prerogative court (such as the Commercials Courts for instance) does not have jurisdiction. The High Court of First instance has jurisdiction where the claim exceeds EUR 7,600; under this amount, the Court of First Instance (*'Tribunal d'Instance'*) has jurisdiction. These courts are composed of professional judges. On appeal, the civil section of the Court of Appeal entertains jurisdiction. Appeals to judgments rendered by the Court of Appeal are heard by the Supreme Court (*'Cour de Cassation'*), which only rules on legal issues, and not on factual findings. The general rules of civil procedure, set out in the Code of Civil Procedure (*'Nouveau Code de Procédure Civile'*) apply to the proceedings before all of these courts.

It should be noted that Administrative Courts have exclusive jurisdiction for the annulment of an administrative act, i.e., when delegated legislation or an act taken by a person acting with prerogatives of public authorities breaches competition law rules.[31] These courts may award damages. Moreover, Criminal Courts have exclusive jurisdiction to award damages for breach of Article 420-6 of the Commercial Code, which provides that '(i)f any natural person fraudulently takes a personal and decisive part in the conception, organization or implementation of the practises referred to in Articles L.420-1 (cartels) and L.420-2 (abuse of a dominant position), this shall be punished by a prison sentence of four years and a fine of 75,000 euros'. However, these courts have a limited role in awarding damages.

Arbitrators may also hear claims for damages based on a breach of competition law.[32] The ECJ held that in such a case, the arbitrators must apply respect the public order rules of competition law.[33]

---

31. *See* C. Momège and N. Bessot, *Comparative Report – France*, p. 4.
32. Cour de Cassation, Chambre Commerciale, *Mors v. Labinal*, 14 February 1995, quoted by C. Momège and N. Bessot, *Comparative Report – France*, op. cit., p. 13.
33. *Eco Swiss China Time Limited v. Benetton International*, Case C-126/97, [1999] *ECJ*, 3055. *See* C. Lucas de Leyssac, 'Arbitrage et concurrence: retour sur *Eco Swiss*', [2000] *Concurrences*, No. 1, p. 1 and C. Nourissat, 'La place de l'arbitrage dans le nouveau paysage communautaire de la concurrence', in *Le nouveau règlement d'application du droit communautaire de la concurrence: un défi pour les juridictions françaises*, [2004] Dalloz, p. 185.

1.   Guiding Principles

The civil proceedings are party controlled (*'principe dispositif'*): the procedures follow the adversarial system and the judge has limited prerogatives, as he is considered as a sort of arbitrator. However, in order to accelerate the proceedings and to obtain a judgment in compliance with the truth, the judge has progressively been given extended powers.

In the proceedings, the *'principe dispositif'* grants the parties important prerogatives as to bringing an action and conducting the lawsuit.[34] The parties conduct the proceeding under the duties incumbent upon them and are obliged to prepare the pleadings according to the rules of procedure within the required time limits.[35] The judge supervises the proper progress of the proceedings; he has the authority to define the time limits and order the necessary measures.[36]

As for the contentious matters, the parties have control over the facts. The parties bear the burden of establishing the facts underlying their claims.[37] The judge may not base his decision on facts that are not in the case, but may however invite the parties to provide factual explanations which he deems necessary for the resolution of the dispute,[38] and may take into consideration, amongst facts in the trial, those that the parties have not specifically put forward to support their claims. Each party must prove the facts which he alleges.[39]

As for the governing rules, the judge must settle the dispute in accordance with the rules of law applicable thereto. He must give or reapply their proper legal definitions to the disputed facts and deeds notwithstanding the interpretations thereof advanced by the parties. However, the judge may not change the construction of the legal terms or ground where the parties, pursuant to an express agreement and in the exercise of such rights which they may freely give, have bound him by legal definitions and legal arguments to which they intend to restrict the debate.[40]

2.   Guarantees

Pursuant to the directly applicable provisions of Article 6 § 1 of the European Convention on Human Rights, '(i)n the determination of his civil rights and obligations or of any criminal charge against him, everyone is entitled to a fair and public hearing within a reasonable time by an independent and impartial tribunal established by law'.

---

34. Article 1 Civil Code of Procedure.
35. Article 2 Civil Code of Procedure.
36. Article 3 Civil Code of Procedure.
37. Article 6 Civil Code of Procedure.
38. Article 8 Civil Code of Procedure.
39. Article 9 Civil Code of Procedure.
40. Article 12 Civil Code of Procedure.

Article 16 of the 1789 Declaration of the Rights of Man and the Citizen provides that '(a)ny society in which no provision is made for guaranteeing rights or for the separation of powers, has no Constitution'. Implementing this provision, the Constitutional Court (*'Conseil Constitutionnel'*) ruled that the right to be heard has a constitutional basis.[41]

The right to an independent court is based on Article 64 of the Constitution. This explains, for instance, the fact that the courts are not bound by the decisions of the French competition authority, the Competition Council (*'Conseil de la Concurrence'*). This principle can potentially, in theory at least, lead to an infringement of the doctrine of effectiveness, as this will have a potential impact on the burden of proof of the breach of competition law rules.

The right to a judgment in a reasonable time is a key element of a fair trial; according to the English adage, 'justice delayed, justice denied'. Order No. 2006-673 of 8 June 2006 provides that judgments must be rendered in a reasonable time. This notion has a variable content and the European Court of Human Rights (ECHR) considers that the matter of delay depends on the details and circumstances of the individual case. The ECHR takes into account a variety of criteria, the combination of which can lead to the finding that Article 6 § 1 has been breached. In France, the length of proceedings will depend on various factors, such as the workload that a court has to deal with, whether appeals are lodged, whether the Competition Council gives an opinion, the way in which the parties cooperate to the case,[42] and the complexity of the case (in particular as an expert may be appointed, especially in competition law cases). The delay before certain courts can be relatively long in France. Moreover, the plaintiff, who may need to request interim measure in emergency procedures (*'procédure de référé'*), will often, in competition cases, not satisfy the very strict conditions applicable in such proceedings.[43] The problem of the length of procedures may be resolved by the specialization of the courts for damages actions for breach of competition rules.

E.   PRINCIPLES OF GERMAN CIVIL PROCEDURE

1.   COMPETITION CASE ALLOCATION

Section 87 of the Act against Restraints on Competition (*Gesetz gegen Wettbewerbsbeschränkungen* – GWB) provides that damages claims for breaches

---

41. Conseil Constitutionnel, decision No. 93-335 DC, 21 January 1994, *JO* 25 January 1994, p. 1382.
42. It should be noted that Article 32-1 of the Civil Code provides that the one who acts in justice in a dilatory or abusive way may be condemned to a civil fine of GB 15 to GB 1.500, in addition to the reparation of damages that would be claimed'. On the grounds of these provisions, an 'intensive and unjustified' use of judicial procedures was condemned (Cour de cassation, 3e Chambre Civile, 12 February 1980, [1980] *JCP*, IV, 168).
43. See Chapter 8 (A) (5) (c).

of EC competition rules shall be adjudicated by the district courts, irrespective of the amount in dispute. Section 89 GWB entitles the State governments to concentrate jurisdiction in civil competition cases on one or more district courts within that State. Most State governments have made use of that provision.[44] Within the district court, the dispute will be conferred to one of the commercial chambers upon request of one of the parties. The general procedural provisions of the German Code of Civil Procedure (*Zivilprozessordnung* – ZPO) and the underlying principles apply.

2.   GERMAN CIVIL PROCEDURE AND THE BASIC LAW

German civil procedural law is to a large extent influenced by the procedural fundamental rights guaranteed under the German constitution, the so-called Basic Law (*Grundgesetz* – GG) and the case law of the *Bundesverfassungsgericht*, the Federal Constitutional Court. Of particular importance for civil proceedings are the *Rechtsstaatsprinzip* (principle of a constitutional state) flowing from Art. 20(3) GG, the *Anspruch of rechtliches Gehör* (right to be heard) according to Art. 103 (1) GG, the right to a fair trial, the *Anspruch auf effektiven Rechtsschutz* (right to effectiveness of justice)[45] and the principle of *Waffengleichheit* (equality of powers).[46] However, most of the principles of German civil procedure do not posses a constitutional basis,[47] and may instead be derived from a number of rules set forth in the ZPO and the Court Constitution Code (*Gerichtsverfassungsgesetz* – GVG). Of these procedural principles, party disposition, party presentation, concentration and immediateness shall be discussed below.

3.   THE RELATIONSHIP BETWEEN JUSTICE, LEGAL CERTAINTY
          AND PARTY AUTONOMY

Art. 20(3) of the Basic Law (Grundgesetz) stipulates:

> The legislature is bound by the constitutional order, the executive and judiciary are bound by statutes and the law.

---

44. *Cf.* Appendix.
45. The right to effectiveness of justice is set forth by Art. 19(4) GG for proceedings against executive measures. It does, however, also apply to civil proceedings by virtue of Art. 20(3), Art. 2(1) GG, BVerfG NJW 1992, 105.
46. According to the Federal Constitutional Court, this principle is derived from Art. 20(3), Art. 103 (1) and the principle of non-discrimination set forth in Art. 3 GG, cf. BVerfG 1979, 1925 (1927).
47. MüKo/*Lüke*, Einleitung, Rn. 161 f.; according to *Stürner*, many of the procedural principles can be cautiously based on the Grundgesetz, cf. R. Stürner, 'Verfahrensgrundsätze des Zivilprozesses und Verfassung' in *Festschrift für Fritz Baur*, W. Grunsky *et al.* (eds) (Mohr, Tübingen, 1981) p. 647 *et seq.*

The Federal Supreme Court has interpreted this so-called *Rechtsstaatsprinzip* (principle of a constitutional State) to include fundamental guarantees for parties to a proceeding, most importantly the right to a fair trial.[48] The Court has also held that both justice and legal certainty are fundamental pillars of the *Rechtsstaatsprinzip*, leaving it in principle to the legislature to find a workable balance if the two demands collide.[49]

The implicit aim of civil procedural law certainly consists of achieving peace under the law and allowing parties to realize their substantive rights on the basis of truth. This notwithstanding, there are two eminent principles of the ZPO which set civil proceedings apart from criminal and administrative proceedings, namely the principle of party disposition (*Dispositionsgrundsatz*) and of party presentation (*Beibringungsgrundsatz*). The principle of party disposition constitutes the parties' control over the proceedings, meaning that it is up to them to initiate, terminate and define the content of civil proceedings. The closely related principle of party presentation signifies that the facts of the case and the requisite means of proof are to be provided by the parties. The court may not base its decision on facts not presented by the parties, unless such facts are obvious (§ 291 ZPO). Thus, the quest for truth and enforcement of the substantive law may be hindered by the parties' decision to suppress facts or to relinquish certain rights.

4.   FUNDAMENTAL RIGHTS OF THE PARTIES

Insofar as a party decides to enforce its substantive rights, it is guaranteed a right to be heard under Art. 103 (1) of the Basic Law, which holds:

Everyone possesses the right to be heard before a court.

The right to be heard includes the entitlement to raise a claim, substantiate it with facts and offer the requisite proof. The right moreover obliges the court to take note of and consider the submissions of the parties. However, it needs to be emphasized that this guarantee does not warrant the right to a specific means of proof or specific types of proof,[50] such as, i.e., disclosure. The right to be heard is also not infinite: Foreclosure provisions designed to concentrate proceedings have been held constitutional by the Federal Constitutional Court, as long as they are interpreted restrictively.[51] Such limitations to the right to be heard are justified by virtue of another fundamental right, namely the effectiveness of justice.

The right to effectiveness of justice mandates a consistent access to the courts which may not be hindered in an unreasonable way.[52] The concept of effectiveness of justice includes a prohibition of court fees that make it virtually

48. BVerfG, NJW 1975, 103; BVerfG, NJW 2000, 1709 *et seq.*
49. BVerfG, NJW 1963, 851; BVerfG, NJW 1969, 1059 (1061).
50. BVerfG, NJW 1996, 3145 (3146); BVerfG, NJW 1981, 1719 (1722).
51. BVerfG, NJW 1984, 2203; BVerfG, NJW 1985, 1150 f.; *cf.* also BGH, NJW 1999, 585.
52. BVerfG, NJW 1992, 105; BVerfG, NJW 1977, 1233.

impossible to raise a claim,[53] the possibility of interim measures[54] and the mandatory completion of proceedings within due time.[55] The Federal Constitutional Court has moreover derived the principle of a fair trial from Art. 20(3) GG,[56] part of which is the concept of *Waffengleichheit*, that is equal standing of the parties before court.[57]

5.   THE PRINCIPLES OF CONCENTRATION AND IMMEDIATENESS

Justice in a procedural sense requires that a judgment be given within reasonable time.[58] Thus, the principle of concentration (*Konzentrationsmaxime* or *Grundsatz der Prozessbeschleunigung*) is set forth by a number of rules of the ZPO (§§ 272, 273, 278, 282, 296, 296a, 349, 358a, 527 *et seq.*). The aim is that both parties and the court prepare the oral hearing in a way that allows the dispute to be resolved in a single hearing. Sanctions for a negligent case management by a party include foreclosure (§§ 296, 527 *et seq.* ZPO) as well as an adverse decision on costs (§§ 95, 97(2) ZPO).

Finally, German civil procedure is based upon the principle of immediateness. Both the oral hearing and the taking of evidence must take place before the trial court. In contrast, the court is not required to always make use of the most immediate means of proof. Admitting information or opinions transmitted by the Commission under Art. 15(1) of Council Regulation 1/2003 as expert advice is therefore not adverse to the principle of immediateness. Section 33 (4) GWB, introduced on 1 June 2005, binds the courts to the findings of the Commission and NCAs regarding a breach of competition rules. This is not a concern under the principle of immediateness, as this principle lacks a constitutional basis[59] and may thus be modified by statute. However, concerns have been raised that the independence of the judges, guaranteed by Art. 97(1) GG, might be impaired.[60] Since the privilege of Art. 97(1) GG only extends to those matters that are up for

---

53. BVerfG, NJW 1980, 1511; BVerfG, NJW 1997, 311 (312).
54. BVerfG, NJW 1978, 693.
55. BVerfG, NJW 1980, 1511; BVerfG,NJW 2000, 797.
56. BVerfG, NJW 1995, 3173 (3175); BVerfG, NJW 1998, 2044 *et seq.* Some scholars hold that the implications of the right to a fair trial might just as well be based on the right to be heard under Art. 103(1) GG, *cf.* W. Waldner, *Der Anspruch auf rechtliches Gehör* (2nd ed, Schmidt, Köln, 2000), para. 27 with further references.
57. G. Lüke, *Münchener Kommentar zur Zivilprozessordnung*, G. Lüke and P. Wax (eds) (2nd edn, C.H. Beck, München, 2000), Einleitung, para. 143 *et seq.* The Federal Constitutional Court bases the concept of *Waffengleichheit* on Art. 3(1), 20(1), 103(1) GG.
58. G. Lüke, *Münchener Kommentar zur Zivilprozessordnung*, G. Lüke and P. Wax (eds) (2nd edn, C.H. Beck, München, 2000), Einleitung, para. 227.
59. G. Lüke, *Münchener Kommentar zur Zivilprozessordnung*, G. Lüke and P. Wax (eds) (2nd edn, C.H. Beck, München, 2000), Einleitung, para. 164.
60. M. Meyer, 'Die Bindung der Zivilgerichte an Entscheidungen im Kartellverwaltungrechtsweg – der neue § 33 IV GWB auf dem Prüfstand', [2006] GRUR, 29.

the decision of the requisite judge,[61] such concerns are unwarranted, as long as the party has been heard by the cartel office and has had the opportunity to seek judicial redress against the cartel office's decision.[62]

6.   CONCLUSION

It is submitted that the above-mentioned principles of German Civil Procedure are in accord with the principles named by the ECJ and Advocate-General *Jacobs* as being able to justify a restriction on the enforcement of community law.

The 'rights of the defence' are clearly covered by the fundamental judicial rights guaranteed under the German Basic Law, that is the right to be heard, the right to a fair trial and the right to effectiveness of justice.

The concept of 'legal certainty' is covered by the *Rechtsstaatsprinzip* under Art. 20(3) GG as interpreted by the Federal Constitutional Court.

Finally, 'proper conduct of procedure' would seem to include rules that aim at achieving effectiveness of justice and that are summarized by the term 'principle of concentration'.

---

61. C. Claasen, *Kommentar zum Grundgesetz*, H. Mangoldt and F. Klein (eds) (Franz Vahlen, 5th edn, München), Art. 97 para. 22.
62. J. Bornkamm, *Kommentar zum deutschen und europäischen Kartellrecht*, vol. 1: *Deutsches Kartellrecht*, E. Langen and H.J. Bunte (eds) (10th ed., Luchterhand, Neuwied, 2006), § 33 para. 4.

Chapter 1

English, French and German Civil Procedure

A.   EC PROCEDURAL ENFORCEMENT PROBLEMS

In this chapter, what might be termed the problem areas of the English French and German systems of civil procedure will be identified in relation to certain of the areas as noted that have been described in both the Commission Green Paper[1] and the Commission Staff Working Paper.[2] Further, there will be a certain number of additional areas, particularly in the English Civil Procedure Rules (CPR) and the Competition Appeal Court (CAT) Rules which although not identified within the aforementioned documents nevertheless arguably may require firstly, the application of the doctrine of effectiveness and secondly, its application in a perhaps novel context: specifically, choosing between what might be termed competing solutions wherein the court must choose the procedural solution which will provide the adequately as opposed to minimally effective enforcement of EC Articles 81 and 82.[3]

---

1. Green Paper SEC (2005) (1732) 19 December 2005 Damages Actions for Breach of EEC Anti-trust Rules.
2. Commission Staff Working Paper COM 672 FINAL: Annex to the Green Paper, Damages Actions for Breach of EEC Anti-trust Rules.
3. W. van Gerven 'Of Rights, Rememdies and Procedures', (2000) 37 CMLRev 500–536; and T. Eilmansberger, 'The Relationship between Rights and Remedies in EC Law: in Search of the Missing Link', (2004) 41 CMLRev 1193–1198. Eilmansberger summarizes his approach as follows on p. 1245–6. 'The traditional approach by the to connect direct applicability and recognition of individual rights works fine in "first generation" cases. . . . However, it is not capable producing the type of individual right that merits and requires protection through substantive remedies. The recipe to fill this void is simple. It is the selection and determination of the holder

B.   ENGLISH CPR AND THE CAT RULES: PROBLEMS
                      CONCERNING ENFORCEMENT OF EC COMPETITION

1.   Costs: The Indemnity Rule – Hourly Calculation of
                      Legal Costs

The Commission Staff Working Paper states at paragraphs 43, 215, 200 and 220
the following with respect to costs:

> Pargaraph 43: 'The study notes the general rule that in all Member States the
> loser pays costs although in practise fees are not fully recoverable. The high
> costs and risks involved in competition actions as well as the length of
> proceedings operate as a disincentive to bringing private actions. This is
> exascerbated by the likelihood of non recovery of all costs (although this
> can also be seen as reducing the risk for the claimant in the event that the
> claim is unsuccessful)'.
>   Paragraph 215: 'As mentioned above the most commonly applied rule for
> cost recovery is the "loser pays" principle. The application of this principle
> will neither act as an incentive nor as a disincentive in those cases in which the
> claimant can be reasonably sure about sinning his case and in which the exact
> rules on cost recovery will allow the successful claimant to recover the entirety
> (or a very large part) of his actual costs'.
>   Paragraph 200: 'The bringing of an action for damages entails costs.
> Economically speaking those costs represent different expenditures necessary
> for the work of the people involved in bringing an action as well as other
> material cots. Although all civil actions have a cost competition related
> damage claims may be particularly costs as they are generally more complex
> and thus more time consuming than other kinds of civil actions'.
>   Paragraph 220: 'In order to prevent the disincentive effect of the "loser
> pays" principle in those cases in which the outcome cannot be clearly assessed
> at the outset of the action, one could make cost recovery dependent always on
> a court order and give the court the power to grant protection from costs
> recovery even if the claimant fails to win on the merits; such "cost protection
> order" could be given at the outset of the action. . . . Such an order could also
> be used to protect economically weak parties from cost exposure thereby
> strengthening their right of access to a court for their damages claims'.

---

and the substance of a right by an analysis of the protective scope of the rule in question. . . . As a
result the division of competences between Community law and national law would become
much clearer and the principle of effectiveness would be easier to apply. . . . Finally, the merely
auxiliary status of national law as provider of the institutions and the procedural framework for
these actions at law would be clarified. While this would obviously by no means eliminate the
complexities and difficulties in the assessment of national restriction, it would at least by clear
that these restrictions can, in principle, only be procedural and may not strike at the existence of
the substantive remedy in question'.

Accordingly, it is clear that the Commission's position is that damages actions for enforcement of EC Articles 81 and 82 are inherently costly. More particularly, the Commission focuses upon the indemnity rule which shifts the costs from the winner to the loser of the litigation as being the procedural mechanism which requires modification in order to ensure enforceability of EC Articles 81 and or 82 as noted in particular in paragraph 220. In reality however, it can be said that in English procedural law, the indemnity rule at best has little or no effect on the access to justice and at worst simply magnifies problems associated with the fundamental problem which is the high legal costs which result from the method of calculation which is hourly based. It is rather that the method of legal cost calculation based upon hours can arguably lead to disproportionate costs which either inherently or when coupled with the indemnity rule may serve to impede the enforceability of EC Articles 81 and or 82. Accordingly, the problem of costs in the English legal system will require a solution other than adjustment to the indemnity rule which the Green Paper and Commission Staff Working Paper propose. The doctrine of effectiveness would seem to require that the solution to the problem of high legal costs with respect to EC Articles 81 and 82 in terms of the Civil Procedure Rules (CPR) take the form of fixed maximum legal costs for both in and out of court legal services: arguably there is no justification for retaining the current method of hourly based calculation fees given its potential for creating excessive and disproportionate costs thereby leading to a reduction in the access to justice.

2.   Conditional Fees

What might be referred to as a category litigation financing related to conditional fees, namely, contingency fees, is raised by the Commission as a possible method of ensuring the greater enforceability of EC Articles 81 and 82 in terms of legal costs. The Commission observes in this regard:

> Paragraph 218: 'Some jurisdictions provide further incentives for bringing an action for damages. Specific cost rules can also serve to provide an incentive. For example, contingency fees are a strong incentive because the financial risk of bringing an action is borne not by the claimant but by private attorneys. The experience of US law suggests that the existence of contingency fees is a factor in the emergence of a claimant bar strongly associated with brining actions for damages. However it must be underlined that contingency fees are not allowed in some Member States and are regulated in others'.

It would appear, however, that the operation of the English conditional fee system pursuant to the CPR may well impede the enforceability of EC Articles 81 and 82: that is, through the combination of the hourly based fee calculations coupled with the indemnity can result in the losing party paying an amount of legal costs which is not proportionate and not foreseeable. Accordingly, the prospect of a losing party being held liable for the winning party's legal costs the amount of which is not foreseeable and not subject to the rule of proportionality may serve to discourage litigants from defending their rights pursuant to EC Articles 81 and or 82. Accordingly, in default of any justification within the CPR, arguably, the doctrine of effectiveness would seem to require that at a minimum the shifting rule for the costs involved in conditional fees be abandoned and that further, a system of maximum legal costs be adopted.

3.   EVIDENTIAL BURDEN: DOCTRINE OF CONSISTENCY

Both the Green Paper and the Commission Staff Working Paper identify the evidential burden as constituting a potential impediment for the enforcement of EC Articles 81 and 82:

> Paragraph 33: 'The Study notes the fact that the burden of proof of causation and damage is on the claimant which in the case in all Member States is an obstacle to private actions. The high standard of proof required in some Member States also exacerbates the difficulties face by claimants particularly where the available evidence may not be very complete. Some Member States lower the standard of proof required in relation to quantification of damage which can be difficult to demonstrate to the requisite standard'.
>   Paragraph 54: 'It has been generally acknowledged that the difficulty for the claimant of obtain evidence of the alleged anti-trust infringement constitute one of the major obstacles to damages actions. That is particularly the case where there is no prior decision from a competition authority finding the infringement. In these so called "stand alone" actions, a lot depends on the possibility for the claimant to oblige the defendant or event a third party to disclose documents in their possession which may constitute evidence by the alleged infringement'.

However, with respect to the UK, both the Green Paper and the Commission Staff Working Paper note that the evidential burden has been reduced for the claimant in English law in various ways: specifically, S 18 and S 20 of the Enterprise Act (2002) which were inserted into the Competition Act (1998) by S 47 A and S 57 A respectively. These sections provide that in money actions, the ordinary court and the CAT are bound by infringement findings made by the OFT concerning EC Articles 81 and or 82: the CAT is in turn bound by a Commission infringement decision concerning those sections once the period of appeal has expired. In contrast, the ordinary court is not bound by a Commission infringement decision. Rather, pursuant to Art. 16.1 EC Reg. 10/2003, the national court is enjoined to avoid rendering a judgment which may conflict with the Commission decision in the same case: 'when national courts rule on agreements, decisions or practises under Articles 81 or 82 which are the subject of a Commission decision, they cannot take decisions running counter to the decision adopted by the Commission'. The Commission goes on to suggest other methods for facilitating access to documents and more generally enforcement in terms of expanding the availability of evidence, be they in the form of Commission decisions in the same case or decisions rendered by the national competition authority: the Commission Staff Working Party proposes at paragraph 98:

> A prior infringement decision of a national competition authority whether domestic or of another EU Member State or of its review court could be used to alleviate the claimant's burden of proving the infringement.

Further, it would seem that the Court of Appeal at least indirectly sought to alleviate the evidential problem of enforcement where no Commission decision exists: effectively, the Court in *Crehan*[4] simply expanded the application of Art. 16.1 EC Reg. 1/2003 by creating what might be termed the duty of deference.

This duty to defer to relevant Commission decisions from other cases and a fortiori to Commission decisions involving the same case as that before the English court was developed with a view to avoiding the entering of judgments which would conflict with relevant Commission decisions and of course Commission decisions in the same case. The result of the now overturned Court of Appeal judgment in *Crehan* was that relevant Commission decisions and or Commission opinions expanded the category of documents which could be introduced as probative evidence in the enforcement of EC Articles 81 and or 82. Arguably, this doctrine of deference served effectively as rule to exclude evidence which would contradict the relevant Commission decisions and thereby had the same effect as S 47 A and S 58 A CA (1998). Accordingly, the doctrine of deference could thereby facilitate enormously the enforcement of EC Articles 81 and 82. However, the House of Lords in its recent judgment of *Inntrepreneur*[5] overturned that of the Court of Appeal in the same case thereby specifically abolishing the doctrine of deference to relevant Commission decisions. Henceforth, relevant Commission decisions and other documents while being admissible as evidence for the content of their opinion cannot serve to exclude any contradictory evidence which the opposing party may wish to lead notably on the matter of infringement of EC Articles 81 or 82. Accordingly, the infringement of these articles must be proved following the normal rules of civil proof in terms of allocation of burden of proof and standard of proof. The result of the House of Lords' judgment in *Inntrepreneur* is that it would seem to make the enforcement of EC Articles 81 and 82 more difficult than was the case under the judgment of the Court of Appeal in *Crehan*. It is submitted, therefore, that the doctrine of effectiveness may intervene to require changes in the rules governing the allocation of the burden of proof and possibly the standard of proof in order to ensure that indeed the normal civil standard of the balance of probabilities is indeed used. The Commission defines this problem in the following manner in the Green Paper:

> S 2.1: Access to Evidence: Question C: Should the claimant's burden of proving the anti-trust infringement in damages actions be alleviated and if

---

4. *Bernard Crehan v. Inntrepreneur Pub Company CPC* (2004) EWCA 1725 Case A3/2003/1725.
5. *Inntrepreneur Pub Company (CPE) & Others v. Crehan* (2006) UK HL 38 on appeal from (2004) EWCA Civ 637.

so how. Option 5: Shifting or lowering the burden of proof in cases of information asymmetry between the claimant and defendant with the aim of redressing that asymmetry.

4.   COLLECTIVE ACTIONS

The Commission notes its concern in the Green Paper with respect to Collective and Representative actions in the following manner:

> Paragraph 2.5: 'Defending Consumer Interests: It will be very unlikely for practical reasons of not impossible that consumers and purchases will bring an action for damages of beach of anti-trust law. Consideration should therefore be given to ways in which these interests can be better protected by collective action. Beyond the specific protection of consumer interest collective actions can serve to consolidate a large number of smaller claims into one action thereby saving time and money. A cause of action for consumer associations without depriving individual consumers from bringing an action. Consideration should be given to uses such as standing (a passive system of registration) the distribution of damages (whether the damages to go the association of the members) and the quantification of the damage'.

The Commission further observes at paragraph 31 of the Staff Commission Working Paper that the absence of collective actions constitutes an obstacle to private enforcement of EC Articles 81 and or 82 in terms of damages actions:

> 1. Collective Actions:
>   31. The Study notes the restrictions on collective actions in the Member States. In particular, the study notes the rarity of collective actions (by which is meant a single action brought on behalf of a group of affected persons) and representative actions (actions brought by representative organization such as consumers' organizations). The Study views this as an obstacle to private actions in so far as it reduces litigation options open to potential claimants.

The CPR at present does not contain any provision for collective actions. Accordingly, in default of any justification in terms of the CPR itself, the doctrine of effectiveness would seem to require that the rules be modified so as to provide for the possibility of a collective action be used in order to ensure effective enforcement of EC Articles 81 and/or 82. It is to be noted however that the S 47 B CA(1998) provides for collective actions at least for the benefit of private consumers. Accordingly, it is possible for private consumers to enforce monetary actions pursuant to S 47A CA(1998) in the CAT by means of a representative action pursuant to S 47 B CA(1998) . In contrast the High Court is unable pursuant to S 58A CA (1998) to provide similarly effective enforcement for private consumers. Indeed CPR 19.r19.1 provides for bringing a representative action when more than one party has the 'same interest' in a claim pursuant to CPR 19 r 19.6 (1) or a Group Litigation Order under CPR 19 r 19.11 where there are multiple claimants and common issues of law or fact. The action pursuant to S 47B CA(1998) differs from those provided by the CPR in that the representative body which under that section has no 'interest' in the proceedings. It would seem therefore that the doctrine of effectiveness and possibly that of non-discrimination would require, in the absence of any justifications in terms of the CPR and its underlying principle of a fair trial, the following: namely, the introduction of a method for private consumers to bring a representative action which would be as effective as that provided by the CAT Rules in order to ensure effective enforcement of EC Articles 81 and 82. Further, apparently no provision exists within S 47B CA (1998) of the CAT Rules for small businesses who do not operate as consumers which would permit them to bring representative – collective actions. This is *a fortiori* the case under the CPR. It would seem that the doctrine of effectiveness may require the creation of a procedural disposition in order to ensure that small businesses, such as those in *Crehan* (the associations of public houses) be able to bring a collective action for monetary claims under both the CPR and the CAT Rules.

5.   CONFIDENTIALITY: CONFIDENTIAL INFORMATION PURSUANT
                  TO EC REG. 1/2003

Before agreeing to communicate with the national courts confidential information in its possession including in particularly business secrets, the Commission will ensure that the national court provides undertakings to ensure the protection of this information.[6] Although a formal privilege to protect confidential information does not exist in the CPR, the English court is, nevertheless, able to provide protection of confidential information on what might be termed and individual or ad hoc basis to prevent disclosure and inspection of the information by non-authorized third parties. However, arguably, correct implementation of Reg. 1/2003 could require the introduction of a formal privilege of confidentiality to apply to enforcement proceedings of EC Articles 81 and or 82. It is submitted that the national principle of legal certainty may require that both the scope of the privilege be defined and the method of its procedural implementation be specified. Further, the principle of effectiveness and non-discrimination will arguably require that the basis for the granting of the privilege of confidentiality be formalized so as to ensure parity of enforcement with the CAT in relation to monetary actions pursuant S 58A CA (1998).

---

6. Commission Notice on Co-operation between the Commission and the Courts of the EU Member States in application of Arts. 81 and 82 EC, C-101/58 (27.4.2004), points 21–26.

6.   ACCESS TO EVIDENCE: COURT SEEKING INFORMATION OF
           ITS OWN MOTION

The Commission Staff Working Paper notes at paragraph 24 the following with
respect to Art. 15 of EC Reg. 1.2003:

> In order to facilitate the application of EC anti trust rules by national courts,
> Art. 15.(1) of the Regulation expressly provides for a number of mechanisms
> by which courts can ask for opinions or information from the Commission.

Art. 15.1 of EC Reg. 1/2003 provides that the national court be able to request the
Commission to provide information in the context of its *Amicus curiae* functions:

> In proceedings for the application of Art.81 and Art. 82 of the Treaty, the
> courts of the Member States may ask the Commission to transmit to them
> information in its possession or its opinion on question concerning the appli-
> cation of the Community competition rules.

This *amicus curiae* intervention by the Commission is to assist the national court
in effectively enforcing EC Articles 81 and 82.[7] Arguably, correct implementation
of this article of the directive will require the modification of the CPR so as to
formalize the possibility of a court seeking information from the Commission on its
own motion: such a rule would define the scope of the court's intervention and
thereby provide legal certainty. It would seem that the doctrine of effectiveness
would intervene to ensure that the English court be able to enforce this directive
effectively by being able to request information of its own motion. Further, it
may well be that the doctrine of non-discrimination will apply to ensure that
EC Articles 81 and 82 can be enforced under Reg. 1/2003 in terms of the CPR
in terms of the court obtaining information *ex officio* as it can as they can by the
CAT. This would be a fortiori the case in so far as the enforcement of monetary
actions are involved pursuant to S 47A CA(1998) for the CAT and S 58A
CA(1998) for the national court are involved.

7.   EXPERT EVIDENCE: ASSESSORS

Both the Green Paper and the Commission Staff Working Paper note that the use of
expert evidence is necessary and that the appointment of a court expert may be
advisable in order to reduce the costs.

> The Commission notes at point 2.9 of the Green Paper:
> Given the complexity of damages actions for infringement of anti trust
> law the use of expertise in the court is particularly important to ensue efficient
> proceedings. If experts were appointed by the court cost saving might result

---

7. Commission Notice on Co-operation between the Commission and the Courts of the EU
    Member States in application of Arts. 81 and 82, C-101/58 (27.4.2004) *ibid.* at points 17–20
    and 31–35.

since fewer experts would be required. This would also reduce the multitude of experts giving conflicting evidence depending upon the client's stand point.

In the Commission Staff Working Paper the following observations are made:

Paragraph 256: 'Use of Expertise in Court: Under Art. 15 of Reg. 1/2003, national courts can ask the Commission for its opinion on question concerning the application of the Community competition rules whenever the national court is apply Article 81 or 82'.

Paragraph 257: 'Recourse to expert evidence in court is in someway possible in all Member States. Nevertheless, important differences persist in many Member States as to the questions of who can nominate an expert, who can be an expert on which issues the expert can give evidence and the relevant evidential value of an expert report'.

Paragraph 260: 'It should be borne in mind that the expertise of the courts will be further increased through the training programmes for national judges in EC competition law first introduced in 2002 by the Commission. The situation could also be further improved were the national courts to make greater use of the existing possibilities of Art. 15 of Reg. 1/2003'.

However, one of the problems of the ordinary English courts as opposed to the CAT is that they are not specialist tribunals. Albeit, as a result of the Practise Direction[8] on the enforcement of EC competition law a specialist body of judges will be gradually formed in the Chancery division. Notwithstanding, there remains a problem which the Commission reports have not identified directly: namely, the evaluation of expert economic evidence by non-specialist judges in the ordinary domestic courts. In England, arguably the non specialist judge can overcome this

---

8. Practise Direction: Competition Law: Claims Relating to the Application of Articles 81 and 82 of the EC Treaty and Chapter I and II of the Competition Act (1998), October 2005:

   'Venue: 2.1 A claim to which this Practise Direction applies –
   a) must be commenced in the High Court at the Royal Courts of Justice and ;
   b) will be assigned to the Chancery Division unless it comes with the scope of Rule 58.1 (2) in which case it will be assigned to the Commercial Court of the Queen's Bench Division'

   CPR 58 r (1) This part applies to claims in the Commercial Court of the Queen's Bench Division (2) In this part and its practise direction 'commercial claim' means any claim arising out of the transaction of trade and commerce and includes any claim relating to:

   a) a business document or contract;
   b) the export or import of goods;
   c) the carriage of goods by land, see, air or pipeline;
   d) the exploitation of oil and gas reserves or other natural resources;
   e) insurance and re-insurance;
   f) banking and financial services;
   g) the operation of markets and exchanges;
   h) the purchase and sale of commodities;
   i) the construction of ships;
   j) business agency;
   k) arbitration.

problem by means of assistance obtained from an assessor appointed under CPR 15.15. As such, it may be that the doctrine of effectiveness will require the court to use its discretion to appoint in appropriate circumstances an assessor to sit with the judge in order to explain the expert evidence in order to ensure that EC Articles 81 and or 82 are enforced effectively to an adequate level as opposed to a minimum level of effective enforcement.[9] Such an application arguably departs from what might be termed the minimum[10] standard of effective enforcement to include new category of enforcement: namely, that of adequate enforcement (that is, more or most effective enforcement) when a choice exists between what might be termed national procedural devices exists which all conform to the basic national principles of procedure.

It is not clear whether the doctrine will require that the assessor be subject to cross examination in order to ensure defence rights pursuant to ECHR Art. 6.1. Further, it is submitted that the doctrine of effectiveness will also apply so as to modify the structure of CPR 35.15 to ensure that the assessor provides only factual information to the court and not evidence: accordingly, the assessor will intervene as part of the court in order to ensure that the judge has access to specialized information which will permit him to evaluate expert evidence in a manner which is as effective as the CAT notably with respect to enforcement of monetary actions pursuant to S 47A and 58 A CA (1998) respectively.[11] The assessor will not however, unlike a court appointed expert, give evidence which is subject to cross examination.

8.   INTERIM INJUNCTIONS

Neither the Green Paper nor the Commission Staff Working Paper mentions the granting of interim relief as constituting a problem. Interim relief is ensured by means of CPR 25. In reality, there are two legal basis for granting the interim relief in the form of a prohibitive injunction: either following the case law of *American Cyanamid*,[12] on the basis of there existing a serious legal issue to be tried; or, on the more traditional basis of the merits of the case as reflected in *R v. Secretary of State ex p Factortame*.[13] It is submitted that the application of the doctrine of effectiveness may be extended so as to effect a choice between the two possible procedural

---

9. W. van Gerven 'Of Rights, Remedies and Procedures', (2000) 37 CMLRev 500–536, op. cit.
10. J. B.ourgeois & T. Baumé in 'Decentralisation of EC Competition Law Enforcement & General Prinicples of Community Law' in 30 Years of European Legal Studies at the College of Europe, (eds) I. Demaret, D. Govaere, D. Hanf, PIE-Peter Lang-Presses Universitaires Européennes, op. cit; at p. 5 see *generally*, W. van Gerven, 'Of Rights, Remedies and Procedures' (2000) 37 CMLRev 500–536 and T. Eilmansberger, 'The relationship between rights and remedies in EC law: in search of the missing link' (2004) 41 CMLRev 1193–98.
11. D. Dwyer 'The Future of Assessors Under the CPR', (2006) (25) CJQ 219, proposes certain modifications to CPR 35.15 in order to ensure that the rule may thereby carryout what she submits are four separate functions currently contained within the rule.
12. *American Cyanamid Co. v. Ethicon* [1975] 1 AC 396.
13. *R v. Secretary of State for Transport ex p Factortame* (No.2) [1991] AC 603.

grounds for the granting of the interim relief; and that further, the application of the doctrine will lead to the choice of the second ground, the merits of the legal case, by reason of it providing more effective enforcement of EC Articles 81 and or 82, that is, adequate as opposed to minimally effective enforcement than the first ground, a serious issue to be tried. The extension of the operation of the doctrine of effectiveness here so as to choose between what might be termed two competing procedural solutions might possibly be justified on the basis that the CPR Overriding Objective does not suffice in itself so effect the choice. Assistance, therefore, is required from the doctrine of effectiveness in the sense of it being extended to provide effective enforcement which is not just minimal but adequate.[14] Accordingly, it is submitted that it might be possible to apply the doctrine of effectiveness in the instant case of the two different legal bases for interim relief in the CPR.

C.   FRENCH CODE OF CIVIL PROCEDURE: PROBLEMS OF
       EC COMPETITION ENFORCEMENT IN TERMS
       OF THE GREEN PAPER

1.   COLLECTIVE ACTIONS

French law does not provide for 'class actions', i.e., civil court procedure under which one party, or a group of parties, may sue as representatives of a larger class of unidentified individuals. Nevertheless, representative actions and actions by associations for the protection of the collective interest they represent are available but under very restrictive conditions.

   The Staff Commission Working Paper observes that the absence of collective actions constitutes an obstacle to private enforcement of Articles 81 and 82 EC Treaty. The French procedural rules in terms of collective actions may therefore breach the doctrine of effectiveness and require an amendment of civil procedure law. However, these rules are justified in terms of the fundamental principles underlying French civil procedure: in particular that the right of action is a personal right.[15] In any event, the French Government is analysing how to introduce class actions in civil procedure, while respecting these fundamental principles.

2.   BURDEN OF PROOF

The decisions rendered by the French Competition Council, do not bind the French courts. Under French Constitutional law and Article 6 § 1 of the European Convention on Human Rights, the courts have to rule in complete independence in disputes between individuals and corporations. Where the Competition Council

---

14. W. van Gerven, 'Of Rights, Remedies and Procedures' (2000) 37 CMLRev 500–536 op. cit.
15. Constitutional Court (*'Conseil Constitutionnel'*), No. 257 DC, 25 July 1989, (1989) *Dr. Soc.*, p. 627.

has made a ruling on agreements, decisions or practises under Articles 81 and/or 82 EC Treaty, the victim will still have the burden of proving the fault. Therefore, a latent conflict underlies the relationship between the administrative bodies implementing EC law and the French courts that have to rule in complete independence.

The burden of proof under French law therefore constitutes a procedural obstacle to the effective enforcement of competition law, but is justified by fundamental principles.

3.   INTERIM MEASURES

The Green Paper does not directly address the problem of interim measures that may be requested by a plaintiff in emergency situations (*'procédure de référé'*). This is however an area which may require the application of the doctrine of effectiveness.

Nevertheless, according to the Commission Staff Working Paper[16] and the case law of the ECJ, the full effectiveness of directly applicable Community law requires that national courts have jurisdiction to grant interim measures as well damages.

Under French civil procedures rules, the president of the Civil or Commercial Court may, when applying Articles 81 and 82 EC Treaty, order injunctions and interim measures in the framework of summary orders.

Pursuant to Articles 808 and 872 of the Code of Civil Procedure, in all cases of emergency, the president of the court may order in an interim procedure all measures which are not challenged or which are justified by the existence of the dispute. Furthermore, Articles 809 and 873 provide for the following two situations: (i) that the president may always order in an interim application such protective measures to return the parties to their status ante as is necessary in order to prevent imminent damage or to abate a manifestly illegal nuisance, and (ii) that in cases where the existence of the cause of action is not seriously challenged, the judge may award an interim payment to the creditor or order the performance of the duty where there is a mandatory duty to act.

The complexity of competition law cases, coupled with the direct application of Article 81(3) EC Treaty, considerably limits the situations in which the French judge will have the power to order, in *prima facie* emergency procedure, interim measures. In particular, in most cases, there will be a 'serious challenge' as to the claims of the plaintiff and it will not be easy to ascertain that a situation causes 'a manifestly illegal nuisance'. This means that the judge will very often have to reject the claims made by the plaintiff. The doctrine of effectiveness of EC law could therefore require that the French rules of procedure in terms of interim measures be modified in the framework of economic litigation characterized by urgency.

---

16. Op. cit., at p. 10.

D. GERMAN CIVIL PROCEDURE: PROBLEMS OF EC
COMPETITION ENFORCEMENT IN RELATION TO
THE COMMISSION GREEN PAPER – DISCLOSURE

1. Access to Evidence

Both the Green Paper and the Commission Staff Working Paper[17] identify
the limited access to documents as a possible set-back for stand-alone claims.
The Green Paper states:[18]

> Actions for damages in antitrust cases regularly require the investigation of a
> broad set of facts. The particular difficulty with this kind of litigation is that
> often the relevant evidence is not easily available and is held by the party
> committing the anti-competitive behaviour. Access by claimants to such
> evidence is the key to making damages claims effective. It must therefore
> be considered whether obligations to turn over documents or otherwise
> provide access to evidence should be introduced.

The Commission's concerns hold certainly true for the German procedural rules.
It is from the afore-mentioned principle of party presentation that the so-called
'*Unzulässigkeit des Ausforschungsbeweises*', the prohibition of exploratory
evidence, is derived. According to the prevailing opinion, a request for evidence
is inadmissible if the evidence is not intended to support the facts pleaded by a
party, but rather aims at exploring facts or revealing as of yet unknown sources of
information which in turn enable a party to plead new facts.[19] The underlying view
is that while § 138 (1) ZPO compels each party to make complete and truthful
submissions, 'no one is obliged to provide the opposing party with weapons'.[20]

This notwithstanding, § 142 ZPO provides that a court may order a party or a
third person to present documents in its possession, in case one of the parties has
referred to the document. However, the effectiveness of this provision is limited for
a number of reasons. First, it was modified relatively recently on 1 January 2002 as
part of a larger reform of the ZPO, and a recent evaluation of that reform has shown
that judges have little willingness to rely on the rule.[21] Second, one of the parties
must specifically refer to the documents in question, meaning that the rule is of no

---

17. Commission Staff Working Paper, COM (2005) 672 final, no. 54 *et seq.*
18. Green Paper – Damages actions for breach of the EC antitrust rules, COM (2005) 672 final, p. 5
     at 2.1.
19. R. Greger, *Zivilprozessordnung*, Zöller (ed.) (25th edn, Otto Schmidt, Köln, 2005), Vor § 284
     ZPO para. 5 with further references.
20. A. Baumbach, W. Lauterbach, J. Albers, P. Hartmann, *Zivilprozessordnung* (64th edn,
     C.H. Beck, München, 2006), Einf. § 284 ZPO n. 29.
21. C. Hommerich, H. Prütting *et al.*, *Rechtstatsächliche Untersuchung zu den Auswirkungen der
     Reform des Zivilprozessrechts auf die gerichtliche Praxis – Evaluation ZPO-Reform*,
     <www.bmj.bund.de/media/archive/1216.pdf>, p. 4.

help if a party is unsure which the relevant documents are[22] (this again, is to prevent the taking of exploratory evidence). Finally, the only sanction in case a party refuses production of the document is the ability of the court to weigh the parties' conduct against it under § 286 ZPO.[23] It is of little consolation that the available sanctions against third parties are much sharper, including fines and imprisonment, cf. § 142(2), 390 ZPO.

Disclosure obligations by one of the parties to civil litigation may also be based upon substantive law, namely § 242 BGB. However, an obligation to provide the other party with information and the rendering of accounts may only arise in the event that a specific legal relationship exists between the parties. The specific link may i.e., arise out of contract or tort, but it is certainly not considered sufficient if the plaintiff solely alleges that a legal connection in the form of a competition infringement exists.[24]

It follows that the proof of a breach of competition law under the German procedural provisions is quite difficult in stand-alone cases, unless the claimant himself is party to the breach and therefore has access to relevant evidence.[25]

22. R. Greger, 'Zweifelsfragen und erste Entscheidungen zur neuen ZPO', [2002] *Neue Juristische Wochenschrift*, 3050; G. Berrisch and M. Burianski, 'Kartellrechtliche Schadensersatzansprüche nach der 7. GWB-Novelle', [2005] WuW, 883; J. Zekoll and J. Bolt, 'Die Pflicht zur Vorlage im Zivilprozess – Amerikanische Verhältnisse in Deutschland?', [2002] NJW, 3130.

23. R. Greger, *Zivilprozessordnung*, Zöller (ed.) (25th edn, Otto Schmidt, Köln, 2005), § 142 ZPO n. 4.

24. BGH, GRUR 1980, 1105, 1111 – *Das Medizinsyndikat III*; GRUR 1986, 62, 64 – *GEMA-Vermutung I*; BGH, NJW 1990, 3151, 3152; OLG Köln, Magazindienst 1998, 945.

25. Monopolkommission, *Das Allgemeine Wettbewerbsrecht in der Siebten GWB-Novelle. Sondergutachten 41* (Bonn, 2004) <www.monopolkommission.de/sg_41/text_s41.pdf>, n. 40.

Chapter 2
English Procedure: Evidence

A.   BURDEN OF PROOF

In the English adversarial system judicial responsibility for ascertaining the facts is limited to reaching a decision on the basis of the evidence presented by the parties. In short, the court is not authorized to find facts beyond those which the evidence produced by the parties has proved.[1] With respect to EC law, normally, a party who raises as the cause of action a breach of statutory duty based upon EC Articles 81 and or 82 bears the legal burden to establish the constitutive elements thereof up to the requisite standard of proof.[2] This is likely to be burdensome where the party must establish the required effect on competition,[3] the interstate effect on trade between Member States and where the court is obliged to consider all the surrounding circumstance of the nature and operation of the relevant economic market or markets.[4] One might add that the discharge of this burden would appear to be particularly complicated when a *Delimitis*[5]

---

1. A.A.S. Zuckerman, *Civil Procedure*, (London, Lexis Nexis, 2003) op. cit. at p 649.
2. *Potato Marketing Board v. Robertsons* (1983) 1 CMLR 93 at 98 (County Ct): also GT –Link v. DSB, Case C-242/95 [1997] ECR I – 4449 where the ECJ held that the question of the burden of proof is a matter for national law subject to the principle of effectiveness and non-discrimination: see also EC Reg. 1/2003 Art. 2.1.
3. *Inntrepreneur Estates v. Boyes* (1993) 2 EGLE 112 at 116 – emphasis of evidence of anti-competitive effect; *Fulton Motors Ltd v. Toyota* (GB) LTd (1998) EuLR 327 (no evidence of anti-competitive effect or effect on trade); *Potatoe Marketing Board v. Hampden Smith* (1997) EuLR 435; it may be that some of these cases would be decided differently in light of the availability of proof through the doctrine of consistency which would seem to subsume *Iberian UK Ltd v. BPB Industries* (1996) 2 CMLR 601.
4. *Bellamy & Child European Community Law of Competition* (5th edn. London, Sweet & Maxwell, 2001) op. cit. at p. 814.
5. *Delimitis v.Henninger Braü AG* C-234/89 [1991] ECR I-935.

distribution network is involved as was the case in *Crehan*.[6] It is recalled that the Delimitis judgment requires not only the establishment of the requisite product market but also an analysis of networks and their possible distortion of inter and intra brand competition notably through the foreclosure of access to new entrants to the product market.

1.   METHODS OF PROOF: FIRST METHOD

Accordingly, there exist at present at least two methods for the discharge of this burden of proof. The first method which is normally used by the ordinary English court in the enforcement of civil matters consists in the use of what might be termed the traditional manner of proof based upon the probative value of the evidence; the second method of proof is based upon the use and probative value of Office of Fair Trading (OFT) and Commission infringement decisions involving EC Articles 81 and 82. By virtue of S 47A CA (1998) OFT and Commission infringements decisions involving notably EC Articles 81 and 82 are made binding on the Competition Appeal Tribunal (CAT) and by means of S 58A (CA), OFT infringements decisions based on those articles bind the ordinary English court.[7] These sections of the CA (1998) provide the basis for what is known as 'follow-on' enforcement or monetary actions. Arguably S 47A and 58A CA (1998) significantly facilitate the discharge of the legal burden of proof of the party wishing to enforce EC Articles 81 and or 82 by eliminating the need to produce any proof beyond the requisite infringement decision made by either the CAT or by the Commission.

In order to better appreciate the operation of the two methods of proof used in the English system of competition law enforcement, it is useful to describe the general legal context of enforcement of EC Articles 81 and 82 in England. There are two venues: first, the ordinary courts and second, the CAT. Pursuant to S 58A CA(1998), the ordinary civil court may be used as noted above in order to enforce a finding of infringement of EC Articles 81 or 82 if produced by the OFT, the European Commission or the CAT. The purpose of enforcement by the ordinary civil court is to produce a remedy in damages for losses caused by the infringement. The court intervenes, therefore, exclusively on the issues of causation and calculation of the loss and damages. Accordingly, where an infringement decision exists the national court may be used in order to provide a remedy in damages. The second method of enforcement is utilized where an infringement decision does not exist as in the instant case of *Crehan*. In those circumstances, the national court must make its own finding of infringement either on the basis of expert evidence produced by the parties. Further, in so doing, the national court applies the normal

---

6. *Courage Ltd v. Crehan* C-453/99 [2001] ECR I-6297; *Crehan v. Inntrepreneur Pub Co* (2003) EWHC 1510 (Ch).
7. EC Dir 1/2003 Art. 16.1 governs the situation of the national courts in relation to Commission decisions rendered in the same matter as that of which the court is seized.

rules of evidence albeit subject to the EC doctrine of effectiveness. This is in contrast to the situation which prevails as noted earlier pursuant to Art. 58A CA (1998) which simplifies the enforcement by making a specified infringement judgment binding on the court.

2.   *CREHAN*: COURT OF APPEAL

Prior to the judgment of the House of Lords in *Crehan*[8] of July 2006, it would appear that the Court of Appeal in its judgment in *Crehan*[9] had established a particular method of proof using relevant Commission decisions and documents. This method of proof could be conveniently called the doctrine of consistency. The Court of Appeal held that following EC Art. 10,[10] Commission Notice of 1993,[11] ECJ[12] and English[13] judgments, the English court had a duty to show deference to relevant Commission infringement decisions and information. While not mentioning either Art. 16.1 Reg. 1/2003 of which the doctrine of consistency could be said to constitute an expansion of the scope or Commission Cooperation Notice of 2004,[14] the Court referred to two matters: in particular to paragraphs 20 and 21 of the 1993 Commission Cooperation Notice[15] and to the concept of 'sincere cooperation' expressed therein as part of the legal basis for

---

8. *Inntrepreneur Pub Co. (CPC) & others v. Crehan* [2006] UKHL 38 on appeal from (2004) EWCA Civ 637.
9. *Bernard Crehan v. Inntrepreneur Pub Co. (CPC)*, Case A3/2003/1725, [2004] EWCA 637.
10. EC Art. 10 provides: Member States shall take all appropriate measures, whether general or particular, to ensure fulfilment of the obligations arising out of the Treaty or resulting from action taken by the institutions of the Community. They shall facilitate the achievement of the Community's tasks. They shall abstain from any measures which could jeopardize the attainment of the objectives of this treaty. They shall abstain from any measures which would jeopardize the attainment of objectives of this Treaty. This the foundation of what is known as the principle of sincere co-operation, being a principle involving obligations and duties of mutual assistance both for Member States and their national courts and for the Community institutions such as the Commission.
11. OJ 1993 C39/06 Notice on Cooperation between the Commission and the National Courts in particular paragraphs 17–20.
12. *Delimitis* C –234/89 [1991] ECIR I-935, *Masterfoods Ltd v. HB Ice Cream* C-344/98 [2000] ECR 1-1369.
13. *Hasselbad GM Ltd v. Orbinson* (1985) & QB 475, *MTV Europe v. BMG Records Ltd* (1997) EuLR 100 at 105, *Iberian UK Ltd v. BPB Industries PLC* (1997) EuLR 1 at 16.
14. OJ 2004 C 101/03 Notice on Cooperation between the Commission and the National Courts.
15. *Bernard Crehan v. Inntrepreneur Pub Co (CPC)*, Case A3/2003/1725, [2004] EWCA Civ 637, op. cit. at para. 97 'In our judgment, in the present case, the English court was obliged under a duty of sincere cooperation to give to the Commission much greater deference than that which the judge was prepared to give'. It would seem that the Court may make a distinction between 'deference' and 'binding' in that at para. 74 referring to the decisions taken by the Whitbread, Bass and Scottish National which were relied upon by Mr Crehan, the Court observed 'It is not in dispute that those decisions did not formally bind anyone not addressed by those decisions'.

the duty to show deference. At point 83 of its judgment, the Court of Appeal observed:

> In paragraph 20 of the Commission Notice, the Commission said that before the national court answers questions whether Art. 81 (1) applies, it should ascertain the opinion or other statements of the Commission.

The Court continued in paragraph 20: 'Such statements provide national courts with significant information for reaching a judgment even if they are not formally bound by them'.

The Court of Appeal further observed in paragraph 21 that: 'if the Commission has not reached an agreement, then the national courts can always be guided in interpreting the Community law question by the case law of the ECJ and the existing decisions of the Commission'.

The Court applied this doctrine of consistency in order to use part of a Commission exemption decision addressed to a third party, Whitbread, in a relevant but different case, in addition to letters directed to the lawyer for Mr Crehan and communications between Inntrepreneur and the Commission.[16]

Indeed, one of the major consequences of the Court of Appeal judgment in *Crehan* was that the doctrine of consistency served apparently as an exclusionary rule of evidence on the issue of breach of EC Articles 81 and 82 where relevant Commission infringement decisions and other documents were used. It thereby fundamentally facilitated the enforcement actions of EC Articles 81 and 82 by reducing the amount of evidence required to prove the cause of action and thereby reducing the costs for litigation. In short, the Court of Appeal judgment had the effect of improving the possibilities for enforcement of EC competition law by the English courts. However, prior to the judgment of the House of Lords, it was also felt that the application of the Court of Appeal's doctrine of consistency would require further clarification with respect to its legal and factual scope: that is, the doctrine seemed to apply to two matters; not only to the law but also to the facts contained in relevant Commission decisions and documents such as letters, advice, etc. In this regard, the Court of Appeal although not enumerating the type of documents to which the doctrine of consistent decisions was to apply referred

---

16. Concerning the evidence the Court of Appeal notes in para. 54 of *Crehan*: 'Mr Crehan called no factual evidence in relation to issues (1) and (2) but relied on decisions of and documents produced by the Commisson and other documentary materials such as reports of the MMC and the OFT at para. 97: 'In our judgment in the present case the English Court was obliged under a duty of sincere cooperation to give to the Commission much greater deference that that which the judge was prepared to give . We accept that the Commission and the ECJ left it to the English court to determine whether the application made by this court on making the reference that the beer tie in the Inntrepreneur lease contravened Art. 81 (1) was correct. However, in the letter of 24 November 1997 to the solicitors, Charles Russell, it is apparent that it expected the English court to take into account its earlier conclusions not only in respect of Inntrepreneur but also in the cases of Whitbread even though not final decisions'.

as noted to Art. 20 of the 1993 Commission Co-operation Notice.[17] Further, the operation of the doctrine appears to have been predicated on the case of *Foto Frost*.[18] In this case the ECJ held that any challenge of the accuracy of a Commission infringement decision must be made exclusively by means of a reference to the ECJ thereby excluding the introduction of any contrary evidence and reinforcing by the national court to contradict the Commission decision. This is clearly related to the principle of legal certainty through consistency. However, concern had also been expressed[19] that the Court of Appeal judgment and the doctrine of consistency reduced the independence of the national courts in terms of venues of enforcement for EC Articles 81 and or 82 in relation to the Commission and its decisions.

3.   *CREHAN*: HOUSE OF LORDS

As events would have it, the House of Lords in its judgment on *Crehan*[20] of 19 July 2006 overturned the Court of Appeal and the latter's application of the doctrine of consistency based upon the principles of legal certainty and loyal co-operation founded upon EC Art. 10 which was comparable as noted to the expansion of the scope of EC Dir 1/2003 Art. 16 (1). In short, the House of Lords held that a Commission decision involving a case other than that before the court constitutes simply admissible evidence which, given the expertise of the Commission, the court may regard as highly persuasive. However, as a matter of law, the Commission decision constitutes only part of the evidence which the court may consider on the issue to be proved and its use does not exclude or preclude other contradictory evidence. The majority opinion, presented by Lord Hoffmann, focussed upon the following matters: first, the absence of any legal basis in EC law for extending the duty of the domestic court to avoid entering a judgment which conflicts with

---

17. The Court referred to the submission of D. Vaughan QC, counsel for Mr Crehan, who endeavoured to limit the scope of the doctrine of consistency at point 96 as follows: 'Mr Vaughan submitted that there are three possible degrees of deference which should be accorded by the national court to the Commission under the duty of sincere co-operation'. The Court then appears to have rejected this attempt at restriction on the scope of the duty of consistency at point 97 in the following terms: 'We do not need to discuss whether or not such degrees of deference are correctly categorised and defined'.
18. *Foto Frost v. Hauptzollamt Lübeck Ost* C-314/85 [1987] ECR 4225 points 11–17.
19. A. Andreangeli, 'Courage Ltd v. *Crehan* and the Enforcement of Art. 81 EC Before the National Courts' (2004) 5 ECLR 758 at 764 'However the approach taken by the Court of Appeal leaves several issues open: in particular with respect to its likely impact on the position of domestic courts in the legal framework established by the Treaty and eventually in their independence. Further guidance should be sought from the ECJ in the future on the interpretation of the duty resulting form Art. 10 to pay due regard to the decisions of the Commission when the latter may be relevant to adjudicate claims grounded on Art. 81 and 82'. See *generally*, A. Andreangeli, 'The Impact of the Modernisation Regulation on the Guarantees of Due Process in Competition Proceedings' (2006) 31 ELRev 342–63
20. *Inntrepreneur Pub Co (CPC) & others v. Crehan* (2006) UKHL 38 op. cit.

Commission decisions beyond the same case as that of which the court is seized; second, the absence of legal grounds for preventing the court from considering evidence which might contradict Commission decisions where there was no duty to avoid conflicting decisions; third, the status of a Commission decision is, henceforth, to be considered simply as that of admissible evidence to which the court may wish to attach significance by reason of the Commission's expertise. Dealing with the absence of legal basis for extending the duty to avoid judgments likely to conflict with Commission decisions Lord Hoffmann held as follows:

> Paragraph 63: 'The law on the relationships between the Commission and the National courts was so to speak codified by Art. 16 of EC 1/2003 on the implementation of the rules on competition laid down in Articles 81 and 82 of the Treaty with effect from 1 May 2004. It was of course not in force at the time of the event but appears accurately to reflect the previous case law'.
>
> Paragraph 64: 'This article makes clear that a relevant conflict exists only when the "agreement, decisions or practise ruled on by the national court have been or are about to be the subject of a Commission decision". It does not apply to other agreements, decisions or practises in the same market'.
>
> Paragraph 65: 'These authorities therefore show that the Commission stated the legal position accurately in its letter to Mr Crehan which I have already quoted (paragraph 32) which said that the question of whether or not Art. 81 (1) applied was "one which the national court is in a position to decide": that it could take into account the views expressed by the Commission in its "general market description" in the Whitbread Art. 19(3) notice: and that "indirect guidance" on questions of law could be derived from the Article 19(3) notice issued after Inntrepreneur's first application. This letter coming soon after the Whitbread noticed would have seen highly misleading if the position was that provided only that the recipients waited for the Commission to adhere to its view in an actual decision in Whitbread and some other case, the issue in the national court would be concluded in their favour'.
>
> Paragraph 66: 'The Court of Appeal accepted at paragraph 67 that the Commission left it to the national court to determine whether 81(1) had been infringed or not. But it said at paragraph 77 that it was clear that the "Commission expected the English Court to follow its view . . . that Art. 81(1) applied". If that means no more than that the Commission thought it was right, I would not think that particularly surprising. But if it means that the Commission thought that the English Court would be obliged as a matter of Community law to follow its view, I think that is neither what the Commission said nor what the authorities required. The Court of Appeal said at paragraph 74 that the Whitbread and other decisions "did not formally bind" Inntrepreneur but nevertheless the judge erred in law by allowing Inntrepreneur "to adduce evidence to show that the Commission was wrong". This suggests a concept of being informally bound which I find difficult to understand. If as the Court of Appeal said, the defendant is precluded from adducing evidence to show that the Commission is wrong the distinction is not visible to the naked eye'.

It would seem that Lord Hoffmann's primary objection to the exclusion by the doctrine of consistency of evidence which could be otherwise introduced in order to contradict a Commission decision is as follows: namely, that preventing a defendant from contradicting a Commission decision in taking of which he had not participated breaches his right to a fair trial. His lordship makes the following observations in this regard in paragraphs 67 and 68 of his opinion:

> Paragraph 67: 'The Court of Appeal said at paragraph 76 that it was left "profoundly uneasy" by the judge's decision to allow Inntrepreneur to challenge the Commission's opinion. But I must confess that I am left profoundly uneasy by the unfairness of the Court of Appeal's decision that Inntrepreneur could not do so. The Court of Appeal said that Inntrepreneur could have raised the matter before the Commission in its own application. It is true that if Inntrepreneur had preserved its application for negative clearance on the old agreements, it could have obtained a ruling and if necessary challenged that ruling in an application for annulment for the Court of First Instance. But the suggestion that it withdraw the application and litigate the matter in England came from the Commission and the Court of Appeal confirmed the judge's decision that his did not induce any abuse of process. For Inntrepreneur to find its main defence shut out by a subsequent decision of the Commission in which it took no part seems to me to be a denial of a fair trial'.
>
> Paragraph 68: 'The Court of Appeal said at paragraph 98 that the judge's decision had created "an irreconcilable inconsistency in the application of the Community's competition policy to the relevant market"; but that again seems to me the opposite of what the Commission said. In its letter to Mr Crehan it said that there was no Community interest which could justify the Commission in deciding whether the old agreements infringed Art. 81(1) or not. If the Commission had thought that it was important to have uniformity of decision on this point, it could have given a decision on the Art. (3) application and subject to annulment that would have bound Inntrepreneur: see *Iberian UK Ltd v. BPP* (1997) EuLR 1. Instead, as an exercise in subsidiarity it left the decision to the national court. To leave a decision to someone else necessarily implies that he may decide it. In my opinion, for the judge to have made his own decision was to respect the policy of the Commission rather than flaunt it'.

Concerning the fact that the judge may consider evidence which contradicts the Commission which therefore need not be followed by reason of deference, his lordship held as follows:

> Paragraph 69: 'There was a great deal of discussion both before the Court of Appeal and in argument before the House of Lords about the degree of "deference" which a national court should show to a decision of the Commission. Mr Vaughan QC is recorded (in paragraph 96 of the judgment of the Court of Appeal) as having constructed a scheme of three degrees of deference (absolute deference, very great deference and deference) which might have to be paid to a decision of the Commission. For my part, I do not find deference

in this context a very helpful expression. It is commonly (if not altogether happily) used in administrative law when a court decides that the decision making powers on a particular question properly belong to someone else and that the court should not substitute its view. But the decision making power on whether Art. 81(1) applies plainly belong to the English court, exercising concurrent jurisdiction and I find it difficult to see how the exercise of this power can be combined with deference to the decision of someone else. The correct position is that when there is no conflict of decisions in the sense which I have discussed the decision of the Commission is simply evidence of properly admissible before the English court which given the expertise of the Commission may well be regarded by the court as highly persuasive. As a matter of law, however, it is only part of the evidence which the court will take into account. If upon the assessment of all evidence the judge comes to the conclusion that the view of the Commission was wrong I do not see how consistently with his judicial oath he can say as a matter of deference he proposes nevertheless to follow the Commission. Only a rule of law in the nature of issue estoppel which obliges him to do so could produce such a result and the Court of Appeal accepts that there was no such rule'.

Paragraph 70: 'Mr Vaughan submits that if his lordship did not accept that the judge was obliged to follow the opinion of the Commission, it should make a reference to the Court of Justice asking whether he was so obliged and alternatively whether in the light of the judge's findings of fact the decision in the Whitbread case was valid. I see little point in either question: on the first issue it is conceded that there is no rule of Community law which required the Court to follow the Commission and on the second the House will either be asking about the validity of a decision about agreements between other parties or else asking the Court of Justice to decide a question of fact which was within the jurisdiction of the national court'.

Paragraph 71: 'In my view therefore the judge was right in deciding that he could decide *Delimits I* for himself and the Court of Appeal was wrong to reverse his decision on the ground that he should have followed the Commission'.

4.   CONSEQUENCES OF THE JUDGMENT OF THE HOUSE OF LORDS IN
           CREHAN FOR THE ENFORCEMENT OF EC ARTICLES 81 AND 82 IN
           INDEPENDENT ACTIONS

The first consequence of the judgment of the House of Lords in *Crehan* is that expert evidence may be admitted in order to contradict a Commission decision decided in a case which is relevant but different from that in issue falling, therefore, without EC Reg. 1/2003 Art. 16(1) as interpreted by their Lordships. Accordingly, a Commission decision constitutes, in terms of probative value, only a piece of evidence which may be used in the matter of proof of an infringement of EC Articles 81 and 82. By reason, however, of the Commission's expertise and competence in matters involving the application of EC Articles 81 and 82 its decisions may well be regarded as possessing significant probative value. However, both the rights of the defence and the absence of any legal basis such as EC Reg. 1/2003 Art. 16(1) permit a party to lead evidence in order to contradict a Commission decision which although relevant nevertheless concerned case different from that of which the national court is seized. Accordingly, the normal English rules of proof apply concerning the use of Commission decisions taken in a case different from that of which the adjudicating English court is seized.

The second consequence is the following: the doctrine of consistency as developed by the Court of Appeal in *Crehan* had the marked effect and, indeed, the advantage of facilitating enforcement in evidential terms of EC Articles 81 and 82 by the national court through the reduction of the amount of evidence which the enforcing party required in order to establish the cause of action. In contrast, the instant judgment of the House of Lords will have the effect of encouraging if not indirectly requiring the use of considerable expert evidence of the type presented at first instance in *Crehan* in order to contradict relevant Commission decisions. Further, this quest for evidence will increase the demands placed upon disclosure. It is of significance to note that in *Crehan*, at first instance, the claimant is recorded by the Court of Appeal as having experienced difficulties in obtaining evidence presumably through disclosure.[21] Accordingly, the net effect of the need for increased expert evidence coupled with greater use of disclosure will lead to the increase of costs involved in the enforcement of EC Articles 81 and 82. This in turn will increase the importance of conditional fees as a method of financing the enforcement proceedings in cases such as that of Mr Crehan who had been financed through legal aid. This could, therefore, under the current rules which govern the operation of conditional fees lead to a disincentive, notably on the part of defendants, to enforce their rights of defence in enforcement proceedings for EC Articles 81 and 82.

The third consequence is that the instant judgment of the House of Lords gives rise to certain legal uncertainties: in this regard, their Lordships do not make clear why *Foto Frost* does not apply, as was noted by the Court of Appeal, so as to prevent the leading of evidence to contradict a Commission decision. It is recalled that the ECJ held in *Foto Frost* the following:

> Paragraph 15: 'On the other hand, those (national) courts do not have the power to declare acts of the Community institutions invalid. As the Court emphasized in the judgment of 13 May 1981 in the case of 66/88 *International Chemical Corporation v. Amministrazione delle Finanze* (1981) ECH 1191, the main purpose of the powers accorded to the court by Art. 177 is to ensure that Community law is applied uniformly by national courts. That requirement of uniformity is particularly imperative when the validity of a community act

---

21. *Bernard Crehan v. Inntrepreneur Pub Company CPC* [2004] EWCA 637 op. cit. at para. 76 'It is apparent that Mr Crehan was frustrated in attempts which he made to obtain evidence by the issue of witness summons. The results is that a judge embarking upon the exercise which Park J. did, perforce makes his assessment on the evidence which the parties choose or are able to put before him and inevitably does so on material less contemporaneous than that which as available to the Commission carrying out its own exhaustive investigation ten years earlier'.

is in question. Differences between courts in the Member States as to the validity of the Community Acts would be liable to place in jeopardy the very unity of the Community legal order and to detract from the fundamental requirement of legal certainty'.

Paragraph 16: 'The same conclusion is dictated by consideration of the necessary coherence of the system of judicial protection established by the Treaty. In that regard, it must be observed that request for preliminary rulings, like actions for annulment constitute reasons for reviewing the legality of acts of the Community institutions'.

Paragraph 17: 'Since Art. 173 gives the Court the exclusive jurisdiction to declare void an act of a Community institution, the coherence of the system required that where the validity of a Community act is challenged before a national court, the power to declare the act invalid must also be reserved to the court of justice'.

It is clear that the evidence which the judgment of the instant House of Lord's judgment in *Crehan* now permits to be adduced has as its objective the contradiction of the Commission decision. The contradiction of the Commission decision in turn has as its underlying objective that of upholding the rights of the defence as noted in paragraph 67 of Lord Hoffmann's speech. It nevertheless remains unclear as to why the rights of the defence cannot be upheld by means of a reference to the Court pursuant to EC Art. 234. Lord Hoffmann dismissed such a possibility but without referring to the exclusive jurisdiction possessed by the ECJ to invalidate acts of Community institutions. It may be, therefore, that a request for a reference to be made to the ECJ on the basis of the latter's exclusive competence to invalidate the acts of Community institutions could avoid Lord Hoffmann's objection: specifically as he observed in paragraph 70 of his speech, that the English court had been charged to decide the matter – understood to mean, in its entirety thereby excluding references. Further, it may be that a request for a reference pursuant to EC 234 as method of upholding the rights of the defence could succeed given that Lord Hoffmann did not consider the role of this article as a method of ensuring such rights. Finally, his Lordship, as noted in paragraph 69 of his opinion, did not deal specifically with the ground accepted by the Court of Appeal and apparently advanced by counsel, Mr. Vaughan QC, for admission of evidence which could, in conjunction with a reference pursuant to EC Art. 234, uphold the rights of the defence: specifically the admission of evidence to prove that a Commission decision should be distinguished from the case at hand. Lord Hoffmann simply observed that the word 'deference' irrespective of the degree thereof was in appropriate. In reality, the advantage is that the process of distinguishing a Commission decision by means of evidence does not contradict the decision or infringe the ECJ judgment of *Foto Frost*. Therefore, evidence can be quite easily led. The Court of Appeal noted specifically:

Paragraph 96: 'Mr Vaughan submitted that there are three positive degrees of deference which should be accorded by the national court to the Commission under the duty of sincere co-operation'.

The second he said is a very great deference in circumstances where the duty of sincere co-operation requires the court to defer entirely to findings of the Commission which apply to the agreement before the Court again subject only to the possibility of a reference but where a party may properly adduce evidence to distinguish the facts of his case form those found by the Commission.

> Paragraph 98: '*Inntrepreneur* in its evidence and submission to the judge did not attempt to distinguish the present case from Whitbread and the other decisions of the Commission going to the applicability of Art. 81(1) in the relevant market'.

Accordingly, it is clear that the objective of the judgment of the House of Lords in *Crehan* is to ensure the protection of the rights of the defence by means of the organization of fair trial. This objective according to Lord Hoffmann may be attained by the introduction of evidence in order to contradict a Commission decision. Notwithstanding this argument, as noted above, it is submitted that it might still be possible to seek to exclude contradictory evidence on the basis of an infringement of *Foto Frost* and to utilize EC Art. 234 in order to ensure the rights of the defence which is quite separate from the operation of EC Reg. 1/2003 and the scope of Art. 16(1) thereof.

The fourth consequence of the instant judgment of the House of Lords is that Lord Hoffmann did not specifically deal with the argument presented by the Court of Appeal concerning the rights of the defence as set forth in paragraph 74 of its judgment. In paragraph 73 thereof, the Court of Appeal noted that one of the reasons which led Park J. to reject the Commission decisions as probative evidence was that Inntrepreneur had not been involved in the process of their taking. It would appear that Lord Hoffmann in paragraph 67 of his opinion previously cited effectively reaffirmed the judge's view in holding that the exclusion of Inntrepreneur's evidence and the use of a decision in which they had never participated would prevent a fair trial. Lord Hoffmann does not indicate, however, why he at least implicitly rejected the Court of Appeal's analysis concerning the matter of Inntrepeneur's indirect participation in the taking of Commission's decision and, therefore, its effect upon the rights of the defence. The Court of Appeal presented its analysis as follows:

> Paragraph 73: 'The judge therefore held that he should decide that question for himself. He gave several reasons'.
>
> Paragraph 74 'The first was that Inntrepreneur was not a party to the proceedings which resulted in the 1999 decision in Whitbread, Bass and Scottish and National and it had no input into the material which the Commission considered. It is not in dispute that those decisions did not formally bind anyone not addressed by those decisions. However, the decisions related to the same market as that in which Inntrepreneur was engaged and it can hardly be said that Inntrepreur had no opportunity to make submissions to the Commission (or to the national competition authorities such as the MMC or the OFT to whose reports the Commission referred) on the question of the foreclosure of the UK market'.

Clearly the Court of Appeal felt that Inntrepreneur had been able to present its views in the context of the Commission's decision making and process and that accordingly, the Inntrepeneur's rights of the defence were not infringed in using these decisions.

The fifth consequence of the House of Lords' judgment is that it will render the enforcement of EC Articles 81 and 82 more difficult in terms of the quantity of proof which the enforcing party must lead in order to establish to the requisite standard the cause of action. Accordingly, as will be discussed below, the judgment may well lead to the intervention of the doctrine of effectiveness in order at a minimum to reallocate the burden of proof so as to ensure overall effective enforcement of EC Articles 81 and 82.

5.   METHODS OF PROOF: TRADITIONAL METHOD

As noted earlier, the traditional or normal method of proof is employed where S 47 A and 58 A CA (1998) cannot be utilized notably by reason of the absence of an infringement decision of either the OFT or the Commission. This is the case in a stand alone action for damages. In short, this traditional or normal method of proof the primacy of which was confirmed by the House of Lords in *Crehan* requires that the party seeking a court judgment prove on the balance of probabilities all the facts which give rise to the right in order to obtain the remedy or order sought.[22] Nevertheless, it is clear that the application of this normal method of proof may result in rendering the discharge thereof more onerous notably in a case where the claimant must adduce himself all of the evidence than would be the case were it possible to invoke the doctrine of consistency as developed by the Court of Appeal. However, there exists some indication that the application of this normal method of proof can be varied and indeed apportioned in English law according to various principles. These principles both explicit and implicit within the Overriding Objective of the CPR would involve considerations of justice and fairness as well as the need to ensure a proportionate use of resources. Arguably, these principles may require in certain circumstances a departure of the normal allocation of the burden of proof such that the burden itself may be distributed between the claimant and the defendant on different issues as opposed to being allocated to exclusively one party. This apportioning may be effected either by the courts or by statute. An example of the statute would be the Employment Rights Act 1996. S 98 of that Act established that in an action for unfair dismissal the employee bears the burden of persuasion to establish that he was dismissed. Nevertheless, it is for the employer to prove that the dismissal was in accordance with the legislative criteria of fair dismissal. With respect to contract, a claimant suing thereon must prove the existence of the contract, its breach and the damage which he has suffered from the

---

22.   *Attheraces Ltd & Anr v. British Horse Racing Board & Anr* (2005) EWHC 3015 (Ch) Case HC
      0500 996, Date of Judgment: 21 December 2005.

breach. However, frustration releases the defendant from the contractual obligation of performance. The claimant has not duty to disprove frustration. The defendant bears the burden of adducing evidence on this issue.[23]

B.   REALLOCATION OF INCIDENCE OF PROOF
                FOLLOWING THE DOCTRINE OF EFFECTIVENESS
                AND NOT DISCRIMINATION

As noted earlier, until the judgment of the House of Lords in *Crehan*, the doctrine of consistency as developed and applied by the Court of Appeal in the same case arguably appeared to have the overall effect of facilitating the enforcement of EC Articles 81 and 82: it sufficed that the enforcing party produce Commission decisions and other documents which although not involving directly the same case as the one of which the national court was seized nevertheless were relevant. Therefore, following the doctrine of consistency unless the Commission decisions could be distinguished the court would find that the infringement alleged was indeed proved to the requisite standard of proof, namely, the balance of probabilities. However, by reason of the judgment of the House of Lords in the instant case of *Crehan*, such a method of proof is no longer possible. As noted earlier, this judgment of the House of Lords has the effect of potentially rendering the enforcement of EC Articles 81 and 82 more difficult by requiring that the enforcing party produce expert evidence notably in stand alone actions where S 47A and S 58A (CA 1998) do not apply. In order to compensate for what might be termed the negative effect of this judgment on the enforcement of EC Articles 81 and 82 in terms of evidence, it may therefore be necessary to consider changes to the distribution of the burden of proof.[24] Arguably, a modification of the burden of proof

---

23.   A.A.S. Zuckerman, *Civil Procedure* (London, Lexis Nexis 2003) see *generally* chapter on evidence.
24.   Reg. 1/2003 Art. 2 provides: 'Burden of Proof: In any national or Community proceedings for the application of Art. 81 and 82 of the Treaty the burden of proving an infringement of Art. 81 (1) or of Art. 82 of the Treaty shall rest on the party or authority alleging the infringement. The undertaking or association of undertaking claiming the benefit of Art. 81 (3) of the Treaty shall bear the burden of proving that the conditions of that paragraph are fulfilled'. Arguably this article represents an attempt at harmonization of the burden of proof in terms of procedural enforcement by the national courts. However, it is submitted that the wording of Art. 2 is to be construed in the sense that the party alleging the infringement bears overall the legal burden of proving the infringement. It is submitted, therefore, that the division of the burden of proof on the issue of the infringement does not contravene Art. 2 provided that the party who claims the infringement bears the overall burden of proof. In so far as Art. 2 does not impose the entire burden upon the party alleging the infringement the regulation does not harmonize completely this procedural issue in terms of precluding national procedural variations as to the division of this burden provided that overall the party claiming the infringement can be said to be have the obligation to discharge this burden overall. See also: *GT-Link v. DBS*, Case C – 242/95 [1997] ECR I 4449 in which the ECJ established that the burden of proof was a matter for the national rules subject to the doctrine of effectiveness and non-discrimination.

may facilitate the enforcement of EC Articles 81 and 82 thereby compensating for the loss of the doctrine of consistency developed by the Court of Appeal in *Crehan*. As such, it is submitted that the doctrine of effectiveness will require that such changes be made unless the principles national English principles of procedure can justify maintaining the normal distribution of the burden of proof.

In *Aalborg*,[25] the ECJ referred to the eventual necessity of reallocation of the burden of proof:

> Paragraph 78: 'As the Council very recently stated in the fifth recital of Reg. (EC) No 1/2003 of 16 Dec 2002, on the implementation of the rules on competition law laid down in Articles 81 and 82 of the Treaty, it should be for the party or the authority alleging an infringement of competition rules to prove the existence thereof and it should be for the undertaking or association of undertakings invoking the benefit of a defence against a finding of infringement to demonstrate that the conditions for applying such a defence are satisfied so that the authority will then have to resort to other evidence'.
>
> Pararaph 79: 'Although according to those principles, the legal burden is born either by the Commission or the undertaking or association concerned, the factual evidence on which a party relies may be of such a kind as to require the other party to provide an explanation or justification failing which it is permissible to conclude that the burden of proof has been discharged'.

Accordingly, it is clear that the method of proof based upon the use of ss 47A and 58A CA (1998) in monetary actions and on the use of the doctrine of consistency until abolished by the House of Lords renders less onerous the matter of proof of an infringement of EC Articles 81 and or 82 than does the traditional or normal method of proof: that is the method wherein the claimant, by default of any such Commission or OFT infringement judgments, must proof each element of the infringement in order to obtain the remedy claimed. However, it is the case that English law can provide for the reallocation of the burden of proof in certain circumstances: notably, by taking into account principles of justice and in particular by ensuring a proportionate allocation of resources. It is submitted that in order to bring enforcement of EC Art. 81 and Art. 82 in terms of free standing actions on an equal playing field with the follow on, monetary actions subject notably to ss 47A and 58A CA (1998) the doctrine of effectiveness and non-discrimination may intervene. It is submitted that this doctrine could lead to the modification of the burden of proof: that is, the burden of proof could be divided between the claimant and the defendant as is in the case of ss 98 Employment Rights Act (1998). This section provides specifically that the burden be divided between the claimant and the defendant.

---

25. *Aalborg Portland et al v. Commission*, joined cases C 204/00, C/205/00, C211/00, C213/00, C217/00; see Commission Staff Working Paper: Annexe to the Green Paper: 'Damages actions for breach of EC anti-trust rules' (COM (2005) 672 Final: <www.europa.eu> paragraphs 78–87.

With respect to EC Art. 81 for example, a possible allocation of the burden of proof between the claimant and the defendant could be as follows: the claimant could be allocated the burden of proving the issue of infringement of competition under EC Art. 81. In the event that this issue were established by the claimant to the requisite level, the burden of proof would then revert to the defendant who would be obliged to disprove a separate issue pursuant to EC Art. 81: namely, the issue of effect on trade between Member States. This procedure is followed apparently in the application of German competition law.[26] Arguably, the allocation of the burden of proof would, thereby, follow the general underlying principles of fairness: that is the division and the distribution of the elements of the burden of proof among the parties is firstly possibly in certain circumstances and secondly, proceeds on the basis of the distribution of the risks of error between the opposing parties. Indeed, it is submitted that 'It is precisely because both parties are entitled to equal protection from the risk of error it makes sense to hold that while one party runs a higher risk on one issue, the opponent must bear the risk on another issue'.[27] It has also been argued that the judgment of the House of Lords in *Crehan* renders the enforcement of EC Art. 81 and or 82 being more difficult than would have been the case under doctrine of consistency developed by the Court of Appeal. By reason of the absence of any English principles to the contrary, it is submitted that the doctrine of effectiveness and non discrimination may intervene so as to ensure effective enforcement of EC Art. 81 and or 82: specifically, the doctrine could intervene so as to approximate the degree of enforceability which could have existed under the doctrine of consistency developed by the Court of Appeal in *Crehan* by reallocating the burden of proof along the lines suggested above in a manner which might approximate the operation of S 20(5) GWB in German competition law.

C.   STANDARD OF PROOF

Finally, it is submitted that it is appropriate that the normal standard of civil proof, namely, the balance of probabilities be utilized in order to establish a breach in a cause of action based upon EC Articles 81 and 82. However, in *Shearson Lehman Hutton*,[28] Webster J states that infringement of EC Art. 81 carries the liability of a

---

26. S 20 (5) of the GWB (German Competition Law) alleviates the claimant's evidentiary burden where the claimant is able to establish a *prima facie* case the defendant is required to clarify those issues which relate to its field of business which cannot be clarified by the claimant but which can be easily clarified by the defendant.
27. A.A. S. Zuckerman, *Civil Procedure* (London, Lexis Nexis, 2003) op. cit. at p. 652.
28. *Shearson Lehman Hutton v. HB Ice Cream Ltd* (1989) 3 CMLR 429 at 570. It would seem that Webster J. may be referring to eventual proceedings before the Commission as opposed to damages in the proceedings before the English court although, with due respect, the relationship between the standard of proof in the English proceedings for damages and Commission proceedings which might result in a finding with damages is not clear in a causal sense: see *Otto v. Postbank Case* C-60/92 at para. 20–21.

penalty and therefore the standard of 'a high degree of probability' should be applied.[29] In contrast, in *Masterfoods Ltd v. HB Ice Cream Ltd*,[30] Kean J. of the Irish court held that the ordinary standard of civil proof, namely, balance of probabilities, applied. In *Crehan*, at first instance, the judge used the balance of probabilities.[31] Again the English court, in *Arkin v. Borchard*[32] applied apparently the civil test of the balance of probabilities but a 'high balance'. In so far as the case law may disclose an attempt by the English court to impose a higher standard of proof than that recognized in the normal test of the balance of probabilities, it is argued that the doctrine of effectiveness coupled with the limb of non-discrimination would intervene. This principle would arguably prevent the imposition of a higher standard. Clearly, there is no apparent justification in terms of procedural principles for treating the enforcement of EC Articles 81 and 82 in civil cases differently from other civil cases event taking account of the eventual imposition of fines by the Commission in eventual enforcement proceedings: first it has been argued that the principle of a fairness requires that all litigants be treated in an equal fashion with respect to the standard of proof;[33] second, in *Hornal*[34] the Court of Appeal held that the civil standard of a preponderance of probability applied in civil cases even if the case involved an allegation of fraud or of a criminal offence; third, in *Re H*(minors)[35] the House of Lords acknowledged that the more serious or improbable

---

29. M. Clough QC & A. McDougall, Ashurst: Study on the Conditions of Claims for Damages: UK Report (2004) <www.europa.eu> op. cit. at p. 12.

30. *Masterfoods Ltd v. HB Ice Cream Ltd* (1992) 3 CMLR 830 at 873.

31. *Bernard Crehan v. Inntrepreneur Pub Co.* (CPC) Case A3/2003/1725 (2004) EWCA 637, op. cit., at paragraph 169 of its judgment, the Court of Appeal refers to paragraph 236 of the judgment at first instance of Park J: 'In paragraph 236 the judge added that it was tacitly accepted by both sides that the issues tended to revolve around whether Mr Crehan would have got through the first three years'. The judge stated his conclusion on paragraph 236: 'Reviewing all of the foregoing matters, I came on the balance of probabilities, to the conclusion in agreement with the opinion of Mr Main that if Mr Crehan had been free of the tie throughout and had been paying a market rent for free-of tie pubs not on an inflated rent for free-tie pubs, his business would have survived the first three critical years'.

32. *Arkin v. Borchard Lines Ltd* (2001) EuLR 232, final judgment *Arkin v. Borchard Line Ltd* (2003) EWHC 687 (Comm Ct).

33. A.A.S. Zuckerman, *Civil Procedure* (London, Lexis Nexis, 2003) op. cit. observes at p. 653–4 'In civil cases proof on the balance of probabilities is all that is required in order to discharge the burden of persuasion. This standard is dictated by considerations of justice. Given that all are equal before the law, there is normally no justification for discriminating between opposing litigants and imposing on one a substantially higher risk of error than on the other'. Any deviation from an even distribution of the risk of error will amount to treating litigants unequally and must therefore be justified. Since the standard of proof on the balance of probabilities represents a just distribution of the risk of error between opposing parties who are entitled to be treated as equals in procedure, the notion that the civil standard should be higher when grave allegations are made must be resisted. See *generally* A. Keene, *The Modern Law of Evidence* (5th ed. 2000 Butterworths, London) p. 96–101.

34. *Hornal v. Neuberger Products Ltd* (1957) 1 QB 247 (Court of Appeal).

35. *Re: H* (minors) (sexual abuse: standard of proof) (1996) AC 563; see also *Attheraces v. British Horse Racing Board* [2006] FSR 201 at paragraph 126 which appears to follow *Re:H* (minors) (sexual abuse: standard of proof)[1996] AC 563 *ibid.* which is cited in terms of standard of proof being the balance of probabilities. 'It is not in dispute that since the legal burden of proof lies on

the allegation of abuse the more convincing the evidence required to prove the allegation had to be. However, what the court must not do is to require a party to prove his case by a higher standard. Therefore, in the absence of any justification in terms of English principles of law, the doctrine of effectiveness would require the English court to apply the normal standard of the balance of probabilities which it applies in all civil cases equally to those involving enforcement of EC Articles 81 and or 82. It is further submitted that the effect of the House of Lords' judgment in *Crehan* is such that the doctrines of effectiveness and non discrimination would imperatively require the use of the normal civil standard of the balance of probabilities in enforcement of EC Articles 81 and 82 by means of civil damages actions.

---

the ATR to establish abuse within Art. 82 and S 18 of the 1988 Act, the burden also lies on ATR to establish each of the analytic steps which are prerequisites to a finding of abuse of dominant position. The standard of proof is the civil standard of balance of probabilities but the seriousness of an infringement of S 18 of the 1998 Act or Art. 82 involves as it may the imposition of financial penalties requires that the proof must be commensurately cogent and convincing see: *re: H* (1996) AC 563–568 Lord Nichols, and Aberdeen Journals Ltd v. OFT (2002) CAT II citing *Napp Pharmaceuticals Ltd v. Director General of Fair Trading* (2002 CAT I at para. 19'. In *Napp*, the CAT held at paragraph 106: 'In our view, the standard of proof to be applied under the Act is to be so decided in accordance with the normal rules of the UK domestic legal system' and at paragraph 107: 'In our view it follows from the speech of Lord Nicholls (with whom Lord Goff and Lord Mustill agreed) in *Re: H*, cited above at 586 & 587, that under the law of England and Wales there are only two standards of proof, the criminal standard and the civil standard . . . with the civil standard however; the more serious the allegation the more cogent should be the evidence before the court considers that the allegation is established on the preponderance of probability'. Arguably, therefore, *Napp* establishes that in proceedings under the C A (1998) although the evidence much be cogent, the standard is the normal civil standard.

Chapter 3
English Procedure: Conditional Costs

In *Campbell*,[1] the House of Lords held that the use of the indemnity rule to transfer the conditional fee with an eventual 100 per cent up lift coupled with an ATE insurance premium to the losing party constitutes a proportionate method to ensure private legal funding. As such, ECHR Art. 11 was not violated. However, their lordships did not decide whether the use of the indemnity rule to transfer a conditional fee with a possible 100 per cent up lift based upon a system of uncapped legal costs may constitute a disproportionate method of private legal funding and thereby violate ECHR Art. 6. Furthermore, this conditional fee system may also contravene the EC doctrine of effective enforcement for the following reason: the system could render the enforcement of EC Articles 81 and or 82 more difficult or almost impossible. Specifically, it might serve, among other things, to discourage a defendant from asserting his rights pursuant to those articles for fear of having to bear the winning party's legal costs with up to a 100 per cent uplift. Therefore, to avoid this financial consequence, the defendant may choose to settle rather than defend the action. Accordingly, in order to prevent such a breach of the doctrine of effectiveness as well as ECHR Art. 6, the English conditional fee system may require modification possibly along the lines of either the rules used in the Competition Appeal Tribunal (CAT) or those of the Court of Session in Scotland.

---

1. *Campbell (Appellant) v. MGN Limited (Respondent)* (2005) UKHL 61 on appeal from (2002) EWCA Civ 1373.

A.   CONDITIONAL FEES IN ENGLAND[2]

In England, the system of conditional fees is provided by S 58 of the Courts and
Legal Services Act (CLSA) which defines Conditional Fee Agreements (CFA).[3]
However, S 27 of Access to Justice Act[4] amends this section so as to make the CFA
a cost which is recoverable from the losing party. The Conditional Fee Agreements
Order[5] provides that CFAs may be used in all litigation[6] except in criminal and
certain family matters. Further, the order fixes the amount of the maximum uplift
of the success fee at one hundred per cent (100%). Until the adoption of the Access
to Justice Act a successful litigant who had utilized the system of conditional fee
agreements was obliged to pay the success fee himself from the costs recoverable
from losing party. He or she was unable to recover the success fee from the losing
party because it was not contained within the definition of the category of recoverable costs. However, the Access to Justice Act changed this situation.[7] S 6 thereof
provides that a costs order made in any proceedings may, subject to the rules of
court, include a provision for the payment of any fees payable under a CFA.

> S 6 provides: A costs order in any proceedings may subject in the case of court
> proceedings to the rules of court include provision requiring the payment of
> any fees payable under a conditional fee agreement for a success fee.
>   S 7 provides: Rules of Court may make provisions with respect to any
> costs which includes fees payable under a conditional fee agreement (includ-
> ing one which provides for a success fee).

Following S 58A of the CLSA,[8] a costs order in any proceedings may subject to
the rules of court include a provision requiring the payment of any fees payable
under a CFA. Under CPR 44 and its accompanying Practise Direction conditional
fees are now normally recoverable from the losing party. S 9.1 of the Practise
Direction accompanying CPR 44 states that 'under an order for payment of costs,
the costs payable will include an additional liability incurred under a costs funding arrangement'. A funding arrangement means a CFA or a policy taken out to
insure against liability to pay the other side's costs, After The Event Insurance
(ATE insurance).

---

2. N. Andrews, 'English Civil Procedure: Three Aspects of the Long Revolution' Centro di Studi e
    Ricerche di Diritto Comparatto et Straniero, diretto da M.J. Bonell (44) Roma (2001).
    <www.w3.uniroma1.it/idc/centro/publications/44andrews.pdf> in particular Section 4 : Condi-
    tional Fees and Contingency Fees.
3. Courts and Legal Services Act (1990).
4. Access to Justice Act (1999).
5. Conditional Fee Agreements Order (2000) (SI 2000/823).
6. Conditional Fee Agreements Order (2000) (SI2000 (823) *ibid.*: does not exclude litigation based
    upon EC Art. 81 and 82.
7. S 6 and S 7 Access to Justice Act (1999) permitted the insertion of the conditional fee within the
    costs recoverable from the losing party.
8. S 27(1) of the Access of Justice Act (1999) inserted S 58 and 58A into the Courts and Legal
    Services Act (1990) concerning conditional fees and their uplifts.

Part 11.8 of the Practise Directions deals with the assessment of the success fee:

11.8.1 In deciding whether a percentage increase is reasonable relevant factors to be taken into account include:
(a) the risk that the circumstances in which the costs, fees and expenses would be payable might or might not occur;
(b) the legal representative's liability for any disbursements;
(c) what other methods of financing the costs were available.

The Court has the power when considering whether a percentage increase is reasonable to allocate different percentages for different items of costs or for different periods during which the costs were incurred.

It is important to note the impact of the recoverability of success fees upon the principle that recoverable costs ought to be incurred and calculated both proportionally and reasonably. Lord Hoffman observes in Campbell:[9] 'As Lord Woolf CJ said in *Lowndes v. Home Office* (Practise Note) (2002) 'the policy is that litigation should be conducted in a proportionate manner and where possible at a proportionate costs'. But the test of proportionality and reasonableness is applied only to the basic costs. It is not applied to the total sum for which the losing party may be liable after the addition of the success fee. This is explicitly recognized in the Practise Direction at Section 11.5.

11.5 In deciding whether the costs are reasonable and (on a standard basis assessment) proportionate, the court will consider the amount of any additional liability separately from the base costs.

Section 11.9 particularizes the consequences of this policy: 'A percentage increase will not be reduced simply on the ground that when added to the basic costs which are relevant (where relevant) proportionate the total appears disproportionate'.

According to Lord Hoffmann, Section 11.9 provides that the aggregate amount of the costs which are shifted to the losing party by the indemnity rule and which is composed of the legal costs in the proceedings coupled with the success fee is not subject to the principle of proportionality.[10] His lordship further observes: 'In Campbell, MGN . . . [sought] a rule of the Appellate Court that they should not be liable to pay any part of the success fee on the ground that they should not be liable to pay any part of the success fee on the ground that in the circumstances of this case, such a liability is so disproportionate as to infringe their right to freedom of expression under Art. 10 of the Convention'.[11] It is to be noted that because the claimant's costs from the three proceedings had not yet been taxed,

---

9. *Campbell v. MGN HL (2005)* op. cit *point 12.*
10. *Campbell v. MGN ibid.* Lord Hope of Craighead observes at point 45 'The effect of these directions is that the exercise of applying the tests of reasonableness and proportionality to the percentage increase is when compared with the task of apply these tests to the base costs a separate exercise'. In reality his lordship, even more so that he indicates his agreement with the analysis of Lord Hoffmann, simply states that the aggregate amount composed of the basic costs and the up lift is not itself subject to the test of proportionality.
11. *Campbell v. MGN ibid.* at point 4 Lord Hoffmann.

MGN was not concerned with the aggregate figures: rather, it raised in advance of the assessment the point of principle concerning their liability for the costs of the proceedings.[12] The ratio of Campbell contains two limbs; the first limb is that there exist two concepts of proportionality: the first one is provided by the CPR when dealing with costs within a particular matter; and the second one relates to the whether the method which a national government chooses in order to ensure access to the courts notably in cases involving defamation can be said to be proportional to that objective: the second limb is that the matter at issue in Campbell concerned proportionality in the sense of the second concept.

His lordship observed: 'But Article 10 is concerned with whether a rule which requires the unsuccessful defendant not only to pay the reasonable and proportionate costs of their adversary in the litigation but also to contribute to the funding of other litigation is a proportionate measure to provide those other litigants with access to justice having regard to its effect on the Art. 10 right to freedom of expression. MGN do not deny that in principle it is open to the legislature to choose to fund access to justice in this way'.[13]

Accordingly, the system of conditional fees coupled with the use of the indemnity rule to shift the payment of costs the aggregate amount of which is not subject to the CPR principle of proportionality constitutes a method of providing for access to justice which is proportionate to that objective. For this reason, ECHR Art. 10 is not violated. However, in reality, Campbell deals with the concept of proportionality in a restricted sense: namely, the use of the CFA coupled with the indemnity system in order to ensure legal funding in general. The judgment does not deal with proportionality in the sense of whether a CFA coupled with uncapped costs imposed upon the losing party by the indemnity rule may be disproportionate to the objective of providing increased access of justice. In contrast with uncapped costs, capped legal costs signify a system by which costs are established and limited either by market forces and agreements or by participants therein or by legislative intervention. Their existence is independent of a costs judge. Arguably, the CFA coupled with the indemnity rule can only become proportionate to its objective of providing increased legal access if the following conditions are fulfilled: where the basic legal costs are capped either through government regulation or by means of market forces as in personal injuries. By reason, therefore, of its lack of proportionality the CFA when based upon uncapped costs and coupled with the indemnity may violate not only ECHR Art. 6 but also the EC principle of effectiveness underlying the procedural enforcement of EC Articles 81 and 82.

---

12. *Campbell v. MGN ibid.* at point 5 Lord Hoffmann.
13. *Campbell v. MGN ibid.* at point 23 Lord Hoffmann.

B.   INADEQUACY OF THE CURRENT SYSTEM OF
       JUDICIAL COST CONTROL

Lord Hoffmann specifically adverts in *Campbell* to what he considers to be the inadequacy of cost control as it pertains to the CFA:

> And I would certainly endorse the sentiments expressed by Brooke LJ in the *King* case. It is however, only a palliative. It does not however deal with problem of incurring substantial . . . costs . . . Further neither capping costs at an early state nor assessing them later deals with having to pay costs at a level which is by definition up to twice the amount which would be reasonable and proportionate.[14]

Lord Hoffmann then observes that there is a real difference between costs in personal injuries litigation 'which are subject to an agreement and costs in defamation proceedings'.[15] As such the real problem is defamation proceedings is 'finding ways of moderating the costs of defamation cases would be in the best interest of all concerned'.[16]

It is useful to consider Lord Hoffmann's observations in Campbell concerning the inadequacy of the method of cost control which is based upon the intervention of the costs judge with his explanation thereof as presented in Callery:[17] in short the reason that prospective cost capping can constitute only a 'palliative' is as follows:

> As I have already said solicitors offering motor accident personal injuries CFAs have no incentive to compete on success fees they charge. So the next question is whether a decision of a costs judge or taxing master as he used to be called is the best way of compensating for the absence of the price competition in the market. The traditional function of the costs judge was to decide what fees were reasonable by reference to his experience of the general levels of fees being charged for comparable work. But this approach only makes sense if the general level of fees is itself directly or indirectly determined by market forces. Otherwise the exercise becomes circular and costs judges will be deciding what is reasonable according to general levels which costs judges have themselves determined. In such circumstances, there is no restraint upon a ratchet effect whereby the highest success fees obtainable from a costs judge are relied upon in subsequent assessments.[18]

His lordship continues:

> The matter becomes even more difficult when a solicitor carrying on litigation business is entitled as the Court of Appeal said to fix success fees to ensure that

---

14. *Campbell v. MGN ibid.* at point 34.
15. *Campbell v. MGN ibid.* at point 36.
16. Campbell *v. MGN ibid.* at point 37.
17. *Stephen Callery (respondent) v. Charles Gray (appellant)* (2002) UKHL 28, 27 June 2002.
18. *Callery v. Gray* House of Lords, *ibid.*; Lord Hoffmann point 32.

the uplifts agreed result in a reasonable overall return having regard to his experience of the work done and the likelihood of success and failure of the particular class of litigation. The costs judge has simply no way of knowing whether a solicitor is carrying on a business on a large enough scale to justify such an approach and still less what level of success fees would give him a 'reasonable overall return'. Such matters are traditionally considered outside the scope of the costs judge.[19]

Lord Hoffmann then proposes a solution for the problem: government intervention which will make will both reduce costs and make them proportionate in an overall manner. His lordship states:

As my noble and learned friend Lord Scott has observed, the criterion prescribed by the CPR for determining whether costs are reasonably framed operate entirely by reference to the facts of the particular case. Once one invokes a global approach designed to produce a reasonable overall return for solicitors, one moves away from the judicial function of the costs judge and into the territory of legislative and administrative decisions. A legislative decision to fix costs at levels calculated to provide adequate access to justice in the most economical way seems to me to be a more rational approach than to leave the matter to an individual costs judge. If it is considered the most appropriate way to secure value for money when the expenditure is borne by the public as a whole (e.g. fixing of graduate fees for criminal legal aid) it should be no less appropriate when the expenditure is born by a section of the public, namely, the motorists. Not only would this be likely to keep the actual costs within reasonable levels but it would also greatly reduce the costs of disputes over costs.[20]

His lordship concludes by observing:

They would be proper to take into account (although the practical difficulties of so doing are considerable) by someone charged with fixing fees for the profession as a whole such as the Lord Chancellor when he determines levels of graduated fees. But a taxing officer in deciding what is a reasonable fee in a particular case must take the general levels of fees as given and use them as a basis of taxation.[21]

It would seem to follow that the solution proposed by Lord Hoffmann corresponds to that proposed by other procedural analysts such as Zuckerman:[22]

19. *Callery v. Gray* House of Lords, *ibid.*; Lord Hoffmann point 33.
20. *Callery v. Gray* House of Lords, *ibid.*; Lord Hoffmann at point 34.
21. *Ibid.*
22. A.A.S. Zuckerman, 'Lord Woolf's Access to Justice: Plus ca change' (1996) MLR 773 at 796 'The history of procedural reform both recent and remote shows the inadequacy of the indirect approach. Attempts to cut down costs by simplifying procedure by judicial pressure or by encouraging clients to resist costs have all been found wanting. There is no alternative to a direct attack on the economic incentives to complicate and protract the litigation process. But a serious challenge to the vested interests of the legal profession cannot come just from a sole reformer however bold and exalted. It must involved determined intervention at the

namely, costs ought to be capped by the government in default of the operation of market forces.

C.   BREACH OF ECHR ARTICLE 6

Accordingly, the following would seem to be the case: *Campbell* establishes generally that a system of conditional fee agreements coupled with the indemnity principle constitutes a proportionate method for improving access to justice. As noted previously, arguably, *Campbell* does not apply where such a system of conditional funding is coupled with the indemnity rule which shifts to the losing party an amount of costs which are not subject to litigation independent control: i.e., are capped. Accordingly, the fundamental question is whether this method of funding is proportional to the objective pursued of increasing access to justice expressed succinctly by Lord Hope in the following manner: 'a reasonable relationship of proportionality between the means employed and the aim sought to be realized'.[23] Following the reasoning of Lord Hoffmann in *Callery*, there appears to be no justification for retaining such an uncontrolled system of costs which produces in turn a method a system of access to justice which is disproportionate to the objective thereof. Perspicuously, methods of legal cost control exist in the form of either legislative intervention or as in personal injuries control through market forces which are more effective than the current method of intervention by a costs judge. Accordingly, with the exception of personal injuries,[24] the apparently unjustifiable use of an ineffective system of cost control is in turn aggravated by the use of the indemnity rule which together produce a method of funding 'which is not proportionate to the objective'. This conclusion would verify As such, it would seem that the analysis of Ashby, Glasser[25] and

---

government level. Until this happens experience will continue to dispel any hopes of improvement and litigation costs will remain as exorbitant as they have been for a very long time'. The Commission Staff Working Paper (Annexe to the Green Paper) COM (2005) 672 19 December 2005, <www.europa.eu.int>, observes at point 212: 'The legal rules regarding costs recovery in the Member States are often of great complexity. Some common themes emerge however from a comparison of these rules. . . . The amount of recoverable fees both for lawyers as well as for experts and other witnesses is often limited by statutory fee schemes'.

23. *Brown v. Stott* (Proc Fiscal Dunferline) (2001) 2 All ER 97 at 103.

24. This field can be arguably exempted for the following reason: the amount of solicitors fees is limited throughout that field by means of agreements between solicitors and insurers which reflect market forces as opposed to government regulation. Where market forces are insufficient to control rates then arguably government intervention is necessary.

25. K. Ashby & C. Glasser 'The Legality of Conditional Fee Uplifts' (2005) 24 CJQ 130 at 135 'Unless the recovery of a success fee can be justified by the nature of the litigation concerned so as to satisfy the Art. 6 criteria, entitlement to an uplift will remain inconsistent with the overriding objective and Lord Woolf's vision of a legal system in which reasonable and proportionate costs are appropriate'.

Zuckerman[26] concerning a breach of ECHR Art. 6. Following these three authors,[27] one method of preventing such a breach would consist in effectively abandoning the use of the indemnity rule. The CFA would be paid by the successful party and not the losing party.

D.   BREACH OF EC DOCTRINE OF EFFECTIVE
            ENFORCEMENT BY CFAS

It may well be that the current CFA system also contravenes the EC doctrine of effective enforcement notably with respect to enforcement of EC Articles 81 and 82 (competition law). As noted earlier, the CFA[28] may be used by litigants who wish to enforce EC Articles 81 and/or 82. A possible example would be a situation such as that which was involved in *Crehan*.[29] In that case, the defendant, Mr Crehan, who was legally aided raised a violation of EC Art. 81 as a defence to a debt arising from a beer supply contract. In short, Mr Crehan claimed that the exclusive purchase provisions of the beer supply contract as well as the lease of public house premises – a tied pub – entered into with the claimant, Courage, contravened EC Art. 81.1 the remedy sought being damages. As the amount of damages

---

26. A.A.S. Zuckerman, Editor's Note, (2005) 24 CJQ 1 at 14 'Beyond personal injury litigation it is difficult to find a proportional relationship between the aims of the CFA scheme and defendant's liability to a success fee. In particular it is difficult to establish proportionality where repeat players are not involved. True CFA's improve access to justice for those who have no ability to pay their lawyers upfront or who are deterred by the risk of losing and having to pay costs. But there seems no argument in fairness that justifies requiring an individual defendant who may be in no better position to should such a burden to pay extra in order to pave the claimant's access to justice. If anything, fairness points the other way because the claimant has a choice of not suing whereas the defendant has not such choice'.

27. K. Ashby & C. Glasser, 'The Legality of Conditional Fee Uplifts' (2005) 24 CJQ 130 op. cit. at 135 'There can be no objection to CFAs where the success fee is restricted to costs normally recovered on a standard basis for work actually done or where any upflit is payable only by the successful party' and A.A.S. Zuckerman, Editor's Note, (2005) (24) CJQ 1 at 15 'It may be possible to reconcile the CFA scheme with Art. 6 by devising a way of avoiding justice to non-CFA litigants. By adding a provision to CFA legislation authorizing the court to dispense with payment of even a reasonable success fee when to do so would cause injustice, it might be possible to resolve the incompatibility issue'. One notes also the Commission Staff Working Paper (Annexe to the Green Paper) (2005) 672 op. cit. at point 213 albeit in relation to Small Claims but nevertheless in the context of the operation of the indemnity rule and costs: 'Art. 14 of the draft regulation establishing a European Small Claims Procedure states that the unsuccessful party shall bear the costs of the proceedings except where this would be unfair or unreasonable thereby limiting cost recover to the notion of reasonableness'.

28. The Commission Staff Working Paper (Annexe to the Green Paper) COM (2005) 672 Final, at point 218 evokes the possible use of conditional fees as a method of facilitating private actions for EC Art. 81 and 82 before national civil courts but defines conditional fees as funding methods whereby ' . . . financial risk for bringing the action is borne not by the claimant but by the private attorney'. No mention is made of a CFA system where the risk is borne by the losing party coupled with a success fee of up to 100 per cent.

29. *Bernard Crehan v. Inntrepeneur Pub Company* CPC, Case A3/2003/1725: Neutral Citation (2004) EWCA 637.

awarded by the Court of Appeal is still on appeal to the House of Lords the aggregate sum of the costs in the case has not yet been calculated. Arguably someone in the situation of Mr Crehan who was funded by the Legal Aid would now seek to avail himself of the CFA in order to enforce EC Articles 81 and or 82. Accordingly, it is appropriate to consider whether CFAs might constitute a problem for the enforcement of EC Articles 81 and or 82.

Various scenarios are possible: for example, one such might consist in a situation where an impecunious claimant without ATE insurance would seek to institute proceedings for damages for breach of EC Articles 81 or 82 such as in *Crehan*; or further, as in *Campbell*, the defendant company is found liable not only for the damages but also for the claimant's costs coupled with the 100 per cent uplift of the CFA. *Crehan* is the first English case to have established that, following a reference to the ECJ,[30] as a matter of English law, breach of EC Articles 81 or 82 will sound in damages. Therefore, at present there is no other reported case resulting in an award of damages for breach of EC Articles 81 and/or 82 in the UK. As such, no large class composed of frequent EC litigators and insurers has emerged such as in field of personal injuries who can negotiate the fixing of fees which reflect market forces. Arguably, EC competition litigation approximates defamation actions even more so that the principles which govern the granting of damages are as noted, under appeal to the House of Lords. In this regard, it remains to be seen whether the application of the principle of effectiveness may lead to the use of a more generous measure of calculating damages than is the normal position with tort.[31]

As noted above, a defendant confronted with the possibility of having to meet a claim for not only a large measure of damages but costs which are increased by 100 per cent as a result of the potentially successful claimant's conditional fee agreement may decide not to defend his action. The situation would be rendered even more onerous for the defendant if the claimant did not have ATE insurance.[32] This financial combination which arises from the operation of the conditional fee system based upon uncapped legal costs coupled with the operation of the indemnity rule may well result in discouraging a defendant company from exercising its own rights of defence under EC Articles 81 and/or 82.[33]

---

30. *Crehan v. Courage* Case C-453/99, (2001) ECR I -6297.
31. Park J., assessed hypothetically the damages of Mr Crehan as of the date of judgment and not at the date of the occurrence of the breach of EC Art. 81. The Court of Appeal reversed this part of the judgment in order to follow the normal English position which requires that the damage suffered be calculated as of the date of loss and that the period during which the claimant is kept from his money be compensated by interest.
32. Such a situation existed in *Turcu v. News Group Newspapers Ltd* (2005) EWCA 799 QP where the claimant did not hold after the event insurance (ATE).
33. The Commission Staff Working Paper (Annexe to the Green Paper) COM (2005) 672 Final op.cit; adverts to the effect of excessive litigation costs on the rights of defendants seeking to enforce their rights under EC Art. 81 and 82: 'The Commission wants to use the debate to find ways to better compensate for anti-trust injuries and increase deterrence while avoiding the situation where defendants settle simply because litigation costs are too high'.

Accordingly, the CFA system would prevent effective enforcement of EC Articles 81 and/or 82 for such a defendant thereby breaching the EC doctrine of effective enforcement. Therefore, in the instant case, one must consider whether CFAs coupled with uncapped costs and the indemnity rule can be justified in terms of the principles and objectives of English civil procedure. As noted previously, there appears to be no justification for the retention of a system of legal costs the control of which is subject neither to market forces nor independent government regulation. Moreover, the lack of cost proportionality created the system of uncapped costs is in turn exacerbated by the use of the indemnity rule.[34] Arguably the enforcement of EC competition law by the CAT and the Scottish civil courts can assist in demonstrating the absence of any justification for the use of the indemnity rule to shift the payment of legal costs of the CFA to the losing party. Therefore, it would seem that the EC principle of effective enforcement would require a modification of the CFA system in England. In order to ascertain the nature of this modification it is helpful to consider the operation of CFAs in Scotland and before the Competition Appeal Tribunal in both England and Scotland in the enforcement of EC Articles 81 and 82.

E.   COSTS AND ENFORCEMENT OF EC ARTICLES
                  81 AND 82 IN THE UK

Within the UK, EC Articles 81 and 82 may be enforced by the national courts, in England, notably, the High Court, Chancery Division[35] or throughout the UK by Competition Appeal Tribunal (CAT) which was established by the Competition Act (1998) (CA). There does exist however a practical difference: the CAT only enforces infringement decisions for money claims in damages rendered either by the Office of Fair Trading (OFT) or the European Commission. In contrast, while they are able to similarly enforce such infringement decisions, civil courts throughout the UK may by virtue of the EC doctrine of direct effect enforce EC Articles 81 and/or 82 by means of an action for damages wherein the burden of proof lies on the claimant to establish the breach. In England, following

---

34. The Commission Staff Working Paper (Annex to the Green Paper) COM (2005) *ibid.* notes at paragraph 43 the eventual dissuasive effect of the operation of the indemnity rule in terms of enforcement of EC Art. 81 and 82: 'The Study notes the general rule that in all Member States the loser pays the costs although in practise fees are not usually fully recoverable. The higher cost and risks involved in competition actions as well as the length of proceedings operate as a disincentive to bringing private actions'.
35. In January 2004 the CPR were amended to provide that all EC competition cases should be brought or transferred to the Chancery Division of the High Court, CPR Part 30.8 accompanied by the Practise Direction on Competition Law, January 2004. The rules of the Court of Session do not apparently contain any rule of procedure similar to the transfer provisions of CPR 30.8. Chapter 87 of the Rules of the Court of Session provide for the intimation of notice to the Office of Fair Trading in the event that an issue involving EC Art. 81 or 82 is raised before the court.

Crehan, the cause of action used to enforce EC Articles 81 and/or 82 both in the CAT and the English courts is a breach of statutory duty with a remedy sounding in damages.

Under S 47A of the CA (1998) parties who have suffered damage caused by an infringement of Articles 81 and or 82 may bring a claim for damages before the CAT. This tribunal will be bound by any prior decision of the OFT and or the Commission. Following S 58 A of the CA (1998) the ordinary UK civil courts are bound by any infringement decision concerning EC Articles 81 and/or 82 made by the Office of Fair Trading. In default of such an infringement decision, the claimant must as noted prove the breach himself relying if possible on either a Commission infringement decision in the matter if such exists or other relevant Commission infringement decisions.[36] Otherwise he must lead expert economic evidence to prove the breach of either EC Articles 81 or 82. Perhaps most interesting from the point of view of the use of a CFA would be the instance where a litigant seeks to enforce an infringement decision concerning EC Articles 81 and/or 82 made either by the OFT or the European Commission. As noted, a potential claimant make seek to enforce this decision either before the CAT or before in the civil courts. However, the choice of rules concerning the CFA vary according to the jurisdiction. In the civil courts in England, as noted, the Courts and Legal Services Act (1990) and Access to Justice Act (1999) will provide for the operation of the Conditional Fee System coupled with the requisite CPR and Practise Directions. In contrast, conditional fees in Scotland, known as speculative fees, although not based upon a system of capped costs are not coupled with the indemnity rule. Accordingly, it is the successful claimant who pays the uplift which he has negotiated with his solicitor and or advocate and not the unsuccessful defendant, the speculative fee not being included within the category of costs recoverable against the unsuccessful party. Following the description of Lord Hope[37] speculative fees are provided for by two statutory instruments: Sederunt (1992) (SI 1992/1897) for advocates and Sederunt (1992) (SI 1992/1879 for solicitors. The primary legislation from which the Lords of Council have derived the power for these acts is S 36(2) of the Law Reform (Miscellaneous Provisions) (Scotland) Act 1990. This section reads as follows:

> S 36(1) An advocate and the person instructing him may agree in relation to a litigation undertaken on a speculative basis that in the event of the litigation being successful the advocate's feel shall be incurred by such percentage as may subject to subsection 2 below be agreed.

---

36. According to *Bernard Crehan v. Inntrepeneur Pub Company* CPC; Case A3/2003/1725, Neutral Citation (2004) EWCA 637, op. cit., the EC duty of consistent judgments enjoins the national court to avoid rendering a judgment which would be inconsistent with Commission decision relevant to the matter before the national court which expands the duty of consistency beyond simply Commission which involve the same matter as the one before the national court.
37. *Campbell v. MGN* (2005) op. cit. paragraphs 40–43 generally.

The percentage increase which may be agreed under subsection (1) above shall not exceed such limit as the court after consultation with the Dean of the Faculty of Advocates prescribed by act of Sederunt.

Lord Hope observes further:

> Under these arrangements, the fee is payable only if the client is successful in litigation. It is open to the advocate and the instructing solicitor and to the solicitor and the client as the case may be to agree that the fee taxed as between party and party (which is the standard basis) or agreed shall be increased by a figure not exceeding 100 per cent. The amount of the permissible uplift was fixed by the Lord President of the Court of Session in 1992 following consultation intended to reflect the degree of risk of non payment of fees which would be involved in undertaking the litigation on the client's behalf. But in contrast to the system which now operates in England, it is the client who must pay the uplift if he is successful in the litigation. It is not recoverable from the losing party.[38]

In contrasting the English and the Scottish system of conditional fee payments, Lord Hope notes:

> The system of conditional fee agreements which was originally introduced in England under S 58 of the Courts and Legal Services Act 1990 did not, of course, provide for the recovery of the uplift or 'success fee' as it was called in S 58(2)(b) from the losing party. But S 58 of the 1990 which was introduced by S 27(1) of the Access to Justice Act (1999) changed all that. . . .
>
> So in contrast to the position in Scotland, litigation may now be conducted in those cases in England on the basis that if the client is successful it will be the losing party that has to pay the success fee'.[39]

Accordingly, the analysis of Lord Hope establishes the following: first, in Scotland, S 36 of the Law Reform Act[40] the costs of the conditional fee are not included within the general heading of costs to be paid by the losing party. Therefore, the indemnity rule cannot operate so as to reallocate their payment by the losing party. In contrast S 27(1) of the Access to Justice Act as previously noted,

---

38. *Campbell v. MGN* (2005) *ibid.* Lord Hope at point 41.
39. *Campbell v. MGN* (2005) *ibid.* Lord Hope at point 42.
40. S 36 Law Reform (Misc Prov) (Scotland) (1990).
     (1) An advocate and the person instructing him may agree in relation to a litigation undertaken on a speculative basis that in the event of the litigation being successful, the advocate's fee shall be increased by such percentage as may be subject to subsection 2 below
     (2) The percentage increase which may be agreed under subsection (1) above shall not exceed such limit as the court after consultation with the Dean of the Faculty of Advocates prescribed by Act of Sederunt
     (3) Where a solicitor and his client have reached an agreement in writing as to the solicitor's fees in respect of any work done or to be done by him for his client it shall not be competent in any litigation arising out of any dispute as to the amount due to be paid under any such agreement for the court to remit the solicitor's account for taxation.

provides that the conditional fee is first a recoverable cost and second, that it may be recovered from the losing party. Conspicuously, in England the indemnity rule operates so as to reallocate the payment of the CFA and ATE to the losing party: secondly, in Scotland the calculation of the amount of the CFA is carried out in relation to the case at hand and in particular as a function of the degree of likelihood of non-payment in the case at hand. In contrast, the use of the indemnity rule and the inclusion of the CFA within costs recoverable from the losing party is calculated in England with a different objective: to ensure that the costs paid by the losing party will permit the lawyers to finance their accepting future claimants whose claim the court may adjudge as unsuccessful. In reality, the essential point is that under the Scottish system it is the successful claimant who accepts to pay costs which the calculation of which may not be capped. Accordingly, the Scottish system would on the one hand ensure the effective enforcement of EC competition law and on the other, avoid a breach of ECHR Art. 6 in the manner proposed by Ashby and Glasser.[41]

It is useful to consider the enforcement of an EC Articles 81 or 82 by means of an OFT infringement decision in two circumstances: first, by the CAT in England as opposed to the CAT in Scotland: and second, the enforcement by the CAT when sitting in England as opposed to the High Court – Chancery Division. It is necessary first to consider the rules for CFAs in the CAT.

The CAT has its own statutorily authorized rules of procedure which were adopted by the Secretary of State in exercise of his powers under S 15 of and Part 2 of Schedule 4 of the Enterprise Act 2002. The Competition Appeal Tribunal Rules 2003 (S1 2003 No 1372) are applicable to all proceedings before the CAT. Concerning CFAs the following is provided:

S 65 of SI 2003 No 1372 establishes:

> S 65: The rules on funding arrangements made under the Civil Procedure Rules SI 1998/3132 as amended apply to proceedings before the tribunal.

Further, the notion of costs is provided for in the following manner:

> S 55(1): For the purposes of these rules 'costs' means costs and expenses recoverable before the Supreme Court of England and Wales, the Court of Session and the Supreme Court of Northern Ireland.

Accordingly, when sitting in England, the CAT uses S 58A of the Courts and Legal Services Act (1990) as modified by S 27(1) of the Access to Justice Act (1999) coupled with CPR 44 and notably Practise Direction 11: that is a success fee which can be increased up to 100 per cent and which can be transferred to the losing party as part of his costs to pay under the indemnity rule. However, the following provision applies to costs when the Tribunal sits in either Scotland or in Northern Ireland.

---

41. See generally K. Ashby & C. Glasser 'The Legality of Conditional Fee Up Lifts': 24 CJQ (2005) W. van Gerven 'Of Rights, Remedies and Procedures' (2000) CMLR 501 op. cit. at 536.

The Guide to Proceedings provides:[42]

> When the Tribunal is sitting as a tribunal in Scotland or Northern Ireland, the costs or expenses recoverable are those which are recoverable in the jurisdiction and will be assessed in accordance with the procedure in that jurisdiction.

However, as noted previously, by reason of the wording of S 36 of the Law Reform (Scotland) Act (1990), the costs of a speculative fee arrangement are not included under the heading of costs which are recoverable from a losing party.

Accordingly, the CAT when sitting in England would normally include the costs of a CFA within the definition of costs as provided by S 58A of the Court and Legal Services Act (1990)[43] In contrast in Scotland, such costs would not be included. Indeed S 17.2 of the Guide to Proceedings reinforces 17.9:

> 17.2 Costs means costs and expenses recoverable in civil proceedings before the Supreme Court in England and Wales, the Court of Session in Scotland and the Court of Appeal in Northern Ireland.

Arguably, this difference would lead to enforcement of EC Articles 81 and/or 82 being less effective in England than in Scotland.[44] However, it may be that the CAT rules provide it with sufficient discretion with respect to the use of the indemnity rule notably in England so as to avoid that consequence. This is of particular significance where a litigant seeks, as noted previously to enforce an OFT infringement decision concerning EC Articles 81 or 82 before the CAT in England as opposed to the High Court – Chancery Division.

Art. 17.1 of the Guide to Proceedings for the CAT provides as follows:

> Unlike the position in some other tribunals where the losing party is not required to pay the costs of the winning party except in exceptional circumstances, Rule 55(c) provides that the Tribunal may at its discretion at any stage of the proceedings make any order it thinks fit in relation to the payment of costs by one party to another in respect of the whole or part of the proceedings. There is no specific rule that costs should follow the event.

---

42. Competition Appeal Tribunal Guide to Proceedings (October 2005).
43. In conjunction with CPR 44 and Practise Direction.
44. The European Commission in Commission Staff Working Paper, op. cit. adverts to this type of unequal enforcement of EC law in the following manner with respect to the remedy of damages in a way which could be applicable to the variation in CFAs before the CAT in England and Scotland and the CAT and the High Court: 'In the European context, not only is clarity desirable but so too is the principle of creating a level playing field of EC rights enforcement across Member States. If a litigant in one Member State faces a better chance of his national court making him a larger award of damages than a litigant in another Member State then the substantive body of Community competition law itself uniform, across the Union, will not be enforced in a uniform way across the Community. It is essential to ensure that rights of European citizens are subject to the same protection across the whole community'.

S 55(2) of SA 2003/1372 provides:

> The tribunal may at its discretion, subject to paragraph (3) at any state of the proceedings, make any order it thinks fit in relation to the payment of costs by one party to another in respect of the whole or part of the proceeding and in determining how much the party is required to pay, the tribunal may take account of the conduct of all the parties in relation to the proceedings.

Further, S 17(3) of the Guidelines deals with the amount of costs if any which the Tribunal may be minded to award:

> Given the specific nature of its jurisdiction, the Tribunal would need to determine in individual decisions the principles on which the discretion as to costs is to be exercised, the principle questions being whether and if so to what extend and in what circumstances costs should be awarded.

The question is how these rules are applied by the CAT in practise. Following its decision *BCL Old Co*,[45] it may be that the CAT would exercise its discretion so as to not award any costs at all to the winning party: that is, not to use the indemnity rule at all.

> The powers under S 55(2) of the Tribunal Rules which is the foundation for the Tribunal to award costs at the level of the proceedings is discretionary. There is no automatic rule that costs follow the event. Since this is the first case under S 47 the Tribunal has not yet to consider and indeed is not in a position to consider how the jurisdiction to award costs under S 55(2) is to be exercises in S 47(A) cases.

The CAT further observes: 'The costs incurred by the Defendants and in particular the Third and Fourth Defendants are wholly disproportionate in the context of the amount to be claimed'.

And finally in the same judgment the tribunal holds:

> More generally the Tribunal notes that this specialised jurisdiction under S 47 1 has been created by Parliament with a view to facilitating claims for damages or restriction on the part of those who have suffered loss as a result of an infringements of domestic or European Competition Law.

In the event that the CAT exercises its discretion so as to not apply the indemnity rule or awarded costs but with a nil uplift, then the following consequences would ensue: first, it would ensure that EC Articles 81 and/or 82 were enforced as effectively in England under the English rules just as in Scotland under the Scots rules; second, it would ensure that EC Articles 81 and 82 were enforced effectively in England by the CAT in conformity with the doctrine of effectiveness in contrast to the situation of the CFA as before the ordinary High Court – Chancery

---

45. *BCL Old Co Ltd* 1028/5/7/04 Judgment: 20 January 2005 at point 37 (judgment for security of costs) website of CAT: <www.cattribunal.org.uk>.

Division.[46] Accordingly, it is submitted that the CFA system provided by S 58 A of the Courts and Legal Services Act (1990) coupled with the indemnity rule and based upon costs which are controlled neither by market forces nor by government intervention would appear to be disproportionate to the objective pursued, namely, increasing access to justice. Indeed, the CFA system may result in a losing party being called upon to pay an amount of costs the calculation of which is not subject to proportionate control by reason of an absence of capping. In turn this sum becomes disproportionate to the objective of providing access to justice both for claimants and defendants. Accordingly, the use of such a disproportionate system of funding in order to ensure access to justice is not justifiable because there exist alternate methods which ensure a proportionate control of costs as demonstrated by the Scottish system of speculative fees and the manner in which the CAT is able to exercise its discretion concerning the application of the indemnity rule in England. By reason, therefore of the absence of any justification for the current system of legal costing in England, the English CFA system contravenes ECHR Art. 6.

Further, this CFA system also breaches the EC doctrine of effective procedural enforcement for the following reasons: firstly, there is no justification for retaining the English CFA system in light of the possibility of using the Scottish system of speculative fees. The Scottish system unlike the English CFA system does not incorporate the up lift within the costs which can be recovered by the successful party from the losing party: secondly, within England itself, the CAT would seem to provide an example of civil procedure where the indemnity rule is not used to automatically shift costs. The doctrine of effectiveness would seem to require, at a minimum, the use of the Scottish system whereby the speculative fee is not included within the costs recoverable by the successful claimant: if on the other hand, the uplift is included within such costs, then it would seem to be necessary to adopt the position of the CAT with respect to the use of the indemnity rule: namely, as the CAT noted in BCL Old 'there is no automatic rule that costs follow the event'. Moreover, the difficulty of the operation of the CFA in England is exacerbated by the absence of any obligation for the claimant to provide ATE insurance.

In conclusion, the operation of the CFA discloses a fundamental problem of the system of legal costing in England which the CPR cannot in itself address: namely, that in order for control of legal costs to be effective and proportionate they must be controlled externally preferably by government intervention in default of market forces.[47]

---

46. It is to be noted that in England the court does not have the discretion to exclude costs under the Practise Direction relating to CPR 44: point 9 'Under an order for payment of costs, the costs payable will include an additional liability incurred under a funding arrangement'.
47. A. Zuckerman, (24) CJQ (2005) 1 at 15. 'However, it is clear that the CFA legislation has merely succeeded in pushing the high costs onto insurance companies, their policy holders and worst of all on unlucky individual defendants. Sure the time has come to try and control the cost of litigation and not just shift it around'. In criminal law costing see: Lord Carter, Procurement of Criminal Defence Services, Market Reforms: Feb 2006: <www.legalaidprocurementreview. gov.uk>.

Chapter 4

English Procedure: Expert Evidence and Assessors

With respect to the use of expert evidence by a national court presided by a non-specialist judge the principle of effectiveness arguably requires that procedural dispositions exist in order to ensure the following objectives: first, that the court be ensured effective access to expert evidence and second, that the court be able to evaluate effectively and efficiently the probative content of the expert evidence.

A.   ACCESS TO EXPERT EVIDENCE: HIGH COURT, CHANCERY DIVISION CPR

CPR 35 governs, generally, what might be termed the court's access to evidence. Expert evidence originates with the parties and not with the court. The use of expert evidence, however, must be approved by the court. The court may only appoint an expert where the parties cannot agree. Further, the court may direct that evidence on a particular subject be given by only one expert. In short, the court is unable to appoint an expert entirely on its own initiative beyond the situation where the parties cannot agree and court intervenes to solve the matter.

CPR 35(4)(1) No party may call an expert or put in evidence an expert's report without the court's permission.

> (7)(1) Where two or more parties wish to submit expert evidence on a particular issue, the court may direct that the evidence on that issue is to be given by one expert only

(3) Where the parties cannot agree who should be the expert the court may –

(a) select the expert from a list prepared or identified by the instructing parties

(b) direct that the expert be selected in such other manner as the court may direct.

Access to Expert Evidence CAT Rules:

In contrast to the CPR, the CAT rules provide direct access to expert evidence in the sense that the Tribunal is able to appoint an expert not only on the request of a party but 'on its own initiative'. There is no limiting factor as in CPR 35(7)(3) such as where the parties cannot agree on the appointment of an expert.

CAT Rule 19(1) The Tribunal may at any time, on the request of a party or on its own initiative, at a case management conference, pre-hearing review or otherwise, give such directions as are provided for in paragraph (2) below or such other directions as it thinks fit to secure the just, expeditious and economical conduct of the proceedings

(2) The Tribunal may give directions –

(1) for the appointment and instruction of experts whether by the Tribunal or by the parties and the manner in which expert evidence is to be given.

At the present time no CAT judgments exist which might indicate how the Tribunal may exercise the full scope of these powers. It would seem however, that in the event that it decides to appoint an expert of its own initiative pursuant to Rule 19(2)(1) the Tribunal could permit cross examination of the expert.

(2)(1) and the manner in which expert evidence is to be given; or 19(1) . . . may give . . . such other directions as it thinks fit to secure the just, expeditious and economical conduct of the proceedings.

However, no cases exist which define the scope of 'such other directions'. Finally, Rule 19(2)(g) provides that the Tribunal may give directions 'as to the examination or cross examination of witnesses'.

The difference between the CAT rules and the CPR with respect to the *ex officio* court appointed expert arguably may have practical significance with respect to the enforcement of money judgments based upon OFT and Commission infringement decisions of EC Articles 81 and 82. Following S 47 A and 58 A CA (1998), an EC Articles 81 or 82 infringement finding made by either the Office of Fair Trading (OFT) or the Commission may be enforced either by the CAT or the national court respectively by mean of a monetary judgment. In this situation of a monetary or follow-on judgment, expert evidence may be introduced to deal notably with the issues of causation and or quantum. In the case of the CAT the Tribunal, as noted, is able to make directions pursuant to Rule 19 for the appointment of experts either by the Tribunal *ex officio* or by the parties. Art. 12. 8 of the CAT Guidelines refer specifically to the Tribunal expert: 'other procedures, including putting written questions to the experts, discussions between experts, the appointment of a single joint expert or of the Tribunal's own expert can equally be envisaged'. It is then necessary to ascertain whether this more limited avail- ability on the access to expert evidence in the CPR is justifiable in terms of the principles of the CPR. In default of such a justification, the principle of effective- ness may apply in order to effect a change of the CPR in order to ensure that EC Articles 81 and 82 money judgments may be effectively enforced.

Lord Woolf in his Interim Report on the Access to Justice[1] describes the fundamental procedural issues underlying the use of expert evidence as follows:

> Impartiality: Most of the problems with expert evidence arise because the expert is initially recruited as part of the team which advances a party's con- tentions and then has to change roles and seek to provide the independent expert evidence which the court requires.

Accordingly, Lord Woolf considers the use of a court expert, that is, an expert appointed by the court *ex officio* as a possible remedy to the problem of the partiality of party lead experts. His lordship observes in the Interim Report at point 20:

> The appointment of a court expert or, as the London Solicitors' Litigation Association, has pointed out to the Inquiry, more appropriately an 'independent expert' is one solution which has been extensively canvassed. It is however a solution which attract strong criticism.

The Report indicates at point 21 the reason for this criticism:

> The unwillingness of parties to take advantage of the court appointed expert is in sharp contrast to the position in civil law jurisdiction where this is the normal course. A number of reasons are given for this by the Bar and the Law Society. The principal reasons are dissatisfaction with the court experts on the Continent, the fact that the expert and not the judge will decide the case, the increased cost incurred by appointing a court expert in addition to the parties own expert and the inability of a court expert to deal with the situation where more than one acceptable view ban be held on a particular issue.

However, Lord Woolf holds that such criticisms are insufficient to outweigh the use of a court appointed expert. His lordship notes at point 23 of the Interim Report:

> The court is perfectly capable of deciding which cases would be appropriate for a court expert and then of appointing an expert with the necessary qual- ification and ensuring that he is used effectively. In the normal way, parties can be left to agree on one expert and if they cannot agree, there are numerous bodies who would be prepared to make an appointment at the request of the court. Rules of the court should allow the court to appoint an independent expert of its own motion and to limit the parties to call any expert except under

---

1. Lord Woolf, Access to Justice, Interim Report, June 1995, <www.dca.gov.uk/civil/reportfr. htm> Expert Evidence, point 5.

the direction of the court. The fact that a court has appointed an expert does not mean that the parties should be deprived of the opportunity to cross examine . . . or in the discretion of the court even to call their own expert if the scale of the case justifies this. While this could mean that three expert might be engaged which might involve additional costs, the third neutral expert will usually justify his appointment by helping to achieve a settlement or in the assistance which he will provide to the judge.

Accordingly, it would seem that an expert appointed by the court of its own motion could assist the court by providing impartial evidence and eventually by accelerating settlement of the dispute. Notwithstanding, Lord Woolf decided in the Final Report of Access to Justice[2] not to propose the introduction of a court expert appointed *ex officio* for the following reasons:

> Point 5. 'My detailed proposals on experts however provoked more opposition than any of my other recommendations; Most respondents favour retaining the full-scale adversarial use of court evidence and resist proposals for wider use of single experts whether court appointed or jointly appointed by the parties'.

His lordship observes at point 16 of the Final Report of Access to Justice, Expert Evidence:

> Since the publication of the interim report resistance to my proposals on single experts has remained particularly strong and it is clear that the idea is anathema to many members of the legal profession in this country who are unwilling to give up their adversarial weapons.[3]

Accordingly, Lord Woolf's Interim and Final Reports would apparently establish that there is no justification in terms of the principles of the CPR for the absence of a rule which would permit the Court to appoint an expert on its own initiative. In particular, the Interim Report clearly indicates that the objections raised against the use of the court appointed expert can be solved by judicial intervention following the overriding principles. Further, the Final Report establishes that this proposed solution to the problems raised by the court appointed expert nevertheless encountered opposition and hostility in the legal community which is apparently not founded upon any principles embodied by the CPR. Therefore, the rule of effectiveness would seem to require that the CPR be modified so as to provide the court with the possibility of appoint a court expert on its own initiative following the rules in CAT and following the original suggestions of Lord Woolf in his Interim Report. As noted by Lord Woolf in the Interim Report, provision would be made following the structure of RSC Or 40 for cross-examination by the parties of the court appointed expert. These modifications would permit the effective enforcement of follow on cases involving money judgments.

---

2. Lord Woolf, Access to Justice, Final Report, July 1996, <www.dca.gov.uk/civil/reportfr.htm>.
3. Lord Woolf, Access to Justice, Final Report, July 1996: *ibid.* point 16.

Further, Jolowicz[4] observes 'The adversarial system as ordinarily understood in this country is the product of several centuries of jury trial in civil cases. Civil trial by jury is now virtually extinct and there is no reason why modern procedure should continue to be bound by its demands. Judicial decisions should in the late 20th century aim at substantive as well as procedural justice. In short it is suggested that judges are normally anxious to do the 'real' that is substantive justice and if they are given the means to do so, even with other purposes in the mind of the legislature, they will in the course of time come to take the opportunities offered . . . Recognition of the reality that no system of procedure can lead to the discover of the objective truth does not mean that all decisions must be based exclusively on what the parties have chosen to lay before the court'.

Moreover, the House of Lords Report on the 'Commission White Paper on Modernization'[5] contains the following observations concerning the use of a court experts:

> Paragraph 68: 'Mr Freeman (Joint Working Party) thought that the civil law system with its inquisitorial approach and ability to seek a court appointed expert and to obtain expert evidence through the bench might be better suited to the germination of Art. 81(3) issues that the common law adversarial style of litigation. Mrs Martin Alegi (CBI) also expressed concerns about the adequacy of procedures and powers of national courts where when compared with the Commission. She said that the national courts while generally having very good powers to obtain evidence from the parties to a dispute before them did not have investigative powers by and large to obtain full information on the economics of the function of international markets'.

The Report states at paragraph 146 in the Conclusions: 'National law and procedures, some quite new in the case of the UK and a number of other Member States, would have to be changed'.

Finally, it is of use to note that historically, the English court possessed the power to appoint experts of its own initiative until the beginning of the 20th century. Dwyer notes[6] that the English courts enjoyed until recently the power to appoint its own experts:

> Power had existed in common law for judges to call witnesses including expert witnesses in order to investigate the truth. This power was removed in 1910 in England with Lord Fletcher arguing that the power to adduce evidence in a civil action rested with the parties and not the court.

---

4. A. Jolowicz, 'The Woolf Report (Interim) and the Adversarial System', (1996) CJQ 198 at 208.
5. House of Lords European Union 4th Report, (session 1999–2000) Sub-Committee E (Law & Institutions) 15 February 2000, on The White Paper on Modernization COM (1999) 101 Final, presided by Lord Hope of Craighead: <www.publications.parliament.uk>.
6. D. Dwyer, 'Changing Approaches to Expert Evidence in England' in International Commentary on Evidence, Vol. 1, No. 2, <www.law.qub.ac.uk/ice/paperslist.htlm> cites Sharpe, *The Law & Medicine in Canada*, 2nd edition, (1987) at p. 142.

Therefore, structurally, in a procedural sense, the appointment of an expert by a court on its own initiative would not seem to constitute an intractable procedural problem or to be fundamentally alien to the operation of the English courts and the method of taking evidence. As such, the doctrine of effectiveness coupled with that of non-discrimination as it applies in relation to enforcement of EC Articles 81 and 82 by the CAT under S 47 A CA (1998) would seem to require the following: namely, introduction of the system of *ex officio* court appointed experts to ensure that EC Articles 81 and 82 can be enforced in the High Courts as effectively as in the CAT in terms of the availability of expert evidence.

B.   EVALUATION OF EXPERT EVIDENCE

1.   High Court, Chancery Division, CPR

Effective enforcement of EC Articles 81 and 82 requires that the national court be able to evaluate the probative value of technically complex expert evidence. In this regard the House of Lords Report contains the following observations concerning the difficulties which the English court may experience with respect to expert evidence required for the enforcement of EC Articles 81 and 82. One notes at paragraph 58:

> The CBI did not consider national courts to be apply 81(3). They were not equipped to deal with the kind of complex economic arguments which that involved . . . Mr Lever and Mr Peretz also drew attention to the large margin of appreciation exercised in the complex assessment needed under Art. 81(3).

They said: 'The training of the general judiciary whether in this country or in other Member States does not equip the judges to engage in such an exercise'. And at point 59: 'That view as shared by Mr Justice Ferris and Mr Justice Laddie. They did not see judges and national courts as the appropriate forum for the application of EC Art 81(3)'.
The Competition Appeal Tribunal (CAT) is in contrast a specialist tribunal. The CAT Guidelines[7] provide as follows:

> The Tribunal is headed by the President who is a senior legally qualified person appointed b the Lord Chancellor and who it appears to the Lord Chancellor has appropriate experience and knowledge of competition law and practise.

Appointments to the panel of chairmen are made by the Lord Chancellor for a period of eight years; Chairmen must be legally qualified and appear to the Lord Chancellor to have appropriate experience and knowledge (either of competition law and practise or any other relevant law and practise).

---

7.   Competition Appeal Tribunal Guide to Proceedings (Oct. 2005).

The ordinary members are appointed for a period of eight years by the Secretary of State and come from a variety of backgrounds. Some are professionally qualified economists, lawyers and accountants whilst others have backgrounds in business, the public service or other relevant experience. Currently, there are 19 ordinary members.

One notes in particular that the judges of the Chancery Division who form part of the panel of chairmen are those to whom all cases involving EC competition law are referred by Competition Law Practise Direction.[8] It is these judges who form a specialist judiciary for the adjudication of competition law claims.

It is to be noted that this practise direction reflects an attempt to constitute a group of judges within the Chancery Division who will acquire specialized knowledge necessary for the enforcement of EC Articles 81 and or 82. In addition in order to ensuring an equal playing field with that of the CAT, the principle of effectiveness may require that the national court consider using one of two procedural devices: the first is provided by CPR 35.15 and consists in the use of an assessor: the second, would consist in the creation of an expert appointed by the court *ex officio* to advise it on expert evidence.

2.   ASSESSORS

CPR 35(15) provides as follows:

> This rule applies when the court appoints one or more persons (an assessor) under S 70 of the Supreme Court Act (1981) or S 63 of the County Courts Act (1984)
>
> The assessor shall assist the court in dealing with a matter in which the assessor has skill and experience
>
> An assessor shall take such part in the proceedings as the court may direct and in particular may –
>
> direct the assessor to prepare a report for the court on any issue in the proceedings
>
> direct the assessor to attend the whole or any part of the trial to advise the court on any such matter
>
> If the assessor prepares a report for the court before the trial has begun –
> the court will send a copy to each of the parties; and
> the parties may use it at the trial
>
> The remuneration to be paid to the assessor for his services shall be determined by the court and shall form part of the costs of the proceedings.

The Practise Direction for CPR 35.15 provides:

An assessor may be appointed to assist the court under rule 35.15. Not less than 21 days before making such an appointment the court will notify each party in

---

8. Practise Direction : Competition Law : Claims relating to the application of Articles 81 and 82 of the EC Treaty, October 2005, in particular Art. 2.1.

writing of the name of the proposed assessor of the matter in respect of which the assistance of the assessor will be sought and of the qualification to the assessor to give that assistance.

Where any person has been proposed for appointment as an assessor objection to him, either personally or in respect of his qualification may be taken by any party.

Any such objection must be make in writing and filed with the court within seven days of receipt of the notification referred to in paragraph 6.1 and will be taken into account by the court in deciding whether or not to make the appointment.

Copies of any report prepared by the assessor will be sent to each of the parties but the assessor will not give oral evidence or be open to cross-examination or questioning.

Lord Woolf sets forth the purpose and in particular the costs advantages of the assessor in the Interim Report at paragraph 24:

> In complex litigation, it could often be of considerable assistance to the judge if he was provided with an assessor. This only happens with any degree of regularity in the Admiralty Court and the practise should be extended. Expense will be involved in employing the expert but this is likely to be justified by substantial savings in the length of the hearing. In particular, it should be possible for the assessor to preside over meetings of the parties' experts and assist them to reach agreement.

In his Final Report Lord Woolf sets forth at paragraphs 58–60 his definitive view on the role of the assessor:

> Paragraph 58: 'In the Interim Report, I recommended that the courts should make wider use of the powers to appoint expert assessors to assist the judge in complex litigation and in appropriate cases to preside over meetings between the parties' experts and help them reach an agreement'.
>
> Paragraph 59: 'There has been some resistance to these proposals largely on the ground that an assessor would usurp the role of the judge. I do not agree that this would necessarily be the case: where there are complex technical issues the assessors function would be to "educate" the judge to enable him to reach a properly informed decision. In the most complex cases, this function could be performed by two assessors, one instructed by each party'.
>
> Paragraph 60: 'Clearly the use of an independent assessor in addition to the parties' experts and the judge will not be cost effective except in the heaviest cases'.

The nature of the intervention of the assessor however is restricted to giving advice to the judge as part of the court concerning technical information but not evidence. Accordingly, the assessor cannot be cross examined as no evidence is presented and the assessor intervenes as part of the court in order to assist the judge in his judicial functions. Blom-Cooper[9] however, argues that this system of providing

---

9. Sir Louis Blom-Cooper QC, 'Experts and Assessors' (2002)(21) CJQ p. 345, at 348.

advice to a judge which is not subject to cross-examination is likely to contravene Art. 6.1 ECHR. He writes:

> The assessor system being advice by an expert not under oath given to the court on matters not disclosable for cross examination by either party would be regarded today as being incompatible under S 3(1) of the Human Rights Act 1988 as a violation of Art 6.1 ECHR.

However, it is submitted that this analysis may possibly not apply in the following situations: first where the assessor provides information which the court uses in order to take judicial notice of non controversial matters:[10] second, in those circumstances where the rights of the defence do not require cross examination, the proposition being that defence rights do not require in all situations the right to cross examination in order to be upheld notably when then are accompanied by an effective system of appeal.

3.   ASSESSORS CPR 35.15 AND PRACTISE DIRECTION 7

Etymologically, assessor signifies a person who is authorized to sit with others in order to assist directly in the taking of decisions. In practise, the role of the assessor may vary widely. Indeed, for some, such as Viscount Simon LC,[11] an assessor may intervene exclusively on matters which require an explanation of the meaning of technical terms. Moreover, an assessor, being unsworn may not give evidence. Others, such as Viscount Dunedin,[12] believe that an assessor may provide a source of facts beyond simply the meaning of words. For Zuckerman, the assessor in providing either the information concerning the meaning of words or more generally, facts, assists the judge in his judicial capacity.[13] Therefore, the assessor cannot be cross examined. Dwyer[14] observes that 'it is settled law that an assessor acting in a normal civil capacity or under a particularly statutory form of proceedings is not an evidentiary source and almost certain constitutes part of the tribunal as scientific adviser under S 70(3) of the Supreme court act (1981) and CPR 35.15'.

---

10. A.A.S. Zuckerman, *Civil Procedure* (London, Lexis Nexis, 2003) op cit ; at 640 'Assessors fulfil a different role from that of expert witnesses. Assessors sit with the judge and assist the court in its deliberations both during the presentation of evidence and argument and after they have been concluded. Since an assessor assists the court in its judicial role, an assessor cannot be cross-examined'.
11. *Richardson v. Redpath Brown & Co. Ltd.* (1944) AC 67, speech of Viscount Simon LC at 70.
12. SS *Australia v. SS Nautilus (Cargo Owners) The Australia* (1927) AC 145 at 150.
13. A.A.S. Zuckerman, *Civil Procedure* (Lexis Nexis, London, 2003) op. cit. at 640.
14. D. Dwyer, 'The Future of Assessors under the CPR' (2006) (25) CJQ 219 at 230 refers to The White Book Service, (Sweet and Maxwell, London, 2006) at p. 962: 'The assessor assists the judge in discharging his judicial role. His function is to educate the judge and to enable him to reach a properly informed decision'. Contrary to Sir Louis Blom-Cooper QC who observes at p. 350 'There has been significant uncertainty as to the status of the advice given to judges by assessors'.

4.   METHOD OF INTERVENTION OF THE ASSESSOR

One method of analysing the function of the assessor is to relate it to the process of judicial notice. Indeed, Lord Denning[15] observed that a judge in using the advice of the assessor 'equips himself in order to take judicial notice'. In terms of a definition judicial notice may be defined as a compendious method of proof. Further, the facts which may be noticed judicially vary between those the veracity of which is indisputable to those which require some type of proof. Restricting judicial notice to the category of indisputable facts entails a procedural advantage: it explains both why an assessor cannot be cross examined and why such absence of cross-examination cannot violate the rights of the defence:[16] namely, that the veracity of the facts noticed judicially is indisputable. If, on the other hand, the concept of judicial notice is expanded so as to include not only indisputable but also disput-able matters as, for example, the meaning of economic terms in EC competition law expert evidence then the rights of the defence may be ensured in two ways: firstly, by means of appeal and secondly, by the right of the parties to respond in some way before judgment to the information given to the judge by the assessor through judicial notice.[17] With regard to the type of facts which may be judicially noticed the distinction is sometimes made between adjudicative facts which are not disputable and legislative facts which are disputable. Indeed, Davis[18] includes both types of facts, legislative and adjudicative, within the concept of judicial notice. Accordingly, it will be argued here that a judge when sitting with the assessor takes judicial notice by means of the information which the assessor provides him of facts some of which are indisputable and others which are disputable.

    In order to ensure that the functions of the assessor correspond to the notion of the judge taking judicial notice, it may be that the doctrine of efficacy and non-discrimination will require certain changes to the structure of CPR 35. 15. One may consider the following:

    First, it is submitted that CPR 35. 15(3) and (4) may be *ultra vires* of the enabling States. The editor of the White Book observes:

> CPR 35(15)(3) provides that an assessor may take part 'in the proceedings as the Court may direct'. This seems wider than the former provisions and

15. *Baldwin & Francis v. Patents Appeal Tribunal* (1959) AC 663 at 691 where Lord Denning explains that the purpose of the appointment of assessors is 'the court is equipping itself for its task by taking judicial notice of all such things as it ought to know in order to do its work properly'.
16. A.A.S. Zuckerman, *Principles of Criminal Evidence* (Oxford Unviersity Press, Oxford, 1989) at p. 98 'Where there can be no reasonable dispute between parties it is wasteful to insist on a full trial of fact. The doctrine of judicial notice relieves the parties of the burden of proving facts which are not reasonably disputable and thereby solves the problems when an indisputable fact is taken for granted it clearly cannot be said that one of the parties has been deprived of the opportunity to present his case'.
17. K.C. Davis, 'Judicial Notice', (1955) (55) *Columbia Law Review* 945 at 978.
18. K.C. Davis, 'Judicial Notice' (1955) (55) *Columbia Law Review* 945 op. cit. at 976.

without the statutory provision . S 70(1) of the 1981 Act says that the Court 'may hear and dispose' of the case 'with their assistance' and S 63(1) of the 1984 Acts states that the assessor 'may sit with the judge'.[19]

In short a court can only direct assessors to 'take part in the proceedings' as in conformity with the Supreme Court Act (1981) and the County Court Act (1984). More particularly, it would seem that CPR 35.15(3) and (4) permit the assessor to provide what could be construed as evidence in so far as the report can be relied upon by the parties. Accordingly, this possibility arguably exceeds the scope of both the SCA (1981) and the CCA (1984) but also tends to obliterate the distinctions as to the appropriate function of a court expert: that is an expert appointed *ex officio* by the court in contrast to the current single expert provided by CPR 35. This would approximate the former court expert under the RSC 40 r 1.[20]

It would seem, therefore, that the elimination of CPR 35. 15(3) and (4) may be required by the doctrine of effectiveness for the following reasons: first to ensure that the operation of the assessor for the enforcement of EC Art 81 and 82 comes squarely within the ambit of SCA (1981) and CCC (1984); and second in order to ensure that the ordinary court has access to the same assistance concerning the explanation of economic terminology in the enforcement of monetary actions under S58A CA (1998) as does the CAT as a specialist tribunal in enforcement of such actions under S47A (CA). Following this analysis above, the restriction of

---

19. Supreme Court Act (1981) S 70 provides: (1) In any cause or matter before the High Court the court may, if it thinks it expedient to do so, call in the aid of one or more assess specially qualified and hear and dispose of the cause or matter wholly or partially with their assistance; (2) The remuneration, if any, to be paid to an assessor for his services under subsection (1) in connection with any proceedings shall be determined by the court and shall form part of the costs of the proceedings;

    (3) Rules of Court shall make provision for the appointment of scientific advisors to assist the Patents Court in proceedings under the Patents Act 1949 and Patents Act 1977 and for regulating the functions of such advisors

    (4) The remuneration of any such adviser shall be determined by the Lord Chancellor with the concurrence of the Minister for the Civil Service and shall be defrayed out of the money provided by Parliament.

20. Sir Louis Blom-Cooper 'Experts and Assessors: Past Present and Future' (2002) CJQ 341 at 347 notes that RSC Or 40 r. 1 which is now replaced by CPR 35 provided

    '1. In any cause or matter which is to be tried without a jury and in which any question for an expert witness arises, the Court may at any time; on the application of any party, appoint an independent expert of if more than once question arises, two or more such experts, to enquire and report on any question of fact or opinion ino involving questions of law or of construction. An expert appointed under this paragraph is referred to as a court expert.

    2. Any court expert in a cause or matter shall, if possible be a person agreed between the parties and failing agreement, shall be nominated by the court.

    3. The question to be submitted to the court expert and the restrictions (if any) given to him shall, failing agreement between the parties, be settled by the court.

    4. In this rule 'expert' in relation to any question arising in a cause or matter means any person who has such knowledge or experience of or in connection with the question that his opinion on it would be admissible in evidence.

    RSC 40 r 1 (2) is the germ of the idea for the single joint expert provision in CPR 35.7 and one wonders why the court appointed expert provision was dropped'.

CPR 35.15 to the parameters of the enabling statutes ensures, thereby, that the role of the assessor is in turn limited to one of assisting the judge to take judicial notice of the meaning of technical words. It is submitted that this restriction of the role of the assessor ensures, thereby, the incorporation of its functions into those of the tribunal. It would seem, therefore, that the assessor operating in this manner may contribute to ensuring that EC Articles 81 and 82 are as effectively enforced in the sense of adequate enforcement by the ordinary court as by the specialist CAT Tribunal.

In order to ensure more fully the reduction in the scope of the assessor which would result from the removal of CPR 35.15(3) and (4), arguably, the doctrine of effectiveness may require an amendment of Practise Direction 7.4:[21] specifically, the words 'copies of any report prepared by the assessor will be sent to each of the parties' would be removed in order to more effectively prevent the production of evidence by an assessor. In the event that the judge feels that his judgment is likely to be influenced by the advice of the assessor with respect to the meaning of particular words then it may be appropriate that he indicate to the parties the nature of this advice before judgment.[22] This will more easily enable the parties to exercise their rights of defence in the following manner: firstly, they are indirectly able to respond to the assessor's advice by commenting thereupon to the judge before judgment despite the exclusion of oral cross-examination of the assessor by S 7.4 of the Practise Direction: and secondly, the parties are able to use this information given by the judge in order to assist in forming eventual grounds of appeal from the judgment.[23] Accordingly, the rights of the defence would

---

21. Sir Louis Blom-Cooper 'Experts and Assessors: Past Present and Future', (2002) CJQ 341 *ibid.* at 352 (footnote 11 *supra*) argues that the 'advice' which the assessor may provide to the judge pursuant to CPR 35.15 in fact is evidence: 'Under 35.15 the 'advice' will qualify as evidence (35.15 (4)(b) and Practise Direction 7.4 and to the extent that a pre-trail report from the assessor is directed by the court, the parties will have sight and the facility to make use of its contents'.

22. *Richardson v. Redpath* (1944) AC 62 at 71, Viscount Simon, 'It would seem desirable in cases where the assessor's advice, within its proper limits, is likely to affect the judge's conclusion for the latter to inform the parties before him of the advice which he has received from the assessor'.

23. Sir Louis Blom-Cooper QC 'Experts and Assessors, Past Present and Future': (2002) 21 CJQ 350 op. cit. and footnote 11 *supra*: 'The assessor system being advice by an expert no under oath given to the court on matters not discloseable for cross examination by either party before judgment and qualifying as evidence would be regarded today as being incompatible under S 3 (1) of the Human Rights Act 1998 as a violation of Art. 6 (1) of the European Convention of Human Rights'. Clearly, this view is based upon an interpretation of EHRC Art. 6 (1) as providing a right to direct oral cross examination as the only method of ensuring the rights of the parties to respond to the case being made against as provided by *van Orshoven v. Belgium* (1997) (26) EHRR 55. However, it is not absolutely clear that Art. 6 (1), and such cases such *as van Orshoven* require that that the right to respond is coterminous with the right to direct oral examination as opposed to the right to respond indirectly coupled with written notice of the information which in turn forms the basis for an eventual appeal. D. Dwyer, in 'The Future of Assessors under the CPR' (2006) 25 CJQ Vol at 219 op. cit. argues at 225 that 'Four distinct functions can be identified for assessors within the current scope of CPR 35.15: tribunal member, court expert, court officer and scientific adviser. The assessor as scientific adviser would seek to clarify technical points of evidence for the judge and might suggest to the judge possible areas for further questioning in relation to a CPR r 35.2 expert's opinion. This appears to be the

appear to be adequately protected by a combination of the aforementioned two provisions : namely, the possibility for the parties to respond directly although not through oral cross examination of the assessor to the information contained in his written report prior to the entry of judgment:[24] and additionally, the opportunity of using the judge's written comments to assist in making an appeal against the judgment where he relied upon the information provided by the assessor in making his judgment. This does not prevent a reference on the matter of the use of the assessor in relation to the rights of the defence pursuant to EC 234 to the ECJ in so far as these proposed amendments apply in relation to the enforcement of EC Articles 81 and 82.

Overall, it may be said that the underlying English principles of the rectitude of the decision coupled with the Overriding Objective of the CPR apply so as to favour the use of the assessor notably in enforcement of EC competition law for the following reasons: recourse to the assessor will ensure firstly, that justice be done particularly in EC competition law cases in the sense that the decision would be accurate as possible in relation to the true facts properly understood by the judge; and secondly, that the decision be taken with a minimum of expense. Indeed, it may be that the use of an assessor is proportionately cheaper and quicker than would be the case if an additional expert were appointed. This reflects what appears to be the historic advantages of the use of the assessor and of judicial notice.[25] As noted, however, the doctrine of effectiveness may also apply in order to ensure that the assessor does not give expert evidence and thereby retains the function of part of the court which does not give evidence and is not subject to cross-examination.

---

type of assessor Mackay J. had in mind in *XYZ v. Schering Health Care* (2002) EWCA 1420 (QB) at 148–49 when consider expert evidence involving algebra'. It would seem the Dwyer feels that the function of scientific adviser which would under her analysis characterize the manner in which an assessor could intervene in enforcement proceedings for EC Art. 81 and 82 may not require cross-examination: she notes at 229 'The final point in applying Art. 6 (1) to the use of assessors is that one must have regard to the extent to which a particular practise might affect the substantive fairness of the process taken as a whole rather than in isolation. Thus the use of assessors to give opinions on the acceptability of the conduct of the parties might reasonably be considered to have a significant effect on the trial and so procedure surrounding such a use should be subject to Art. 6 (1) scrutiny. On the other hand, the use of assessors to advise the judge in general terms or to suggest further lines of question might be see has having significantly less impact on the case as a whole'. See generally D. Dwyer, 'Changing Approaches to Expert Evidence in England and Italy' (2003) Intl. Commentary on Evidence: <www.law.qub.ac.uk/ice/papers/expert2pdf> op. cit.

24. It is useful to note that the CAT Rules restrict the availability of cross examination: the CAT Guidelines (2005) provide at 3.4 (IV) The Tribunal will pay close attention to the probative value of documentary evidence. When there are essential evidential issues that cannot be resolved without cross examination, the Tribunal may permit oral examination of the witness.

25. K. K. Davis, (1955) (55) *Columbia Law Review* op. cit. *945 at 983 and J. Dickey, 'Assessors' (1970) MLR 494 at 501.*

Accordingly, it is submitted that the doctrine may apply to eliminate, thereby, CPR 35.15(3) and (4) in conjunction with Art 7.4 of the Practise Direction.[26]

C.   COMPETITION APPEAL TRIBUNAL

The CAT Rule 19(2)(1) as noted earlier, provides for the appointment of an expert *ex officio* by the court or on the request of the parties. There is no explicit provision however for the provision of an assessor by means of a separate rule such as CPR 35.15 which makes explicit reference to an 'assessor' as opposed to an 'expert'. Notwithstanding, it is necessary to consider whether CAT Rule 19(1) would provide the Tribunal with the possibility of making such an appoint: 'The Tribunal may at any time, on the request of a party or of its own initiative, at a case management conference, pre-hearing review or otherwise, . . . give such directions as it thinks fit to secure the just, expeditious and economical conduct of the proceedings'. It will be argued however, that CAT Rule 19(1) is unlikely to possess the scope necessary in order to provide for the appointment of an assessor by the Tribunal for the following reasons: first, it is submitted that the fact that CAT Rule 19(2)(1) does not contain specific mention to an assessor and that further there is no additional specific rule such as CPR 35.15 which deals with the appointment of an assessor is attributable to the specialist nature of the Tribunal. As indicated by the CAT Guidelines, the ordinary members of the Tribunal are specialists in areas such as economics. Accordingly, normally, the Tribunal unlike the ordinary court possesses the requisite specialist knowledge in order to understand expert evidence in the field of EC competition law. The second reason, is that by reason of the Tribunal's expertise with respect to the evaluating economic evidence CAT Rule 19(1) is unlikely to possess the requisite scope to permit the appointment of an assessor; or if that article does possess the requisite scope that the CAT Tribunal is most unlikely to make such an appointment by reason of its inherent specialist expertise which arises from its ordinary members so as to supplement CAT Rule 19(2)(1). In short, in the circumstances, such a function would be superfluous. The third reason is that, as is recalled, the CAT Rules and the CPR although drawing on similar principles nevertheless do have differences as pointed out in the Guidelines: the CAT Rules do not therefore constitute a duplicate of the CPR either in terms of its rules or the principles of interpretation. The Guidelines state as follows:

> 3.3 However, it should be borne in mind that the Tribunal Rules are different in various respects. Parties should not assume that the CPR and the rules of procedure of the CFI apply to a particular procedural issue.

---

26. Sir Louis Blom-Cooper Q.C., 'Experts and Assessors' (2002) (21) CJQ 345 op. cit. at 354 notes: 'Why can the court not use the assessor system under part 35.15 as a court appointed expert? With Case Management in force the appointment of an assessor under CPR 35.15 can be made before trial. Is it not time for the courts to use the new modified assessor system at least where the expert issue is complex?' This view appears to be shared by J. A. Jolowicz Q. C. in 'A Note on Experts' (2004) CJQ 408 at 410.

Accordingly, it is submitted the CAT Rules do not provide for the appointment of an assessor unlike the CPR for the following reasons:

1. no express provision exists to that effect in CAT Rule 19(2)(1);
2. CAT Rule 19(1) is unlikely to possess the scope necessary to supplement it 19(2)(1) and or the CAT is unlikely to use its discretion to use the rule if it does possess the requisite scope to permit the appointment of an assessor.

Both of these explanations are attributable to one factor: namely, the specialist nature of the CAT Tribunal which renders the use of an assessor a superfluous duplication. Arguably, in those circumstances, the presence of an assessor in the context of the CAT would be likely to infringe the very principles contained with CAT Rule 19(1) itself: specifically those which require the application of the principle of proportionality in the use of resources in order to save costs. The Guidelines give some indication as to the specialist nature of the background of the CAT members in the following:

> 1.9 The ordinary members are appointed for a period of eight years by the Secretary of State from a variety of backgrounds. Some are professionally qualified economists, lawyers or accountants whilst others have backgrounds in business, the public service and other relevant experience.

Accordingly, it is submitted that for these reasons and in contrast to the CPR no change would be required by the doctrine of effectiveness with respect to the appointment of an assessor in the context of the CAT Rules.

Chapter 5

English Procedure: Disclosure

A.   ACCESS TO INFORMATION

1.   CPR: Implementation of EC Reg. 1/2003[1] Article 15.1

Art 15.1 Reg. 1/2003 provides as follows:

> In proceedings for the application of Articles 81 or 82 of the Treaty, courts of
> the Member States may ask the Commission to transmit to them information in
> its possession or its opinion on questions concerning the application of the
> Community competition rules. This may be referred to as the *Amicus curiae*
> provision.

The current Practise Direction[2] arguably implements only Art. 15.2[3] and Art. 15.3
of Reg. 1/2003 but not Art 15.1 thereof. Further, the Practise Direction appears to

---

1. Regulation 1/2003 (16.12.2002) OJ L1/1 (4.1.2003), <www.eur-lex.europa.en>.
2. Practise Direction : Competition Law: Claims Relating to the Application of Art. 81 and 82 of the
   EC Treaty and Chapters 1 and II of the Competition Act (1998).
3. Art. 15 (2) Reg. 1/2003 'Member States shall forward to the Commission a copy of any written
   judgment of national courts deciding on the application of Art. 81 or Art. 82 of the Treaty. Such
   copy shall be forwarded without delay after the full written judgment is notified to the parties'.
       Art. 15 (3) Reg. 1/2003 'Competition authorities of the Member States acting on their own
   initiative may submit written observations to the national courts of their Member States on issues
   relating to the application of Art. 81 or Art. 82 of the Treaty. With the permission of the court in
   question, they may also submit oral observations to the national courts of their Member State.
   Where the coherent application of Art. 81 or 82 of the Treaty so requires, the Commission, acting
   on its own initiative may submit written observations to courts of the Member States. With the
   permission of the Court in question, it may also make oral observations'.

be restricted to post action commencement. The Practise Direction provides as follows:

> PRACTISE DIRECTION: Case Management: Competition Law
>
> Attention is drawn to the provisions of Art. 15.3 of the Competition Regulation (cooperation with the national courts) which entitles competition authorities to submit written observations to national courts on issues relative to the application of Art 81 or 82 and with the permission of the court in question to submit oral observations.
>
>   . . .
>
> 4.3 An application by a national competition authority or the Commission for permission to make oral representation at the hearing of a claim must be made by a letter to the Chancery Chambers at the earliest opportunity identifying the claim and indicating why the applicant wishes to make oral representations
>
> 4.4 If a national competition authority or the Commission files a notice under para. 4.2 or an application under 4.3 it must at the same time serve a copy of the notice or application on every party to the claim.
>
>   . . .
>
> 4.6 Where the court receives a notice under para. 4.2 it may give case management directions to the national competition authority or the Commission including directions about the date by which any written observations are to be filed.
>
>   . . .
>
> 4.8 In any claim to which this practise direction applies the court shall direct a pre-trial review to take place shortly before the trial if possible before the judge who will be conducting the trial.

2.   CAT RULES

In contrast, the CAT Rules provide:

> Rule 19(1) The Tribunal may at any time on the request of a party or of its own initiative at a case management conference, pre trial hearing or otherwise give such directions as are provided for in paragraph (2) below or such other direction as it thinks fit to secure the just expeditious and economical conduct of the proceedings.
>
> Rule 19(3) The Tribunal may in particular of its own initiative:
>
> (c) ask the parties or third parties for information or particulars
>
> (d) ask for documents or any papers relating to the case to be produced.

It would appear that CAT Rules 19(1) and (3) would permit the Tribunal to ask a third party, namely, the Commission, at any time, either post-commencement, or pre-commencement, and either on its own initiative or on the request of one of the parties for either documents or information from the Commission relevant to the case. BCL Old[4] appears to establish the availability of at least third party requests for information from the OFT. Accordingly, CAT Rules 19(1) and (3) would seem to permit the Tribunal to obtain information from the Commission pursuant to Art. 15.1 Reg. 1/2003 in enforcing a money action involving either a Commission or OFT infringement finding involving EC Articles 81 and or 82.

3.   CHANGES: DOCTRINE OF EFFECTIVENESS

Accordingly, it is clear that the current Practise Directive does not permit the High Court to obtain any information pursuant to Art. 15.1 Reg. 1/2003 either of its own motion or upon the request of the parties. It is submitted that the regulation requires both possibilities on a normal construction thereof. Further, it would appear therefore that the doctrine of effectiveness would require the CPR to be modified in order to ensure the Art. 15.1 could be properly implemented unless there is some procedural justification in terms of the Overriding Principles or the underlying principle concerning a fair trial[5] which justifies the current situation. Given that no such justification is apparent it would appear that the CPR or more particularly the Practise Direction would require modification in order to ensure that Art. 15.1 be fully implemented. It may well be that the doctrine of non-discrimination would apply to ensure that the CPR be modified to ensure implementation of Art. 15.1 in a manner equivalent to the CAT Rules notably with respect to enforcement of monetary actions pursuant to S 47A and S 58A CA (1998) respectively.[6] Further, it is submitted that the doctrine of effectiveness would also apply so as to require modification of Practise Direction which governs appeals in the Court of Appeal so as to ensure that the Court is able to ask the Commission *ex officio* or at the request of the parties for information pursuant to Art 15(3) of

---

4. *(1) BCL Old Ltd (2) DFL Old CO Ltd (3) PFF Old Co Ltd v. (1) Aventis SA (2) Rhodia Ltd (3) F Hoffmann-La Roche AG (4) Roche Products Ltd, CAT*, Case 1028/5/7/04; Date of Registration: 26 February 2004.

5. *Bellamy & Child European Community Law of Competition* (5th edn. 2001 Sweet & Maxwell, London) footnote 42 on p. 773 'while there is no formal provision in the CPR for such requests, English courts have made such request by a letter from the court to the Commission (Zwartveld Orders)'.

6. It may be however that the scope of the doctrine of non-discrimination being limited to the same category of legal context: that is, unless the CPR and the CAT Rules were considered as forming effectively one system for the enforcement of EC Art. 81 and 82 in the UK, then in order to make a comparison for the doctrine to apply it would be necessary to consider the rules within the CPR and the CAT separately: the rules in the two systems could therefore not be compared as the systems are different which would seem to prevent the application of the doctrine of non-discrimination: *Palmisani v. INDS*; Case C-261/95 [1997] ECR I 4025; *EDIS v. Ministero delle Finanze* Case C-281/96 [1998] ECR I 7141.

Reg. 1/2003. The relevant sections of the Practise Direction for the Court of Appeal are as follows:

PRACTISE DIRECTION 52 APPEALS:
S 21.10A APPEALS RELATION TO THE APPLICATION OF Arts. 81 AND 82 OF THE EC TREATY AND CHAPTER I AND II OF PART I OF THE COMPETITION ACT (1998)

(6) If a national competition authority or the Commission intends to make written observation to the Court of Appeal it must give notice of its intention to do so by letter to the Civil Appeals Office at the earliest opportunity;

(7) An application by a national competition authority or the Commission for permission to make oral representation at the hearing of an appeal must be made by letter to the Civil Appeals Office at the earliest opportunity, identifying the appeal and indicating only the applicant wishes to make oral representation;

(8) If a national competition authority or the Commission files a notice under sub-paragraph (6) or an application under paragraph (7) it must be at the same time serve a copy of the nature or application on every party to the appeal;

(9) Any request by a national competition authority on the Commission for the Court to send it any documents should be made at the same time as filing a notice under sub-paragraph (6) or an application under sub-paragraph (7);

(10) When the Court of appeal receives a notice under sub-paragraph (6) it may give case management directions to the national competition authority or the Commission, including directions about the date by which any written observations are to be filed.

4.   SPECIFIC CHANGES TO THE CPR

In reality, the specific procedural form of the modifications to the CPR will be determined, in large measure by the scope of Art. 15.1 Reg. 1/2003. The following elements will be considered:

a.   **Court Request: *Ex officio* and/or at Party Request**

Accordingly, it is necessary to ascertain whether Art. 15.1 establishes that the court be able to make a request both on its own initiative to the Commission or whether the request is to be made at the request of the parties to the court. In this regard, the Commission Notice[7] would seem to establish that the court be able to request information both *ex officio* and at the request of the parties:

Point 19 indicates: In fulfilling its duty under Art. 10 EC of assisting national courts in the application of EC competition law, the Commission is committed

---

7. Commission Notice (co-operation) 2004/C 101/04, (27.4.2004).

to remaining neutral and objective in its assistance. Indeed, the Commission's assistance to the national courts is part of its duty to defend the public interest. It has therefore no intention to serve the private interest of the parties involved in the case pending before the national court. As a consequence, the Commission will not hear any of the parties in the case pending before the court on issues which are before the court about its assistance to the national court. In case the Commission has been contacted by any of the parties on issues which are raised before the national court, it will inform the national court thereof independently of whether these contacts took place before or after the national court's request for cooperation.

This would seem to indicate that the court, if it has sought the opinion of the Commission on its own initiative as opposed upon the request of one of the parties may consider whether the rights of the defence require disclosure of the report to the parties as pursuant to CPR 35.14 with the assessor. Further, restricting the ability of the court to seeking information from the Commission to the condition of a previous request made by one the parties would prevent the court from obtaining information in the absence of such a request to the court: that is, of its own initiative independently of the parties. In this regard one notes that the Court of Appeal in *Crehan* held at point 96:

> The judge rightly acknowledged that he could not possibly embark upon a detailed research investigation himself and that to do so would be inconsistent with the role of the judge in civil litigation in this jurisdiction. That is why such investigations have been entrusted to bodies such as the Commission, the MMC and Competition Commission and the OFT.

Arguably, it would seem that the Court of Appeal whilst upholding the traditional non-inquisitorial role nevertheless does not object to the judge seeking information from specialized bodies such as the Commission and the OFT. The House of Lords in its judgment in *Crehan* did not deal specifically the point of the 'role of the judge in civil litigation in this jurisdiction'.

Therefore it would seem that the scope of the terms 'the courts . . . may ask' includes two possibilities: first that the national courts may *ex officio* request information from the Commission and second, that the national court may subsequent to a request by the parties ask the Commission for information. Accordingly, it is submitted that effective implementation of Art. 15.1 Reg. 1/2003 may require that the court be empowered to make requests to the Commission of its own motion. The doctrine of effective enforcement would seem to require that at a minimum the Practise Direction and possibly the CPR be modified so as to permit the High Court to seek information from the Commission *ex officio*. It is submitted that this modification is required for the following reason: namely that the express principles of the Overriding Objective of the CPR and the underlying principles of a fair trail would not suffice to justify the absence of a provision permitting a court to seek information from the

Commission *ex officio* where the absence thereof may impede completely the implementation of EC Art. 15.1.[8]

Upon receipt of the Commission's opinion, in order to ensure the rights of the defence, then following CPR 35.14 and the Practise Direction it would be appropriate for the court to consider communicating this information to the parties where such information was obtained on the court's own initiative.

b.   Scope

Article 15.1 provides: 'In proceedings . . . courts of the Member States may ask the Commission to transmit to them information in its possession or its opinion on questions concerning the application of the Community competition rules'.

It would seem that the term 'information' in Art. 15.1 refers to documents as defined in the CPR. However, it is not clear whether these are documents which are immediately relevant or whether it is possible to obtain documents which might be

---

8. *Peterbroeck van Campenhout SCS & Cie v. Belgium*, Case C-312/93 [1994] ECR I-4599 at para. 14 and *van Schijndel v. Stichting Pensionenfonds voor Fysiotherapeuten* (1995) C-430/93 C-431/93 op. cit; see also J. Bellhouse & L. Lavers (2004) CJQ Vol 23 17 at 190 'The traditional function of the *amicus curiae* in the English courts can then be summarized: it has been a practise whereby arguments on points of law or information may be presented before the tribunal with its permission and often by its active invitation which would not otherwise be heard because the information did not form part of the respective cases of the litigants represented'. In 2001, the then Attorney General, Lord Williams, in consultation with the Lord Chief Justice, Lord Woolf, set up a working party to re-appraise and regularize the *amicus curiae* function. The new name is Advocate to the Court. The working group produced a guidance in the forma of a Memorandum to Judges issued on Dec 201/2001. The new memorandum is entitled: Requests for the Appointment of an Advocate to the Court and makes the following points . . .

   1. In most cases, an Advocate to the Court is appointed by the Attorney – General following a request by the court.
        . . .
   3. A court may properly seek the assistance of an Advocate to the Court when there is a danger of an important and difficult point of law being decided without the court hearing relevant argument.
   4. An Advocate to the Court represents no one.
   5. The function of the Advocate to the Court is to give the court such assistance as he or she is able on the relevant law and its application to the facts of the case
        . . .
   8. The court should request the appointment of an Advocate to the Court as soon as it becomes aware of the need for assistance, setting out the circumstances and the point of law on which help is needed. The court should consider whether written submissions would be sufficient.

   . . . Lord Goldmsith also provided interesting statistics on the *amicus curiae* in the last three years before the reform. There were 26 request in 1999, 22 in 2000 and 31 in 2001 which the Attorney – General described as a 'modest increase' and which he illuminated with the observation that 'many of the cases in which the Courts have asked for the assistance of an *amicus curiae* have involved issues as to the compatibility of legislation or practises with the Human Rights Act 1998'.

so, that is wider than the scope provided by English procedure. Arguably the scope of the request will be decided by the Commission subject to appeal by the national court to the ECJ.

Concerning the scope of the opinion which a national court may seek from the Commission pursuant to Art. 15.1, following Point 29 of the Commission Notice it would seem that the following is the case: although a national court may ask the Commission for its opinion on the application of EC Articles 81 or 82 nevertheless the Commission will not give its view on the merits of the case. The Notice provides as follows:

> Point 29. 'When giving its opinion, the Commission will limit itself to providing the national court with the factual information or the economic or legal clarification asked for without considering the merits of the case pending before a national court. Moreover, unlike the authoritative interpretation of Community law, but the Community Courts, the opinion of the Commission does not legally bind the national court'.

It is to be noted that Point 29 reaffirms that the opinion is to be given post-commencement and not pre-action. Second, it is noted that there is an attempt to make a distinction between a legal opinion on the interpretation of EC Articles 81 or 82 and its application to the facts of the case – that is 'the merits of the case'. Clarification of this distinction can perhaps be sought in The Commission Annual Report on Competition (2004) at point 112: 'Art. 15(1) of Reg. EC 1/2003 gives national judges the option of asking the Commission for information in its possess or for an opinion on questions concerning application of the EU competition rules. In 2004, the Commission received nine requests for an opinion. Six requests emanated from the Spanish courts and all dealt with a similar type of distribution agreement in the energy sector. These agreements mainly raised questions as to the distinction between agent and retailer with the meaning of EU competition law and contained both clauses relating to the setting of a maximum full retail price and non compete clauses for fuel that might result in the foreclosure of the market. The Commission's replies to these six requests were largely based on its preliminary assessment in the *Pepsol* Case'.

Further, Point 19 of the Notice establishes that:

> In fulfilling its duty under Art. 10 of assisting national courts, in the application of EC competition rules, the Commission is committed to remaining neutral and objective in its assistance . . . Indeed the Commission's assistance to national courts is part of its duty to defend the public interest. It has therefore no intention to serve the parties involved in the case pending before the court.

It is not clear whether, bearing in mind Points 19 and 29 of the Notice, the scope of the documents and in particular, the nature of the opinion which a court could seek from the Commission pursuant to Art. 15.1 would approximate the information which was presented to the High Court and considered by the Court of Appeal in *Crehan*: it is to be noted however, that this information was obtained by

Mr Crehan's solicitor from the Commission in the course of what appears to be the Commission's decision to refer enforcement to the English court. The Court of Appeal observed at paragraph 97 of its judgment:

> However it is apparent from what the Commission said in the letter of 24 January 1997 to Charles Russell & Co. that it expected the English Court to take into account its earlier conclusions not only in respect of *Inntrepeneur* but also in cases such as Whitbread even though not final decisions. The fact that it was considered unnecessary and therefore undesirable for the Commission itself formally to give the decision as to whether Art 81(1) applied when the English court was in a position to give the decision and to award compensation which the Commission could not do so did not leave the judge free to reconsider the Commission's earlier conclusion afresh. Still less was the judge free so to do in 2003 by which time the *Whitbread, Bass* and *Scottish & National* decisions with its conclusions, central to those decisions, on the foreclosure of the relevant market had been published and the comfort letter of 24 January 2000 relating to retail link had been issued. We accept that it is read inference from that letter that in the Commission's view Art. 81(1) applied to the Inntrepreneur leases throughout the period relevant to Mr Crehan's case'.[9]

Given, however, that the Commission will determine the scope of the type of information which will be given in the opinion subject to an appeal to the ECJ it would seem appropriate to use the terminology in the CAT Rule in the Practise Direction: namely, information.[10]

---

9. *Bernard Crehan v. Inntrepreneur Pub Company CPC* (2004) EWCA 637, Case No A3/2003/ 1725, paragraph 97.
10. No specified requirements are necessary concerning the rules of evidence in order to accommodate the status of information obtained by the court from the Commission. Following *Bernard Crehan v. Inntreprneur Pub Company CPC* (2004) EWCA 637, op. cit., it would appear that the status of Commission opinions and OFT reports constitutes documentary evidence which can be introduced pursuant to the Civil Evidence Act (1995). The Court of Appeal at paragraph 54 observes: 'Mr Crehan called no factual evidence in relation to issues (1) and (2) but relied upon decisions of and documents produced by the Commission and on other documentary materials such as reports of the MMC and OFT. To some extent Inntrepeneur also relied upon similar documentary material and very sensibly Inntrepeneur's solicitors by letter date 14 January 2003 suggested that neither party would take any point on the absence of notice under the Civil Evidence Act (1995) and CPR 33. 2.(3) when making submission as to the weight to be given to hearsay statement and that each party would be free to rely upon the failure of the other to call a witness to give oral evidence and to be available for cross examination as a reason why less weight should be given to that evidence'. The House of Lords *in Inntrepreneur Pub Co. (CPC) et al v. Crehan* (2006) UKHL 38, *op. cit.* upheld this position: see Lord Hoffmann at paragraph 69 of his opinion: 'The correct position is that when there is no conflict of decisions in the sense which I have discussed, the decision of the Commission is simply evidence properly admissible before the English Court which given the expertise of the Commission, may well be regarded by the Court has highly persuasive. As a matter of law it is only part of the evidence which the Court will take into account'.

c. **Time: Pre-action**

It is not clear that Reg. 1/2003 provides for pre-action enforcement. The Commission Note states at Point 28: 'When called upon to apply EC competition rule to a case pending before it, the national court'. This would seem to indicate that Art. 15.1 Reg. 1/2003 applies only post action commencement. Further, the current Practise Direction appears notably in S. 8.1 to apply only post commencement: that is to actions pending. In the event however, that Art. 15.1 Reg. 1/2003 were construed to apply to pre-action enforcement of EC Articles 81 and or 82, then arguably the Practise Direction would require modification pursuant to application of the doctrine of effectiveness so as to provide such a disposition: it would appear that such modification would be possible by means of the S. 8 of the Civil Procedure Act (1997): The Lord Chancellor may by order amend the provisions of S 33(2) of the Supreme Court Act 1981 or S 52(2) of the County Court Act (1984)...so as to extend the provisions to circumstances where other claims may be made.

B.   PRIVILEGE: CONFIDENTIALITY

In communicating information to the national court pursuant to Art. 15.1 EC Reg. 1/2003, the Commission indicates in its Notice on Co-operation[11] that the national court must provide effective protection for confidential information. In default of an undertaking by the national court to provide such protection, the Commission will not communicate the requested information. The Commission Notice specifies as follows:

> Point 23: 'In transmitting information to the national courts, the Commission has to uphold the guarantees given to natural and legal persons by EC Art. 287 (*Delimitis* C-234/89 (1991) ECR I-935, para. 53). EC Art. 287 prevent members, officials and other staff of the Commission from disclosing information covered by the obligation of professional secrecy. The information covered by professional secrecy may be both confidential information and business secrets. Business secrets are information of which not only disclosure to the public but also mere transmission to a person other than the one that provided the information might seriously harm the latter's interests (*Postbank* T 353/94 (1996) ECR II-921, para. 86–87)'.
> Point 25: 'Consequently, before transmitting information covered by professional secrecy to a national court the Commission will remind the court of its obligation under community law to uphold rights which EC Art. 287 confers on natural and legal persons and will ask the court whether it can and will guarantee protection of business secrets. If the national court cannot offer such a guarantee the Commission shall not transmit the

---

11.   Commission Notice on Co-operation 2004/C 101/04 (27.4.2004) op. cit. points 23 and 25.

information covered by professional secrecy to the national court. Only when the national court has offered a guarantee that it will protect the confidential information and business secrets will the Commission transmit the information requested indicting those parts which are covered by professional secrecy and which parts are not and can therefore be disclosed'.

In terms of implementation of this protection by the CPR, two aspects must be considered: first the scope of the protection available for confidential information: second, the procedural method by which this protection is afforded.

1.   PRIVILEGE OF CONFIDENTIALITY AND THE CPR

Generally, it may be said that a privilege protecting confidential information does not exist in English law.[12] Indeed, subject to certain well defined exceptions such as legal professional privilege and the privilege against self-incrimination, no person has a right to withhold from the court information that is relevant to an issue before the court. Neither a party nor a non-party is entitled to invoke privacy or an obligation of confidentiality as a reason for refusing disclosure of documents or providing information which is required in legal process.[13] Notwithstanding the absence of a privilege of confidentiality, as a matter of general principle the court may accord protection to interests of privacy and confidentiality to the extent that it can be done without compromising the administration of justice in terms of ECHR Art. 6.1.[14] In this regard, the court may hold proceedings behind closed doors in order to maintain the secrecy of sensitive commercial information. Accordingly, such a procedure enables the court to consider the confidential material when

12. P. Gardner, in 'Human Rights Act: Future Impact' Feb. 2003, <www.moncton.com> argues that Art. 8 ECHR provides a privilege against inspection of confidential documents as established in *Funke v. France*, 16 EHRR 277, and ECtHR, *Société Colas Est et al v. France*, application 37971/97, Judgment : 16 April 2002, followed by the ECJ in *Roquette Frères*: Case C-94/00 [2002] ECR I – 9011 at point 29, belonging to both private individuals and companies, although the protection of the latter may be less extensive than that of the former.
13. A.A.S. Zuckerman, *Civil Procedure* (Lexis Nexis, London, 2003) op. cit. at p. 103 ECHR Art. 6.1, the right to a fair trial, provides among others 'a right to an adversarial process which means a right to be informed of all the evidence adduced in the case and the arguments presented and an opportunity to respond. The ECt HR has recognized that the right to be heard is not absolute and that necessity may justify exceptions. (*Keegan v. Ireland* (1994 18 EHRR 342) However an exception may only be made for legitimate purposes, it must be strictly limited and it must be proportionate in the circumstances'. One of the exceptions involves denial of access to evidence or information where material is withheld from a party but disclosed to the party's legal representatives or experts.
14. M. Clough QC & A. McDougal, Actions for Damages, UK Report (2004) observe with regard to the absence of the privilege for confidentiality in the CPR 'It is interesting to note in this context that the CAT will be in a better position to protect confidential information and business secrets communicated to it by the European Commission under Art. 15 (1) of Reg. 1/2003 and the notice on Cooperation with National Courts than the ordinary civil courts where the judges will have to rely on their power to control disclosure as there is no category of privilege from disclosure applicable to confidential information'.

deciding the issues without harming its secrecy. Similarly, the court may consider the need to protect privacy and confidentiality when making inter partes orders of disclosure and inspection or when it is asked to order a non-party to disclose documents or other information.[15] Pursuant to Art. 15.1 Reg. 1/2003 it is the Commission which decides which information it considers to be confidential and not the national court. Accordingly, it would seem that the Commission would ask the English court following Point 28 of its Notice whether the court would be able to provide guarantees to effectively protect the confidential information. Further, it appears that the English court would be able to provide such guarantees through combination of inspection restricted to the legal representatives and or experts and proceedings held within camera. However, it is not clear that such an informal system ensures the enforcement of EC Articles 81 and 82 in the most effective manner particularly compared to the CAT Rule 53 which provide specifically for protection of confidential information. Accordingly, it is appropriate to consider both CPR and the CAT Rules as they pertain to the protection of confidential information.

2. PROCEDURAL PROTECTION OF CONFIDENTIAL
    INFORMATION BY THE CPR

The CPR provides for a party to request that a document be withheld from inspection but does not specify confidentiality as a ground for the application:

> CPR 19(3): 'A person who wishes to claim that he has a right or a duty to withhold inspection of a document or part of a document must state in writing that he has such a right or duty; or the grounds on which he claims that right or duty
> (4) The State referred to in paragraph (3) must be made
> (a) in the list in which the document is disclosed
> (b) if there is no list to the person wishing to inspect the document'.

Accordingly, CPR 19(3) would not suffice unless accompanied by the court's inherent discretion to provide the undertaking required to implement Art. 15.1 EC Reg. 1/2003 as interpreted by Points 23 and 25 of the Commission Notice on Co-operation. CPR 19(3) provides for eventual protection of confidential information only at the request of one of the parties. Therefore, it empowers the court to provide an undertaking to the Commission to protect confidential information following a request for assistance made by the court to the Commission pursuant to Art. 15.1 EC Reg. 1/2003. Accordingly, it is submitted that the doctrine of effectiveness would require at a minimum that Practise Direction for the enforcement of EC Reg. 1/2003 be modified so as to ensure two possibilities: first that the court, as noted earlier, be able to request information and assistance from the

---

15. A.A. S. Zuckerman, *Civil Procedure* (Lexis Nexis, London, 2003) op. cit., see *generally*, Ch. 2 Fair Trial and Ch. 14 Disclosure Sections 14.50 to 14.70.

Commission both *ex officio* as well as upon the request of the parties; and second, that in so doing that the court be able *ex officio* to provide the Commission with the requisite undertaking so as to ensure effective protection of confidential information communicated to it pursuant to Art. 15.1 EC Reg. 1/2003.

3.   PROCEDURE FOR THE PROTECTION OF CONFIDENTIAL
                INFORMATION BY THE CAT

The CAT Rules provide first, protection for confidential information, and second, a procedural mechanism to ensure the implementation of Art. 15 EC Reg. 1/2003.
The CAT Rule 53 provides as follows:

> 53(1) A request for confidential treatment of any document or part of a document filed in connection with proceedings before the Tribunal shall be made in writing by the person who submitted the document at the latest within 14 days after filing the document indicating the relevant words, figures or passages for which confidentiality is claimed and supported in each case by specific reasons and if so directed by the Registrar, the person making the request must supply a confidential version of the relevant document.

No request for confidential treatment made in disregard of this rule or outside the period provided under paragraph (1) shall be permitted unless the Tribunal considers that the circumstances are exceptional. In the event of a dispute as to whether confidential treatment should be accorded, the Tribunal shall decide the matter after hearing the parties taking into account the matter referred to in paragraph (2) of Schedule 4 of the 2002 Act.

It would seem from Rule 53(2) that confidential information is to be dealt with primarily by that rule and secondarily where the conditions for the application of the rule are not made out with the discretion of the Tribunal. It may be that in such circumstances the Tribunal may follow Rule 19(1) and in particular: 'The Tribunal may at any time, on the request of a party or of its own initiative at a case management conference or otherwise, give . . . or such other directions as it thinks fit to secure the just, expeditious and economical conduction of the proceedings'.

In so far as Rule 53 governs confidential information it would appear that the doctrine of effectiveness would require the following modifications in order to ensure the implementation of Art. 15.1 Reg. 1/2002: first, that the scope of the term 'person' in Rule 53(1) be expanded so as to include 'The Commission' with respect to a request made by the Tribunal to the Commission pursuant to Art. 15. 1 EC Reg. 1/2003; second, that Rule 53(3) be amended with respect to applications made pursuant to Art. 15.1 EC Reg. 1/2003 so as to conform with *Zwartveld*[16] and the Preamble to EC Reg. 1/2003. It is the Commission which decides the matter of confidentiality and not the Tribunal. In the event of dispute, the

---

16. *Zwartveld* Case C 2-88 (1990) ECR-I – 4405 at points 10 & 11.

Tribunal would be able to appeal the Commission's decision concerning confidentiality[17] to the ECJ.

The scope of the protection which CAT is apparently able to provide for confidential information is provided as noted in CAT Rule 53(3) by Art. 1(2) of Schedule 4 of the EA (2002):

> 1.(2) In preparing that document, the Tribunal shall have regard to the need for excluding, so far as practicable –
>
> a) information the disclosure of which would be in its opinion contrary to the public interest;
>
> b) commercial information, the disclosure of which would or might in it is opinion significantly harm his interests;
>
> c) information relating to the private affairs of an individual the disclosure of which would or might in its opinion, significantly harm his interests.

The procedure which is currently followed when a person makes a request for a request for confidential treatment for documents is provided by Section 13 of the CAT GUIDELINES and in particular by the following sections:

> Rule 53 provides that if a person wishes to request confidential treatment for any document or part of a document filed in the proceedings he must do so preferably in the document in question but in any event in writing within 14 days of sending the document to the registrar indicating the relevant words, figures or passages over which confidentiality is claimed together with his reasons for doing so.

If the Registrar so requires the appellant must provide a non-confidential version of the document. In broad terms, confidential information is information the disclosure of which would be contrary to the public interest: commercial information the disclosure of which could significantly harm the legitimate business interests of the undertaking to which it relates; or information relating to the private affairs of an individual the disclosure for which could significantly harm his interest (see para. 1(2) Sch. 4 to the 2002 Act). Whether particular information is to be regarded as confidential is a matter for the Tribunal to decide in the circumstance of the individual case.

Even if the information is confidential the Tribunal must when drafting its judgment take into account the extent to which disclosure is necessary for the purpose of explaining the reasons for its decision (para. 1(3) of Sch. 4 to the 2002 Act).

> 13.8 In practise, a request for confidential treatment is therefore mainly relevant to the possible disclosure of confidential information to third parties either in the context of the intervention procedure or during the hearings of the Tribunal.
>
> 13.10 The need for disclosure in the interests of fairness on the one hand and a legitimate claim to the confidentiality of (commercially) sensitive

---

17. Preamble 33 of EC Reg. 1/2003 'Since all the decisions taken by the Commission under this Regulation are subject to review by the Court of Justice in accordance with the Treaty'.

information, on the other may, in appropriate circumstance be accommodated where, with the consent of the parties and with appropriate protective orders or undertakings, disclosure is made solely within a 'confidentiality ring' normally comprising the parties' named legal representatives and, possibly, other external advisers or experts such as accountants and economists rather than to the parties themselves.

13.11 As regards hearing, the Tribunal will sit in private for any part of a public hearing where it is satisfied that it will be considering confidential information in accordance with Rule 50. Similarly the Tribunal will if it thinks it appropriate in the circumstances exclude such confidential information form any publicly available version of its final judgment after hearing the principal parties.

It would appear that with the exception of Art. 13.4, the CAT Guidelines in conjunction with CAT Rules 19.1 and 53 and Art 1.1 of Schedule 4 of the EA (2002) would permit the Tribunal to implement Art. 15.1 EC Reg. 1/2003 and notably to provide the requisite protection required by the Commission in paragraphs 27 and 28 of its Notice. Arguably, the principle of effectiveness and non discrimination would require a modification of the CPR Practise Direction on the Implementation of EC Regulation 1/2003 so as to introduce a system of protection for confidential information similar to that used by CAT: that is, the CAT Rules and Guidelines of the scope of confidential information and the procedural method of protection permit a greater degree of legal certainty not only for the Commission but also eventual parties who wish to enforce EC Articles 81 or 82 than that provided by the CPR. Arguably, therefore, the legal certainty afforded by the CAT Rules provide a more effective system of enforcement for EC Articles 81 and 82 than the CPR with respect to the treatment of confidential information. Additionally, the introduction of a system such as that used by the CAT would fulfil more effectively the overriding objective of the CPR: namely, the just, expeditious and economical conduct of the proceedings. Arguably, the principle of non-discrimination as well as that of effectiveness would intervene so as to require the aforementioned modifications in order to ensure the following: that monetary actions concerning either Commission or OFT infringements decisions of EC Articles 81 and 82 can be enforced as effectively by the ordinary court under S 58A CA (1998) as by the CAT pursuant to S 47A CA (1998) in terms of protecting confidential information. The principle of effectiveness alone would intervene in order to ensure that the ordinary court may enforce as effectively as possible EC Articles 81 and 82 in free standing damages actions in terms of protecting confidential information.

4.   APPLICATION OF THE DOCTRINE OF EFFECTIVENESS TO THE CAT RULES AND CPR TREATMENT OF CONFIDENTIALITY

Both the CAT Rules and the CPR are able to afford protection for confidential information provided to the Tribunal and the Court respectively by the

Commission pursuant to Art. 15.1 EC Reg. 1/2003. However, the difference between the two systems of procedure turns on the use by the CAT of Rules 53 which defines the scope of the protection available pursuant to paragraph 1(2) of Schedule 4 of the 2002 Enterprise Act. It is not clear at the present time that in practise the scope of protection provided by the CAT and the court is functionally different. Rather, the advantage which CAT Rule 53 provides is that of legal certainty in that in conjunction with Art. 1(2) of Schedule 4: first, with respect to the scope of the protection; and second, with respect to the manner in which the protection is to be sought. Arguably, the doctrine of effectiveness would require for reasons of legal certainty as system such as that provided by CAT Rule 53 coupled with Art. 1(2) of Schedule 4 in order to ensure the implementation of Art. 15.1 of Reg. 1/2003.

C.	THE PRIVILEGE AGAINST SELF-INCRIMINATION AND DISCLOSURE

In order to consider the operation of the privilege against self-incrimination in the enforcement of EC Articles 81 and 82 by the English courts and the CAT, in terms of disclosure both in the context of Reg. 1/2003 and in damages actions, it is necessary to consider the following: first the scope of the privilege as provided by English law independent of the cases of the European Court of Human Rights (ECtHR); second, the scope of the privilege as provided by the cases of the ECtHR; and third the scope of the privilege as defined by the case of the European Court of Justice (ECJ) and Court of First Instance (CFI) and notably by *SGL Carbon*.[18]

1.	ENGLISH LAW

In English law, the scope of the privilege against self-incrimination applies both to the testimony and to the disclosure and inspection of documents. The privilege provides immunity against being compelled to provide evidence or information of a self-incriminating or potentially self-incriminating nature.[19] Accordingly, a person who is called as a witness is entitled to refuse to answer any question if to do so would tend to expose him to proceedings for either a criminal offence or for recovery of a penalty pursuant to UK law.[20] Further,

---

18. *Commission v. SGL Carbon Co. Ltd.* Case C-301/04 P Opinion of Advocate-General Geelhoed.
19. *Versailles Trade Finance Ltd (in administrative receivership) v. Clough* (2001) EXCA Civ 1509 Civil Evidence Act (1968), s 14.
20. *Blunt v. Park Lane Hotel* (1942) 2 KB 253: Civil Evidence Act (1968).
    KB 253; Civil Evidence Act 1968, s 14. See *generally* Phipson on Evidence (16th edn, Sweet & Maxwell, London, 2005) para. 24-40: Cross & Tapper on Evidence (10th edn, Blackstone Press, London, 2004) pp. 445.

a witness is entitled to claim the privilege in relation to any statement which is sought from him and which the authorities may use against him with a view to sustaining a criminal charge[21] or in deciding to prosecute him.[22] A person who seeks to raise the privilege against self-incrimination must satisfy the court that there is a real risk of prosecution or the imposition of a penalty. The test is whether there is a 'real and appreciable risk of criminal proceedings[23] ... being taken against' the person.[24] A remote or slight possibility of such consequences would be insufficient in order to invoke the privilege and to justify refusing to respond to the question.[25] In short, the privilege applies to prevent a witness from being obliged to reply to incriminating questions. It is only by extension for this testamentary protection that a witness is similarly protected from having to disclose or produce documents which may serve to incriminate the witness.[26] Moreover, as is evidenced by the case of *Westinghouse*,[27] a legal person may benefit from the protection of the privilege notably in the enforcement of EC Articles 81 and 82 by the ordinary English court. Accordingly, the scope of the English privilege is apparently wide. However, prior to the adoption of the Human Rights Act (1998) (HRA), the English courts sought to restrict the scope of this wide privilege at least in civil proceedings. Therefore, while recognizing that Parliament alone could abolish the privilege in civil proceedings, the House of Lords nevertheless approved at least one method whereby the operation of the privilege may be restricted: *AT & T Istel.*[28] Arguably, this desire on the part of the English courts to restrict the application of the privilege has now been countered by the application of the HRA (1998) and its concomitant introduction of the ECtHR case law concerning notably the privilege against self-incrimination. It is submitted however, that there may be the possibility of restricting the operation of the privilege against self-incrimination in English enforcement proceedings of EC Articles 81 and 82 in the following manner: first, it may be that as a result of *Otto v. Post*

---

21. *Blunt v. Park Lane Hotel* (1942) 2 KB; Civil Evidence Act (1968) S 14; See *generally* Phipson on Evidence (16th edition) (2005) para. 24–46; Cross & Tapper on Evidence (10th edition) (2004) pp. 445.
22. *A T & T Istel Ltd v. Tully* (1993) AC 45, *Den Norske Bank ASA v. Antonatos* (1997) QB 271.
23. *Blunt v. Park Lane Hotel* (1942) 2 KB 253; Civil Evidence Act (1968) S 14: See *generally* Phipson on Evidence (16th edition) (2005) para. 20–26; Cross and Tapper on Evidence (10th edition) (2004) pp. 445.
24. *Rank Film Distributors Ltd v. Video Information Centre* (1982) AC 380 at pp. 441 and *Sociedade Nacional de Combustiveis de Angola UEE v. Lundquist* (1991) 2 QB 310.
25. *R v. Boyes* (1861) 1 B & S 311, 121 ER 730 at 738; *Den Norske Bank SAS v. Antonatos* (1998) 3 All ER 74.
26. A.A.S. Zuckerman, Civil Procedure (Lexis Nexis, London, 2003) op. cit. *generally* Ch. 17.
27. A.A.S. Zuckerman, Civil Procedure (Lexis Nexis, London, 2003) *ibid.* 578–583.
28. *AT & T Istel Ltd v. Tully* (1993) AC 45.

Bank,[29] the Commission may not be able to use information from national proceedings.[30] In that judgment the ECJ held as follows:

> Paragraph 18: 'Post Bank claims however that if the limitation on the Commission's power of investigation under Regulation 17/62 is not applied in the national proceedings that limitation would be deprived of any practical effect since the Commission could obtain through the national proceedings the information which it cannot obtain directly under the procedure governed by Regulation 17/62'.
>
> Paragraph 19: 'That argument must be rejected'.
>
> Paragraph 20: 'Information obtained in the course of such proceedings may indeed be brought to the attention of the Commission in particular by an interested party. However, it follows from the *Orkem* judgment that the Commission or for that matter a national authority cannot use that information to establish an infringement of the competition rules in proceedings which may result in the imposition of penalties or as evidence justifying the initiation of an investigation prior to such proceedings'.

It would seem that this principle corresponds to the situation which prevails pursuant to S 15. 3 of Reg. 1/2003, second sub-paragraph as will be analysed below. Second, it may be that in the event that the Commission has already rendered a decision and exercises it fining powers it would not be possible to raise the privilege against self-incrimination. This may be the case with respect, notably, to monetary judgments pursuant to S 47A and 58A CA (1998). In both of these situations, it would seem that notwithstanding *Westinghouse*, the English privilege against self-incrimination cannot, in principle, be raised for the simple reason that there is no likelihood of the imposition of a fine by the Commission: either because

---

29. *Otto v. Post Bank* Case C-60/92 (1993) ECR I 5663.
30. See also M. Clough QC & A. McDougal Actions for Damages, UK Report (2004) at p. 15 : 'The House of Lords held in *Westinghouse* (Rio Tinto) that a party could claim a privilege from discovery and disclosure of documents by involving the Civil Evidence Act S 14 on the grounds that to do so might incriminate him and make him vulnerable to the imposition of a fine by the European Commission for breach of Art. 81 and 82. It is unclear whether the same approach would be followed where the Commission or the OFT had already adopted a decision finding an infringement and exercises their fining powers'. *Bellamy & Child European Community Law of Competition* (5th Ed. Sweet & Maxwell, London, 2001) observe at p. 811 footnote 12: 'In *Westinghouse* (1978) the House of Lords held that such a privilege (privilege against self-incrimination) could be claimed: However, Westinghouse concerned third party discover in aid of US proceedings and the English law of privilege against self-incrimination in civil proceedings has subsequently been refined: see *AT & T Istel v. Tully* (1993) AC: Further, the ECJ has held that the Commission cannot use directly incriminating information obtained in the course of civil proceedings before a national court as evidence of a breach of competition rules: Case C – 60/92 *Otto v. Postbank* (1993) ECR I 5683 note: 12 -022: in *Otto v. Postbank*, the ECJ held that national courts are not required as a matter of Community law to apply the *Orkem* principle in ordinary civil proceedings which do not lead to the imposition of a penalty. But it followed that the Commission was not entitled to use information obtain in that in the course of national proceedings which may come to its attention in order to establish an infringement or as evidence justifying the initiation of an investigation'.

the Commission cannot use the information or because a fine has already been imposed. However, both of these situations appear to turn on the use of the incriminating documents as the basis for raising the privilege, notably in the former perhaps more than the latter. Accordingly, the fact that the incriminating information cannot be used thereby prevents the raising of the privilege in English law. However, by reason of the introduction of the case law of the European Court of Human Rights (ECtHR) into English law by virtue of S 4 of the Human Rights Act (HRA) (1998)[31] it is necessary to ascertain more clearly the scope of the English privilege against self incrimination notably as it could affect enforcement proceedings for EC Articles 81 and 82. In particular, it will be necessary to consider the effect of *J.B. v. Switzerland*[32] which seems to establish, in the line of *Funke*[33] as opposed to *Saunders*,[34] that EC Art 6.1 may be violated even if incriminating documents are not used. Arguably, *J.B. v. Switzerland* and *Funke* appear to extend the scope of the privilege in civil cases to not only the production of incriminating documents but also the disclosure. These three cases are of particular significance notably in relation to the recent ECJ judgment of *SGL Carbon*.[35] It will also be necessary to consider the effect of the doctrine of effectiveness and supremacy of EC law in terms of the effect of *SGL Carbon* on the scope of the privilege against self-incrimination in enforcement proceedings by the English court of EC Art. 81 and 82. In short, it is submitted that the application of this doctrine will require the use of the *Orkem* privilege at least in those circumstances where the privilege can be raised in the enforcement of EC Articles 81 and 82.

2.   PRIVILEGE AGAINST SELF-INCRIMINATION AND CASES OF
           THE EUROPEAN COURT OF HUMAN RIGHTS

In *Funke*, the French customs authorities having found certain documents at Mr Funke's house requested him to produce further specified documents. Having initially said that he would do so, Mr Funke changed his mind and refused to produce them. Upon being sentenced to pay a penalty for the refusal to produce the documents, Mr Funke claimed that ECHR Art 6.1 entitled him to refuse to produce the documents. The Court held:

> The Customs secured Mr Funke's conviction in order to obtain certain documents which they believed must exist, although they were not certain of that

---

31. By reason of the S 2(1) HRA (1998) one must take account of the case law of the ECtHR the case. S 2(1) HRA (1998) provides:

    '2 (1) A court or tribunal determining a question which has arisen in connection with a Convention right must take into account any:
    (a) judgment, decision, declaratory or advisory opinion of the European Court of Human Rights'.
32. *J.B. v. Switzerland* Case 31827/96 (2001) ECHR 324 (3.5. 2001).
33. *Funke v. France* (1993) 16 EHRR 297.
34. *Saunders v. United Kingdom* (1996) 23 EHRR 313.
35. *Commission v. SGL Carbon Co. Ltd.,* Case C-301/04P Judgment: 29 June 2006, <www.curia.eu>.

fact. Being unable or unwilling to produce them by some other means, they attempted to compel the applicant himself to provide evidence of the offences which he had allegedly committed. The special feature of the Custom's law-
. . . cannot justify such an infringement of the right of anyone 'charged with a criminal offence within the autonomous meaning of this expression in Art 6(1) to remain silent and not to incriminate himself'.

In *Saunders*, the Secretary of State appointed inspectors with the power to compel the production of documents and information in order to investigate irregularities in the business take over of Argyl. The file of the inspectors was transferred to the Crown Prosecution Service. At Mr Saunder's trial for theft and conspiracy, the prosecution relied mainly on the transcripts of his evidence to the Department of Trade and Industry (DTI) to refute the evidence which he gave at trial. Mr Saunders was convicted and applied to the ECtHR on the grounds that the use made at trial of evidence given to the DTI inspectors under their compulsory powers deprived him of the right to a fair trial contrary to Art. 6(1) of the ECHR. The ECtHR held that the exercise of the inspectors' powers did not infringe Art. 6.1 because their function was essentially investigative rather than adjudicative. The Court held as follows:

> The right to not incriminate oneself in particular presupposes without resort to evidence obtained through methods of coercion or oppression in defiance of the will of the accused. In this sense the right is closely linked to the presumption of innocence contained in Art. 6(2) of the Convention.
>
> The right not to incriminate oneself is primarily concerned however with respecting the will of an accused person to remain silent. As commonly understood in the legal systems of the contracting parties to the Convention and elsewhere it does not extend to the use in criminal proceedings of material which may be obtained from the accused through the use of compulsory powers but which have an existence independent of the will of the suspect such as, *inter alia*, documents acquired pursuant to a warrant, breath blood and urine samples and bodily samples for the purpose of DNA testing. In the present case the court is called upon to decide whether the use made by the prosecution of statements obtained from the applicant by the inspectors amounts to an unjustifiable infringement of the right.

In *J.B. v. Switzerland*, the taxpayer, J.B. challenged the imposition on him of a fine by the Swiss tax authorities for his refusal to provide information as in Funke to the authorities concerning his income. The ECtHR held:

> Paragraph 65: 'In the present case, when on 4 December 1987 the X district office instituted tax evasion proceedings against the applicant, he was requested to submit all documents concerning the companies in which he had invested money. When the applicant failed to do so, he was requested on three further occasions to declare the source of the income invested. The applicant not having reacted to those requests a disciplinary fine of CHF 1000 was imposed on 28 February 1989'.

Paragraph 66: 'The Court notes that in its judgment of 7 July 1995 the Federal Court referred to various provisions in criminal proceedings obliging a person to act in a particular way so as to enable the authorities to obtain his conviction, for instance, the obligation to install a tachograph in lorries or to submit to a blood or urine test. In the Court's opinion however, the present case does not involve material of this nature which like that in Saunders has an existence independent of the person concerned and is not therefore obtained by means of coercion or in defiance of the will of that person'.

3.   COMPARISON OF THE SCOPE OF *ORKEM, FUNKE, SAUNDERS* AND *J.B. V. SWITZERLAND*

At the present time there are contradictory views as to the scope of the privilege against self-incrimination as developed by the ECtHR. Accordingly, its scope would not seem to be entirely clear. Ward, Gardner[36] and Willis[37] assert that *J.B. v. Switzerland* has reaffirmed *Funke*. Therefore, the scope of the privilege is wide and applies not only to interrogatories, but also to both disclosure and to production of documents which already exist. Ward and Gardner observe:

> Having considered the effect of *J.B. v. Switzerland*, namely, that it effectively reaffirms *Funke* to the detriment of *Saunders*: does the privilege against self-incrimination apply to documents which have existence independent of the will of the accused and which are sought through the use of compulsory powers? *Saunders* suggests not. But *Funke* and *J.B.* support the contrary view.[38]

However, it is to be noted that Ward and Gardner recognize that the ECtHR appears to have been influenced by the facts of the case: namely, that the Swiss authorities were seeking not only the production of the incriminating documents but also that Mr J.B. produce through interrogatories, statements which could be incriminatory. From the text of the judgment in English, it would seem that the ECtHR may have conflated the two requests, namely, the production of documents and the interrogatories into one request: specifically as noted previously in the judgment at paragraph:

> When the applicant failed to do so (produce documents) he was requested on three further occasions to declare the source of the income invested. The applicant not having reacted to those requests, a disciplinary fine of CHF 1000 was imposed.

---

36. T. Ward & P. Gardner, 'The Privilege Against Self-Incrimination: In Search of Legal Certainty' (2003) EHRLR (4) 388, <www.monckton.com>.
37. P. Willis, 'The Privilege Against Self-Incrimination in Competition Investigations' University of Oxford Centre for Competition Law & Policy, 27 January 2006, <www.denning.law.ox. ac.uk>.
38. T. Ward & P. Gardner, 'The Privilege Against Self-Incrimination: In Search of Legal Certainty' (2003) EHRLR (4) 388 op. cit. at 395.

In any event, the ECtHR held that the documents which the Swiss authorities sought were different from those referred to in *Saunders* which were not protected by the privilege against self-incrimination. Accordingly, on the facts of *J.B. v. Switzerland*, it is not clear how the ECtHR made the distinction between the documents in that case and in Saunders. By distinguishing *J.B. v. Switzerland* from *Saunders*, the ECtHR upheld implicitly that the privilege against self-incrimination does not apply to documents which exist independently of the will of the accused. Arguably, the finding of the House of Lords in *Green*[39] concerning the scope of the privilege against self-incrimination as concerns following the line of cases constituted by *J.B. v. Switzerland* and *Funke* may no longer be accurate: specifically that the privilege against self-incrimination pursuant to Art. 6(1) does not apply to prevent the production of previously existing documents which may be incriminatory.

Similarly Willis observes:

> Paragraph 28: 'However, neither of these rationales really explain the conflicting treatment of documentary requests in *Funke & Saunders* or address *Orkem* where the ECJ placed no limitation on the request for documents or Saunders where the production of documents was not in issue. It is submitted that the basis supported by case law is that the rationale set out in Saunders . . . namely that what is offensive is the use of the material that the accused is compelled to produce for the purpose which does not already exist. The extent of the right of privilege against self-incrimination following *Orkem, Funke Saunders* and *J.B.* is therefore not entirely clear. What is clear is that as a matter of Convention law *Orkem* is no longer good law under *Funke* or *Saunders*'.

Accordingly, it is useful to consider *SGL Carbon* in order to ascertain the relationship between *Funke, Saunders, J.B. v. Switzerland* and *Orkem* notably in the context of the doctrine of effectiveness.

4.   THE PRIVILEGE AGAINST SELF-INCRIMINATION AND ECJ CASE LAW

a.   *Orkem*

The EC privilege against self-incrimination was established in the case of *Orkem*.[40] In that case, *Orkem* challenged a Commission decision requesting information under EC Reg. 17/62. It submitted that the Commission had infringed the general principle that no one may be compelled to give evidence against himself.

---

39. R *v. Hertfordshire CC ex p Green Environmental Industries Ltd* (2002) 2 AC 412 per Lord Hoffmann at 423 'Art. 6 (1) is firmly anchored to the fairness of the tiral and is not concerned with extra judicial enquiries. Such impacts as Art. 6 (1) may have is upon the use of such evidence at a criminal trial'.
40. *Orkem v. Commission*, Case C-374/87 [1989] ECR 3283.

According to *Orkem*, that principle formed part of the Community legal order as a principle expressed in ECHR Art. 6.1. The ECJ noted that EC Reg. 17/62[41] does not contain a right to silence. Although holding that ECHR Art. 6.1 could be relied upon by an undertaking subject to an investigation related to competition law it did not consider that the wording of Art. 6 or the case law of the ECtHR established a right not to give evidence against oneself. In the absence therefore of any guarantee in the ECtHR case, the ECJ considered whether Community law imposes limitations on the Commission powers of investigations. The ECJ concluded:

> While the Commission is entitled . . . to compel an undertaking to provide all necessary information concerning such facts as may be known to it and to disclose it if necessary, such documents relating thereto as are in its possession even if the latter may be used to establish against it or another undertaking the existence of anti-competitive conduct, it may not by means of a decision call for information undermine the rights of the defence of the undertaking concerned.
>
> Thus the Commission may not compel an undertaking to provide it with answers which might involve an admission on its part of the existence of an infringement which it is incumbent upon the Commission to prove.[42]

The scope of the privilege against self-incrimination as established by the ECJ in *Orkem* is narrow in that it extends only to a testamentary obligation. The *Orkem* privilege prevents a witness from being obliged to reply to questions which involve admissions of infringement of EC Articles 81 or 82 but not to facts. It arguably does not extend to disclosure or inspection of documents.[43] In *Orkem* the ECJ held that the scope of the privilege is as follows:

> Point 34: 'Accordingly, whilst the Commission is entitled in order to preserve the useful effect of Art. 11(2) and (5) of Reg. 17, to compel an undertaking to provide all necessary information concerning such facts concerning such as facts as may be know to it and to disclose if necessary such documents relating thereto as are in its possession eve if the latter may be used to establish against it or another undertaking, the existence of anti competitive conduct, it may be by means of a decision calling for information, undermine the rights of defence of the undertaking concerned'.

---

41. Nor does EC Reg. 1/2003.
42. *Orkem v. Comission*, Case C-374/87 [1989] ECR 3283 op. cit. at para. 34.
43. P. Willis, 'The Privilege Against Self-Incrimination in Competition Investigation', University of Oxford Centre for Competition Law & Policy, 27 1 06, <www.denning.law.ox.ac.uk>, op. cit. at point 62: states concerning the EC privilege against self-incrimination: 'It may allow a person or an undertaking under investigation not to hand over documents where to do so would involve testimonial self-incrimination (*Saunders v. UK, US v. Doe*)'. Arguably, *Orkem v. Commission*, Case C-374/87 (1989) ECR 3283 op. cit, at para. 34 sustained by the interpretation of *A-G Geelhoed* in Case C-301/04P, *Commission v. SGL Carbon Co. Ltd.* at para. 47 specifically excludes the disclosure of incriminating documents from the scope of the privilege.

>Point 35: 'Thus the Commission may not compel an undertaking to provide it with answers which might involve an admission on its part of the existence of an infringement which it is incumbent upon the Commission to prove'.

In *Mannesmann*[44] the Court of First Instance (CFI) invokes the EC treaty obligation of enforcement of competition law as a justification for limiting the scope of the privilege against self-incrimination:

>Paragraph 66: 'To acknowledge the existence of an absolute right to silence, as claimed by the applicants would go beyond what is necessary in order to preserve the rights of the defence of undertakings and would constitute an unjustified hindrance to the Commission's performance of its duty under Art. 89 EC (now Art. 85) to ensure that the rules of competition within the Common Market are observed'.

In *SGL Carbon AG*,[45] Advocate General Geelhoed interpreted the scope of the *Orkem* privilege as follows:

>Paragraph 47 (Opinion): 'In that regard the Court of Justice drew a distinction between providing answers to questions on the one hand and producing documents on the other. As to the former, the Court of Justice drew a further distinction. It held that the Commission has the power to compel an undertaking to answer questions of a factual nature but that it odes not have the power to compel an undertaking to provide it with answers which might involve an admission on its part of the existence of an infringement. It is the latter aspect against which an undertaking can invoke its right to remain silent as part of its rights of defence. As regards documents, the Court of Justice did not limit the Commission's investigatory power. The undertaking involved must disclose documents that already exist and relate to the subject matter of the investigation even if these documents may be used to establish the existence of an infringement if requested to do so'.

The Advocate General then goes on to explain in *SGL Carbon* why, in his opinion, the narrow scope of the EC privilege against self-incrimination should not be expanded beyond that established by the ECJ in *Orkem* despite the various judgments of the ECtHR such as *J.B. v. Switzerland*. He concludes there is no need to depart from *Orkem* in light of more recent EChHR case law which is in fact concerned with criminal procedure against individuals: for the following reasons: first, it is not inherently possible to simply transpose this privilege which provides protection for individuals in criminal proceedings to procedures involving undertakings in primarily civil proceedings; second, although the ECtHR seeks to extend the privilege to companies in so doing it recognizes the possibility of greater restrictions thereof than is the case with individual persons; third, significantly,

---

44. *Mannesmannröhren Werke v. The Commission*, Case T-112/98 (2001) ECHR II 729.
45. *Commission v. SGL Carbon Co. Ltd.*, Case C-301/04 P, <www.curia.eu> op. cit.

under *Saunders*, a request to produce already existing documents does not contravene the right to silence: in this regard the defence may exercise its rights of defence by contradicting the meaning ascribed to the documents by the Commission: and finally, the relationship between fundamental rights and competition enforcement constitutes a balancing exercise which prevent therefore, the complete transposition of the ECtHR case law into the field of EC competition law enforcement.

b.   **SGL Carbon (SGL)[46] and the Privilege against Self-Incrimination**

In the *Commission v. SGL Carbon*, the ECJ, following the Opinion of Advocate General Geelhoed, reaffirmed that the scope of the *Orkem* privilege against self incrimination was compatible with that of the ECtHR in *Funke, Saunders and J.B. v. Switzerland*. More particularly, the basis of *SGL Carbon* was an appeal from the Court of First Instance (CFI) judgment in Graphite Electrodes wherein SGL had appealed against a decision of the Commission. The Commission had imposed a fine of EUR 80.2 million on SGL for its part in the graphite electrodes cartel. One of the arguments of SGL was that the Commission had given it insufficient credit for having volunteered information beyond what was required in terms of the privilege against self-incrimination. SGL had volunteered the information in order to benefit from the Commission's leniency programme. The Commission had argued that SGL had provided information to it in a response to a request for information pursuant to EC Reg. 17/62 and that further, the information was not provided voluntarily because it was not protected by the privilege against self-incrimination. Therefore, SGL ought not to be entitled to a reduction of its fine. The CFI noted that the ECJ had not changed its privilege against self-incrimination in light of *Funke, Saunders* and *J.B. v. Switzerland*. It confirmed the requirement on the part of SGL to answer purely factual questions and to produce documents already in existence. However, the CFI added that the group of documents which related to the directly incriminating interrogatories were covered by the privilege. Therefore SGL was not entitled to a reduction of its fine because it had not been obliged to disclose these documents.

In *SGL Carbon*, the ECJ found that the CFI had committed an error in law by seeking to extend the privilege against self-incrimination established in *Orkem* so as to include the documents which related to the directly incriminating interrogatories. Moreover, the ECJ reaffirmed that *Orkem* does not protect documents and that the scope of the privilege in this regard corresponds to that in *Funke, Saunders* and *J.B. v. Switzerland*. In holding that the CFI had made an error in law in restricting the applicability of *Orkem* so as to protect certain documents the ECJ concluded by reaffirming previous case law to the effect that the scope of the

46.   *Commission v. SGL Carbon Co. Ltd*, Case C-301/04, <www.curia.eu>.

privilege of *Orkem* was effectively compatible with that of *Funke, Saunders* and *J.B. v. Switzerland*. The ECJ held as follows:

> Paragraph 43: 'It must be added that the Court of Justice in paragraphs 274–76 of the judgment in *Limburgse v. Commission* observed that since the judgment of *Orkem v. Commission* there have been further developments in the case law of the European Court of Human Rights which the Community judicature must take into account when interpreting the fundamental rights. The Court of Justice stated however in that regard that those developments were not such as to put in question these statements of principle in *Orkem v. Commission*'.

It is to be recalled that in *Limburgse Vinyl*[47] to which it refers in its judgment the ECJ specifically referred to the cases of *Funke, Saunders* and *J.B. v. Switzerland*.

> Paragraph 274: 'The parties agree that since *Orkem* there have been further developments in the case law of the European Court of Human Rights which the Community Judicature must take into account when interpreting the fundamental rights as introduced by the judgment in *Funke* cited above on which the appellants rely and the judgments of 17 December 1996 in Saunders and of 3 May 2001 in *J.B. v. Switzerland*'.
>
> Paragraph 275: 'However both the *Orkem* judgment and the recent case law of the European Court of Human Rights requires the exercise of coercion against the suspect in order to obtain information from him and second, establishment of the existence of an actual interference with the right which they define'.
>
> Paragraph 276: 'Examined in the light of that finding and the specific circumstances of the present case the ground of appeal alleging infringement of the privilege against self-incrimination does not permit annulment of the contested judgment on the basis of the developments in the case law of the European Court of Human Rights'.

The ECJ then concluded its judgment in *SGL Carbon* by reaffirming *Orkem*:

> Paragraph 45: 'It is important to point out also that the Court of First Instance itself in paragraph 405 of the judgment under appeal expressly referred to the principles stated in *Orkem v. Commission* and to the fact that the Court of Justice has not reversed its case law on this point'.

Arguably, by reaffirming *Limburgse Vinyl* which established that *J.B. Switzerland* did not introduce any change into the line of cases established by *Funke* and *Saunders*, the ECJ judgment in *SGL Carbon* produces the following consequences: first, that at least for the ECJ, *J.B. v. Switzerland* does not contradict Saunders which established that privilege against self-incrimination does not prevent the disclosure and inspection of previously existing documents; second, it would seem to follow, once again, at least for the ECJ, that there is no conflict in the scope of the

---

47. *Limburgse Vinyl Maatschappij & Others v. Commission* Case C-238/99P etc (2002) ECR I 8735.

privilege under *J.B. v. Switzerland* and *Saunders* on the one hand and *Orkem* on the other. The ECJ specifically followed its established case law as presented by Advocate General Geelhoed at paragraph 65 of his Opinion: he states specifically states that *J.B. v. Switzerland* does not alter the *Saunders* line of cases focussing on the part of the decision in which the ECtHR distinguished the facts in *J.B. v. Switzerland* and the ratio of *Saunders*.

> Paragraph 65: 'Third, what is decisive, however, so far as Art. 6 of the Convention is concerned is that a request for documents is not contrary to the right to remain silent. The European Court of Human Rights did not recognize an absolute right to remain silent. It held in *Sanders* that "the right not to incriminate oneself is primarily concerned with respecting the will of the accused person to remain silent". As commonly understood in the legal system of the contracting parties, the Convention and elsewhere, it does not extend to the use in criminal proceedings of material which may be obtained from the accused through the use of compulsory powers but which has an existence independent of the will of the suspect such as inter alia, documents acquired pursuant to a warrant, breath, blood and urine samples and bodily tissues for the purpose of DNA testing'.

That finding has been recently confirmed in *J.B. v. Switzerland*.

The result of this process is therefore, that according to the ECJ and its most recent judgment in *SGL Carbon* coupled with the opinion of its Advocate General, a request for existing documents neither violates the *Orkem* privilege nor the privilege as established by the European Court of Human Rights.[48] There remains,

---

48. Although not dealt with specifically in *SGL Carbon*, the ECJ implicitly reaffirms its position in *Mannesmannröhren-Werke* Case T/112/98 (2001) ECR II 729, op. cit. at paragraph 75 ('suffice it to repeat that the applicant cannot directly invoke the Convention before the courts') concerning the relationship between ECtHR case law and the ECHR Art. 6.1 on the one hand and on the other, the ECJ privilege against self-incrimination as embodied in *Orkem*. The solution is simply that Art. 6.1 ECHR and in particular the ECtHR case law cannot be relied upon directly by a litigant before a Community Court. Arguably, the ECJ will choose the *Orkem* privilege against self-incrimination in the event of a conflict, which is not the case according to *SGL Carbon*, between the scope of its privilege against self-incrimination and that of the ECtHR based upon ECHR Art. 6.1. It is submitted that the ECJ in the instant case dealt indirectly with what may be a difference in the scope of the privilege against self-incrimination between the ECJ and the ECtHR by stating that in fact there was no such conflict. Therefore, it was not necessary for the ECJ to follow a possible second line of argument which it developed notably in *Mannesmannröhren-Werke*: namely that an applicant may not rely directly on the ECHR convention: the ECJ could have pursued the second line of argument which appears to resolve potential conflict between the scope of the privilege on the basis that the interpretations of the Convention made by the ECtHR are effectively not binding upon the ECJ.

    Paragraph 39: 'The applicant claims that on the basis of Art. 6(1) of the Convention it may lawfully refrain from any positive action that would compel it to give evidence directly against itself in an investigation procedure quite independently of whether or not in light of the principle recognised in *Orkem* such action would lead it to supply incriminating evidence or to admit unlawful objectives'.

however, perhaps one difficulty: the ECJ did not state, explicitly, in *SGL Carbon* that the scope of the two privileges against self-incrimination, that of *Orkem* and that of the ECtHR, is identical. The implication is, nevertheless, that the scope of the two privileges is indeed the same at least with respect to ECJ judgments. Accordingly, it is submitted that in order to ensure the effective enforcement of EC Articles 81 and 82 the doctrines of supremacy and effectiveness will require the following; first that the interpretation of the relationship which the ECJ has presented in *SGL Carbon* in terms of the scope of *Orkem*, on the one hand and on the other, that of *J.B. Switzerland*, be followed by the ordinary court and the CAT in enforcing EC Articles 81 and 82; secondly, that the *Orkem* privilege of self-incrimination be applied to ensure the following: specifically, that the privilege against self-incrimination be restricted to preventing replies to directly incriminating interrogatories such that it would not apply to either the disclosure or the production of incriminating documents which exist.

5.   The ECtHR Control of the ECJ Privilege against Self-Incrimination in Enforcement of EC Articles 81 and 82 by Member States

Before concluding this matter, it is necessary to consider more fully the method by which the scope of the privilege against self-incrimination is to be determined for the enforcement of EC Articles 81 and 82 by the ordinary courts and by the CAT: in short, whether the doctrine of effectiveness is the exclusive determinant in the choice of the scope of the privilege against

---

The reaction of the CFI was that an applicant could not directly enforce the Convention and implicitly the ECtHR case law before it.

Paragraph 59: 'It must be emphasized at the outset that the Court of First Instance has no jurisdiction to apply the Covenant when reviewing an investigation under competition law in much as the Convention is not part of Community law'.

Paragraph 60: 'However it is settled case law that fundamental rights form an integral part of the general principles of Community law where observance is ensured by the Community judicature. For that purpose the Court of Justice and the European Court of Human Rights draw inspiration from the constitutional tradition common to the Member State and from guidelines supplied by International Treaties for the protection of Human Rights on which the Member States have collaborated and to which they are signatories. The Convention has special significance in that respect. Furthermore, paragraph 2 of Article F of the Treaty of the European Union provides that the Union shall protect fundamental rights as guaranteed by the Convention and as they result from the constitutional traditions common to the Member States as general principles of common law'.

Paragraph 61: 'As for the arguments that Art. 6 (1) and (2) of the Convention enables a person in receipt of a request for information to refrain from answering the questions asked even if purely factual and to refuse to produce documents to the Commission it is sufficient to note that the applicant may not rely direct on the Convention before the Community Courts'.

self-incrimination in such proceedings. *Willis*[49] implicitly accepts that the doctrine of effectiveness applies so as to determine that the *Orkem* privilege be used by the national court EC Articles 81 and 82 proceedings both under EC Reg. 1/2003[50] and also in free standing enforcement proceedings. Notwithstanding, Willis poses the question[51] as to whether a national court might decide to apply the ECtHR case law concerning the privilege against self-incrimination as opposed to the ECJ *Orkem* privilege. Further, both Willis[52] and Riley[53] advance an alternative view: specifically, that national court implementation of Art. 20(6)–(8) EC Reg. 1/2003, and implicitly, enforcement of EC Articles 81 and 82 by free standing damages actions in terms of the scope of the privilege against self incrimination may be subject to not simply the doctrine of effectiveness. Rather, this enforcement process may also be susceptible to control by the ECtHR through the doctrine of equivalent protection as developed in the ECtHR case of *Matthews*.[54] Arguably, however, ECtHR intervention under *Matthews* is restricted to those situations where the ECJ is unable to effect control of primary legislation[55] by want of express jurisdiction. Notwithstanding, if, which is not clear, the doctrine of equivalent protection were to apply as suggested by Willis and Riley, it would be necessary to consider the scope of the ECtHR case of *Bosphorus*.[56] It is submitted that *Bosphorus* establishes a presumption that protection of ECHR rights by the ECJ is equivalent although not identical to that of the ECtHR. Disproof of this presumption to the level of manifest deficiency will permit the ECtHR to review acts which the Member States have adopted in order to implement EU law on the basis of a contravention of ECHR rights in a

---

49. P. Willis, 'The Privilege Against Self-Incrimination in Competition Investigations', University of Oxford Centre for Competition Law and Policy (27.01.06), <www.denning.law.ox.ac.uk> op. cit. at paragraph 62.
50. Assistance given by the national court to the Commission pursuant to EC Reg. 1/2002 S 20.
51. P. Willis, 'The Privilege Against Self Incrimination in Competition Investigations', University of Oxford Centre for Competition Law and Policy (27.01.06), <www.denning.law.ox.ac.uk> *ibid.* at paragraph 41.
52. P. Willis, 'The Privilege Against Self Incrimination in Competition Investigations', University of Oxford Centre for Competition Law and Policy (27.01.06), <www.denning.law.ox.ac.uk> *ibid.* at paragraph 63.
53. A. Riley, 'ECHR Implications of the Investigation Provisions of the Draft Competition Regulation Draft Competition Regulation' (2002) 51 ICQL 55 at pp 77–78, <www.iclq.oxford-journals.org/cgi/repri/51/1/55>.
54. Mathews v. the UK, ECtHR A 24833/94 (18.12.99), <www.echr.coe.eu>.
55. K. Lenaerts in 'Fundamental Rights in the European Union' (2000) 25 ELRev 575 at 578 'The judgment looks classical at first sign in that it confirms implicitly the equivalent protection test excluding direct European Union Member State liability under the Convention in relation to the "normal community cast" subject to judicial review inside the Community order. But at the same time, the judgment indicates that in the absence of such a possibility of judicial review, the Member States may be held responsible under the Convention for any infringement of the provisions of the latter resulting from 'international instruments which they freely entered into'.
56. *Bosphorus Hava Yollari Turizm v. Ireland*, (2006) 42 EHRR 1, A 45036/98 (30.6.2005), <www.echr.coe.eu>.

particular circumstance: that is, provided that the Member States do not have any discretion in the implementation thereof.[57] Accordingly, in order for the doctrine of equivalent protection to apply so as to permit the ECtHR to review the scope of the privilege against self-incrimination used by the national court in the aforementioned situations it would be necessary to consider the following: namely, whether the EC doctrine of supremacy and effectiveness constitutes part of a Member State's EU strict legal obligations in a specific sense: specifically, that these doctrines eliminate the discretion of the national court to apply anything other than ECJ case law concerning the privilege against self incrimination in the enforcement of EC Articles 81 and 82 by damages actions and notably EC Reg. 1/2003.[58] Arguably, the national court does not enjoy discretion to choose anything other than the ECJ *Orkem* privilege for the following reason: namely, the combined effect of EC Art. 10, EC 226, and the doctrines of supremacy and effectiveness coupled with the cases of *SGL Carbon* and *Mannesmannröhren-Werke*. It is by means of these legal obligations that the EU is able to ensure in the absence of[59] a harmonized code of civil procedure, the effective decentralized enforcement of EC Articles 81 and 82 by national courts using their specific codes of civil procedure. Accordingly, if in those circumstances the *Bosphorus* doctrine of equivalent protection were to apply, the next question would be the following: specifically, whether an applicant may displace the presumption of ECJ equivalent but not identical protection of ECHR rights concerning self-incrimination in cases involving the enforcement of EC Articles 81 and 82 by the national court. It is submitted that such a displacement of the presumption is unlikely. In reality the ECJ protection afforded would appear to be equivalent in the following circumstances to that offered by the ECtHR and the ECHR: where the national court pursuant to EC Art. 10 and the EC doctrines of effectiveness and supremacy had proceeded in the following manner: that is, the court had applied the ECJ *Orkem* privilege against self-incrimination following, notably, *SGL Carbon* and *Mannesmannröhren* while possibly making an EC 234 reference on that point.

---

57. See *Borphorus* paragraphs 156 and 157; C. Costello in 'Bosphorus Ruling of the European Court of Human Rights: Fundamental and Blurred Boundaries in Europe' (2006) HRLRev 6(1) 87–130, S. Douglas-Scott, *'Bosphorus v. Ireland*: Case Note:' (2006) 43 CMLR 243–54, S. Douglas-Scott, 'A Tale of Two Courts: *Luxembourg, Strasbourg* and the Growing European Human Rights Acquis' (2006) 43 CMLR 629–665.
58. Wouter Wills, 'Powers of Investigation and Procedural Rights and Guarantees in EU Anti-Trust Enforcement', First Lisbon Conference on Competition Law and Economics, 3–4 November 2005, <www.autoridadaconcorrencia.pt> at paragraph 23 as to the intervention by the Commission pursuant to EC Art. 226 to ensure that the national court implement EC Art. 1/2003 effectively notably in terms of the privilege against self-incrimination.
59. See *generally*: A.G.F. Jacobs 'ECHR Case law in the Jurisprudence of the European Court of Justice' in The Future of the European Judicial System, Conference on European Constitutional Law Network, Berlin 2–4 November 2005; <www.ecln.net/elements//conferences/book_ berlin/jacobs.pdf>.

In contrast, were the EU doctrine of supremacy and effectiveness not to preclude the national courts from using their discretion both with respect to the implementation of Directive 1/2003 and the method of enforcement of EC Arts. 81 and 82 then arguably, the following might occur: pursuant to a case such as *Cantoni*[60] it might be possible to bring an action against the UK for failure to secure ECHR Art. 6.1 rights in terms of implementation of EU legislation. Douglas-Scott observes in this regard in *Bospohorus*:[61] 'Where the Member State has discretion as to how it carries out its EU obligations, it appears that the Court of Human Rights can treat the act as if it were an ordinary Member State act'.

It is submitted, however, that in such a case as that involving the method of enforcement of EC Articles 81 and 82 it is not clear that the ECtHR would find a violation of ECHR Art. 6.1 for two reasons; first, it would be necessary for the ECtHR to establish that a national court, in application of the doctrines of supremacy and effectiveness, had erred in law by applying the ECJ *Orkem* privilege rather than the ECtHR case law concerning the ECHR Art. 6.1 privilege; second, following Advocate-General Geelhoed in his Opinion in *SGL Carbon*,[62] it is not apparent on what ground the ECtHR would seek to extend the privilege which it developed to protect a human defendant in the context of classical criminal proceedings to companies involved in competition enforcement proceedings In this regard, the Advocate General observed as follows in his Opinion:

> Paragraph 63: 'First, it must be borne in mind that the case law concerned natural persons in the context of classical criminal proceedings. Competition law concerns undertakings. The Commission is only allowed to impose fines for violations of Art. 81 EC and 82 EC. It is not possible simply to transpose findings of the European Court of Human Rights without more to legal persons or undertakings. In that regard, I would refer to other jurisdictions in which the right not to incriminate oneself is reserved solely to a natural person and cannot involved the Fifth Amendment to the United States Constitution. The Fifth Amendment Clause states that "no person shall be compelled to be a witness against himself in any criminal case." This right or privilege against self-incrimination is a personal one. It applies to individual human beings only. A corporation cannot plead the Fifth Amendment in order to keep silent; in other words a corporation has to produce documents if requested to do so'.
>
> Paragraph 64: 'Second there is no dispute that the European Court of Human Rights extended certain rights and freedoms to companies and other corporate entities; the same is true of under Community law and under the Charter of Fundamental Rights of the European Union. That being said, the European Court of Human Rights also makes a distinction

60. *Cantoni v. France*, Application 17862/91, (15.11.1996)
61. S. Douglas-Scott, '*Bospohorus Hava Yollari Turizm Ve Ticaret Anonim Sirketi v. Ireland* application: No. 45036/98 ECtHR, Case Note, (2006) 43 CMLR 243–254 op. cit. at p. 249.
62. *Commission v. SGL Carbon*, Case C-301/04P, Opinion of Advocate General Geelhoed (delivered 19.1.2006), <www.curia.europa.eu>.

between the level of protection conferred on natural persons on the one hand and legal persons on the other'.

Paragraph 67: 'Lastly, it must be said that the interplay between the fundamental rights of legal persons and competition enforcement remains a balancing exercise; at stake are the protection of fundamental rights versus effective enforcement of Community Competition law. As the Court of Justice held in ECO Swiss, Art. 81 is a fundamental provision which is essential for the accomplishment of the takes entrusted to the Community and in particular for the functioning of the internal market. Art. 81 EC forms part of the public policy of the Community is no longer empowered to request the production of documents its enforcement of competition law in the Community legal order will become heavily dependent on either the voluntary co-operation or on the use of other means of coercion as for example dawn raids. It is self evident that he effective enforcement with reasonable means of the basic tenants of the Community public legal order should remain possible just as it is evident that the rights of the defence should be respected too. In my view, the latter is the case. As case law now stands, a defendant is still able either during the administrative procedure or in the proceedings before the Community courts to contend that the documents produced have a different meaning from that ascribed to them by the Commission'.

Finally, Douglas-Scott[63] observes that any difference in scope which may exist between the ECJ privilege and that of the ECtHR may well both acceptable and justified Indeed, the ECtHR may well defer to such a difference where it arises from the application by the ECJ of its doctrine of supremacy of EU law. Douglas-Scott makes the following two points in this regard:

> Yet the Court of Human Rights does now seem to be more aware of the ECJ and more willing to refer to it. In the absence of accession to the EU to the ECHR, EU law would appear to have the same status as any body of law which is not that of a contracting party.... The Court of Human Rights has also seemed to take a fairly deferential approach to the EC generally, shoring up the principles of supremacy and uniformity of EC law.[64]
>
> So, for example, in the 2006 case of *SGL Carbon*, Advocate General Geelhoed suggested that "it is not possible simply to transpose the findings of the European Court of Human Rights without more to undertaking" also noting that case law from other jurisdictions such as that under the US Fifth Amendment right against self incrimination, could not be invoked by companies. From time to time fear has been expressed about the dangers of conflicting rulings from *Strasbourg* and *Luxembourg*. However, the different context of these two courts with *Strasbourg* acting as freestanding human

---

63. S. Douglas-Scott, 'A Tale of Two Courts: *Luxembourg, Strasbourg* and the Growing European Human Rights Acquis' (2006) 43 CMLR 629–665, op. cit. at p. 642.
64. S. Douglas-Scott, 'A Tale of Two Courts: *Luxembourg, Strasbourg* and the Growing European Human Rights Acquis' (2006) 43 CMLR 629, *ibid.* at pp. 642 and 644 respectively.

rights court and *Luxembourg* possessing a much wider jurisdiction comprising a very large number of (sometimes competing) policies should not be over looked as a factor constraining and sometimes shaping human rights interpretations.[65]

Accordingly, if, as has been argued, the doctrine of effectiveness can be applied as the exclusively determinative principle for the enforcement of EC competition by the English courts and the CAT it will require the use of the *Orkem* privilege against self-incrimination. However, as was also previously noted, the application of the doctrine of effectiveness is subject to the principles of the national procedure. In short, it is submitted that the application of the doctrine of effective enforcement with respect to the choice of the *Orkem* privilege would be justified in relation to the national principles for the following reasons: first, the HRA (1998) does not render the judgments of the ECtHR binding on the English courts in the sense that S 47A and S 57A of the CA (1998) bind the CAT and the High Court respectively with respect to OFT infringement decisions on EC Articles 81 or 82. The courts need only 'take account' pursuant to SS 3(2) and 2(1) HRA of the ECtHR decisions. Notwithstanding, the effect of ss 3(2) 'take account' has been described by Lord Slynn[66] as follows:

> Although the [HRA] 1998 Act does not provide that a national court is bound by these decisions it is obliged to take account of them so far they are relevant. In the absence of some special circumstances it seems to me that the court should follow a clear and constant jurisprudence of the European Court of Human Rights. If it does not do so there is at least a possibility that the case will go to that court which is likely in the ordinary case to follow its own constant jurisprudence.

Following his lordship's opinion, the doctrine of effectiveness would, arguably, provide a good reason for not following the judgments of the ECtHR with respect to the enforcement of EC Articles 81 or 82. The second reason is simply the absence of any preponderant justification for the use of the wide privilege in the enforcement of EC Articles 81 and 82 in English proceedings: specifically, the wide ECtHR privilege may well have the effect of preventing disclosure of documents and thereby rendering impossible or exceedingly difficult the enforcement of EC Articles 81 or 82.[67] The third reason[68] is that there would be appear to be no real basis for in the historical development of the principle[69] for justifying the

---

65. S. Douglas-Scott, 'A Tale of Two Courts: *Luxembourg, Strasbourg* and the Growing European Human Rights Acquis' (2006) 43 CMLR *ibid.* at 649.
66. *R v. Secretary of State for the Environment*, Transport and the Regions (2001) UKHL 23 at 26.
67. *Bernard Crehan v. Inntreprenuer Pub Co CPC* (2004) EWCA 637, op. cit. in which the Court of Appeal referred to the Mr Crehan's difficult in obtain evidence which seems to have been related to the use of the privilege in disclosure.
68. A.A.S. Zuckerman, *Civil Procedure* (2003, Lexis Nexis, London) op. cit; see *generally* pp. Ch. 14 and 17
69. A. Mac Culloch, 'The Privilege Against Self-Incrimination in Competition Investigations' (2006) 25 *Legal Studies* 2. 'The most convincing justification for the existence of the privilege

use of the wide privilege notably in the enforcement of EC Articles 81 and 82 in civil actions. In this regard, it may be said that the duty to produce documents has traditionally be considered to constitute a testimonial obligation; that is, in order to obtain the production of documents form non-parties normally a *subpoena duces tecum* was utilized. This necessitated the swearing in of the bearer of the documents prior to the production thereof.[70] Disclosure pursuant to CPR 31.2 provides that a 'party discloses a document by stating that the document exists or has existed'. Further, CPR 31.23 provides that a person who knowingly makes a false disclosure statement may be liable in contempt.

Accordingly, the logic is as follows: disclosure and production appear to be considered as constituting testimonial obligations. Therefore, the privilege against self-incrimination constitutes an immunity against testifying. Following this analysis, the privilege against self-incrimination may attach to the disclosure and production of documents. However, in reality, the extension of the privilege to disclosure of documents is not justifiable for the following reasons: first, disclosure and production testimonials constitute only what might be termed technical as opposed to substantive testimonial obligations. The probative value of the documents turns not on what the producer of the documents states but on the contents of the documents themselves. Indeed, if the documents can be procured without the assistance of the 'producer', they may be admitted for their full value at trial; second, arguably, the privilege has no serious justification with respect to disclosure in civil proceedings: in *AT&T Istel*, Lord Templeman stated that the justification for the privilege against self-incrimination was that 'it discourages ill-treatment of a suspect and second that it discourage the production of dubious confessions'.[71] His lordship added that these considerations have no value in civil proceedings. Similarly, Lord Griffiths observed in the same case: 'I can for myself see no argument in favour of the privilege against producing a document the contents of which may go to show that the holder has committed a criminal offence. The contents of the document will speak for itself and there is no risk of the false confession which underlies the privilege against having to answer questions that may incriminate the speaker'.[72] The third reason that the extension of the privilege to the disclosure of documents in civil proceedings is not justified is that it leads to an irrevocably contradictory situation: a criminal search warrant can produce

---

is to protect the privacy of the person. Where there are arguments that legal persons should not benefit from the privilege in the same way as natural persons as they do not have the same 'central zone of privacy' there are other arguments to suggest that the privilege is a functional necessity within any investigatory system. Even if that is accepted, the privilege should not attach to any pre-existing document or recorded information: in the same manner it does not attach to the evidence outside the mind of the accused. The limited privilege that is justified is restricted to testimonial information created by compulsion. Therefore there is no distinction in this regard between spoken and written testimony'.

70. See CPR 34.2 (1) (b).
71. *AT&T Istel Ltd v. Tully* (1993) AC 45 at point 53.
72. *AT&T Istel Ltd v. Tully* (1993) AC 45 *ibid.* at point 57.

incriminating documents unlike a civil warrant. All of these documents may be used for their full probative value in a criminal trial.[73] The fourth reason is, arguably, that the natural tendency of English civil procedure is to limit the scope of the privilege against self-incrimination. This is indicated in the case of *AT & T Istel* which arguably corresponds to the operation of the privilege in *Orkem*[74] in addition to the judgments of Lords Templeman and Griffiths: the privilege against self-incrimination is available in order to prevent unreliable testimony in criminal trials.[75] Accordingly, there is no purpose in seeking to transpose its use to civil trials and notably to extend its use to disclosure and production of documents. In summary, no principle, historic or contemporary, appears to exist which can justify the use of the wide ECtHR privilege against self-incrimination in enforcement proceedings of EC Articles 81 and 82 by the ordinary English courts. Therefore, the doctrine of effectiveness would require that the narrow *Orkem* privilege be used in such enforcement proceedings in order to ensure minimally effective enforcement thereof.[76] Moreover, the *Orkem* privilege has the added advantage of providing also provides a measured policy reduction of the scope of the interpretation of ECHR Art. 6.1 in favour of the public benefit which arises from the unimpeded enforcement of EC Articles 81 and or 82.[77] The utilization of the *Orkem* privilege against self incrimination will arguably ensure effective enforcement also pursuant to Reg. 1/2003.

---

73. A.A.S. Zuckerman, *Civil Procedure* (2003 Lexis Nexis, London) op. cit. at p. 581 'The application of the privilege to civil search orders is even more difficult to justify because it verges on the absurd. Suppose that the defendant has been running a fraudulent business using fraudulent invoices and accounts. The documents would be immune from disclosure and from seizure under a civil search order because they may assist the defendant's convection for fraud. Yet, in criminal proceedings, a criminal search order can be obtained to seize evidence of fraudulent practise (PACE ss 8, 19): Against a criminal search order the defendant has no privilege against self-incrimination because the execution of a criminal search order authorises the police to enter, search and seize without the suspect's consent and therefore imposes no testimonial obligation on the suspect. It would appear therefore that while the defendant is immune from a civil search order lest incriminating documents would be found which could later be used in criminal proceedings, he has no immunity in criminal proceedings from the forcible seizure of the same documents which once in the hands of the police would be admissible in evidence at the defendant's criminal trial'.
74. *Orkem v. Commission* Case 374/87 (1989) ECR 3283 : specifically the Commission is prevented from using any incriminating evidence emanating from the civil proceedings before the national court just as the CPS undertook not to use any incriminating evidence emanating from the civil proceedings for fraud.
75. A. Mac Culloch, 'The Privilege Against Self-Incrimination in Competition Investigations' (2006) 26 *Legal Studies* 2, <www.blackwell-synergy.com> op. cit. feels that the operation of the statutory restriction of the privilege is facilitated by the exclusionary discretion enjoyed by the court pursuant to S 78 PACE (1984).
76. See *generally*: A. Mac Culloch 'The Privilege Against Self-Incrimination in Competition Investigations' (2006) 26 *Legal Studies* 2, <www.blackwell-synergy.com> *ibid.*
77. See dissenting judgment of Judge Martens in *Saunders v. The UK* (1996) 23 EHRR 313, op. cit. : in particular para. 2, 3 and 22.

6.   PRIVILEGE AGAINST SELF-INCRIMINATION: S 15(3) REG. 1/2003

It is submitted that the application of the *Orkem* privilege against self-incrimination has the advantage of ensuring the effective implementation of S 15(3) Reg. 1/2003. The purpose of this section which coupled with *Otto v. Post Bank*[78] is to prevent the Commission from using potentially incriminating information obtained in national proceedings in its own proceedings. The second paragraph of S 15(3) Reg. 1/2003 which provides as follows:

> For the purpose of the preparation of their observations only, the competition authorities of the Member State and the Commission may request the relevant court of the Member State to transmit or to ensure the transmission to them of any documents necessary for the assessment of the case.

The Commission Notice states with respect to the above sub-paragraph: In order to enable the Commission to submit useful observation, the national court may be asked to transmit or ensure the transmission to the Commission of a copy of all documents that are necessary for that case. In line with Art. 15(3) second sub-paragraph of the regulation, the Commission will only use those document for the preparation of its observations.

It is submitted that S 15(3) of Reg. 1/2003, which apparently prevents the Commission using any information which it might receive following a request to the national court for purposes other than the preparation of its observation would prevent the raising of the English privilege against self-incrimination. In this regard, the prohibition on the Commission from using the information other than the formulation of its observations appears, perhaps, more clearly in the French and the German text of S 15(3) and in point 33 than in the English translation of the Regulation which has just be cited:

> 15.3 Afin de leur permettre leurs observations, et à cette fin uniquement, les autorités ... et la Commission ...
>
> 33. Conformément à l'article 15, paragraphe 3, second aliéna du règlement, la Commission n'utilisera ces documents que pour préparer ses observations.
>
> 15.3 Zum ausschliesslichen Zweck des Ausarbeitung ihrer Stellungnahme ...
>
> 33. Gemäss Artikel 15, Absatz 3, zweiter Unterabsatz der Verordnung, verwendet die Kommission dies Schriftstück ausschliesslich zum Zwecke des Ausarbeitung ihrer Stellungnahme.
>
> (5) Restrictions on the availability of the privilege against self incrimination in English proceedings brought to assist the Commission pursuant to S 20(6)–(8) Reg. 1/2003.

Finally, if the scope of the privilege against self incrimination used for the enforcement of EC Articles 81 and or 82 by the English courts is indeed already that which

---

78. *Otto BV v. Postbank NV*, Case C-60/92 [1993] ECR I-5863.

is required by the doctrine of effectiveness, namely, that of *Orkem*, then it is submitted that the following occurs: the English court will be able to enforce the Commission requests which involve the privilege against self-incrimination. Indeed, it is submitted that the doctrine of effectiveness will require, as will be demonstrated, that the national Court in providing assistance to the Commission pursuant to S 20 Reg. 1/2003, an EC regulation, use the *Orkem* privilege against self-incrimination. Pursuant to S 20(6)–(8) Reg. 1/2003 the national judicial authorities must assist the Commission where an investigation order by Commission decision is opposed by the addressee of the decision. Under S 20(7) Reg.1/2003. The assistance sought may include seeking an order from the relevant national court on an anticipatory basis. The intervention of the national court is governed by *Hoechst*[79] and followed in *Roquette Frères*.[80]

In *Hoechst*, the ECJ held:

> Paragraph 33: 'In that regard, the Member States are required to ensure that the Commission's action is effective ... It follows that within those limits the appropriate procedural rules designed to ensure respect for undertakings' rights are those laid down by national law'.
>
> Paragraph 34: 'Consequently, if the Commission intends with the assistance of the national authorities to carry out an investigation other than with the co-operation of the undertakings concerned it is required to respect the relevant procedural guarantees laid down by national law'.

Following *Hoechst* and *Roquette Frères* it would seem that beyond the control of the Community law principles of proportionality, legality and effectiveness, the national court is to apply the national rules in enforcing S 20(6)–(8) Reg. 1/2003 and notably in granting search warrants under CPR 25 and PD 25. This would involve provision for the privilege of self-incrimination.[81] That being said, it would appear that following *Hoechst* and *Roquette Frères* the doctrine of effectiveness would apply in order to ensure that that the Commission's search pursuant to this regulation were at least minimally effective in so far as enforcement of EC Articles 81 and 82 are involved. Further, this doctrine would arguably require the use of the *Orkem* privilege against self-incrimination unless the principles of the CPR or underlying Common Law principles such as the search for truth[82] justified the use of the wide ECtHR privilege. As noted earlier, no such justifications appear to exist in terms of the national principles.

In conclusion, it would seem, therefore, that in the enforcement of EC Reg. 1/2003, and notably inspections ordered by the Commission, the scope of the privilege against self-incrimination would be subject to the doctrine of

---

79. *Hoechst AG v. Commission*, Cases C-46/87 and C-227/88 [1989] ECR 2859.
80. *Roquettes Frères*, Case C-94/00 [2002] ECR –I 9011.
81. The Civil Procedure Act (1997) S. 7(7) places civil search orders on a statutory basis and expressly state that the section does not affect the right to refuse to do anything on grounds of self-incrimination.
82. A.A.S. Zuckerman, *Civil Procedure* (London, Lexis Nexis, 2003) op. cit. pp. 5–7.

effectiveness.[83] Further, this principle would result in the English court applying the *Orkem* privilege with respect to the implementation to Commission order searches following S 20(6)–(8) EC Reg. 1/2003 as well as requests for information by the Commission directed to the national court pursuant to Art. 15.2 Reg. 1/2003.[84]

---

83. P. Willis 'The Privilege Against Self-Incrimination in Competition Investigations' *University of Oxford Centre for Competition Law & Policy*, 27 January 2006, <www.denning.law.ox.ac.uk> op. cit. see in particular W. Wills op. cit. in footnote 44 *supra* in particular the possible use of EC Art. 226 by the Commission to ensure that searches carried out by the national court be effective. See *Hoechst AG v. Commission*, Cases C-461/87 and C-227/88 [1989] ECR I 7141 op. cit. para. 33.
84. Arguably the privilege could not be raised following *Otto BV v. Post Bank NV*, Case C-60/92 op. cit. in which the ECJ held that the Commission could not use information obtained from the national court in its own enforcement proceedings; see note 34 infra.

Chapter 6
English Procedure: Costs

A. COSTS AND THE CPR

The Commission Green Paper[1] and the Commission Staff Working Paper[2] raise the issue of costs as constituting a potential obstacle to the enforcement of EC Articles 81 and or 82 by the national courts. Both of these documents focus upon the indemnity rule as constituting a major factor which may serve to impede enforcement of EC competition law and propose various methods for attenuating its effects. Further, the recommendations contained within the documents are limited to restricting the application of the indemnity rule so as to protect an eventual unsuccessful complainant in EC competition proceedings.

Both the CPR and the CAT Rules provide for the use of the indemnity principle in the sense of the winner recovering his lawyer's costs from the loser. Notwithstanding, it is not clear that the indemnity rule in itself suffices to explain the problems which arise in terms of costs in terms of the CPR. First, both the CAT Rules and its case law establish that the CAT does not inflexibly apply the indemnity rule. Second, in terms of the CPR the precise effect of the indemnity rule is at best ambiguous. Zuckerman[3] argues with respect to the CPR that at least in first instance the indemnity rule can indeed exercise a nugatory and dissuasive effect upon the use of court proceedings in order to enforce legal rights. This can, he argues, lead to an invidious situation in which the mere likelihood of having to bear the payment of the opponent's legal costs may dissuade an impecunious

---

1. Green Paper: Damages Actions for Breach of the EC Anti-Trust Rules (SEC (2005) COM (2005) 672 Final.
2. Commission Staff Working Paper: Annexe to the Green Paper: Damages Action s for Breach of EC Anti-Trust Rules: (COM) (2005) 672 Final: SEC (2005) 1732 (19.12.2006).
3. A.A.S. Zuckerman, 'Devices for Controlling the Cost of Litigation' in (2005) 24 CJQ 3.

litigant. However, perversely, once the litigation has commenced, the indemnity principle may serve to encourage if not augment legal costs. Sustained by the possibility of collecting his legal costs as well as the legal remedy sought from his opponent, a litigant may seek by reason of what might be termed the principle of emulation, to duplicate if not exceed the legal efforts and expenditures effected by his opponent in the hope of achieving a legal victory and thereby recovery of his costs. Zuckerman observes:[4]

> The indemnity principle combines with those forensic incentives to increase the cost of litigation. Litigants' fear of costs act as a deterrent to litigation. But once it is clear that a dispute is destined to go to trial the indemnity principle tends to erode resistance to costs. Given that success brings with it not only the sum claimed but also the expenses laid out, a litigant who believes that an increase in the amount spent on litigation will increase his chances of success and run a greater risk of having to pay the other party's costs as well as losing the subject matter of the dispute. It is therefore not uncommon for litigation to reach a point where the parties would have reason to persist with investment on litigation not so much for the sake of favourable judgment on the merits as for the purpose of recovering the money already expended in the dispute which may well exceed the value of the subject matter in issue. Even before the proceedings have commenced a claimant may feel obliged to invest considerable resources in pre-action activity in order to persuade a defendant to enter into serious negotiations. It is clear therefore that the high cost of litigation could itself general further upward pressure on costs.

With respect to the CPR, it would appear that the major cost factors involving the enforcement of legal remedies including actions for damages for breach of EC Articles 81 and or 82 are the following: first the manner in which lawyers are remunerated for both in and out of court services, namely on a hourly basis;[5] and second, the system of controls based upon judicial intervention through judicial case management coupled with at best prospective budgeting which deals exclusively with party to party costs based upon hourly legal remuneration.[6]

---

4. A.A.S. Zuckerman, 'Devices for Controlling the Cost of Litigation' in (2005) 24 CJQ 3 *ibid.*
5. A.A.S. Zuckerman, 'Devices for Controlling the cost of Litigation' in (2005) 24 CJQ 3 *ibid.* identifies the following two problems in Devices for controlling the cost of Litigation: 'The failure of the present system to curb costs is due to two factors: first, costs are determined by reference to what is considered by the profession to be reasonably necessary work and by the prevailing standards of hourly fees and overheads; In other words, the judicial pitching of costs follows the forensic practises and expectations and not the other way around. Secondly, taxation is conduction retrospectively so that it reflects the way in which the parties chose to conduct the case. In other words, retrospective taxation does not influence the steps taken in the litigation'.
6. M. Zander Q.C. in 'Where are we now on Conditional Fees or why this Emperor' (2002) 65 MLR 919 at 927: 'The CPR, Lord Hoffmann said, required assessment entirely by reference to the facts of the case. Once one involved a global approach designed to produce a reasonable over all return for solicitors one moved away from the judicial function and into the territory of the legislature or the administrative decision. In his view, it would be more rational to have levels of costs at a

Accordingly, the EC doctrine of effectiveness could intervene so as to require that procedural cost controls be applied in a manner so as to ensure effective enforcement of EC Articles 81 and or 82 unless there is some type of justification within the principles of the CPR. It would seem, therefore, that the doctrine of effectiveness could lead to the following situation where the costing practises applied by the CPR restrict the enforcement of EC competition law either by making it impossible or – as is more likely – exceedingly difficult by analogy to the difficulties experienced in commercial litigation on the Multi Track. First, that prospective budgeting be applied to not only party to party costs but also to solicitor to client costs; second, that a system of fixed maximum costs be established to cover both party to party and solicitor to client costs. This system would simply extend, thereby, the current regime which applies on the current CPR Fast Track; and, finally, that the application of the indemnity principle by the CAT be followed in the High Court.

B. EFFECT OF COSTS IN ENGLISH ENFORCEMENT
    PROCEEDINGS OF EC ARTICLES 81 AND 82

At present, no studies exist concerning the costs specifically associated with the enforcement of EC Articles 81 and 82 using either the CPR or the CAT Rules. Arguably this absence of data is attributable at least in part to the fact that until the ECJ judgment in *Crehan*[7] and its application by the High Court,[8] Court of Appeal[9] and the House of Lords,[10] no case in damages had been decided by an English court involving a breach of EC Articles 81 and or 82. Notwithstanding, it would appear that costs can potentially seriously restrict enforcement of EC competition particularly in free standing actions for the following reasons: costs apparently continue to constitute a major difficulty in provision of legal services generally under the CPR. In this regard, there exists the study undertaken by Peysner and Seneviratne[11] which demonstrates perhaps not unexpectedly that the use of the system of judicial case management introduced by the CPR has lead to an increase in the cost of litigation. The CPR principles of Case Management of the CPR necessarily apply to the enforcement of EC competition law by the English courts. Peysner and

---

reasonable level but also reduce disputes about cots. Lord Hoffmann's speech exposed to public gaze the complete intellectual emptiness of the Court of Appeal's approach to the fixing of success fees which has now been endorsed by the House of Lords. The hole business is based on string and mirrors; There is nothing solid there at all'.

7. *Courage Ltd v. Crehan*, Case C-453/99 [2001] ECR I 6297.
8. *Bernard Crehan v. Inntreprneur Pub Co (CPC) et al.* [2003] EWHC (CH) Case 1998 C801.
9. *Bernard Crehan v. Inntrepeneur Pub Company CPC* (2004) EWCA 637 A3/2003/1725 21 May 2004.
10. *Inntrepreneur Pub Company (CPC) v. Crehan* [2006] UKHL 38, <www.publications.parliament.uk>.
11. J. Peysner, & M. Senviratne, The Management of Civil Cases : the Courts and the Post – Woolf Landscape (Dec 2005), <www.dca.gov.uk/research/2005/9_2005.htm>.

Seneviratne observe at page 80 of their report the following with respect to costs and Case Management:

> We found that the effect of the CPR including the extensive range of pre-action protocols, unsurprisingly front loaded costs. For the many case that under the pre CPR regime would have settled before or just after issue, the impact of the arrangements in the CPR to divert cases from litigation or to ensure that that litigation cases were better prepared and disclosed more information relevant to liability and quantum not least so that an opponent could make a better informed offer to settle, the inevitable result was that costs per case were higher. . . . In effect we draw the same conclusion as RAND that case management which in this case includes pre-action protocols, the Fast Track and individual case control is effective in cutting delay but it is ineffective in cutting costs or indeed may increase costs. Rules alone cannot achieve proportionality, economy certainty and predictability of costs: policy solutions are required.[12]

Peysner and Seneviratne continue at page 98:

> Costs were felt to have increased overall as a result of the CPR and in particular costs are now 'front loaded'. Also the cost per case is higher than pre CPR. Judges felt that the costs particularly on the Fast Track were disproportionate. In areas outside personal injury work or simple monetary claims, it was accepted that the demands of the CPR required substantial work. There were mixed views about the merits of fixed costs with judges tending to support them for Fast Track case. The cost estimation rules were not being followed or enforced. Costs remain a problem and these have increased. In conclusion, the case management court dispute resolution system is delivering quality at a much improved pace but probably at higher cost.

---

12. See also, Rand Corporation, Rand Institute for Civil Justice, 'An Evaluation of Judicial Case Management Under the Civil Justice Reform Act', (1996), J. Kalakik, T. Dunworth, L. Hill, D. McCaffery, M. Oshiro, N. Pace, M. V; M. Vaiana; <www.rand.org/icj/pubs/admin.htm>; Zander Q.C., 'The Woolf Report: Forwards or Backwards for the New Lord Chancellor' (1997) (16) CJQ 208 at 215 'The idea that judicial case management is the answer to the twin evils of cost and delay in civil litigation has in recent years taken hold not just here but in other common law countries'. and at p. 219 'But in the ordinary run of the mill cases it is not true. Judicial case management does not save money, it positively adds to costs. The recent RAND study both establishes that as a fact and explains the reasons. Early judicial cases management (also) is associated with significantly increases costs to litigants as measured by attorney work hours. The reason? Case management generates more work for lawyers'.; and Zuckerman on the likelihood of the CPR case management system leading to an increase of costs. The Ashurst Report (National Report – UK) observes at p. 34: 'The most important development in England is the case management approach to procedure and the strict time limits followed by the CAT'.

This study would seem to confirm empirically the observation made by Zuckerman as to the most effective method of controlling litigation costs generally:

> The history of procedural reform both recent and remote, shows the ineptness of the indirect approach. Attempts to cut down costs by simplifying procedure by judicial pressure or by encouraging clients to resist rising costs have all be tried and found wanting. There is no alternative to a direct attack on the economic incentive to complicate and protract the litigation process. But a serious challenge to the vested interests of the legal profession cannot come from just a lone reformer, however bold and exalted. It must involved determined intervention at government level. Until this happens experience will continue to dispel our hopes of improvement and litigation costs will remain as exorbitant as they have been for a very long time.[13]

In so far as the CPR case management is used for Multi Track litigation for enforcement of EC Articles 81 and 82 it would seem likely that the conclusion of Peysner and Seneveritne may well apply with respect notably to the increase of costs of enforcement of EC competition law. This eventuality may well be aggravated by the abolition of civil legal aid and its replacement by the conditional fee with the entirety of the costs and the uplift shifted to the losing party. Indeed, the use of the conditional fee coupled with the success fee the amount of which is decided by the claimant and his lawyer all of which is shifted to the unsuccessful defendant may well lead to the following two consequences: first a general increase in the costs of litigation in that the claimant is no longer concerned about the amount thereof as the entire burden will be shifted to the defendant;[14] Peysner and Seviratne observe at page 65 of their report with respect to personal injury claims:

> The abolition of legal aid, the front loading of claims under the CPR, pre-action protocols and the introduction of conditional fees with recoverable elements under Access to Justice (1998) created an unprecedented hike in the costs of negotiating the claims and a breakdown in normal settlement procedures. In 2003 the Civil Justice Council helped to negotiate an industry wide agreement for fixed recoverable costs in the most contentious areas. The agreement

---

13. A.A.S. Zuckerman, 'Lord Woolf's Access to Justice' (1996) 59 MLR 773 at 796.
14. A.A.S. Zuckerman, 'Devices for Controlling the Costs of Litigation', (2005) 24 CJQ p. 3–4; 'What was not predictable at the time of the Woolf Report was that the structure of the CFA legislation would combine with the existing inflationary factors to inflame the situation. This is because the adverse incentive possessed by lawyers to complicate and protract the litigation process could in some situations be magnified by the size of the success fees. For if the success fee is 100 per cent every billable hour charged at a certain rate could yield twice as much. Of course the risk of losing might discourage lawyers from investing too much time in the case. But this may not always be the case. Lawyers tend to take cases in which they feel confident of success. Even where success is uncertain they may reckon that the investing more in the process they would increase the chances of their success or at least impress the opponent in the case the risk of such a high costs order in the event that their client is successful that the opponent may be induced to settle'.

was a system which calculated costs not on a normal system of hours times hourly rates but with a matrix based on the settlement figure.

The second consequence is the shifting of the burden for payment of the costs including payment of a success fee of up to 100 per cent may serve to discourage following the experience in the defamation cases, defendants from exercising their rights pursuant to EC Articles 81 and or 82. The costs shifted will of course be calculated on a hourly basis and be subject to the current CPR controls which it is submitted are insufficient so as to ensure proper access for those parties who wish to enforce their rights pursuant to EC Articles 81 and or 82.

C.   NATURE OF THE COSTS PROBLEM IN
                ENGLISH LITIGATION

Lord Woolf in his Interim Report on Access to Justice (1995)[15] defined the nature of the problem concerning high legal costs in England in the following manner in Chapter 25:

> Point 5: 'There is a misconceived view that the entire problem is due to the scale of the lawyer's costs. This is not so. It is however, the case that market forces which in other contexts have acted as a restraint on prices operate rather weekly in relation to the supply of professional legal services. Factors associated with legal charging are to be found in this field: notably the restrictions on access to the market and the regulating controls necessary to maintain proper professional standards and the integrity of the legal system'.
>   Point 6: 'While I do not regard it is part of my remit to comment generally on the relationship between clients and their own lawyers in connection with litigation, there are areas where that relations affects the costs of litigation'.
>   Point 8: 'In Chapter 3, I refer to the common practise of lawyers charging their clients by the hour (or by the day in the case of barristers). I believe that this has an inflationary effect on costs. Regular litigators appreciating this, are moving towards costs agreed in advance for a range of legal services. . . . In addition to requiring information to be given as to fees, the professional bodies should encourage lawyers to enter into fixed fee agreements where practical'.
>   Point 10: 'In the second stage to my enquiry, I hope to examine an approach to taxation of costs. I am concerned that the system while controlling levels of fees which are out of line with those of the profession in fact ratifies a general level of costs which is over generous for the work done'.

Therefore, according to his lordship, there are various factors which explain the existence of high costs in English legal proceedings; first, the inability of market

---

15. Lord Woolf, Interim Report Access to Justice, (1995), <www.dca.gov.uk/civil/interim/chap25.htm>.

forces to function within the field of legal services by reason among other things of lack of client information; second, the manner in which lawyers calculate their costs namely on an hourly or daily basis; third, post litigation assessment of costs through judicial taxation ratifies the high level of costs.

Zuckerman identifies the source of the problem of costs in the following manner:

> The failure of the present system to curbs costs is due to two factors: first, costs are determined by reference to what is considered by the profession to be reasonably necessary work and by the prevailing standards of fees and overheads. In other words, the judicial pitching of costs follows the forensic practise and expectations and not the other way around. Secondly, taxation is conducted retrospectively so that it reflects the way in which the parties chose to conduct the case. In order words, retrospective taxation does not influence the steps taken in the litigation.[16]

Lord Hoffmann noted that the problem of costs could be analysed in the followed manner:

> As my noble and learned friend Lord Scott has observed, the criterion prescribed by the CPR for determining whether costs are reasonably framed operate entirely by reference to the facts of the particular case. Once one invokes a global approach designed to produce a reasonable overall return for solicitors, one moves away from the judicial function of the costs judge and into the territory of legislative and administrative decisions. A legislative decision to fix costs at levels calculated to provide adequate access to justice in the most economical way seems to me to be a more rational approach than to leave the matter to an individual costs judge. If it is considered the most appropriate way to secure value for money when the expenditure is borne by the public as a whole (e.g. fixing of graduate fees for criminal legal aid) it should be no less appropriate when the expenditure is born by a section of the public, namely, the motorists. Not only would this be likely to keep the actual costs within reasonable levels but it would also greatly reduce the costs of disputes over costs.[17]
>
> His lordship concludes by observing: 'They would be proper to take into account (although the practical difficulties of so doing are considerable) by someone charged with fixing fees for the profession as a whole such as the Lord Chancellor when he determines levels of graduated fees. But a taxing

---

16. A.A.S. Zuckerman, 'Devices for controlling the Cost of Litigation through Taxation': paper presented to the Woolf Inquiry Team, (1996) JILT (1), <www.warwick.ac.uk/fac/soc/law/elj/jilt/1996_/woolf/costs>.
17. *Callery v. Gray House of Lords ibid.* Lord Hoffmann point 34.

officer in deciding what is a reasonable fee in a particular case must take the general levels of fees as given and use them as a basis of taxation'.[18]

The Commission undertook studies on competition in the field of professional services in 2003[19] and 2004.[20] In its Follow Up Paper of 2005[21] the Commission defines the problem with respect to liberal professions including law as generally one in which excessive regulation prevents the operation of market forces. It observes at page 4 of the Follow Up Paper:

Point 6: 'The Commission focussed upon six professions including lawyers'.

Point 7: 'In many instances tradition restrictive rules in these areas are serving to restrict competition. Such regulation may eliminate or limit competition between service providers and thereby reduce the incentives between service providers and thus reduce the incentives for professional to work cost efficiently, lower price increase, quality or to offer mother market services'.

However the Commission then goes on to observe at page 5 of the same document:
BETTER DEFINING OF THE PUBLIC INTEREST:

There are reasons why some carefully targeted regulation of professional services may be necessary:

Firstly, because there is an asymmetry of information between customers and service providers of professional services in that they require practitioners to display a high level of technical knowledge. Consumers may not have this knowledge and therefore find it difficult to judge the quality of services.

Secondly, the concept of externalities whereby the provision of a service may have an impact on third parties as well as the purchaser of the service.

Thirdly, certain professional services are deemed to produce 'goods' that are of value for society in general. For example the correct administration of justice. It is possible that without regulation there might be an inadequate or under supply of these services.

---

18. *Callery v. Gray House of Lords ibid.* Lord Hoffmann at point 34, see *generally* M. Zander QC, 'The Government's Plans for Civil Justice' (1998) MLR 382, <www.blackwell-synergy.com>.
19. Institut für Höhre Studien, Economic Impact of Regulation in the field of Liberal Profession in Different Member State for the European Commission DG Competition: Wien, Jan 2003. It is necessary to consider the critique of this report made in particular by RBB Economics, Economic Impact of Regulation in Liberal Professions: A Critique of the IHS Report, 9 September 2003, <www.ccbe.org/doc/En/rbb_ihs_critique_en.pdf>.
20. EC Commission Report on Competition in Professional Services COM (2004) 83 9 February 2004.
21. EC Commission Follow up Report on Competition in Professional Services COM (2005) 405 Final SEC (2005) 1064.

In its Commission Staff Working Document[22] the Commission makes the following observation apparently in relation to the information provided in the previous analyses:

KEY FINDING OF ANALYSIS:

21. A further differentiation of the markets of professional services would allow a better identification of the public interest involved and of the degree of regulation indispensable to protect this. This can be arrived at by assisting what is needed for the different types of customers or users. The above analysis shows that one off users – generally individual customers and households may have a greater nee of some carefully targeted protection (e.g. price regulation may be needed) for the lower paid to ensure proper access to legal advice and representation in certain areas of law. On the other hand the main users of business services – business and public sector – may have no or little need given that they are better equipped to chose providers that best suit their needs. The position of small business is not entirely clear and further economic analysis is needed to arrive at a conclusion on the facts.

Accordingly, despite its emphasis upon introduction of market forces facilitated through deregulation, the Commission nevertheless apparently recognizes that some regulation of costs may be necessary in order to ensure that specific categories of users, e.g. individual users and small businesses, are protected.[23]

D. ECJ CASE LAW: POSSIBLE SOLUTIONS TO THE PROBLEM OF ENGLISH COSTS IN CONFORMITY WITH EC CASE LAW

1. PRINCIPLE OF EFFECTIVENESS AND THE NATIONAL RULES ON COSTS

Clean Car Autoservice[24] establishes that the EC principle of effectiveness indeed applies to the national rules of procedure concerning costs. In *Clean Car*

---

22. Commission Staff Working Document COM (2005) 405 Final IHS study which the Commission commissioned in 2003 undertaken.

23. See Ogus 'Some Reflections on the Woolf Interim Report' *Journal of Current Legal Issues*, <www.ncl.ac.uk/-nlaw>; and B. Main & A. Peacock 'What price civil Justice' (1998) Hume Institute, <www.econ.ed.ac.uk/papers/confmp3.pdf> at p. 6, 'There are two types of purchases of civil legal services. The first is the one time buyer whom the costs of obtain and evaluating information on the range and quality of legal services can be high. Purchases are therefore typically make on faith and for this type of buyer legal service is a credence good where it can be argued that some kind of third party regulation is beneficial. The second type is a professional or repeat buyer who may be a business enterprise. Here there is ample opportunity to gain information on the nature of supplies and to make informed purchases based upon experience. To these buyers legal services are an experienced good where the normal stricture of caveat emptor leads to an efficient outcome'.

24. *Clean Car Autoservice v. Stadt Wien* C-472/99 [2001] ECR – I 9687.

Autoservice, although not finding that the Austrian rules concerning fixed costs violated the principle of effectiveness, the ECJ nevertheless observed that costs rules, as part of the national procedure, must comply with the EC Principle of effectiveness. The ECJ held as follows:

> Paragraph 27: 'It follows from the foregoing that as Community law stands at present, it is in principle for the internal order of each Member State to determine rules applicable to the payment of costs by the parties in the main proceedings when a reference is made for a preliminary ruling'.
>
> Paragraph 28: 'However as the Advocate General observes in point 26 of his Opinion, although in the absence of Community legislation governing the matter, it is for the domestic legal system of each Member State to lay down the detailed procedural rules governing court action for safeguarding rights which individuals derive from Community law: such rules must not be less favourable than those governing similar domestic actions (principle of equivalence) and must not render virtually impossible or excessively difficult the exercise of the rights conferred by Community law (principle of effectiveness)'.

Accordingly, it is clear that the rules of the CPR which deal with costs must conform with the EC principle of effective and non discriminatory enforcement.

2.   COMPLIANCE OF COSTS RULES WITH RESPECT TO
                 EC COMPETITION LAW

In addition, both the content and the application of the national procedural rules on costs must not infringe EC competition law, in particular, EC Art. 81.

a.   **Fixed Maximum and Minimum Legal Costs**

ARDUINO: In *Arduino*[25] the ECJ held that although EC Art. 81 applies only to private undertakings and not government measures. Nevertheless both EC Articles 10 and 81 could be violated by a government measure in two circumstances: first, where the government had delegated control to a private operator or second, the government measure tended to accentuate anti-competitive effects.

It would appear that, in contrast to the Advocate General's opinion, the Court based its judgment exclusively on the two factors: first, whether or not the State had delegated control to a private party and whether the measure had any anti-competitive effects.[26] 'Article 5 and 85 of the EC Treaty (now Articles 10 EC and 81 EC) do not preclude a Member State from adopting a law or regulation which approves on the basis of a draft produced by a professional body of members of the Bar, a tariff fixing minimum and maximum fees for members of the profession

---

25. *Arduino* Case C-35/99 (2002) ECR I 1529, <www.curia.europa.eu> (reference to the ECJ).
26. *Arduino* Case C-35/99 [2002] ECR I 1529, <www.curia.europa.eu> *ibid.*

where that State measure forms part of the procedure as that laid down in Royal Decree Law No. 1578 of 27 12 1933 as amended'.

Advocate General Léger in contrast specifically considered the measures sought to achieve as an element of public policy: specifically the quality of legal services. *A priori* therefore measures related to such a policy objective would be justifiable as public policy and not contravene EC Art. 81. However, the Advocate General then goes to decide that in the instant case the use of fixed legal fees notably minimum fees was not demonstrably related to the achievement of such and objective ipso facto and second, was in any event not proportionate: the appropriate method of quality control was through proper training, legal complaints. Notwithstanding, the Advocate-General concluded that a State system of minimum and maximum costs would not contravene either EC Art. 10 or EC Art. 81. In short, the ECJ held that EC Art. 10 and notably 81 did not apply to a government legislation which the regulated legal fees albeit on the basis pro-positions made by the Italian Bar Council. The legislation provided for the fixing of both minimum and maximum fees arguably for both court and non court services although this latter point was taken in the subsequent cases of *Macrino* and *Cipolla*.

WOUTERS: In *Wouters*[27] ECJ held that the concept of 'association' in EC Art. 81 could apply to a private regulatory system in the instant case, the Dutch Bar, because the State had effectively delegated its regulatory power. However, because of the legitimacy of the measure adopted, namely, the prohibition of mixed group-ings of lawyers and accountancy sought to ensure professional standards, neither EC Art. 81 nor Art 10 applied.[28]

AMOK: In *AMOK*[29] the ECJ held that EC Art. 49 and EC Dir. 77/249 should be interpreted so as not to prevent the application of the BRAGO[30] rule which provided a maximum amount for the reimbursement of lawyers fees thereby lim-iting the amount which the successful party could claim for his Austrian lawyer's in court work. However, the BRAGO rule which prevented the inclusion of the fees of the supernumerary German lawyer whose presence was necessary in order to ensure that the Austrian lawyer could present his case effectively before the German court required modification in order to prevent infringement of EC Art. 49.

---

27. *Wouters v. Algemene Raad van de Nederlandse Orde van Advocaten*, Case C-309/99 [2002] ECR I 1577, <www.curia.europa.eu>.
28. I. Forrester QC in 'The Relationship between Competition Law and the Liberal Professions, 9th Annual EU Competition Law and Policy Workshop, European University Institute 2006 feels that Arduino and Wouters may "represent an important judicial milestone for competition lawyers." For at least 20 years lawyers have been encouraging the Commission to adopt a less expansive approach to the application of the competition rules. It has been suggested that the Commission should recalibrate the breach of EV Art. 81 (1) and as a result rely less on Art. 81(3). Quaere whether this is restricted to professions and in particular the legal profession as opposed to constituting a new method of applying EC Art. 81 restrictively'. See also L. Idot, 'Avocats et Doit de la Concurrence' (2002) (Mai) *Europe* 7.
29. AMOK Verlags GmbH & A&R Gastronomie GmbH Case C-289/02, <www.curia.europa.eu>.
30. Bundesgebührenordnung für Rechtsanwälte (1957) now replaced.

3.   COMPLIANCE WITH EC COMPETITION LAW AND THE PRINCIPLE OF
             FREEDOM OF SERVICES

a.   **Fixed Maximum and Minimum Costs in
             Out-of-Court Legal Services**

In *Macrino, Capodarte v. Maloni*[31] and *Cipolla v. Fazari*,[32] Advocate General
Poiares Maduro was of the opinion that the ratio of the *Arduino* judgment applied
to the fixing of out of court fees. This is based upon the state nature of the Italian
legislation as a whole and not on the specific nature of its potential anti competitive
effects. The Advocate General concluded that a measure which fixes a scale for
lawyer's fees for out of court services is compatible with community competition
law provided that it is subject to effective supervision by the State and the power to
derogate from that scale where it rules on a dispute in the amount of the fees is
interpreted in accordance with Community law in a way that limits its anti-
competitive effect. On the question of the prohibition on derogation from the
fee scale, the Advocate General concluded such a measure did not constitute a
breach of the EC competition laws.

         With respect to the freedom to provide legal services, the Advocate General
concluded that the imposition of a scale providing for minimum fees does constitute an unjustifiable restriction. The Advocate General observed first that although
the scale of fees applies irrespective of nationality, to all lawyers wishing to provide services in Italy, it is established by taking into account only the situation and
the expenses incurred by the Italian lawyers. The minimum fees fixed by the scale
therefore prevent lawyers established outside of Italy from providing legal services
in Italy at rates below those minimum levels. In addition, Italian citizens wishing to
instruct foreign lawyers are unable to benefit fully from the advantages of the
common market because access to legal services at a cost below that fixed by
the Italian scale is denied to them even though those services are available in
the Member State. The minimum fees therefore constitute a restriction on the
freedom to provide services because they neutralize the competitive advantage
of lawyers established outside of Italy. That reason is not restricted by an overriding reason in the public interest. Although the objective of ensuring the proper
operation of the legal profession is legitimate, Italy was unable to demonstrate how
the fixing of minimum fees is appropriate for attaining it.

b.   **Effect of *Arduino, Macrino* and *Cipolla* on
             a National Rule Fixing Legal Fees**

The Advocate General reaffirms the judgment of the ECJ in *Arduino* in the
following manner: first, he construes the preliminary questions of the Italian
court as seeking to ascertain the scope of the judgment. In short, it would seem

---

31. *Macrino and Capodarte v. Maloni*, Case C-202/04, <www.curia.eu>.
32. *Cipolla v. Fazari*, Case C-94/04, <www.curia.eu> judgment rendered on 5 December 2006.

that the Advocate General feels in response to the Commission that the objectives set forth in terms of the public interest justify the extension of the ratio of Arduino to extra legal services and to the prohibition on party to party derogation from the fee schedule.

Advocate General Poiares Maduro, therefore, concludes noting in particular the possibility for the Italian court to exercise its discretion so as to derogate from the fixed fee schedule. Accordingly, the Advocate General concludes that the Italian system does not infringe EC Art. 10 or EC Art. 81: in particular, the system does not exercise an anti-competitive effect notably by reason of the Italian courts ability to exercise its discretion so as to derogate from the fee schedule. Therefore, the Advocate General effectively interprets EC Art. 81 in a restrictive manner.[33] However the Advocate General then counters his narrow interpretation of EC Art. 81 by what might be termed a wide interpretation of EC Art. 49 with consequences which are perhaps somewhat reminiscent of the debate on the scope of EC Art. 81.[34] In short Advocate General Poiares Maduro uses what seems to constitute a wide interpretation of barrier and therefore starts from the position that fixed fees constitute a barrier to the provision of legal services on a transnational basis. Advocate General Poiares Maduro begins his analysis of the concept of barrier at paragraph 58 of his opinion by citing as authority his own opinion in *Marks & Spencer*:[35]

> The common line adopted in those cases appears to be that any national policy that results in treating transnational situations less favourable than purely national situations constitutes a restriction on the freedom of movement.

Then at paragraph 59:

> The less favourable treatment of transnational situations may take various forms. Often it manifests itself as an obstacle to the national market either by protecting positions acquired in the market or by making it more difficult for cross border service providers to participate in the market.

The Advocate General observes at paragraph 60:

> In the present although the scale of lawyers fees established by legislation applies indiscriminately to both lawyers established in Italy and those established in other Member States who wish to provide services in Italy, it gives rise to restriction on freedom to provide services in a number of situation in

---

33. The opinion of Advocate General Poiares Maduro does not indicate why in terms of cannons of interpretation the strict method could not be used in the instant case at least a start of the analysis: specifically, that on the facts, the Court rendered its judgment specifically mentioning that the Italian State decree provided for lawyers fees both in court and out of court. Therefore, arguably, there is nothing in the judgment to indicate that the ECJ's conclusion was not intended to apply to the entire Italian legislation as cited in the body of the judgment.

34. See *generally*, V. Korah, An Introductory Guide to EC Competition Law and Practise (8th edn., Hart Publishing, Oxford, 2003).

35. *Marks & Spencer*, Case C-446/03, (2005) ECR-I 6000, (reference pursuant to EC Art. 234).

which the latter are placed in a less favourable situation than their Italian counterparts.

Accordingly, the operative part of the concept is that it is any measure which discriminates by making it more difficult for cross border service providers to participate in the market. This is so because at paragraph 61:

> First it is clear that the scale is drawn up taking into account only Italian lawyers and not transnational situations. It is therefore appropriate to consider whether the criterion adopted in fixing fees are specific to lawyers established in Italy or whether they are applicable to lawyers established in other Member States.

Assuming that these national Italian criterions for fixing fees are applied to lawyers from other Member States specific problems arise according as to whether there are minimum or maximum fee scales.

c.   **Fixed Minimum Fees**

The Advocate General describes the barrier created by minimum fees in the following manner:

> Paragraph 63: 'It is clear from well established case law of the Court that State price control systems including a prohibition on selling below a minimum price do not in themselves constitute measures having an effect equivalent to a quantitative restriction but may have such an effect when prices are fixed at a level such that imported products are placed at a disadvantage compared to identical national products either because they cannot profitably be marketed on the conditions laid down or because the competitive advantages conferred by lower costs prices is cancelled out'.

It is clear however that for this reasoning to apply, the services involved in the case of the Italian and non-Italian lawyers must be the same – i.e., 'to identical national products'.

> Paragraph 64: 'This reasoning was transposed by the Court from the area of free movement of goods to the area of the right of establishment in *Caixa Bank v. France*. Similarly in respect of freedom to provide services it is necessary to ensure that the competitive advantage of lawyers established outside Italy is not cancelled out by the legislation of that Member State. The comparison should be between the situation of lawyers established in other Member States and that of their counterparts already established in Italy'.

Having extended the reasoning to the provision of legal services the Advocate General then concludes at point 65 with respect to fixed minimum fees:

> The minimum fees fixed in the scale prevent lawyers established in Member States other than the Italian Republic from providing legal services in that State for fees below those minimum even if they had the opportunity to do so,

for example by reason of their specializing in a particular field. The Advocate General observes in his footnote 50: 'No account is taken of the fact that foreign lawyers might have lower costs.

Advocate General Poiares Maduro then deals with the matter of causation in paragraph 65:

> The minimum fees therefore constitute a restriction on the freedom to provide services in so far as they cancel out the competitive of a lawyer established outside of Italy . . . Consequently Italian citizens wishing to call on the services of a lawyer established in another Member State are unable to benefit full from the advantages of the Common Market because access to legal services at a cost below that fixed by the Italian State are denied them even though those services are available in another Member State.

With due respect, the argument of the Advocate General presents certain problems: first, as noted above, part of the definition used requires that the national products in question be identical: that is, Italian and non-Italian lawyers must offer the same legal services. Second, they must compete in the same market defined in terms of product demand. It is not clear, however, from the Advocate General's opinion that these requirements are fulfilled with respect to the Italian legal market for services as they pertain to fixed minimum fees. On the contrary, the Copenhagen Report[36] notes that at least with respect to Denmark and apparently Norway, there are at least two different markets for legal services according to the nature of the demand and the product itself: the market for national law which is reinforced by the use of the Danish language. Therefore, the first condition of the definition is not fulfilled at least with respect to the market in national law: non Danish lawyers and Danish lawyers do not offer the same legal products. Arguably the same is the case with respect to the market for national law in Italy: Italian lawyers and non-Italian lawyers do not offer the same products.

The Copenhagen Report, The Legal Profession: Competition and Liberalization,[37] observes at page 37:

> However, several aspects limit the international competition between lawyers. Lawyers need an in depth knowledge of the legislation of the country and clients often refer a local lawyer (NOU (2002) 'Right to Justice: Norwegian Ministry of Justice JD NOU 2002 18 and Ziirsen (2003) Investigation for Private Clients: Part 1 Citizens Need for and use of Legal Services) and language barriers will limit the scope of export and import. But in large transaction, the contract language will be English and in reality there is no language barrier and in such cases the legal basis will primarily be EU legislation which

---

36. Copenhagen Economics, 'The Legal Profession: Competition and Liberalisation', January 2006, <www.copenhageneconomics.com/publications/The_legal_profession.pdf>.
37. Copenhagen Economics, 'The Legal Profession: Competition and Liberalisation', January 2006, <www.compenhageneconomics.com/publications/The_legal_profession.pdf>, *ibid.*

reduces the need for knowledge of national legislation. It is therefore primarily a question of national markets.

Second, even if the condition of identity of products were fulfilled, which it is not, the next problem is whether price is the decisive element in competition between lawyers either within the same Member State or lawyers in different Member States. The Advocate General does not indicate on what basis price was chosen as constituting the essential element in competition. More particularly, he does not indicate on what factual basis he rejects the contention of the German government that competition between lawyers involves quality rather more than price. Advocate General Poiares Maduro simply observes in this regard at paragraph 65:

> The minimum fees constitute a restriction on freedom to provide services in so far as they cancel out the competitive advantage of lawyers established outside Italy. Contrary to what the German government contends that finding is not altered by the fact that competition between lawyers does not have effect only on prices but also on the quality of the services provided.

Notwithstanding the use of the expression 'that fact', Advocate General Poiares Maduro does not advance any economic opinion to sustain his claim that competition in lawyers between Member States involves price. On the contrary, the Copenhagen Report concludes that competition between lawyers does not concern price:

> Page 22: 'The marketing analysis institute, Ziirsen Research, has examined the demand for legal services from clients. The survey shows that the most important concern when choosing a lawyer is professional capability. Further to this, the reputation of the lawyer and the fact that the lawyer is local are important parameters for private clients when choosing a lawyer. A Norwegian survey shows the same pattern. Professional capacities and personal relations are more important than price. This means that lawyers have to compete more on professional capabilities and reputation than on price. Price therefore is not the most important competition parameter for lawyers nor will it be following a liberalization of the legal profession'.[38]

Accordingly, the analysis of Advocate General Poiraes Maduro fails to take account of the nature of the demand within one of the particular markets, namely, that of individual and small business, the existence of which he implicitly recognized in paragraph 41 of his opinion when dealing with asymmetries of information:

> It could be argued that the market in out of court legal services differs from the market in legal services provided in the context of proceedings before a court. In the former case, there is less asymmetry of information between a lawyer and his clients because the recipients of the services refer to a lawyer more

---

38. Copenhagen Economics: 'The Legal Profession: Competition and Liberalisation'; January 2006, at page 22, <www.copenhageneconomics.com/publications/The_legal_profession.pdf> *ibid.*

frequently, and are therefore in a better position to assess the quality of the services provided.

Certainly, the Advocate General does utilize the economic concept of market in his analysis as noted from the paragraphs above as well as competition. Accordingly, it is not clear why there is no economic definition of the markets.

Third, it is not clear from his Opinion how the Advocate General relates the discretion enjoyed by the Italian court to derogate from application of fixed fees both minimum and maximum to his conclusion notably in the above-cited footnote 50: 'No account is taken of the fact that foreign lawyers might have lower costs'. Rather it would seem to be the case that the Italian court is indeed able to apply the system to both in court and out of court fees is able to consider such information. Certainly in paragraph 45 the Advocate General specifically exhorted the Italian court to exercise its discretionary powers of derogation in order to ensure effective enforcement of EC competition law.

> Paragraph 45: 'However, a national court has a duty when interpreting national law to select where it has some discretion in the matter the interpretation that forms most closely to Community law and is most likely to attain its objective. Art. 60 of the Decree Law state that a court is free to fix at its discretion fee for out of court services within maximum and minimum limits of the scale. Consequently in order to increase the anti-competitive effect of the scale, the national court will be required so far as possible to use its discretion when it decides a dispute concerning the amount of fees laid down in that scale for out of court services'.

It is recalled that even under EC Art. 49 the Advocate General advances competition as being the essential concern as noted above, albeit competition in prices. It is submitted that it is also clear from the opinion and specifically from the footnote cited that the Advocate General clearly considers the system of fixed fees applies and not just how it is constituted. Further, the case cited by the Advocate General in his definition of minimum prices at paragraph 63 specifically establishes that the effect must be considered: 'they do not in themselves constitute measures having an effect equivalent to a quantitative restriction but may have such an effect'. This would suggest that the Advocate General is applying a very wide interpretation of quantitative restriction so as to include minimum prices irrespective of their effect and that therefore one must consider whether, following the Commission, such restrictions are justifiable in terms of public policy. If this is so, the opinion does not indicate on what basis this wide interpretation of quantitative restriction can be justified.[39] In short, the opinion does not establish that the application of the system of minimum fees contained within the Decree law indeed causes the problem complained of in paragraph 65.

---

39. This seems once again to suggest a parallel with the position described by Professor Korah concerning in particular the Commission wide interpretation of EC Art. 81 (formerly 85) notably prior to the Modernization Regulation; see *generally*, V. Korah, An Introductory Guide to EC Competition Law and Practise (8th edn, Oxford, Hart Publishing, 2003).

The Advocate General then proceeds in paragraph 71 to enumerate various provisions of the Italian decree law which are said to exacerbate the infringement of EC Art. 49 caused by the fixed minimum fees:

> Under the ministerial decree whether that of 1990 or of 1994 lawyers practising in Italy are required to invoice their services on the basis of a closed list set out in the scale. They are therefore in principle prevented from fixing the amount of time by another method, e.g. on the basis of the amount of time spent preparing the case by each lawyer according to his level of expertise. However, these two systems give the client the opportunity to understand the amount of the fees he will have to pay and also help to reduce the asymmetry of information that exists between lawyers and a client.

The Advocate General, however, does not advance any facts to sustain his assertion that for example, hourly calculation of fees, will assist in the reduction in the asymmetry of information or whether, even if they might so do, such calculation can lead to unfortunate consequences in terms of raising costs and diminishing access to justice.

The Copenhagen Economics report[40] observes as follows:

> Page 13: 'The Competition Authority has suggested that lawyers must break down their hours and hourly rates such that clients have a better view of what they are paying for. Such a rule will improve transparency but can on the other hand give other problems. Fees calculated only from hours used could give some lawyers a vested interest in using more hours in a case than necessary. There is a risk that fees calculated from hours used lead to complaints regarding the amount of hours used by lawyers (Polinsky A M and D L Rubinfield (2001) 'Aligning Interests of Lawyers & Clients' The Berkley Law & Economics Working Papers, Vol 2001 Issue 2 Fall 2001)'.

Having decided that the minimum fees constitute a barrier the Advocate-General then goes on at paragraph 83 to consider whether there might be some justification thereof in terms of public policy:

> The major argument put forward by the Italian Government and the German Government at the hearing concerns the likelihood that fierce competition between lawyers would lead to price competition resulting in the quality of the services provided to the detriment of consumers. That likelihood would be all the greater since the market in legal services is characterised by asymmetry of information between lawyers and consumers since the latter do not have the necessary criterion for assessing the quality of the services provided. (with regard to the asymmetry of information which characterises the market in professional services see opinion in *Arduino* at pp. 112).

---

40. Copenhagen Economics, 'The Legal Profession: Competition and Liberalisation', January 2006, <www.copenhageneconomics.com/publications/The_legal_profession.pdf> *ibid.*

The Advocate General, however, expresses some dubiety as to the efficacy of minimum prices to control this problem and cites at paragraph 86:

> Although the Court did not consider this point in *Arduino*, Advocate General Leger raises in his opinion the question whether it was possible to justify the adoption of minimum fees in order to ensure the quality of services provided by lawyers.

At paragraph 117 of his opinion, he expressed his doubts in the following terms: 'I fail to see how a system of mandatory prices would prevent members of the profession offering inadequate services if, in any event, they lacked qualification, competence or moral conscience'.

The Advocate General then observes at paragraph 86:

> Advocate General Léger's doubts are shared by economic literature which considers that it is by no means demonstrated that the abolition of minimum fees would necessarily lead to a deterioration in the quality of legal services provided. Although unable to address any evidence, the German government has tried to plead a negative causal link which it considers results from the fact that below a certain level of fees the quality of services is no longer guaranteed. This presupposes knowing that it would be guaranteed above a certain level. This . . . is not moreover sufficient to justify fixing minimum fees. It is necessary to demonstrate that the abolition of minimum fixed fees would automatically lead to a reduction of quality of legal services.

It would seem that the Advocate General is focussing on the issue of 'adverse selection'. Van den Bergh[41] provides arguably a more balanced view of the operation of adverse selection in relation to quality control of legal services:

> First of all fee regulation can be a useful tool to prevent the problem of 'adverse selection'. Consumers cannot judge the quality of services provided by professionals. Therefore consumers will base their decision to purchase certain services mainly on price and will not be willing to pay higher prices for higher quality. As a result providers of higher quality services (with a higher price) may be driven out of the market and entry of new high quality service providers may be discouraged by the low income levels.

However, Van den Bergh then makes the following observation as to the manner in which minimum fees can or should be used in order to further this objective:

> A fixed or minimum fee may then overcome this problem and maintain the quality of services provided. Policy makers should be fully aware of the adverse selection problem and refrain from introducing price competition as long as instruments to assess quality have not sufficiently been developed.

---

41. R. Van den Bergh & Y. Montangie, 'Theory and Evidence on the Regulation of the Latin Notary Profession'; Erasmus Competition and Regulation Institute, Erasmus University – Rotterdam, ECRI Report 0604 June 2006 at p. 56, <www.seor.nl>.

In markets characterised by serious information asymmetries where quality assessment does not (yet) reach the minimum level required to avoid adverse selection, fixed price may be preferred to fee tariffs.[42]

Van den Bergh then states as follows:

While critics of fee restrictions acknowledge that competition on fees may lead to adverse selection and moral hazards problems they argue that rules on fees may not be the appropriate tool to address these questions. For example, setting minimum fees or fixed fees does not in itself guarantee that a desired level of quality of the services will be offered. An alternative method which is less restrictive of competition and would thus present less negative effects is the mandatory publication of adequate information on quality and fees on behalf of the consumer.[43]

However, Van den Bergh then concludes: 'From an economic point of view, these negative effects of fee regulation should be put in perspective and should not be overestimated'.[44]

At its strongest therefore, the Advocate General has presented apparently only one view which apparently exists among experts concerning how to deal with the problem of adverse selection and the use of minimum fees as a method of ensuring quality in a market characterized by asymmetry of consumer information. It would have been helpful if the Advocate General's opinion had presented both views on the matter in order to demonstrate more fully the justification for the conclusion: that is how the use of minimum fees in the circumstances, particularly with legislation which provides for the use of judicial discretion to derogate from the scale, constitutes an unjustifiable barrier to the free movement of lawyers. In short, the criticisms of RBB raised with respect to the IHS report seem relevant to the approach adopted by the Advocate-General. The RBB report states: 'the theoretical overview seems to have a bias towards the contra-regulation theories as the authors do not even consider the possibility that there could be too little regulation'.[45]

Or as Van den Bergh summarizes the criticisms made of the IHS approach to regulation of the legal professions including the fixing of fees: 'Second it can be argued that the HIS Study shows a certain bias in favour of contra regulation theories. The study seems to depart from the view that there may be too much

---

42. R. Van den Bergh & Y. Montangie, 'Theory and Evidence on the Regulation of the Latin Notary Profession', Erasmus Competition and Regulation Institute, Erasmus University – Rotterdam ECRI, Report 0604, June 2006 *ibid.* at p. 56.

43. R. Van den Bergh & Y. Montangie, 'Theory and Evidence on the Regulation of the Latin Notary Profession', Erasmus Competition and Regulation Institute, Erasmus University – Rotterdam, ECRI, Report 0604, June 2006, *ibid.*, at p. 58.

44. R. Van den Bergh & Y. Montangie, 'Theory and Evidence on the Regulation of the Latin Notary Profession' Erasmus Competition and Regulation Institute, Erasmus University – Rotterdam, ECRI, Report 0604, June 2006, *ibid.* at p. 58.

45. RBB Economics, 'Economic Impact of Regulation in Liberal Profession: a Critique of the IHS Report' 9 9 2003 op. cit. at p. 18, <www.ccbe.org>.

regulation and does not ask the more general and neutral question of what the optimal level of regulation should be'.[46]

d.   **Fixed Maximum Fees**

In contrast to minimum fees, the Advocate General appears to be generally more restrained in his analysis concerning maximum fees. He nevertheless commences his analysis by observing at paragraph 67 that maximum fees fixed fees can apparently constitute a barrier to the provision of legal services and that at paragraph 68 AMOK applies only to in court costs:

> The Court has already considered pricing systems containing maximum prices. It is clear from case law that where the effect on the maximum prices is to reduce the gross profit margin of importers who must deduct from that price their imports that price conflicts with the free movement of goods. The ensure on maximum prices is expressed in general terms: a restriction on free movement is found to exist 'where prices are fixed at such a level that the scale of imported products becomes either impossible or more difficult than domestic products.
>
> Paragraph 68: 'The judgment in *AMOK* cited by the German government at the hearing in order to dispute the fact that the scale brought about a restriction on freedom to provide services is not relevant in the present case. In *AMOK* the Court considered a German procedural rule which limited the recoverable costs to the rates which apply to lawyers established in Germany. Unlike the legislation at issue here however, the German scale does not preclude foreign lawyers and their clients from fixing the level of fees freely'.

However, the reason of the opinion is not perhaps clear on the following matters: first, the Advocate General states that maximum fees constitute a barrier. It is not clear however, that the ECJ in *AMOK* held that the maximum fee necessarily constituted a barrier even in the restricted case of in court fees.

The ECJ held at paragraph 27 in AMOK:

> Art. 49 EC prohibits restrictions in the freedom to provide services within the Community. It cannot be ruled out that the imposition of an upper limit on the reimbursable fees of a lawyer established in another Member State may in the case where the fees are higher than those resulting from the scale used by the latter State be liable to render less attractive the provision by lawyers of their services across borders.

It would have been helpful to understand why the Advocate General had apparently chosen to apply the concept of barrier very widely at least with respect to out of court fees whereas the ECJ has clearly provided a potentially narrower definition

---

46. R. Van den Bergh & Y. Montangie, 'Theory and Evidence on the Regulation of the Latin Notary Profession' Erasmus Competition and Regulation Institute, Erasmus University – Rotterdam, ECRI, Report 0604, June 2006, *ibid.* at p. 37.

thereof. Second, it is not clear why having decided that *AMOK* applies exclusively to in court fees, the Advocate General apparently refuses to extend the ratio of *AMOK* as was done with respect to *Arduino* so as to include out of court fees. Apparently the problem with the Italian decree turns on the fact that the parties are not free to decide their own maximum. Once again, no mention is made of the Italian court's discretion to derogate from the fixed out of court maximum and minimum costs.

It is perhaps of significance that Van den Bergh concludes that over all in relation to both minimum and maximum fees there is an insufficiency of empirical studies concerning the effect of mandatory fixed fees and their effect on legal services. Accordingly, this absence of empirical analysis would seem to justify a prudent approach to observations concerning the effect of obligatory fixed fees. Van den Bergh notes specifically:

> While a number of arguments both in favour of and against fee schedules have been presented, there is only a limited amount of empirical evidence on the subject. The limited empirical evidence does not allow drawing hard conclusions on the positive or negative effects of fee regulation and certainly does not confirm the arguments claiming that such regulation mainly has negative effects.[47]

Nevertheless, the Advocate General having decided that maximum fees constitute a barrier nevertheless expressly restricts his opinion to fixed minimum fees for the following reason for the following reasons: 'However, the national court has not touched on that aspect (maximum fees). Also an assessment of the possible justification for maximum fees is more complex and delicate than that of minimum fees. Therefore that point has not been discussed'.

In reality, it would seem that when closely analysed, the opinion clearly suggests that maximum fees for lawyers fees and for conditional fees may not contravene the principle of freedom to provide services at least in certain circumstances for the following reasons: first, the Advocate-General observes generally at point 81 'It is clear from this that the objective 'to make rules relating to organization, qualification and professional ethics, supervision and liability in order to ensure that the ultimate consumers of legal services and the sound administration may justify a restriction on the freedom to provide services'. Second, in footnote 77 of his opinion, the Advocate General clearly links the question of maximum legal fees to objective of ensuring equal access to the courts: 'Also the question of maximum fees is more complex and delicate than minimum fees. In particular with regard to their consequences for equal access to courts'. Third, he observes at paragraph 80:

> However, it is not clear how the fixing of minimum fees helps to ensure equal access to courts for all citizens. On the contrary, as the Commission stated at

---

47.   R. Van den Bergh & Y. Montangie, 'Theory and Evidence and the Regulation of the Latin Notary Profession' Erasmus Competition and Regulation Institute, Erasmus University–Rotterdam, ECRI Report 0604, June 2006, op. cit., at p. 60.

the hearing, if that were the objective of the Italian legislation in question in the main proceedings, it would on be necessary to fix maximum fees in order to prevent the level of fees from exceeding a certain threshold.

Fourth, with regard to conditional fees, the Advocate General notes at paragraph 94:

Also, with regards the justification based on access to the courts, the possibility of fixing the success fees might on the contrary, improve such access by enable parties who have no financial resources to have access to the courts with the risk being borne by the lawyer. In some cases it is even the existence of success fees which makes it possible to bring a class action.

Fifth, the Advocate General notes at paragraph 80:

However it is not clear how the fixing of minimum fees helps to ensure equal access to courts for all citizens. On the contrary, as the Commission state at the hearing, if that were the objective of the Italian legislation in question, in the main proceedings, it would only be necessary to fix maximum fees in order to prevent the level of fees from exceeding a certain threshold.

Finally, it is useful to consider the conclusions of van den Bergh: 'A maximum fee schedule may be helpful in dealing with the problems of the moral hazard. Since a consumer of professional services, by lack of complete information cannot estimate the desired quality level, a professional may be included to provide services of too high a quality and charge excessive fees even if his client would be adequately served with a lower quality at a lower price. A maximum fee schedule may protect consumers against such excessive charges'.

Therefore, it is concluded that a strict interpretation of *Arduino* establishes that a State implemented and controlled policy to fix maximum legal fees for in court proceedings or extra court consultations does not constitute a breach of EC Art. 10 and 81; second, the Advocate-General suggests in *Cipolla* that both he and the Commission feel that in certain circumstances the fixing of maximum fees would constitute a justifiable economic restriction necessary in order to facilitate in certain cases access to justice. Further it would seem that support could be found in the observation made by the European Commission correspond to the observations attributed thereto by the Advocate General.

E.   CONSEQUENCES OF *ARDUINO* AND *WOUTERS* CONCERNING REGULATION OF LEGAL SERVICES IN ENGLAND

It would seem that at present there are at least two possible methods of State regulation of legal fees in England which could come within the parameters of *Wouters*: the first would be through a regulatory body as might result from the studies of Sir David Clementi.[48] The second might be through the Civil Justice Council provided that either or both complied with the ECJ case law in *Arduino* and *Wouters*. With respect to regulation of the legal profession in the UK in relation to the EC competition regulations, advisers to Sir David Clementi were of the following opinion:

> 17. We are asked to consider on the assumption that the promotion of competition was one of the objectives which could underpin the regulatory regime what impact the judgments of the European Court of Justice in case C-309/99 *Wouters* and Case C-35/99 *Arduino* might have on that objective.

In those two cases the Court distinguished between cases where rules of professional conduct were to be considered as State measures and there they were to be considered as decisions of association of undertaking. In the former case (the rules for setting legal fees in Italy considered in *Arduino*), the Court found that they were State measures and consequently that the competition rules for undertakings, that is EC Articles 81 and 82, did not apply. This was on the basis that the State laid down the general principles and retained substantial decision making power and power of control. In the latter case (the rules of the Dutch Bar in *Wouters*) the Court found that the rules were subject to the competition rules applicable to undertakings. The distinction is not clear cut as can be seen from the facts of the two cases. If the competition aspect of the regulatory regime adopted is covered by the principles set out in *Wouters*, the competition principles would apply automatically by virtue of the application of Art. 81 or Ch.1 of the Competition Act 1998. If however, the competition aspect of the regime is covered by the principles of Arduino, it would be perfect possible to enshrine the objective of the promotion of competition by requiring that the rules be scrutinized by the Office of Fair Trading prior to their adoption with that objective in mind.[49]

It is noted that the Civil Justice Council in its report, Improved Access to Justice,[50] recommended that a 'costs council' be established. It is not clear at this point whether such a body would fulfil the criterion established in the *Arduino* and *Wouters* cases. Notwithstanding, the Council makes the following recommendation:

> Recommendation 20: 'A costs council should be established to oversee the introduction, implementation and monitoring of reforms we recommend and in particular to establish and review the recoverable fixed fees in the fast track and guideline hourly rates between the parties in the multi-track. Membership in the costs council should include representatives of the leading stake holder

---

48. Sir David Clementi, Report of the Review of the Regulatory Framework for Legal Services in England and Wales, Dec 2004; <www.legal-services-review.org.uk/content/report/index.htm>.
49. Opinion of Slaughter & May for Sir David Clementi <www.legal-services.org.uk/content/report-app.pdf>.
50. Civil Justice Council, Improved Access to Justice: Report and Recommendations: August 2005; <www.costsdebate.civiljusticecouncil.gov.uk>.

organizations involved in the funding and payment of costs and should be chaired by a member of the judiciary'.

F.   APPLICATION OF THE EC DOCTRINE OF
             EFFECTIVENESS TO METHODS OF COST
             CONTROL IN THE CPR

As noted earlier, the Clear Car establishes that the principle of effectiveness applies to the matter of costs. Accordingly, it is appropriate to consider how this principle might apply to the matter to the issue of cost in order to ensure the effective enforcement of EC Articles 81 and or 82: in short, it is appropriate to consider the types of possible methods of cost control which might be required in order to ensure effective enforcement of the EC competition regulations.

The first possible method would be that proposed by the Civil Justice Council (CJC) in its report 'Improved Access to Justice'. The CJC recommends at page 26 the following methods to improve control of costs:

> With regard to estimates, cost capping and budgeting as a variety of mechanisms for controlling costs, the CJC is of the view that:
> – Costs in the person injury cases in the Fast Track should be controlled by extending the predictable costs regime;
> – Costs in non personal injury cases in the Fast Track and Multi-Track cases below GB 1 million costs capping and budgeting should not apply unless the court order otherwise;
> – In Multi-Track cases below GB1 million costs should be controlled by estimates with strengthened sanctions;
> – There should be a rebutable presumption for costs budgeting and capping in Multi-Track cases above GB 1 million;
> – In Multi-Track cases above GB 1 million where the costs are likely to be very significant, costs budgeting / capping is appropriate as a means of control and proportionality.

The Civil Justice Council further recommends with respect to the extension of the Fast Track predictable fixed costs regime that:

> Recommendation 2: 'Fast Track for personal injuries be increased to GB 25,000 with an opt in for cases up to GB 50,000'.
>   Recommendation 3: 'Predictable Costs currently restricted to Road Traffic Accident cases below GB 10,000 be extended to include all personal injury cases in the increased Fast Track and should include fixed costs from the pre-action protocol steps through the post issue process and including trial with an escape route for exceptional cases. Fixed success fee and fixed guidelines ATE premiums and fixed guideline disbursements should also be part of the scheme'.

Recommendation 5: 'Non personal injury cases can be included in Recommendation 2'.

The CJC apparently motivates its recommendation for the extension of the system of fixed costs by reason of its beneficial effect on the development of the After The Event (ATE) insurance premium market. The CJC observes at page 18 of its report:

> In a post legal aid environment where conditional fees are the main means of bringing a claim, a strong ATE market that receives premium income in large numbers of lower value claims is vital to provide underwriting support for ATE insurance of medium and large claims. Access to Justice can only be achieved through the mechanism of the ATE supported by conditional fees on the basis that the 'many have to pay for the few'. The delicate balance of this crucially important economic equation will be assisted by widening the scope of predictable costs in person injury claims to include more claims at the lower end value. This can be readily achieved by extending the Fast Track limit from GB 15,000 to GB 25,000 for person injuries.

Accordingly, it would seem that the recommendations of the CJC are of two types: first, fixed fees, and second, cost capping. However, it is to be noted that the fixed fees apply only to party to party fees. The question is whether the doctrine of effectiveness may apply so as to require the regulation of party to solicitor fees or out of court fees. It would seem that the doctrine of effectiveness in the sense of requiring both minimum and adequate implementation of EC Articles 81 and 82 may require the introduction of fixed maximum fees for both in and out of court lawyer's fees. This is particularly the case where the prospect of high legal fees, notably out of court legal fees, may dissuade a potential litigant from enforcing his rights pursuant to EC Articles 81 and 82 notably in a free-standing action. In such a situation it would seem that the effect of the current costs regime is to render impossible if not exceedingly difficult the enforcement of EC law and notably EC Articles 81 and 82. However, it is first useful to consider the objections to the extension of the fixed fees to solicitor own client or out of court fees. In this regard Peysner[51] observes:

> The indemnity rule means that between parties the costs are discounted against and can never be more than the costs charged by the solicitor to his own client. In practise clients are often advices that they will be unable to recover all of their costs. In principle this would complete the cost capping scheme because otherwise the solicitor can simply shift excessive costs over the cap to their client thus defeating the overall requirement of proportionality. However, while the right to obtain costs from the loser springs from a court order, the solicitor's charges to a client are based upon a retainer. In many cases this may be an academic point as the client is unable to pay but in complex multi track matter involving commercial clients, the temptation to pass onto to the client and avoid the discipline which the court wishes to impose may be high.

---

51. J. Peysner, 'Predictability and Budgeting', (2004) CJQ (23), 15 at p. 23.

In practise this may be more difficult than it appears. If the client fails to agree to accept liability for the balance this can be tested by a Solicitors Act detailed assessment . . . If the client has given informed consent in advance to pay a deficiency that is purely a matter between the solicitor and client.

Accordingly, Peysner advocates post litigation assessment by the professional body and secondly, apparently by market forces. Zander[52] implicitly criticizes limitation of fees to simply party to party costs in observing the following:

Another critical question is whether appropriately fixed costs would really bring down the costs of litigation as opposed to merely allowing the unsuc- cessful defendant (often effectively an insurance company) to pay less by way of fixed costs. Woolf recognised that fixed costs would not necessarily prevent lawyers from charging their own clients more. But he hoped that restricting the amount that could be recovered by the loser would result in lawyers not charging their clients more; It is difficult to see that basis for this hope other than wish fulfilment . . . Fixed costs as proposed by Woolf Middleton and the Government only control recovery of costs from the other side.

Accordingly, the control must include out of court costs as well. Further it is not clear that Peysner's method of cost control for out of court costs would be justified for the following reasons: first, such a system would be apparently based upon a hourly method of calculation: following the criticism of Lord Hoffman, Lord Woolf and Zuckerman, it is less than apparent that such a method of calculation serves to reduce costs: rather, it can serve to increase costs. Second, following Lord Woolf, the European Commission report on professional services, and Peacock, it would appear that there exists a market for legal services in which the asymmetry of information of such is that regulation is required.

It is submitted that in English law, the regulation of legal costs which is required must fulfil two requirements. On one hand, calculation of legal fees on a basis other than exclusively hourly basis as for example by fixing fees on a basis which is proportional to the amount of value in issue. On the other hand extension of this method of calculation to both client own solicitor or out of court costs and party to party costs. Moreover, it would appear appropriate to extend this tariff in order to ensure effective access in particular to the non-repeat clients identified in the European Commission in litigation of up to GB one million on the multi-track. Arguably this extension would be necessary in order to ensure that the category of possibly one off litigants, namely, individuals and small businesses would be able to effectively enforce their rights pursuant to EC Articles 81 and or 82 in terms of legal costs. In order to diminish any possible anti-competitive effects it may be appropriate to ensure that the Court is able to exercise its discretion to ensure that in the particular case, the aggregate amount of fees is indeed proportionate to the value involved.

---

52. M. Zander QC, 'The Government's Plans for Civil Justice' (1998) MLR 382, op. cit. at p. 386.

It would appear that following CPR 44. 3(1)–(5), the Court enjoys such discretion to depart from the fixed schedule. Finally, it would appear that following *Arduino*, *AMOK* and the opinion in *Cepolla*, it is possible in terms of ECJ case law to extend the system of fixed fees so as to include maximum fees for not only in court costs but also out of court fees. This extension would ensure that the system of conditional fees would function effectively. Thereby the legal certainty which will result from the fixed legal maximum amounts will provide that the ATE fee market may develop with respect to enforcement of EC competition because the fee disbursements will become predictable. It is clear however, that the establishment of the fee structure must be carried in a manner which conforms with *Wouters* and *Arduino*. In this regard, it may be that the method for the establishment by fixed fees as currently provided in the CPR could be carried out with the additional protection that they be scrutinized for anti-competitive effect by the Office of Fair Trading prior to formal adoption.

Interestingly, Zander[53] an opponent of the Case Management system embodied by the CPR would seem nevertheless to admit the necessity of system of fixed fees although doubting whether it could be implemented politically at present. 'The trouble as Lord Hoffmann convincingly point out is that however carefully they watch the developments, the cost judges, the circuit judges and the Court of Appeal do not and will not have the tools to do this job. Nor is it likely that the Lord Chancellor will accept Lord Hoffmann's suggestion that the government should intervene to regulate the field'.

Arguably, therefore the doctrine of effectiveness which may require the government to regulate the fees in the manner which has been suggested. In conclusion, it would seem that the CPR principles of proportionality and ensuring access to justice coupled with the EC doctrine of effectiveness would required the current CPR system of fixed maximum costs to be extended in the following manner. First to litigation involving amounts of up to GB1 million; second, to litigation concerning EC Articles 81 and or 82; third, that this system continue to be subject to judicial discretion as is currently the case; fourth, that the system of fixed costs be extended to include both in court and out of court provision of legal services; and finally, that this protection be limited at least in first instance to two categories of litigants: individuals and small businesses.

Finally, as to the actual form, it is to be noted that variations on the system of control of legal costs as presented could be envisaged in order to obtain the most effective solution. Zuckerman[54] has proposed two possibilities in this regard:

> 21. Fixed costs regime may take a number of forms but they have one common feature: lawyers are expected to provide litigation services at a fixed cost. That is, lawyers are expected to provide litigation services at a fixed cost.

---

53. M. Zander QC, 'Where are we now with Conditional Fees' (2002) (26) MLR 919 at p. 930.
54. A.A.S. Zuckerman, 'Devices for Controlling the Cost of Ligitation,' paper presented to the Woolf Inquiry Team; Access to Justice: available on (1996) Journal of Information Law & Technology, <www2.warwick.ac.uk/fac/soc/law/elj/jilt/1996_1/woolf/costs>.

22. There are several ways in which a fixed costs regime could operate: a) a fixed fee for the litigation as a whole.

23. The fixed fee can be determined as a general rule for all case. For instance we could have a pre-determined scale of fees under which legal fees are fixed as a proportion of the value of the subject matter in dispute.

24. Alternatively the fixed fees can be determined on a case by case basis.

25. There is also the possibility of a combination of these two methods . The combined method would involve a pre-determined scale of fees the exact calculation of which could then be done on a case by case basis. For instance, the scale would determine claims for 10–20 K which would be between 10–20 per cent leaving the exact level to the judge in charge of the case.

b) Fees fixed by reference to procedural activity.

26. Under this system the legal fees for each procedural step are determined in advance as a matter of rule. A system of this kind exists in the county court under Scale 1 costs (see The County Court Practise 19995, PP 1622, 1663) Under Scale 1, a certain sum is payable for preparation of documents for interlocutory proceedings, for preparation for trial and so on. Further, so much is payable per typed page.

27. This system may be operated with a ceiling so that costs may not exceed a certain proportion of the value of the claim or some other pre-determined sum. Or it can operate with no ceiling unlike now however, there would be a limit on the procedural activity.

c) Mixed systems

28. One can have a mixed system, consisting of fixed costs for the preliminary stage and activity costs for the stages following the case management conference. The costs for serving a statement of claim and defence and preparing for the case management conference will be fixed by regulation (possibly as a proportion of the value of the claim). Thereafter, costs will be charged on the activity basis in respect of the activities sanctioned by the procedural judge.

29. Such a system will obviate the danger of front loading and at the same time allow some flexibility subject to a ceiling in the preparation for trial'.

Furthermore, it is to be observed that a system of fixing of fees for both party to party and client own solicitor is apparently not unknown in both Northern Ireland and in Scotland.[55] In so far as those systems could practically be used to enforce the EC competition rules in those respective jurisdictions it would seem that the principle of non-discrimination would require a level playing field be established

---

55. Civil Justice Council Improved Access to Justice: Founding Options and Proportionate Costs: Report and Recommendations August (2005) op. cit. at p. 90; 'Until 1992, the Court regulated not only the level of fees recoverable from a paying party but also the level of fees a solicitor could charge his client in litigation. Since that time it is only the inter parties which are regulated by the court. Solicitors are free to charge their clients at whatever hourly rate they consider appropriate. The rates recommended by the Law Society of Scotland are generally in excess of the prescribed judicial rate'.

so as to ensure equally effective enforcement of the EC Articles 81 and 82 in terms of cost in England. Legal costs are also fixed in varying degrees in Germany.[56]

Beyond the amount of GB 1 million arguably the principle of effectiveness would not require intervention as the clients will be able to exercise market power to control costs through budget agreements.

---

56. N. Cahill, Comparative Research Paper on Legal Costs, <www.justice.ie/80256E010039C5AF/ vWeb/+1JUSQ6L4LJS-en/$File/ComparResearch.pdf> February 2005 at p. 71: 'The Rechtsan-waltvergultingsgesetz/RVG/ was introduced to regulate the remuneration of lawyers/ The RVG contains statutory scales that can be charged for legal services; It also allows the lawyer the option of charging negotiated fees; However the negotiated fee cannot be lower than the statutory minimum . . . These can be fixed fees or fees within a fixed range. Fees within a fixed range may depend upon the value of the dispute. The level of these fees are set out in a fee scale in an annex to the RVG and are called *Satznehmengebürhen*. Alternatively, a minimum and a maximum amount may be prescribed and these are referred to as *Betragsrahmengebühren*. When the legal services do not involve court proceedings, the fees were completely liberalized as of 1 July 2004. The RVG introduced a provision permitting lawyers to enter into agreements regarding such fees. If no agreement is formed, fees will be calculated on the basis of civil law. By way of example, if the client is a consumer and there is no fee agreement, the lawyer's fee for advice and legal expertise not involving court proceedings must not exceed Euros 250. The fee for the initial legal advice to a consumer in such circumstances must be no higher than Euro 190. For non-litigation related legal services the RVG does set a fee range scale (*Geschäftsgebuhr*). This . . . Is 0.5 – 2.5 of the fee scale. However, the RVG specifically state that a lawyer can only charge a fee which is higher than 1.3 if his legal work was extensive or difficult . . . There are two types of legal fees for litigation related services: fees for proceedings (*Verfahrensgebühr*) and a fee for the Court hearings and meetings with the lawyers of the opposing party (*Terminsgebühr*). It should be recalled that legal costs consist of Court fees and disbursements on the one hand and out of court costs on the other. The out of court costs consist of layers fees and disbursements and the parties' other cots. As regards lawyer's fees, the unsuccessful party is only liable to pay the opposing lawyer's fees as set out by the RVG and not any higher level of fees which the opponent may have agreed to pay his lawyer. The costs that can be recovered are those costs which were necessary for brining or defending an action and these are to be kept as low as possible'.

Chapter 7

English Interim Injunctions and Representative Actions

A.   INTERIM ORDERS PURSUANT TO THE CPR

The Ashurst[1] UK report on damages actions states that applications may be made for interim injunctions to the ordinary courts[2] in order to enforce EC competition law following the principles of *American Cyanamid*.[3] Bellamy & Child[4] similarly observe that 'In cases where the claimant seeks an interim injunction to enforce his contractual rights and the defendant alleges that the agreement is prohibited by Art. 81, the English court will apply the usual principles relating to a serious issue to be tried and the balance of convenience'. However, it is submitted that it is appropriate, in light of the criticisms of that case, to consider the following two matters: first, whether the guidelines of *American Cyanamid* indeed constitute the most appropriate basis for granting an interim injunction; and second, whether the ECJ doctrine of effective enforcement may in some way affect the choice of the guidelines or principles upon which the interim injunction is granted.

For the purposes of this analysis, one might define an interim injunction as follows: a provisional order granted by a court to an applicant who seeks to protect

---

1. M. Clough QC & A. McDougal, UK Report for the European Commission Study on Damages (2004) at p. 9 'Infringement of Art. 81 and 82 can be subject to applications for injunctive relief at the suit of an injured party before the Courts. The onus is on the party to satisfy the basic conditions which need to be satisfied if a court is to exercise this discretionary remedy: see *American Cyanamid*'. <www.europa.eu>.
2. Infringements of EC Art. 81 and or 82 can be the subject of injunctive relief before the ordinary civil courts but not the Competition Appeal Tribunal.
3. *American Cyanamid Co. v. Ethicon* (1975) 1 AC 396.
4. Bellamy & Child, *European Community Law of Competition* (5th edn, London, Sweet & Maxwell, 2001) p. 809; see also footnote 2 on that page 809.

a legal enforceable right either from actual or apprehended infringement by the defendant prior to a full judicial determination of the matter by means of a full trial. While the historical origin of the interim injunction is Equity, the court now obtains its power and discretion to grant or to refuse the order pursuant to S 31 of the Supreme Court Act 1981 which is implemented by CPR 25 which provides:

> CPR 25(1) The Court may grant the following interim remedies:
> an interim injunction
>
> . . .
>
> According to Lord Bridge in *Factortame*[5] the purpose of the injunction is to protect the rights of the applicants. In granting the order the Court must be vigilant to avoid creating harm to the parties.

Therefore, it is useful to relate the purpose of the injunction to the choice between what effectively constitutes two different sets of principles or guidelines which may serve as the basis for granting an interim injunction pursuant to CPR 25. The first set of guidelines uses the merits of the case in terms of the law and the facts; and second set of guidelines consists in the purely utilitarian principle of the balance of convenience: that is, who will suffer the greater harm if the injunction is either granted or refused. The recent history of the granting of interlocutory relief is one in which the use of the principle based upon the merits of the case has been in large measured reduced through the influence of Lord Diplock in the case of *American Cyanamid*. Indeed, in order to avoid the difficulties attendant upon evaluating legal merits exclusively on affidavit evidence, Lord Diplock[6] sought to eliminate the use of the guidelines based on the merits of the case by substituting those of the balance of convenience. His lordship observed:

> The object of the interlocutory injunction is to protect the plaintiff against injury by violation of his right to which he could not be adequately compensate in damages recoverable in the action if the uncertainty were resolved in his favour at the trial; but the plaintiff's need for such protection must be weighed against the corresponding need of the defendant to be protected against injury resulting from his having been prevented from exercising his own legal rights from which he could not be adequately compensated under the plaintiff's undertaking in damages if the uncertainty were resolved in the defendants

---

5. *R v. Secretary of State for Transport exp Factortame (No 2)* (1991) 1 AC 603 at 659: Lord Bridge states: 'If in the end, the claimant succeeds in a case where interim relief has been refused, he will have suffered an injustice. If, in the end, he fails in a case where interim relief has been granted, injustice will have been done to the other party. The objective that underlies the principles by which the discretion is to be guided must always be to ensure that the Court shall choose the course, which in all circumstances, appears to offer the best prospect that an eventual injustice will be avoided or minimised'.
6. American Cyanamid Co v. Ethicon (1975) 1 AC 396 op. cit. at 408 and 510 respectively wherein Lord Diplock held 'It is not part of the court's function at this stage of the litigation to try to resolve conflicts of evidence on affidavit as to facts on which the claims of either party may ultimately depend nor to decide difficult questions of law which call for detailed argument and mature considerations. These are matters to be dealt with at the trial'.

favour at the trial. The court must weigh one need against another and determine where 'the balance of convince' lies.

However, perhaps most significantly, Lord Diplock added what seemed to constitute a restriction on the court's discretion to grant interim relief:

> It is no part of the court's function at this stage of the litigation to try to resolve
> conflicts of evidence on affidavit as to facts on which the claims of either party
> may ultimately depend nor to decide difficult questions of law which call for
> detailed argument and mature considerations. There are matters to be dealt
> with at the trial.

Zuckerman[7] observes:

> This statement was later interpreted to mean that beyond ensuring that the
> applicant had an arguable case, the strength of the parties claims and their
> respective chances of success on the merits had no role to play in the exercise
> of the jurisdiction...Criticism of the *American Cyanamid* case was not
> slow to come...More significantly, no sooner was judgment in *American
> Cyanamid* delivered than the courts started discovering exception to the
> principle that a consideration of the merits should be confined to the question
> whether the applicant has shown a serious question to be tried.

One of the first exceptions was defamation. It was decided that *American
Cyanamid* did not affect the old rule whereby an injunction would not be granted
in defamation proceedings if the defendant proposes to plead justification except
where the statement in question is obviously false and therefore libellous. The
reason given was that the freedom of speech should not be easily restricted before
a claimant has proved his case of defamation at trial.[8] Further, the *American
Cyanamid* principles did not apply where the facts of the case were clear or
where there was not material dispute about them.[9]

Moreover, Lord Diplock did not exclude the possibility of considering the
merits in the case where the balance of convenience did not suffice to make an
assessment of the appropriateness of granting or withholding an injunction:

> If the extent of the incompensable disadvantage to each party would not differ
> widely, it may not be improper to take into account in tipping the balance the

---

7. A.A.S. Zuckerman, *Civil Procedure* (London, Lexis Nexis, 2003) at p. 277.
8. *Bonnard v. Perryman* (1891) 2 Ch 269 at 284 per Lord Coleridge CJ 'The right of free speech is
   one which it is for the public interest that individuals should possess and indeed, that they should
   exercise without impediment so long as no wrongful act is done; and unless an alleged libel is
   untrue, there is no wrong committed; but, on the contrary, often a very wholesome act is performed in the publication and repetition of an alleged libel. Until it is clear than alleged libel is
   untrue it is not clear than any right at all has been infringed; and the importance of leaving free
   speech unfettered is a strong reason in cases for libel for dealing most cautiously and warily with
   the granting of interim injunctions'. See subsequently *Bestobell Paints Ltd v. Bigg* (1975) FSR
   421; *Cambridge Nutrition v. BBC* (1990) 3 All ER 523 (CA).
9. *Smith v. Inner London Education Authority* (1978) 1 All ER 411; *David (Lawrence) Ltd v. Ashton*
   (1991) 1 All ER 385 at 393.

relative strength of each party's case as revealed by the affidavit evidence
adduced at the hearing of the application . . . this should be done only where it
is apparent on the facts disclosed by the evidence as to which there is no
credible dispute that the strength of one party's case is disproportionate to
that of the other party.[10]

A further long standing exception exists where the granting of the interim injunction is likely to dispose finally of the dispute. Lord Diplock recognized in a
subsequent case, *NWL Ltd v. Woods*[11] that where 'the grant or the refusal of the
interim injunction will have the practical effect of putting an end to the
action . . . the degree of likelihood that the plaintiff would have succeeded in establishing his right to an injunction if the action had gone to trial is a facto to be
brought into the balance'.

Moreover, a ban on the use of the merits has never applied to the granting of
mandatory as opposed to prohibitory injunctions. The granting of a mandatory
injunction has always required that the merits of the case be examined. This situation was reaffirmed in *Bryanston*[12] which was decided subsequent to *American
Cyanamid*.

Additionally, it is submitted that the case *R v. Secretary of State for Transport
exp Factortame (No 2)*[13] has further restricted the applicability of *American
Cyanamid* beyond the exceptions considered thus far: in short, this case establishes
that *American Cyanamid* effectively constitutes a guideline which expands the
court's discretion to grant an injunction where the merits of the case cannot be
satisfactorily discerned on affidavit evidence. In *Factortame* the House of Lords
was asked to grant an interim injunction against the Crown in order to restrain it

---

10. *American Cyanamid Co. v. Ethicon* (1975) AC 396 op. cit. at p. 409 and 511 respectively.
11. *NWL Ltd v. Woods* (1979) 3 All ER 614 (1979) at 626; RC Simpson in 'A Case Note on NWL',
     (1980) MLR (43) at 325 states that the prohibitory injunction in Scotland known as the interdict
     does not use the *American Cyanamid* principles: 'Since Cyanamid does not apply to Scotland,
     Lord Fraser concluded that the reason S 17(2) was not apply to Scotland was that it is unnec-
     essary since 17(2) merely established the existing position in Scotland law where the practise is
     to try the relative strength of each party's case at the interlocutory state (Lord Fraser p. 880–81'.
     In considering whether the interim interdict should be grated it would seem that Scottish court
     firstly determines whether a *prima facie* case has been made out. In determining whether a
     prima facie case exists the court will investigate the merits of the case: *Malden Timber Ltd v.
     McLeish* (1992) SLT 727. It is submitted that it would be appropriate for the English court to
     consider the legal basis upon which the Scottish interim interdict is granted along with other
     principles which underlie English civil procedure in order to ensure adequate as opposed to
     minimal enforcement of EC Art. 81 and 82 in terms of an interim injunction.
12. *Bryanston Finance Ltd v. de Vries (No2)* (1976) Ch. 63.
13. In the earlier (or first) judgment, *R v. Secretary of State for Transport exp Factortame Ltd* (1990)
     2 AC 85 the House of Lords had decided that there was no jurisdiction to grant an interim
     injunction against the Crown or to suspend the coming into force of an Act of Parliament. The
     matter was referred to the ECJ which decided that the English courts did have the power to grant
     interim injunctions in support of EC law and could accordingly order the suspension of an Act of
     Parliament. The matter was remitted to the House of Lords for a decision as to whether on the
     facts an interim injunction ought to be granted pending litigation in the ECJ concerning the Act
     of Parliament.

from giving effect to an Act of Parliament which denied foreign-owned British fishing boats the right to fish under British fishing quotas. It was clear that both parties were exposed to loss from an unfavourable decision at the interim state. If it emerged at the end of the day that the law suspended by the interim injunction was in fact valid, the public interest would have been harmed notably that of the British fisherman whose share of the quotas would have been diminished by the applicant's fishing. Similarly, if an injunction were refused and it eventuated that the law were invalid, the applicants would have suffered serious loss for which they would not be entitled to compensation. As Lord Bridge remarked: 'the injustices (which each party was likely to suffer from an unfavourable interim decision) are so different in kind that (it is) . . . very difficult to weight the one against the other'.

His lordship concluded that 'in the circumstances . . . the most logical course in seeking a decision least likely to occasion injustice is to make the best prediction we can of the final outcome and give to that prediction decisive weight in resolving the interlocutory issue'. In the event the House of Lords granted an interim injunction which suspended the act in question because it was likely that judgment in the ECJ would be favourable to the applicants. Because the issue involved law, namely, the validity of an act of Parliament in relation to EC law, Lord Diplock's principles were not departed from and there was no assessment of the parties' respective chances based on affidavit evidence. Although the House of Lords did stress the continuity of the principles of *American Cyanamid*, nevertheless it did minimize the restriction on evaluating the merits of the case. Perhaps most significantly, Lord Goff stated that the primary purpose of *American Cyanamid* was as follows: 'to remove a fetter which appeared to have been imposed in certain previous cases, viz. that a party seeking an interlocutory injunction had to establish a *prima facie* case for substantive relief'.[14]

Finally, the attempt to further reduce the application of the American Cyanamid ban on the examination of the merits of the case was continued in Series 5 Software[15] by Laddie J. who held as follows:

> In my view Lord Diplock did not intend by the last quoted passage to exclude consideration of the strength of the cases in most applications for interlocutory relief. It appears to me that what is intended is that the court should not attempt to solve difficult issues of fact or law on an application for interlocutory relief. If, on the other hand, the court is able to come to a view as to the strength of the party's case on the credible evidence, then it can do so . . . if it is apparent from that material (the affidavits) that one party's case is much stronger than the other's then that is a matter the court should not ignore. To suggest otherwise

---

14. *R v. Secretary of State for Transport (No2)* (1991) 1 AC 603 at 660; his lordship also observed at p. 671: 'In the end the matter is for the discretion of the court taking into consideration all of the circumstances of the case. Even so the court should not restrain a public authority by interim injunction from enforcing an apparently authentic law unless it is satisfied having regard to all the circumstances that the challenge to validity of the law is *prima facie* so firmly based as to justify so exceptional a course being taken'.
15. *Series 5 Software v. Philip Clarke* (1996) 1 All ER 853.

would be to exclude from consideration an important factor and such exclusion would fly in the face of the flexibility advocated earlier in *American Cyanamid*. As Lord Diplock points out in Hoffmann–La Roche, one of the purposes of the cross-undertaking in damages is to safeguard the defendant if this preliminary view of the strength of the plaintiff's case proves to be wrong.[16]

Accordingly, it is submitted that these exceptions undermine the principle established in *American Cyanamid*.[17] In short, the exceptions establish that there remains a need for an examination of the merits remains irrespective of the type of injunction sought: that is, whether or not there is a mandatory or a prohibitory, whether or not the injunction is likely or not to dispose of the issues finally, whether or not the facts of the case are clear as opposed to disputed or whether or not the factors of convenience are equally balanced between the parties.

1.   DOCTRINE OF EFFECTIVENESS

As noted, the application of the *American Cyanamid* principles is restricted to those situations which are not covered by the exceptional cases listed. It is also submitted that the preferred basis for the granting of the injunction is the 'merits of the case' as opposed to 'the balance of convenience' for two reasons: first, the speech of Lord Goff clearly establishes that the principles in *American Cyanamid* simply serve to extend the discretion of the court to grant an injunction: clearly, the merits of the case constitute the normal principles in what are termed the exceptional cases. Arguably, following Lord Goff, the court retains the discretion to grant injunctions even beyond those cases to ones involving difficult questions of law and fact but using if it wishes the principles of the balance of convenience. Following Laddie J., the court enjoys discretion even in such cases to use the principles based upon the merits of the case: that is 'if, on the other hand, the court is able to come to a view as to the strength of the party's case on the credible evidence, then it can do so . . . if it is apparent from that material (the

---

16. *Series 5 Software v. Philip Clarke* (1996) 1 All ER 853, *ibid.* at 865.
17. A.A.S. Zuckerman, *Civil Procedure* (London, Lexis Nexis, 2003) op. cit. argues at 277 'Ignoring the probability of the success limb may therefore result in the interim decision increasing rather than decreasing the likelihood of harm pending proceedings'; see *generally* Prof. A. Keay, 'Whither American Cyanamid?: Interim Injunctions in the 21st Century (2004) 23 CJQ 132; see also *GMG Radio Holdings Ltd v. Tokyo Project Ltd* (2005) EWHC 2188, (2006) FSR 15 at paragraph 24 in which Kitchin J. specifically considers the merits of the case in the context of applying generally the *American Cyanamid* guidelines as opposed to restricting his inquiry to the guideline of a serious issue to be tried: 'Taking into account all of these considerations, I have reached the conclusion on the materials before me that the claimants will have considerable difficulty in making good their claim in passing off at trial. In my judgment the risk of deception and confusion occurring is relatively low. Nevertheless, particularly in light of the statements made by Mr Doyle and Mr Brooks, and the results of the survey the claimants have done enough to establish that there is an issue to be tried'.

affidavits) that one party's case is much stronger than the other's then that is a matter the court should not ignore'.[18] Second, the special cases themselves where the use of the merits of the case are required undermine the necessity of using the principles of the balance of convenience in other cases. Third the use of the merits of the case corresponds to the method described by Lord Bridge as the one least likely to cause injustice: that is, to ensure fairness for both parties and the rights of the defence: 'the most logical course in seeking a decision least likely to occasion injustice is to come the best prediction we can of the final outcome and give to that prediction decisive weight in resolving the interlocutory issue'.[19]

Further, with respect to the granting of interim prohibitory injunctions pursuant to CPR 25 for the enforcement of EC Articles 81 and or 82 it would seem that the following conditions would apply. First, where the facts of the litigation are such that they are covered by one of the special cases noted earlier, then arguably the court will use the principles consisting in examining the merits of the case contained in the affidavit evidence. If however, the litigation is not covered by one the special cases then arguably the doctrine of effectiveness might intervene in order to assist the court in justifying the decision to apply the principles based also on the merits of the case as opposed to the balance of convenience for the following reason: one notes that neither the use of the principles of the merits of the case nor the balance of convenience makes the enforcement of EC Articles 81 and or 82 impossible or exceedingly difficulty. It is submitted that the use of these principles can lead to enforcement which is adequately effective as opposed to minimally effective.[20] Indeed, it would appear that the use of the principles of the merits of the case overall lead, overall, to more adequately effective enforcement of EC Articles 81 and or 82 than will the balance of convenience for the following reason: the criterion of the merits of the case is less likely to cause injustice and therefore more likely to ensure fairness between the parties because it upholds two of the underlying principles of both English and EC law, namely, respect for both the rights of the defence and legal certainty. In the instant case it is submitted that the possible use of the doctrine of effectiveness to assist the court in choosing between the two competing sets of

---

18. *Series 5 Software v. Philip Clarke* (1996) 1 All ER 853 op. cit. at 857.
19. *R v. Secretary of State for Transport, exp Factortame* (No.2) (1991) 1 AC 603 op. cit. at 659 *sub nom Factortame Ltd v. Secretary of State for Transport (No 2)* (1991) 1 All ER 70 at 108.
20. G. Deburca 'National Procedural Rules and Remedies: the Hanging Approach of the Court of Justice' in J. Lonbay & A Biondi (eds), *Remedies for Breach of EC Law* (London, Wiley, 1997) 37 at 45 observes: 'On the other hand as Advocate General Jacobs suggested in his opinion, this general balancing approach by the Court may be seen to reflect the principles of proportionality and subsidiarity. While it represents a move away from the tone of earlier rulings in which the Court expressed the principle of supremacy very strong and categorically, it does appear to be in more accordance with the current Community mood – political judicial and institutional of deference towards national choices and variations'. It is suggested that the intervention of the doctrine of effectiveness in order to choose between a more as opposed to a less effective solution does not represent a departure from the deference to 'national choices and variations' observed by De Burca: specifically, the 'choices' between the more effective as opposed to the less effective method of enforcement already exist within the system itself prior to the application of the doctrine of effectiveness.

principles goes beyond what might be termed minimally effective enforcement of the directly effective rights of EC Articles 81 and or 82. It, therefore, perhaps most clearly exemplifies the concept discussed earlier of adequately effective enforcement as opposed to minimally effective enforcement.

Before concluding, it is perhaps useful to consider the cases of *Zuckerfabrik*[21] and the *House of Lords Tobacco*[22] judgment with respect to the standard to be used by a national court when enforcing EC law. In *Zuckerfabrik* a reference had been made to the ECJ to ascertain under what conditions a national court could suspend the application of a regulation the validity of which was being examined by the ECJ. A restrictive interpretation of this judgment would lead to the following conclusion: following paragraph 27 of the judgment, the ECJ intervened so as to impose its own standards for granting an injunction on the national courts when the national courts operate in a function comparable to that of the ECJ when it grants an injunction to suspend the application of EC legislation the legality of which it reviews: it is necessary to bear in mind that only the ECJ can review the legality of EC legislation. The ECJ observed in paragraph 27 the following:

> Since the power of national courts to grant such supervision corresponds to the jurisdiction reserved to the Court of Justice by Art. 185 in the context of actions brought under Art. 173 those courts may grant such relief only on a condition which must be satisfied for the Court of Justice to allow an application to it for interim measures.

In paragraph 25 the ECJ observed that the national courts were free to choose their own rules of procedure.

> Paragraph 25: 'As regards the other conditions concerning suspension of enforcement of administrative measures, it must be observed that the rules of procedure of the courts are determined by the national law and that those conditions differ according to the national law governing them which may jeopardize the uniform application of Community law'.

Nevertheless, national courts when called upon to enforce Community law must follow paragraph 30 'ensure that full effect is given to Community law'.

> Paragraph 30: 'It should be added that a national court called upon to apply within the limits of jurisdiction, the provisions of Community law is under an obligation to ensure that full effect is given to Community law and consequently where there is some doubt to the validity of Community regulations to take account of the interest of the Community, namely, such regulations should not be set aside without proper guarantees'.

---

21. *Zuckerfabrik v. Commission* C-143/88 and C-92/89, (1991) ECR 415, <www.curia.europa.eu>.
22. *R v. Secretary of State for Health ex p Imperial Tobacco Ltd & others* House of Lords, Session 2000/01 Publications on Internet, 7 December 2000 <www.publications.parliament.uk/ pa/ id200001/1djugmt/jd/207/tobacc-1.htm>; see Court of Appeal judgment at: <www.hmcourt-service.gov.uk/judgmentsfiles /j460/tobacco5.htm> in date of 16 December 1999.

According to the ECJ, the essential problem is that the diversity in the procedure may undermine the effectiveness of the enforcement of Community notably through its lack of uniform application. Therefore, the enforcement of Community law by the national courts must be subject to the following conditions:

> Paragraph 26: 'Such uniform application is a fundamental requirement of the Community legal order. It therefore follows that the suspension of enforcement of administrative measures based upon a Community regulation whilst it is governed by national procedure law, in particular as regards the making and examination of the application must in all Member States be subject at the very least to conditions which are uniform so far as granting of such relief is concerned'.

Having thus held that the minimum conditions for effective enforcement of EC law by national rules of procedure is uniformity the ECJ simply applies without explanation the conditions which govern the granting of an interim measure in its own rules of procedure: as noted above in paragraph 27: 'those courts may grant relief only on conditions which must be satisfied for the Court of Justice to allow an application to it for interim measures'.

In paragraph 33 the ECJ established the principles which are to be obligatorily followed by a national court: 'It follows from the foregoing that the reply to the second part of the first question put to the Court by the Finanzgericht Hamburg must be that suspension of enforcement of a national measure adopted in the implementation of a Community regulation may be granted by a national court only'. If that Court entertains serious doubts as to the validity of the community measure and should the question of the validity of the contested measures not already have been brought before the Court itself refer that question to the Court, if there is urgency and a threat of serious and irreparable damage to the applicant and if the national court takes account of the Community's interest. The expression 'serious doubts' is taken to mean a strong case on the merits.[23]

It is unclear as to why the ECJ did not explicitly refer to other legal sources such as the rules of the Member States in order to establish a uniform standard for enforcement; or at a minimum, justify the choice of the standard provided by its own rule in relation to the standard which can be said to exist in the national rules.[24]

---

23. S. Moore, 'This test has strong similarities with the domestic law test – crucial issues both as a matter of domestic and EC law, are the strength of the legal challenge and the level of potential damages.... That is to say that an applicant must show a strong case on the merits and that it would suffer serious and irreparable harm if the relief were not granted'. <www.11kw.com/inex.php?category_id=6&art_id=76>.

24. Arguably, if the ECJ had explicitly considered the conditions which apply in the national legal systems they may have arrived at a conclusion which would have provided uniform efficacy without violating the principle of national procedural autonomy. In short standards which would perhaps be somewhat different from that of the interim relief granted in the ECJ but corresponding more generally to the rules in the national courts; see K. Laenaerts, 'Interlocking Legal Orders in the European Union and Comparative Law' (2003) 52 ICLQ 873 at 905–906, 'Whether the comparative law method is used to confront rules of

Accordingly, the judgment on this point would appear to lack legal certainty as to the application of the principles of effectiveness, non-discrimination and uniformity. Arguably, in *Zuckerfabrik*, the ECJ effectively eliminated the discretion enjoyed by the national courts under the principle of subsidiarity and its own case law to choose the substantive content of the rules of procedure to enforce EC law in conformity with the doctrine of effectiveness and non-discrimination. At a minimum, this position would seem to contravene the principles which the ECJ established for itself in Express Dairy[25] where it observed: 'in the regrettable absence of Community provisions harmonizing procedure and time limits, the Court finds that this situation entails differences in treatment on a Community scale. It is not for the Court to issue general rules of substance or procedural provisions which only the competent institution may adopt'.

Further, Dänzer-Vanotti[26] argues that the ECJ usurped the powers of the Council to establish uniform rules of procedure. In contrast, Apte[27] asserts that 'the Court did nothing more than fill a gap left by the Treaty as it has done traditionally since its land mark case of *van Gend en Loss*'. Indeed, Apte seeks to justify the ECJ's interventions as in the following:

> Leaving aside for the moment the obligation to refer questions of validity for a preliminary ruling show a rationale is closely connected to the Court's exclusive jurisdiction to declare Community acts invalid, it has been suggested that the uniform conditions equivalent to those applied by the Court itself under Art 242 and 243 of the Treaty are visibly drawn from common principles common to the law of the Member States (W. van Gerven Bridging

---

national law or to compare the Community legal order and one or more other legal orders (whether national or international) it is always inspired by the same objective: to uphold the rule of law in the Community legal order as prescribed in Article 220 EC. Its purpose is not just to fill lacunae in the Community construction, but rather, after having carefully "taken the pulse" of the national legal systems, to find the best solution in the "middle-line" or compromise solution, which should enjoy credibility and acceptability in the Member States and which will ensure the effectiveness of Community law. Depending on the circumstances, this solution – which is the fruit of a subtle putting into balance of the interests of the evolution of the Community and the acceptability of this evolution in the domestic legal orders – can take the form of a principle, a fundamental rights, an interpretation or a construction of Community law based on a legal concept sufficiently common to the Member States. In the absence of a 'fundis communis', the Community courts can develop an autonomous Community solution where they find contradictions in the national legal systems or may import into the Community legal order a 'proven national solution, or else may impose on a national legal order the obligation, within acceptable limits, to bear the "consequences of Community law' of its own internal choices".

25. Express Dairy Foods Ltd v. Intervention Board for Agricultural Produce, Case 130/79 [1980] ECR 1987.
26. W. Dänzer-Vanotti (1991), Der Gerichtshof der Europaïsichen Gemeinshaften beschränkt vorlaüfigen Rechstschutz (1991) *Betriebs-Berater* 1015 cited in P. Oliver, Interim Measures: Some Recent Developments, (1992) 29 CMLR 113.
27. S. Apte in 'Interim Measures in EC Law' (2003) EJCL Vol 2.7 <www.ejcl.org/72/art72-1 .html>.

the Gaps Between Community and National law: Towards Principles of Homogeneity (1995) CMLRev (32) 679 at p 688).

Notwithstanding, it would appear that there are some insuperable difficulties with the analysis presented by both Apte and van Gerven: first, the existence of the two different standards in English injunctions known as a 'serious issue to be tried' and a 'strong case on the merits', demonstrates that the principles within the Member States and in particular within the legal system of a single Member State may differ on this point: they are not necessarily identical or 'common'. Second, it is submitted that the fundamental problem with *Zukerfabrik* as previously noted is that it provides not for minimum standards but rather for absolute enforcement standards by eliminating the national court's discretion to modify those conditions or choose other conditions. In so doing, the ECJ effectively contradicts paragraph 25 of the judgment itself. Third, the ECJ in *Zuckerfabrik* specifically omits to indicate how the principle of uniformity is to be balanced with the application by the national courts of the doctrine of effectiveness and non-discrimination. In this regard one notes that van Gerven in his article 'Of Rights, Remedies and Procedures'[28] written sometime subsequent to 'Bridging the Gaps Between Community and National law: Towards Principles of Homogeneity', specifically remarks on the point of balancing:

> Of course it remains true that it is for the Member States to lay down remedial rules but such competence must be reconciled with the principle of effective remedies in national courts and the fundamental (although not 'absolute') requirement of uniform application. This involves a balancing act as will be emphasized hereafter with the aim of finding the right balance between the national and the Community interests involved.

Clearly, *Zuckerfabrik* does not indicate, as noted above, how the balancing of these issues is to take place thereby creating problems of legal certainty. In short, in order to clarify the status of *Zuckerfabrik* and the balancing required between the doctrines of uniformity and those effectiveness and non-discrimination in the context of national enforcement, it would seem that following the House of Lords in Tobacco a reference on the point to the ECJ for a preliminary ruling would be appropriate. Overall, it would seem that the House of Lords effectively expanded the ratio of *Zuckerfabrik* in its Tobacco judgment with the following result: namely, the replacement of the so-called normal standard established in *American Cyanamid* for injunctions by that of the ECJ, namely, a case on the merits. The Tobacco case turned on whether the EC Directive 98/43 prohibiting the advertising of tobacco and which the UK sought to implement was *ultra vires*. Accordingly, its validity was on challenge to the ECJ. The appellant, Imperial Tobacco sought to restrain the UK government from adopting implementing legislation whilst the ECJ was considering the validity of EC Directive 98/43. At first instance,

---

28. W. van Gerven 'Of Rights, Remedies and Procedures' (2000) 37 CMLR 530 op. cit.

Turner J had granted Imperial Tobacco such an injunction using the principles of *American Cyanamid*. The Court of Appeal overturned this judgment and substituted as the grounds for the injunction that of the ECJ as established in *Zuckerfabrik*, namely, a strong case on the merits as opposed to a serious issue to be tried. The House of Lords upheld the judgment of the Court of Appeal. The reasoning of the majority as expressed by Lord Slynn of Hadley was that preventing the UK govt. from implementing an EC Directive concerning tobacco the validity of which was on challenge to the ECJ concerned the application of EC law. Therefore, following *Zukerfabrik* this application in order to be effective required uniformity of national procedure and therefore the House of Lords applied the higher standard of *Zuckerfabrik*: a case on the merits, which arguably is the traditional standard adopted by the English courts in those situations where *American Cyanamid* does not apply.

Lord Slynn of Hadley speaking for the majority concluded as follows:

> If the grant of the injunction was to depend wholly on domestic law, the principle laid down in e.g. *American Cyanamid Co. v. Ethicon* (1975) *AC and R v. Secretary of State v. Factortame* are to be followed. But the essential question is whether domestic law only is relevant or whether Community has any application. That it seems to me plainly to involve a question of Community law. The granting of interim relief has already been considered a number of times by the European Court of Justice. Thus in *Factortame (No 2)* the European Court of Justice held that in a case concerning Community law where interim relief was sought if a national court considered that the only obstacle which precluded such relief was a rule of national law, it had to see that rule aside. In *Zuckerfabrik* (C-143/88 and C-92/89) the Court was specifically asked to say under what conditions national courts may order the suspension of enforcement of a national administrative measure based on a Community regulation. It seems to me, therefore, that Community law is a relevant factor or at least it is not clear beyond a reasonable doubt that it is not a relevant factor and that as a starting point the conditions referred to in *Zuckerfabrik* (and followed in Atlanta C 465/93) should be applied. It is not necessary to set them out. How far a difference between those conditions and the *American Cyanamid* principles case has been much debated before your lordships . . . I think that it is at least arguable that if a Directive is implemented in national law before the prescribed final date any application for interim relief to suspend the operation of the Directive would be a matter for Community law and that the position would be the same on an application for interim relief to prevent the Directive being adopted.

In his opinion, Lord Hoffmann described the difference between the two litigants with respect to the grounds for the granting of the injunction as follows: 'the position of Counsel for the Secretary of State (Mr Vaja QC) was on the merits, the appellants had an arguable case but no more. Mr Sumption QC for the appellants (Imperial Tobacco) argued that the case was a very strong one'.

However, the majority recognized that a reference to the ECJ on this question would be required. Lord Slynn observed:

> I am firmly of the view that if in order to give judgment in this appeal, it had been necessary to consider whether a) Community law applied and b) what was the scope of its application in the present case, it would have been necessary to refer a question to the ECJ under art 234.

Further, Lord Nichols held: 'I have reached this conclusion with reluctance because it means that the present appeal will not provide the answer to the important question of law. The question will have to remain then for another occasion'.

Accordingly, it is submitted that the Tobacco case is best restricted to its facts until a reference is made to the ECJ concerning the manner in which the principles of uniformity are to be balanced in relation to the doctrine of effectiveness and non-discrimination as applied by the national courts.

Therefore, the concluding remarks concerning the relationship of *Zuckerfabrik* and the Tobacco judgment to the granting of interim relief by the ordinary courts under CPR in order to enforce EC Articles 81 and 82 would be as follows: arguably, if the concept of balancing of national principles in relation to the concepts of effectiveness and non-discrimination as developed in *Peterbroeck* and *van Schijndel* were applied in *Zuckerfabrik* notably in relation to uniform application of EC law it is likely that the result would be that an English court, in order to ensure the adequate as opposed to minimum effective enforcement of EC Articles 81 and 82 would used the standard of a 'serious case on the merits' which corresponds to the English principle of legal certainty and has the advantage of approximating the standard used by the ECJ in granting interim relief. More in particular, it is submitted that *Zuckerfabrik* requires as a result of cases such as *Peterbroeck* and *van Schijndel* as well as the terms of the judgment itself, the application of balancing of the national principles in the context of effectiveness and non-discrimination and uniform application of EC law.[29]

Finally, although injunctive relief as provided by CPR 25 is not available in the CAT, nevertheless a form of interim relief is available pursuant to Rule 61. Of interest is that fact that pursuant to Rule 61(6)(c) an application for interim relief must present a *prima facie* case:

- power to make interim relief;
- the tribunal may make an order on an interim basis suspending in whole or in part the effect of any decision which is the subject matter of proceedings before;

---

29. S. Apte, 'Interim Measures in EC Law' (2003) EJCL Vol 2.7 op. cit. observes in this regard: 'In the author's view, the transposition in totem of the ZAP (Zuckerfabrik) condition to a Factortame type of situation does not appear a prior to be a very reasonable option. The Community provision legal protection in individuals should not be left entirely to the different procedural law system of the Member States. However there is no reason for imposing the strict ZAP (*Zuckerfabrik*) conditions, evaluation guidelines and criteria where the need to avoid over enthusiastic suspension of enforcement of uniformly applicable norms whose validity is contested like in action for annulment under Art. 230, does not exist'

- in the case of an appeal under S 46 or 47 of the 1998 Act varying the conditions or obligations attached to an exception;
- granting any remedy which the Tribunal would have power to grant in its final decision;
- without prejudice to the generally by the foregoing if the Tribunal considers it necessary as a matter of urgency for the purpose of preventing serious irreparable damage to a particular person or category of persons or protecting the public interest the Tribunal may give such direction as it considers appropriate for that purpose.

The Tribunal shall exercise its power under this rule taking into account all of the relevant circumstances including the urgency of the matter; the effect on the party making the request of the relief sought is not granted; the effect on competition if relief is granted. The request for interim relief shall state the subject matter of the proceedings. In the case of a request for a direction present to para. (2) the circumstances giving rise to the urgency the factual and legal grounds establishing a *prima facie* case for the granting of interim relief by the Tribunal.

B.   REPRESENTATIVE ACTIONS

The Commission Green Paper notes that the availability of representative actions is likely to increase the enforceability of EC competition law.

> Defending Consumer Interests: it will be very unlikely for practical reasons if not impossible that consumers and purchasers with small claim will bring an action for damages for breach of anti trust law. Consideration should therefore be given to ways in which these interests can be better protected by collateral action. Beyond the specific protection of consumer interests and collective actions can serve to consolidate large number of smaller claims into one action thereby saving time and money.[30]

Advocate General Jacobs observed in Osterreicher:[31]

> Collective rights of action are an equally common feature of modern judicial systems. They are most encountered in areas such as consumer protection, labour law, unfair competition law or protection of the environment. The law grants associations or their representative bodies the right to bring cases either in the interest of persons which they represent or in the public interest. This further private enforcement of rules adopted in the public interest and supports individual complainants who are often badly equipped to face well organized and financially stronger opponents.

---

30. *Commission Green Paper*, op. cit. at point 2.5 page 8.
31. *Osterreichsicher Gewerkshaftsbund v. Austria*, Case C-195/98 [2000] ECR I-10947 at paragraph 47 and footnote 121 for paragraph 191 in the Commission Staff Working Paper op. cit.

In English law, it is said that the impediment to representative actions may be explained as follows:

> In England, a party representing others may sue to vindicate not only his personal interest but also the rights of those who are similarly affected by the defendant's breach of duty. This is a representative action which has a long history. However, a representative cannot use this procedure to make a claim if he does not have a cause of action in his own right . . . Damages cannot be awarded at large or globally without reference to the particular loss. This is the nub of the matter and the reason why the English representative action remains a procedural backwater.[32]

Accordingly, it would seem that a representative action pursuant to CPR 19.6 may only be brought where the relief sought is by its nature beneficial to all whom the claimant, including himself, seeks to represent by bringing the action.

CPR 19 r 6 provides:

> Where more than one person has the same interest in a claim
>   (a) the claim may be begun;
>   (b) the court may order that the claim be continued by or against one or more of the persons who have the same interest as representatives of any other persons who have that interest
>   The court may direct that any person may not act as a representative. Any party may apply to the court for an order under paragraph (2) unless the court otherwise directs any judgment order given in a claim in which a party is acting as a representative under this rule is binding on all person represented in the claim but may only be enforced by or against a person who is not a party to the claim with the permission of the court.

Notwithstanding these limitation, the CAT rules do provide for a representative action in the context of monetary claims brought to enforce infringement decisions of either the EC Commission or the OFT which involve EC Articles 81 or 82.

Pursuant to S 47 B CA (1998) representative bodies may bring actions on behalf of individual consumers. However, the representative body must be appointed by order of the Secretary of State. Indeed, S 47 B CA (1998) provides that a 'specified body' may subject to the provisions of the Competition Act 1998 and the CAT Rules, commence proceedings in the CAT which consist in 'consumer claims' taken on behalf of at least two individuals as pursuant to S 47 B(1) or with the consent of the individual concerned following S 47 B(3). 'Specified' person means a body such as the Consumer's Association, specified in an order made by the Secretary of State for the purpose of this section S 49 B(9). 'Consumer Claim' means a claim to which S 47 A applies and where an individual has in respect of an infringement affecting indirectly or indirectly

---

32. N. Andrews, 'Multi-party proceedings in England' (2000) *Duke Journal of Comparative and International Law* (11) at 249.

goods or services to which S 49 B(7) applies. S 47 B applies to goods and services which a) the individual received or sought to received otherwise than in the course of a business carried out by him (notwithstanding that he received or sought to receive them with a view to carrying on a business and b) were or would have been supplied to the individual (in the case of goods whether by way of sale otherwise) in the course of business carried on by the person who supplied or would have supplied them. A business includes, first, a professional practise, second, any other undertaking carried on for such a reward and c) or undertaking in the course of which goods or services are supplied otherwise than free of charge (S 47 b(4) and (5).

One notes that by virtue of S 11 of the Enterprise Act (2002) enables consumer groups designated by the Secretary of State to submit consumer complaints to the OFT.

The rules provide as follows:

S 47 B Claims brought by consumers:

After S 47 B Claims of the 1998 Act (which is inserted by S 18) there is inserted:

47 B Claims brought by consumers:

1) A specified body may (subject to the provisions of this Act and Tribunal Rules) bring proceedings before the Tribunal which comprise consumer claims make or contained on behalf of at least two individuals

2) In this section 'consumer claims' means a claim to which Section 47 A applies which an individual has in respect of an infringement affecting (directly or indirectly) goods or services to which subsection 7 applies

3) A consumer claim may be included in proceedings under this section if it is:
   a) a claim made in the proceedings on behalf of the individual concerned by the specified body, or
   b) a claim made by the individual concerned under S 47 A which is contained in the proceedings on his behalf by the specified body and such claim may only be made or contained in proceedings with the consent of the individual concerned

4) The consumer claims included in the proceedings under this section must all relate to the same infringement

5) The provisions or other sum (not being costs or expenses) awarded in respect of a consumer claim included in proceedings under this section must be awarded to the individual concerned: but the tribunal may with the consent of the specified body order that the sum awarded must be paid to the specified body (acting on behalf of the individuals)

6) Any damages or other sum (not being costs or expenses) awarded in respect of a consumer claim included in proceedings under this section must be awarded to the individual concerned: but the Tribunal may with the consent of the specified body and the individual, order that the sum awarded must be paid to the specified body (acting on behalf of the individual)

7) This subsection applies to goods or services which
   a) the individual received or sought to receive otherwise than in the course of business carried on by him (notwithstanding that he received or sought to receive them with a view to carrying on the business and
   b) were or would have been supplied to the individual (in the case of goods whether by way of sale or otherwise) in the course of business carried on by the person who supplied or would have supplied them
8) a business includes:
   - professional practise
   - any other undertaking carried on for gain or reward
   - any undertaking in the cause of which goods or services are supplied otherwise than free of charge
9) 'Specified' means specified in an order made by the Secretary of State in accordance with criterion to be published by the Secretary of State for the purpose of this section
10) An application by a boy to be specified in an order under this section is to be made in a form approved by the Secretary of State for this purpose.

The essential limitation however of this representative cause of action is that following ss 47 B(1)–(3) it applies only to consumers as provided for in subsection (3). Arguably, as demonstrated by *Crehan*, enforcement of EC Art 81 and 82 may well involve not only individual consumers but also small businesses. The judgment of the Court of Appeal in *Crehan*[33] makes reference to representative groups such as the National Association of Inntrepreneur Lessees who complained to the Commission pursuant to EC Reg. 17/62 concerning their leases with *Inntrepreneur*. The judgment also states 'In 1994 the firm of solicitors Charles Russell applied to the Commission on behalf of 48 current and former *Inntrepreneur* tenants'.[34] Finally, the judgment states: 'We are told that there are about 600 dissatisfied Inntrepreneur tenants'.[35] It is of interest to note the position adopted by the Department of Trade and Industry in its consultation paper dealing with representative actions.[36] 'We believe representative actions should be brought on behalf of domestic consumers rather than businesses or individuals purchasing goods for use in a business context. We consider that business or traders should be sufficiently competent to act on their own behalf'.

The doctrine of effectiveness and non-discrimination would intervene in the following circumstances: first to require that infringement decisions involving EC Articles 81 and or 82 by means of a monetary action be enforceable by means of a representative action not only by the CAT as provided by Rule but also by the CPR: in the case of CPR, it is submitted that the doctrine of effectiveness and non-discrimination would require at a minimum a rule drafted equivalently to that

---

33. *Bernard Crehan v. Inntrepreneur Pub Co.* (CPR) [2004] EWCA 637
34. *Bernard Crehan v. Inntrepreneur Pub Co.* (CPR) [2004] EWCA 637 at para. 31.
35. *Bernard Crehan v. Inntrepreneur Pub Co.* (CPR) [2004] EWCA 677 *ibid.* at paragraph 56.
36. Department of Trade & Industry: Consultation: Representative Actions in Consumer Protection Legislation (12 July 2006) <www. dti.gov.uk/files/files31886.pdf>, at paragraph 4.

of S 47 B CA (1998). Second, it is submitted that the doctrine of effectiveness would require that the representative action be expanded to include not only private consumers as defined in S 47B CA (1998) but also business in order to provide for enforcement in circumstances as in *Crehan* where several small business which to enforce their rights pursuant to EC Articles 81 and or 82. One notes in this regard the facts as presented by the Court of Appeal in its judgment in *Crehan*[37] concerning the multitude of potential claimants who could have more effectively enforced their rights if arguably, a representative action existed in order to permit the bringing of a full action for damages for breach of EC Art. 81. Accordingly, the doctrine of effectiveness would seem to require that provision be made in terms of the CPR to ensure the availability of representative actions for both consumers and small businesses and possibly business in general in so far as the enforcement of EC Articles 81 and 82 are concerned. There is arguably no bar in terms of the overriding objective or the underlying principles of a fair trial which can serve to justify a refusal to extend the representative action first, to consumers who wish to enforce the monetary claims before the High Court pursuant to S58A CA (1998); and second, to small businesses who similarly wish to avail themselves of monetary claims provided by that section; and third, the creation of a representative action based upon S 47B CA (1998) in order to ensure that both consumers and small businesses may be able to use a representative action in order to enforce claims for damages for breach of EC Articles 81 and 82. Further, it is submitted that the principle of non-discrimination would apply: this is because enforcement of money actions by the CAT under S 47A and by the national court under S 58A CA (1998) arguably involve the same category of action. Accordingly, there is no justification in terms of procedural principles for providing more favourable enforcement of EC Articles 81 and 82 by the CAT than by the ordinary courts under the CPR.

---

37. *Bernard Crehan v. Inntrepreneur Pub Company CPC*, [2004] EWCA 637 op. cit; at para. 38 'That left outstanding the application made by the 48 dissatisfied Inntrepreneur tenants under Art. 3 of Reg. 17'; and at para. 40: 'There was also an understanding that when the Community law issues raised by the tenants did go to trial, Mr Crehan's case would be the lead case'; and at para. 56: 'We are told that there are about 600 dissatisfied Inntrepreneur tenants. Whilst the value of the claims will depend on the facts of their case, it is apparent that the outcome of their appeal may have very significant financial consequences for Mr Crehan and for Inntrepreneur'.

Chapter 8
French Civil Procedure

A. CASE ALLOCATIONS AND REPRESENTATIVE
    ACTIONS

Before analysing the French procedural rules, one has to observe the rareness of
damages actions for breach of the antitrust rules brought before the French courts.[1]
The reason for this rareness is that the victims of anti-competitive practises are
reluctant to take legal action for damages because of the long and expensive
proceedings. The victims therefore tend to refer competition law cases to the competition authorities, which are able to collect the necessary elements of proof of the
anticompetitive behaviours.[2] Another reason for the rareness of reported cases
could be that the claimants often find a settlement out of court.[3]

   Neelie Kroes, Member of the European Commission in charge of Competition
Policy, observes that the obstacles to private enforcement include 'uncertainty as to
ability to prove the infringement, given that most of the evidence is usually in the
hands of the defendant. Uncertainty as to the result of an action in court, combined
with the risk of having to bear all costs that are related to the procedures if one loses
the case, is probably one of the main reasons why potential plaintiffs decide against
going to court, even when they have a good case'.[4]

---

1. M. Chagny, 'La place des dommages-intérêts dans le contentieux des pratiques anticoncurrentielles' [2005] *Revue Lamy de la concurrence*, No. 4, 186.
2. M.A. Frison-Roche and M.S. Payet, *Droit de la concurrence* [2006] Dalloz, p. 278.
3. C. Momège and N. Bessot, *Comparative Report – France*, p. 1, on the website of the
   Commission.
4. N. Kroes, 'Damages Actions for Breaches of EU Competition Rules: Realities and Potentials',
   Speech/05/613 at the conference on 'La réparation du préjudice causé par une pratique
   anti-concurentielle en France et à l'étranger: bilan et perspectives', Cour de Cassation, Paris,
   17 October 2005.

The French civil procedure rules have been modified in order to reduce the obstacles to private enforcement and thus achieve the aim set out by Regulation 1/2003. An important amendment concerns the creation of specialized courts, which exclusive jurisdiction as to the implementation of competition law.

1.   THE SPECIALIZATION OF THE FRENCH COURTS

The new mission assigned to the national courts in the application of Art. 81 and 81 EC Treaty requires that judges be trained in the implementation of economic law and in the particular techniques of economic law enforcement.[5] The specialization of the courts rationalizes the training of the judges in these 'techniques'.[6] The absence of specialized courts for damages actions therefore appears to constitute a major procedural obstacle to the effective enforcement of competition law.[7]

The NER (*'Loi sur les Nouvelles Régulations Economiques'* ('Loi NRE') – Law on the New Economic Regulations) of 15 May 2001, provides for the creation of specialized courts for the enforcement of competition law actions.[8] Pursuant to Article L.420-7 of the French Commercial Code, as amended by the NER, litigations relating to the application of the domestic French competition rules contained in Articles L.420-1 to L.420-5 and the EC rules contained in Articles 81 and 82 EC Treaty may only be brought before specific High Courts of First Instance (*'Tribunaux de Grande Instance'*, i.e., civil courts) and Commercial Courts (*'Tribunaux de Commerce'*). Article L.420-7 also provides that the list of these courts is to be set out in a Conseil d'Etat Decree. The Decree is to determine the province and scope of jurisdiction of the court(s) of appeal which are competent to take cognisance of judgments pronounced by those jurisdictions.

Decree 2005-1756 determining the competent courts for competition cases was adopted on 30 December 2005. This Decree provides that eight High Courts of First Instance and eight Commercial Courts have jurisdiction to hear litigation in competition cases; these courts are located in Paris, Lille, Nancy, Marseille, Bordeaux, Fort-de-France, Lyon and Rennes. Moreover, the Paris Court of Appeal is the only court competent to hear appeals in these cases. Article L.420-7 refers to 'disputes in relation to the application of the rules laid down in Articles L.420-1 to L.420-5 (of the Commercial Code) and Articles 81 and 82 of the Founding Treaty of the European Community, and those in which the said provisions are invoked'. Therefore, when counter-claims, whether main or accessory, relating to competition law are made in cases concerning a different matter, are based on provisions of competition law, it seems that only a specialized jurisdiction has jurisdiction to

---

5. Véronique Sélinsky, 'Quand les juges du commerce appliquent le droit de la concurrence...', *Revue Lamy de la Concurrence*, May/July 2005, 21.
6. G. Canivet, 'L'organisation des juridictions nationals pour l'application du droit communautaire de la concurrence', *Concurrence – RDLC*, December 2004, No. 1, p. 27.
7. Clearly & Gottlieb law firm, 'Damages, Incentives, Legal Action – Lessons from practical experience: France', Conference 9 March 2005.
8. Law No. 2001-420, published in the French Official Journal (*'OJ'*) of 16 May 2001.

hear these counter-claims.[9] Given the rapid evolution of case law and the importance of economic issues, this exclusive jurisdiction appears to be logical and necessary. Indeed, the specialization of the courts should ensure that judges trained in competition law deal with the competition law cases.[10]

The specialization of the courts, as we will see in our developments, constitutes a major step in the adaptation of French law to comply with the doctrine of effectiveness of EC competition law and ensure fostering private enforcement.

2.   *LOCUS STANDI*: REPRESENTATIVE ACTIONS

The Commission Staff Working Paper observes that:

> There is a merit in fostering claims by final consumers, because these contribute directly to the overarching aims of compensation and increased deterrence, as well as to the development of a competition culture. Costs, delays and administrative burdens involved in ordinary judicial proceedings can certainly discourage consumers who suffer a relatively minor economic loss from seeking a judgment against undertakings engaging in anticompetitive conduct. To enable consumers to be viable litigants, some facilitating instruments may be required.[11]

According to the Green Paper, consumers and purchasers with small claims will not be able, in practise, to bring actions for breach of anti trust law; the Green Paper underlines that 'consideration should therefore be given to ways in which these interests can be better protected by collateral action'.[12] Moreover, Advocate General Jacobs observes that collective rights of actions support 'individual claimants who are often badly equipped to face well organized and financially stronger opponents'.[13]

There is no equivalent to the US 'class action' in French law. The Comparative Report on the conditions of claims in case of infringement of EC competition rules defined 'Class actions' as 'a civil court procedure under which one party, or a group of parties, may sue as representatives of a larger class of unidentified individuals. Members of the class may exclude themselves from the proceedings. Only the class members who opt out are not bound by the judgment in the case. Any damages resulting from the action will be awarded to the members of the class

---

9. Valérie Michel-Amsellem, *Concurrence*, No.1, 2006, 'Procédures – Chroniques', p. 185.
10. *Ibid.*
11. Commission Staff Working Paper: Annexe to the Green Paper: Damages Actions for Breach of EC Anti-Trust Rules: (COM) (2005) 672 Final: SEC (2005) 1732 (19.12.2006), p. 53.
12. Commission Green Paper, 'Damages actions for breach of the EC antitrust rules Damages actions for breach of the EC antitrust rules', COM(2005) 672 final.
13. In *Osterreichsicher Gewerkshaftsbund v. Austria*, Case C-195/98 (2000) ECR I-10947 at paragraph 47.

as a whole i.e., individual awards will not be made to the different members of the class although each will be entitled to a part of the award'.[14] For certain lobbying groups, this type of procedure is used as a an instrument for political action as well as a more conventional jurisdictional instrument.

Such a procedural device has not yet been introduced into French law, despite the efforts in this direction. Indeed, the French judge may only settle individual disputes, the right to bring an action being an individual right.[15]

The general rule concerning *locus standi* is set out in Article 31 of the French Code of Civil Procedure ('Nouveau Code de Procédure Civile'): 'The right of action is available to all those who have a legitimate interest in the success or dismissal of a claim, without prejudice to those cases where the law confers the right of action solely upon persons whom it authorizes to raise or oppose a claim, or to defend a particular interest'.

In situations in which no specific statute applies, the associations therefore only have the right to act for the defence of personal interests and to represent their members in the exercise of their actions subject to the holder of the action giving the associations a specific mandate.[16] It should be noted that if these rules are strictly applied by the criminal courts, certain civil courts have given associations the right to act for the defence of a collective interest, analysed as the sum of the individual interests of their members. These actions were brought to obtain the reparation of the prejudice of the members of the association as opposed to the

---

14. D. Waelbroek, D. Slater and G. Even-Shoshan, 'Study on the conditions of claims in case of infringement of EC competition rules – Comparative Report', 31 August 2004, p. 43. Taking into account the diversity of legal systems in the EU, the Report also proposed the following definitions relating to group litigation:

Public interest litigation: litigation, usually by a representative organization, that is not done on behalf of any identified individuals but for the benefit of the public at large. Any damages awarded in the context of such claims are in some way given to the general public. This differs from class actions and collective claims in that the proceedings are brought on behalf of the public at large rather than a group of individuals (either identified or unidentified).

Collective claim: single claim brought on behalf of a group of identified/identifiable individuals. Any award resulting from the action will be made to the group as a whole i.e., individual awards will not be made to the different members of the group.

Representative actions: single claim brought by, for example, an association on behalf of a group of identified individuals (usually its members). Any award resulting from the action will made to the individual members.

Joint action: set of claims brought by several plaintiffs together or joined by the judge hearing the claims due to some link between them (e.g. same defendant, damages resulting from same facts). This type of action differs from class actions or collective claims in that the joining of the cases is procedural and at the end, although a single judgment may be made covering the cases of all the plaintiffs, the plaintiffs claims will be treated separately within that judgment and awards will be made individually to the different plaintiffs.

Assignment of claims: possibility for potential plaintiffs to assign their right of claim to an unconnected third party.

15. Constitutional Court (*Conseil Constitutionnel*), No. 257 DC, 25 July 1989, *Dr. soc.* 1989, p. 627.

16. Cour de cassation, Chambres réunies, 15 June 1923, *DP* 1924, 1, p. 153, and Cour de cassation, 1re Chambre civile, 16 January 1985, *Bulletin civil* I, No. 25.

prejudice suffered by the association itself. These judgments are therefore *contra legem.*[17]

However, certain statutes allow representative actions, i.e., single claims brought by an association on behalf of a group of identified individuals. Nevertheless, the conditions set out in these statutes are very strict.

Specific statutes have granted certain associations – in particular consumer associations – the right to bring representation actions and actions for the protection of the collective interest. These representative actions ('actions en représentation conjointe' – 'action in joint representation') are based on Article L.422-1 Consumer Code, which provides that:

> Where several consumers, identified as natural persons, have suffered individual damages caused by the same business act and which have a common origin, any approved association recognized as been representative on a national level in application of the provisions of the part I may, if its has been duly authorized by at least two of the consumers concerned, institute legal proceedings to obtain reparation before any court on behalf of these consumers.
>
> The mandate may not be solicited by means of a public appeal on radio or television, nor by means of posting of information, by tract or personalized letter. Authorization must be given in writing by each consumer.

It is therefore possible for certain associations to institute proceedings in order to represent either several individual interests or a collective interest, but the action has to satisfy very strict conditions. In particular, pursuant to Article L.422-2 Consumer Code, an association may only represent the interests of its individual members if it has received an explicit mandate from each consumer it represents. Moreover, the associations may not publicly ask for mandates in the press; and the associations are not granted the right to act in the name of others. The system is based on a contractual representation: the association does not exercise its own right of action, but the action of its members.[18] It acts in the interest and for the benefit of the representatives who have to be identified in the proceedings, and the judge will render a judgment ruling on each prejudice taken individually.

Because of these very restrictive conditions, it seems that these actions have not yet been used in damages actions for breach of competition law, whether French or EC law.[19] The Ashurst Report for France explains that this could also be explained by the fact that 'the requirement that an association must be duly authorized (which is fulfilled in by only a limited number of associations) and by

---

17. Generally on this question, see S. Guinchard *et al*ii, *Droit et pratique de la procédure civile*, Dalloz, Dalloz Action, 2006–2007, No. 102.152 *et seq.*
18. S. Guinchard *et alii*, op. cit., No. 102.84.
19. C. Momège and N. Bessot, *Comparative Report – France*, p. 7, on the website of the Commission. Moreover, the Competition council (*Avis relatif à l'introduction de l'action de groupe en matière concurrentielle*, 21 September 2006, p. 6 to 8, published on the website of the Competition Council, <www.conseil-concurrence.fr>) notes that very few actions have been introduced before the Council by consumers associations (21 decisions and 4 opinions).

the fact that these actions are aiming at the protection of consumer interests, whereas competition cases for damages are mainly exercised by competitors'.[20] The Competition Council observes, from its experience, that the cases in which group actions could usefully be engaged against restrictive agreements or abuses of a dominant position are limited, and that collective action will not solve certain difficulties related to the implementation of civil procedures.[21] The Competition Council considers that the choice of a collective action will only be useful in cases in which the victim is a direct consumer, as it increases the likelihood of establishing a relationship between the anticompetitive behaviour and the prejudice. It gives as examples the cartel of banks on the renegotiation of real estate loans,[22] or the cartel of the French mobile telephone operators.[23]

It should be noted that the conditions for a representation action are much less restrictive before the administrative courts. The Ashurst Report for France, observes that the *Conseil d'Etat* (the Administrative Supreme Court) 'has admitted that associations may bring actions before such courts either to defend their own interest or to defend the collective interest they represent.[24] Unlike in civil and commercial proceedings, these associations do not need to be 'authorized'.[25]

Actions by associations for the protection of the collective interest they represent, as opposed to the representative actions, are also available. Associations may act by exercising the rights recognized to the party claiming damages in a criminal case ('partie civile'), which necessarily implies the existence of a criminal offence causing a direct or indirect prejudice to the interest of consumers, for instance cartels or abuses sanctioned by Article L.420-6 of the Commercial Code.[26] Article L.421-1 of the Consumer Code indeed provides that 'Duly declared associations whose statutory object specifies the protection of consumer interests may, if they are approved for this purpose, exercise the rights conferred upon civil parties in respect of events directly, or indirectly, prejudicing the collective interest of consumers'. Pursuant to these provisions, associations are therefore not allowed to act before a civil court. Parléani observes that the French rules should be modified to be in 'harmony' with the spirit of the 1/2003 Regulation, which favours a private enforcement approach.[27]

It should be noted that consumer associations are also empowered to act directly to ask the judge to order a stop order. Pursuant to Article L.421-2 of

---

20. C. Momège and N. Bessot, op. cit., p. 7, footnote 28.
21. Avis relatif à l'introduction de l'action de groupe en matière concurrentielle, op. cit.
22. Decision No. 00-D-28, 19 September 2000, <www.conseil-concurrence.fr>.
23. Decision No. 05-D-65, 30 November 2005, <www.conseil-concurrence.fr>.
24. See for instance, Conseil d'Etat, 28 December 1906, *Syndicat des patrons-coiffeurs de Limoges*, No. 25521, *Recueil Lebon*.
25. *Comparative Report – France*, op. cit., p. 7.
26. Article L.420-6 'If any natural person fraudulently takes a personal and decisive part in the conception, organization or implementation of the practises referred to in Articles L.420-1 and L.420-2 (cartel and abuses of dominant position), this shall be punished by a prison sentence of four years and a fine of 75,000 euros'.
27. G. Parléani, 'Actualité de la sanction judiciaire des pratiques anticoncurrentielles', *Petites Affiches*, 20 January 2006, No. 14, 3.

the Consumer Code, the approved consumer associations acting in accordance with the conditions specified in this article, may ask the civil court or the criminal court ruling on civil actions, to order the counsel for the defence or the defendant, where appropriate subject to penalty, for any measure intended to stop illicit actions or to remove illicit clauses from the contract or the standard contract offered to consumers.[28] The approved consumer associations also have the right to ask the Competition Council to give its opinion on issues concerning competition.[29]

The absence of class actions in French law, as well as the fact that the existing collective legal actions are only possible under very strict conditions, has been viewed as being an obstacle to obtaining damages.[30] A government bill[31] proposes an intermediary solution, which would improve the current mechanism while creating a system in which the consumers would be associated to the action with having to give a mandate. Pursuant to this proposal, only an association approved and recognized as being representative on a national scale could introduce an action. The associations would be entitled to ask for the reparation of any loss related to a contractual breach from a professional party.[32] However the French Minister of Justice specified that the cases relating to complex laws would be excluded from the class action mechanism, such as environmental offences, damages relating to employment law and personal injury; this could exclude infringement to competition rules. A report relating to class action, drafted by the working group set up by the Ministries of Economy and Justice and published in December 2005,[33] states that the President of the Competition Council

---

28. C. Momège and N. Bessot, op. cit., p. 1, also observe that 'an action more similar to what is defined as public interest litigation action exist (Article L.442-6 of the Commercial Code), whereby the public prosecutor (*Procureur de la République*), the Minister for Economic Affairs or the Chairman of the Competition Council can bring an action for damages on behalf of individuals. However, this action is only open where damages arise from a restrictive practise (Article 442-1 *et seq*. Commercial Code for which no textual equivalent exists in EC law: discriminatory conditions of sales, abuse of purchase power in order to obtain undue or disproportionate commercial advantages,, etc.), and form an anticompetitive practise.
29. Article L.462-1 of the Commercial Code.
30. Clearly & Gottlieb law firm, 'Damages, Incentives, Legal Action – Lessons from practical experience: France', Conference 9 March 2005.
31. P. Clément, Minister of Justice, Speech at the Conference '*Action de groupe*', Senate, 12 September 2006, <www.justice.gouv.fr/discours/d120906>.
32. Pursuant to this proposal, certain High Courts of First Instances would be designated, and the procedure would be the following: the judge would rule on the liability of the professional but would not take a decision on the loss suffered by the consumers, who are not, at this stage, parties to the proceedings. Should the professional be declared as being liable, the decision would be made public and the judge would postpone judgment on the assessment of the individual prejudices of the consumers. The consumers would then have a delay to send to the professional a claim for indemnity. At this stage, the professional would be obliged to make an offer accompanied by a cheque to each consumer. At the end of the postponement, certain claims have not been satisfied, the judge will rule following a simplified procedure, without any compulsory hearing not representation by a lawyer. The representation by a lawyer is obligatory only during the first stage.
33. Report on Group Action, Report given to the Minister of Economy, Finance and Industry and to the Minister of Justice, 16 December 2005.

underlined the legal difficulties relating to the implementation of such an action on the grounds of competition law, in particular because competition law constitutes a technical type of litigation, which necessitates particular expertise.

However, following the publication of this report, the Competition Council was invited to give its comments in an Opinion: in this document,[34] it announced that it is in favour of class action, under certain conditions, for consumers victim of anticompetitive practises. The Competition Council explained that class actions can contribute to improve damages in compensation for losses sustained by consumers as the result of anticompetitive practises, by restoring a balance between powerful companies, which are often large groups, and consumers, who are by nature isolated.[35] The Competition Council also considers that class actions mechanisms can effectively contribute to strengthen deterrence.[36]

We have noted that because of the very restrictive conditions relating to group actions, it seems that these actions have not yet been used in damages actions for breach of competition law.[37] The Staff Working Paper notes that it considers that this rarity of collective actions (i.e., a single claim brought on behalf of a group of affected people) and representative actions (i.e., actions brought by representative organizations, such as consumer organizations) 'is an obstacle to private actions in so far as it reduces the litigation options open to potential claimants'.[38] One could therefore consider that the French rules breach the doctrine of effectiveness. However, nothing in the ECJ's case law seems to indicate that the principle the procedural law of the Member States to provide for actions securing the collective interests of consumers in competition cases.[39]

Moreover, in any event, an important principle in French law is that the courts are not allowed to issue, through their judgments, regulations and rules, which would be the case if class actions were accepted. The Constitutional Court ('*Conseil Constitutionnel*') ruled that courts may only settle disputes concerning individual litigations, and that the right to action is a freedom of the person.[40] Therefore, even though the French rules are very restrictive, there is a strong justification underlying the French civil procedure rules, i.e., the French rules render the application of Articles 81 and 82 EC Treaty more difficult as regards

---

34. *Avis relatif à l'introduction de l'action de groupe en matière concurrentielle*, 21 September 2006, published on the website of the Competition Council, <www.conseil-concurrence.fr>.
35. *Ibid.*
36. In the same Opinion, the Competition Council specified that class action mechanisms require on one hand, a satisfactory coordination between public and private actions an on the other hand, the preservation of leniency programmes (*Avis relatif à l'introduction de l'action de groupe en matière concurrentielle*, op. cit.).
37. C. Momège and N. Bessot, op. cit., p. 7.
38. Commission Staff Working Paper: Annexe to the Green Paper: Damages Actions for Breach of EC Anti-Trust Rules: (COM) (2005) 672 Final: SEC (2005) 1732 (19.12.2006), p. 12.
39. See *below*, Germany, IV, 'Representative Actions'.
40. Constitutional Court (*Conseil Constitutionnel*), No. 257 DC, 25 July 1989, *Dr. soc.* 1989, p. 627.

collective actions, but are nevertheless justified in terms of the French fundamental principles underlying civil procedure rules.[41]

As the ECJ held in *van Schijndel*, 'For the purposes of applying these principles, each case which raises the question whether a national procedural provision renders application of the Community law impossible or excessively difficulty must be analysed by reference to the role of that provision in the procedure, its progress and its special features viewed as a whole before the various national instances. In the light of that analysis the basic principles of the domestic judicial system such as the protection of the rights of the defence, the principle of legal certainty and the proper conduct of the procedure must where appropriate be taken into consideration'.[42]

---

41. Generally on this question, see *above*, the Introduction, and M. Struys, 'Le Droit communautaire et l'application des règles procédurales nationales' (2000) J.T.D.E. No. 67.
42. *van Shinjndel v. Stichting Penioen Fonds voor Fysiotherapeuten*, Case C-430, 431/93 (1995) ECR I 4705 at para. 19 and *Peterbroeck v. Belgian State* Case C-312/93 [1995] ECR I-4599 at para. 20.

Chapter 9

French Procedure: Proof and Evidence

A.   BURDEN OF PROOF

Any person, whether an individual or a legal person, who suffers a damage due to anti-competitive practises can claim damages before the competent French courts on the grounds of civil liability, whether contractual liability/deception[1] or tort (Article 1382 of the Civil Code).[2]

Pursuant to the rules applicable to civil liability, the plaintiff has to prove the existence of (i) a fault (violation of a duty or a statutory obligation), (ii) a damage and (iii) a causal connection between the fault and the damage suffered.

1.   BURDEN OF PROOF OF AN INFRINGEMENT OF ARTICLE 81(1) OR OF ARTICLE 82 OF THE TREATY

Pursuant to Article 2 Regulation 1/2003, 'In any national or Community proceedings for the application of Articles 81 and 82 of the Treaty, the burden of proving an infringement of Article 81(1) or of Article 82 of the Treaty shall rest on the party or the authority alleging the infringement. The undertaking or association of

---

1. Article 1116 of the French Civil Code provides that 'Deception is a ground for annulment of a contract where the schemes used by one of the parties are such that it is obvious that, without them, the other party would not have entered into the contract. It may not be presumed, and must be proved'.
2. Article 1382 of the French Civil Code provides that 'Any act whatever of man, which causes damage to another, obliges the one by whose fault it occurred, to compensate it'.

undertakings claiming the benefit of Article 81(3) of the Treaty shall bear the burden of proving that the conditions of that paragraph are fulfilled'.

These provisions seem put an end to certain 'hesitations' of French case law. If the Supreme Court generally applies the principles of civil procedure in terms of burden of proof to competition law, the Supreme Court has shifted, in two different types of situations, the burden of proof to the defendant. The Commercial Chamber of the Supreme Court (*'Cour de Cassation'*) had ruled that a company holding exclusive intellectual property rights had to bring evidence showing that it exploited the rights in compliance with EC competition law.[3] The Supreme Court also reversed the burden of proof by requiring producers and manufacturers to prove the lawfulness of franchise contracts, making it easier for a plaintiff to establish illegality.[4]

Pursuant to Regulation 1/2003, it seems clear that the claimant will in all cases have the burden of proving the infringement, damage and causation. The burden of proof is however shifted to the other party where a party establishes a *prima facie* case. The Ashurst Report for France observes that: 'The Judge may consider, even in the absence of one decisive evidence, that an allegation is presumed to be true taking into account several elements or pieces of evidence provided by the claimant. Such a presumption would thus shift the burden of proof to the other party'.[5]

Moreover, the judge, who is sovereign in the assessment of evidence, may take into account a party's refusal to produce documents. In this way, Article 11 of the Code of Civil Procedure provides that 'The parties are held to cooperate for the implementation of the investigation measures, and the judge may draw conclusions from abstention or refusal to do so'. The Ashurst Report for France however observes that no application of this principle to EC competition law related cases seem to have been reported, which may also be explained by the shortage of private enforcement actions. The Report further notes that even though the refusal of a party to produce a document will in itself lead the judge to the conclusion that the document exists, and that it contains decisive information supporting the other party's arguments, such a refusal may be decisive where it comes in addition to other evidence.[6]

The Commission Staff Working Paper[7] observes, concerning cases of information asymmetry, i.e., where one party has in its control or access to more evidence relating to a given claim, that the ECJ held, in Aalborg Portland, after paraphrasing Article 2 Regulation 1/2003, that: 'Although according to those principles the legal burden of proof is borne either by the Commission or the undertaking or association concerned, the factual evidence on which a party relies

---

3. Cour de cassation, Chambre Commerciale, 20 March 1990, No. 85-15.224, *Bulletin Civil* IV, No. 85, p. 56.
4. See C. Momège and N. Bessot, *Comparative Report – France*, p. 12.
5. *Ibid.*
6. *Ibid.*
7. Commission Staff Working Paper: Annexe to the Green Paper: Damages Actions for Breach of EC Anti-Trust Rules: (COM) (2005) 672 Final: SEC (2005) 1732 (19.12.2006), p. 26.

may be of such a kind as to require the other party to provide an explanation or justification, failing which it is permissible to conclude that the burden of proof has been discharged'.[8]

The Commission Staff Working Paper[9] considers that 'in situations of information asymmetry, it would be sufficient for the claimant to present facts which may constitute evidence of an infringement of the EC competition rules. The burden would then be on the defendant to adduce the necessary explanations or justifications to proof that those facts do not constitute an infringement of the EC competition rules.

Under French law, where information asymmetry exists, the claimant still has the burden of proving that the defendant infringed the applicable competition rules. However, in the event the claimant is able to bring a *prima facie* case, the defendant will often, in practise, be put in a situation where he will have to prove that the facts do not constitute an infringement of the competition rules.[10]

Moreover, in follow-on actions (i.e., cases in which the civil action is brought after a competition authority has found an infringement), a decision of the Commission or of the Competition Council will definitely help the claimant to prove the fault. In this regard, the provisions of Regulation 1/2003 implement the case law of the ECJ developed in *Delimitis*[11] and *Masterfoods*.[12]

Article 16(1) of the Regulation 1/2003 provides:

> When national courts rule on agreements, decisions or practises under Article 81 or Article 82 of the Treaty which are already the subject of a Commission decision, they cannot take decisions running counter to the decision adopted by the Commission. They must also avoid giving decisions which would conflict with a decision contemplated by the Commission in proceedings it has initiated. To that effect, the national court may assess whether it is necessary to postpone judgment. This obligation is without prejudice to the rights and obligations under Article 234 of the Treaty.

Point 13 of the Cooperation Notice (Communication) specifies that if a national court has some doubt on the lawfulness of a decision rendered by the Commission, it may not avoid the effects of Article 16(1) where the ECJ has not ruled the contrary. Therefore, should a national court wish to go against a decision of the Commission, it will have to refer the matter to the ECJ on the grounds of Article 234 EC Treaty in the framework of a preliminary ruling.

When a national court renders a decision before the Commission does, it must avoid taking a decision that would go against the decision envisaged by the

---

8. Joined Cases C-204/00, C-211/00, C-213-00, C-217/00 and C-219/00, *Aalborg Portland and others v. Commission* [2004] ECR I-123, pra 79.
9. Commission Staff Working Paper: Annexe to the Green Paper: Damages Actions for Breach of EC Anti-Trust Rules: (COM) (2005) 672 Final: SEC (2005) 1732 (19.12.2006), p. 26.
10. See Cour de cassation, 2^e Chambre Civile, 13 October 1971, [1972] *Dalloz*, 117.
11. Case C-234-89 [1991] ECR p. 6689.
12. Case C-344/98 [2000] ECR I, p. 935.

Commission. Point 14 of the Communication on the Cooperation between the Commission and the national courts clarifies the applicable procedure.

However, the decisions rendered by the French competition authority, the Competition Council, do not bind the national courts. This constitutes an important difference with English law where an OFT or a CAT infringement decision concerning either Article 81 or 82 'binds' the national court.[13] French courts may therefore render decisions in contradiction with rulings of the Competition Council. Kroes observes that:

> With regard to Commission decisions, the Court of Justice came to the plaintiff's aid by declaring in the *Masterfoods* case – and this has been codified in Regulation 1/2003 – that a national court cannot take a decision which runs counter to the Commission's decision. The plaintiff could thus use the Commission decision finding an infringement to stand as evidence of the violation. Why shouldn't we take the logic of this system a step further and apply the *Masterfoods* case law to decisions of NCAs?[14]

It is difficult to assess how such a step could be taken in French law. Under French Constitutional law and Article 6§ 1 of the European Convention on Human Rights, the courts have to rule in complete independence in disputes between individuals and corporations.[15] Therefore, a latent conflict underlies the relationship between the administrative bodies implementing EC law and the French courts which have to rule in complete independence.[16] As a consequence of the absence of *res judicata*, where the Competition Council has rendered a ruling on agreements, decisions or practises under Articles 81 and/or 82 EC Treaty, the victim will still have the burden – in theory at least – to prove the fault of the defendant, i.e., the infringement of Articles 81 or 82 EC Treaty or Articles L.420-1 or L.420-2 of the Commercial Code.

However, a court will logically consider that a legally binding decision rendered by the Competition Council, or even possibly a decision rendered by a national authority from another EU Member State,[17] will constitute the necessary element of proof of the infringement, and therefore of the fault.[18] In practise, the trend is to give such a decision an automatic and compulsory effect on the existence

---

13. See Chapter 3 ('Burden of proof' under English law) *supra*.
14. N. Kroes,' Damages Actions for Breaches of EU Competition Rules: Realities and Potentials', Speech/05/613 at the conference on 'La réparation du préjudice causé par une pratique anti-concurrentielle en France et à l'étranger: bilan et perspectives', Cour de Cassation, Paris, 17th October 2005.
15. See, *for example*, S. Guinchard *et alii*, *Droit et pratique de la procédure civile*, Dalloz, Dalloz Action, 2006–2007, No. 211-61 *et seq.*
16. G. Canivet, 'L'organisation des jurisdictions nationals pour l'application du droit communautaire de la concurrence', *Concurrence – RDLC*, December 2004, No. 1, p. 21.
17. The Ashurst Report (C. Momège and N. Bessot, *Comparative Report – France*, p. 17) notes howhever that there are no reported court judgments mentioning decisions if national competition authorities from other Member States other than factual.
18. P. de Montalembert and M. Henry, 'Indemnisation du préjudice causé par des pratiques anti-concurrentielles: risques et opportunités', *Option Finance*, 6 June 2006, 43.

of a fault,[19] but this should not in theory be the case, especially if the decision has not been subject to the control of the competent court of appeal (i.e., the Court of Appeal of Paris).[20] The Ashurst report for France observes that in practise 'When a practise has been sanctioned by the European Commission or the French Competition Council, proof of the infringement, and thus of the fault, is already made'.[21] The Working Paper therefore observes that France is a legal system which seems to facilitate, in this respect, private enforcement of competition law since fault does not present a hurdle to the claimant.

The requirement concerning the proof of a fault is easily overcome, as the anticompetitive practise will constitute in itself a presumption of fault. The burden of proof under French law is therefore alleviated in follow-on actions, and does not seem to constitute a procedural obstacle to the effective enforcement of competition law.

2.   BURDEN OF PROOF OF CAUSATION AND DAMAGE

Pursuant to the French civil liability rules, the plaintiff has not only to prove the existence of a fault, i.e., infringement of Article 81(1) or of Article 82 of the Treaty, but also a damage and a causal connection between the fault and the damage suffered.

The Commission Staff Working Paper notes states that 'the fact that the burden of proof of causation and damage is on the claimant, which is the case in all Member States, is an obstacle to private actions'.[22] The Working Paper therefore seems to make a distinction between the proof of the infraction to EC competition, for which, in application of Article 2 Regulation 1/2003, the claimant bares the burden of proof, and the proof of causation and damage. Where national law provides that the claimant bares the proof of causation and damage, the Working Paper seems to consider that there would be a breach of the principle of effectiveness.

However, according to *van Schijndel*, in order to apply the principle of effectiveness, it is necessary to analyse the provision in question by reference to the role of that provision in the procedure viewed as a whole, and to take into consideration, where appropriate, the basic principles of the domestic judicial system such as the principle of legal certainty.[23] The French Supreme Court held that the principle is that the claimant must establish the causal effect between

---

19. See *for example* Commercial Court of Paris, *Peugeot v. Eco System*, 22 October 1996.

20. R. Bout, *et alii*, *Lamy Droit Economique*, June 2006, 2244.

21. C. Momège and N. Bessot, *Comparative Report – France*, p. 10, on the website of the Commission.

22. Commission Staff Working Paper: Annexe to the Green Paper: Damages Actions for Breach of EC Anti-Trust Rules: (COM) (2005) 672 Final: SEC (2005) 1732 (19.12.2006), p. 12.

23. *van Shinjndel v. Stichting Penioen Fonds voor Fysiotherapeuten*, Case C-430, 431/93 (1995) ECR I 4705 at para. 19 and *Peterbroeck v. Belgian State* Case C-312/93 [1995] ECR I-4599 at para. 20.

the fault and the damage,[24] which means that any doubt as to the existence of this relationship will in principle benefit the defendant.[25] The rule, which at least partially based on legal certainty and justice, is an important principle of the French legal system.

However, one must not exaggerate the importance of the proof required.[26] In a first phase of the proceedings, the claimant may bring 'more or less' elements of proof, which is sufficient to reverse to burden of proof, putting the defendant in a position where he has to prove that, in reality, causation necessary to obtain reparation of the damage is lacking.[27] Moreover, in practise, the courts sometimes base their decision on presumptions of causation.[28] The plaintiff will however regularly experience difficulties in demonstrating the damage suffered.[29]

Furthermore, the Working Paper states that 'The high standard of proof required in some Member States also exacerbates the difficulties faced by the claimants, particularly where the available evidence may not be complete'.[30] The Working Paper further observes that 'The normal rule under the national laws of the Member States is that the burden of proving all elements of the claim rests on the claimant. This means that the claimant in all cases has to prove the infringement, the causal connection between infringement and damage, and the quantum of damages. The burden of proving a defence to an action rests on the defendant. As a matter of Community law, Article 2 of Regulation 1/2003 states these rules for actions based on EC antitrust rules'.[31]

It is therefore possible to consider that the principle of effectiveness will be infringed by national law only where the burden of proof of damage and causation lies on the claimant (which is the case in all Member States) and where, at the same time, the national law not only requires a high standard of proof but also does not give the claimant efficient means to access evidence.

B.   STANDARD OF PROOF

The Working Paper[32] recalls that Article 2 Regulation 1/2003 does not regulate the standard of proof, which remains regulated by national laws.

Under French law, the only criterion is that the evidence presented by parties must, like in most civil law countries, 'win the conviction of the judge' ('*emporter*

---

24.   Cour de Cassation, 2ᵉ Chambre Civile, 1 April 1963, [1963] *Dalloz*, 403.
25.   Cour de Cassation, 2ᵉ Chambre Civile, 21 April 1966, [1966] *JCP*, II, 14710.
26.   F. Terré, P. Simler, Y. Lequette, *Les obligations, Dalloz*, p. 757.
27.   Cour de cassation, 2ᵉ Chambre Civile, 13 October 1971, [1972] *Dalloz*, 117.
28.   Cour de cassation, 2ᵉ Chambre Civile, 19 Febuary 1964, *Bulletin Civil* II, No. 150.
29.   *Ibid.*
30.   Commission Staff Working Paper, op. cit., p. 12.
31.   *Ibid.*
32.   Commission Staff Working Paper, op. cit., p. 26.

la conviction du juge'). As noted by the Ashurst Report for France, this is a general principle of French law, with no specific legal basis.[33] In practise, 'winning the conviction of the judge' means that 'the parties need to place the judge in the situation where he does not need any additional facts to be proven by the parties, in order for him to decide a case in a certain way. In any event, the applicable principle is the one of free evaluation of evidence by the judge. In practise, this means that the judge evaluates the respective importance of the different pieces of evidence at his disposal according to his own conscience'.[34] In *Mors v. Labinal*, for instance, the judgment mentioned that the expert's opinion had convinced the judge as to the elements of the damage suffered by one of the parties.[35]

It should be noted that the Competition Council may, before giving an opinion to a court, launch an enquiry.[36] Such an enquiry will give a much more efficient result in searching for evidence than the result that can be expected from the Commission's opinion, where the Commission will theoretically simply analyse the documents transmitted by the court in order to give its opinion.[37]

The standard by which the claimant must win the conviction of the judge is stricter than the 'balance of probabilities' test in existence in common law jurisdictions. However, comparing the two standards, the Working Paper expresses the view that 'in the individual case there may not be any significant difference between the two tests, since the judge may require being convinced that one explanation is more likely than the other'.[38]

In practise, the French rules concerning the burden of proof and the test by which the parties have to 'win the conviction of the judge' do not appear to infringe the effectiveness principle in itself. These rules would, however, infringe the effectiveness principle, where combined with a difficulty in obtaining evidence. The French legislator, in particular by creating specialized courts, has however set out the necessary conditions to improve access to evidence, thus, hopefully, creating the necessary conditions to improve damage actions and render the action more efficient.[39]

---

33. C. Momège and N. Bessot, op. cit., p. 12. The report quotes J.L. Aubert, *Introduction au droit, Armand Colin*, 9th edition, p. 233 *et seq.*
34. C. Momège and N. Bessot, op. cit., p. 13.
35. Quoted by C. Momège and N. Bessot, op. cit., p. 13.
36. Court of Appeal of Paris, *Ugap v. Camif*, 13 January 1998, *UGAP v. CAMIF*, [1998] *JCP G*, II, 10217.
37. J. Riffault-Silk, 'Les actions privées en droit de la concurrence: obstacles de procédure et de fond', [2006] *Revue Lamy de la Concurrence*, p. 89.
38. Commission Staff Working Paper, op. cit., p. 25.
39. For an optimistic view on the expected consequences of the specialization, see *for example* M. Malaurie Vignal, 'L'hyper-technicité et la proximité du droit', [2006] *Concurrence Contrats Consommation*, February 2006, p. 1 and J. Riffault-Silk, 'Les actions privées en droit de la concurrence: obstacles de procédure et de fond', op. cit., p. 89.

C.   ACCESS TO EVIDENCE AND INFORMATION

The Green Paper observes 'Actions for damages in antitrust cases regularly require the investigation of a broad set of facts. The particular difficulty with this kind of litigation is that often the relevant evidence is not easily available and is held by the party committing the anti-competitive behaviour. Access by claimants to such evidence is the key to making damages claims effective. It must therefore be considered whether obligations to turn over documents or otherwise provide access to evidence should be introduced'.[40]

Producing evidence will not be an easy task for the victim of an infringement to EC competition law where the victim cannot force the other party to produce certain documents.[41] Under French law, there are no pre-trial disclosure requirements which would oblige a party to produce all the evidence relating to the case. In any event, third parties may hold evidence and the discovery system will therefore not always be useful.

However, the French judge has powers to investigate. The judge may also ask, under certain conditions, the Commission and the Council for documents and information.

1.   THE INVESTIGATION POWERS OF THE FRENCH JUDGE AND
                      THE ROLE OF PARTIES

Under the EC principles, the national rules of procedure should neither render excessively difficult nor almost impossible the enforcement of EC competition law.[42] According to the Green Paper, access by claimants to the relevant evidence, which is often held by the party committing the anti-competitive behaviour, and which is not, therefore, easily available, 'is the key to making damages claims effective. It must therefore be considered whether obligations to turn over documents or otherwise provide access to evidence should be introduced'.[43]

The judge needs all the relevant evidence before the pre-trial examination phase of the proceedings is closed, as evidence may not be communicated after the closure of this phase.[44] Even though the French courts do not have the same investigation powers as the Commission and the Competition Council, the French

---

40. Commission Green Paper, 'Damages actions for breach of the EC antitrust rules Damages actions for breach of the EC antitrust rules', COM(2005) 672 final.
41. R. Bout, *et alii, Lamy Droit Economique*, June 2006, 2249.
42. See *Van Schijndel v. Stichting Pensionenfonds voor Fysiotherapeuthen*, Case C-430/93, 431/93 [1995] ECR I-4705 and *Peterbroeck van Campenhout SCS & Co. v. Belgium*, Case C-312/93 [1995] ECR I-4599.
43. Commission Green Paper, op. cit.
44. Pursuant to Article 782 of the Code of Civil Procedure, the closure of the pre-trial examination is pronounced by a non-reasoned order, which is not subject to appeal. A copy of that order is then delivered to the advocates. Article 783 provides that after the pronouncement of closure, 'no further pleadings may be filed nor any new document be produced in the hearings, under penalty of inadmissibility to be pronounced *sua sponte*'.

judges do have at their disposal useful provisions in the Code of Civil Procedure, which allow them to have an active role in the research of evidence during the pre-trial examination phase. At the present time, damage actions are still relatively rare in France, and it is mainly the doctrine that has suggested that the judges use these provisions.[45] It is therefore uncertain whether the judges will fully implement these provisions in damages actions. Indeed, during the pre-trial examination phase, the judge in charge of the examination (the 'pre-trial judge') is often overloaded with work and does not usually have time to read the briefs of the parties and to acquaint himself with the evidence produced by the parties. However, the parties will have an important role to play in particular in asking the judge, during the procedural phase of the proceedings, to implement these provisions, thus making him take this active role. Moreover, the Decree 2005-1756 determining the competent courts for competition cases, adopted on 30 December 2005, has created specialized courts, and may therefore have a positive effect on the judge accepting to take an active part in the research of relevant evidence, which would hopefully facilitate civil actions based on the violation of EC competition law.

The judge may have an active role during the investigations before the proceedings are engaged and, of course, during the pre-trial phase of the proceedings once they have commenced.

2.　　　　　INVESTIGATIONS BEFORE THE COMMENCEMENT OF
　　　　　LEGAL PROCEEDINGS

Before the proceedings are engaged before the court, the research of evidence may be asked for in a summary proceeding or by way of a petition, before the president of the competent Civil Court (*'Tribunal de Grande Instance'*) or the president of the competent Commercial Court (*'Tribunal de Commerce'*).

Article 145 of the Code of Civil Procedure provides that 'If there is a legitimate reason to preserve or to establish, before any legal process, the evidence of the facts upon which the resolution of the dispute depends, legally permissible preparatory inquiries may be ordered at the request of any interested party, by way of a petition or by way of a summary procedure'.

However, this summary proceeding may be engaged even if proceedings on the merits of the case are not brought before the court (the Civil Court or the Commercial Court, as opposed to the summary proceeding before the president of the Civil Court or the Commercial Court). This constitutes an advantage compared to the situation before the Competition Council where the request for measures of conservation is an accessory to proceedings on the merits. Nevertheless, where proceedings before the court have already been launched, Article 145 may not be implemented.

---

45. See *for instance*, Jean-Louis Lesquins, 'La sanction judiciaire des pratiques anticoncurrentielles', *Decideurs Stratégie Finance Droit*, June 2004, No. 55, 79 and R. Bout, *et alii*, *Lamy Droit Economique*, June 2006, 2250.

In application of Article 145, the judge may order a measure to research a specific document as long as its existence is at least possible.[46] The victim will therefore have to already have a precise idea of what he is looking for, since the object of the future proceedings must be outlined in his claim and the investigation must not be imprecise.[47] The Article 145 action ('in futurum') must have as a purpose the research of elements of proof that are lacking or the conservation of documents that might disappear: this research must be useful in the perspective of a future or possible litigation. Failing that, the claim is inadmissible.[48]

In taking his decision, the judge must take into consideration the legitimate interests of the defendant. The claim must therefore be rejected where the measures requested might undermine confidential information or business secrets.[49]

3.   THE INVESTIGATIONS DURING THE PROCEEDINGS

Pursuant to Article 9 Code of Civil Procedure, each party must prove, according to the law, the facts necessary for the success of his claim.

Even though, according to Article 9, the plaintiff is supposed to bring all necessary elements of proof in the proceedings on the merits, Article 10 empowers the judge to order *sua sponte* any legally appropriate investigation measures in terms of obtaining documents. The judge can therefore order one of the parties to produce elements of proofs, but his power is limited by the existence of a legitimate obstacle, such as banking secrecy[50] or business secrecy for instance.

Moreover, Article 11 provides that: 'The parties are held to cooperate for the implementation of the investigation measures, and the judge may draw conclusions from abstention or refusal to do so.

Where a party holds evidence material, the judge may, upon the petition of the other party, order him to produce it, where necessary subject to a periodic penalty payment. He may, at the request of one of the parties, request or order, where necessary subject to the same penalty, the production of all documents held by third parties where there is no legitimate impediment to doing so'.

The judge may not order *sua sponte* the production of a document held by a third party, whereas Article 10 allows him to do so concerning all other measures of instruction: the concerned party will have to make a request to the judge and identify precisely, in his claim, the documents and deeds requested.[51]

---

46. Court of Appeal of Paris, 20 February 2002, *BICC* 1 March 2003, p. 56, No. 244.
47. Court of Appeal of Paris, 26 December 1986, [1987] *Dalloz*, p. 344. See J.L. Lesquins, 'L'établissement des pratiques anticoncurrentielles lors du procès civil, *in* Les sanctions judiciaires des pratiques anticoncurrentielles, *Petites Affiches* 20 January 2005, 17.
48. Court of Appeal of Paris, 26 December 1986, [1987] *Dalloz*, p. 344.
49. See Cour de cassation, 2e Chambre Civile, 14 March 1984, [1987] *RTD Civ.*, p. 561.
50. Cour de cassation, Chambre Sociale, 27 January 1999, [1999], No. 214.
51. Cour de cassation, 2e Chambre Civile, 15 March 1979, Bulletin Civile, II, No. 88.

An important condition for the implementation of Article 11 is the absence of a legitimate obstacle to the production of the requested elements. Article 138 of the Code of Civil Procedure gives a more precise answer to this question, providing that if, during the proceeding, a party wishes to rely on a notarial deed or a contract to which he was not a party or a document held by a third party, he may request the judge, to whom the matter is referred, to order the delivery of a certified copy or to lodge the deed or the document with the court. Pursuant to Article 139, the request may be made without any specific procedural formality. The judge, if he considers that the request is well founded, may order the delivery or the production of the original, copy or extract of the deed, as the case may be, under the conditions and guarantees that he determines, if necessary, under a periodic penalty payment.

In the event of a justifiable objection,[52] the judge will refuse the request. The judge may assess this reasonableness either when the request is presented or if the third party raises an objection. The judge has discretionary power to decide whether the production of the element of proof is legitimate[53] and will decide whether the delivery requested is contrary to a higher interest, such as professional secrecy.

According to Article 140, in case of difficulty, or if a reasonable objection is raised, the judge who ordered the delivery or the production in court may, on informal request being made to him, retract or modify his decision. The third party may appeal against the new decision within 15 day as from its pronouncement. Should the president order the disclosure and production of confidential documents, the person who was ordered to disclose the document, may, under Article 140, ask the judge to retract or modify his decision, it being specified that confidentiality will not constitute an obstacle to the search for evidence necessary to the judge who remains free to decide whether the solution of the case requires such disclosure. Therefore, the third party will not systematically be able to refuse the disclosure and inspection of the requested documents.

The provisions of Article 140 are particularly useful in damage actions based on the infringement of Articles 81 or 82 EC Treaty, where corporations will certainly oppose the disclosure of documents by claiming that they are covered by business secrecy.

4.   INQUIRY MEASURES

Articles 143 and 144 empower the judge to take any and all necessary measures of investigation. Pursuant to Article 143, the factual circumstances upon which the resolution of the dispute depends, may, at the request of the parties or *sua sponte*, be subjected to any legally permissible preparatory inquiry. In any event, the preparatory inquiries may be ordered when the judge is not supplied with sufficient

---

52. Articles 11 and 141.
53. Cour de Cassation, 2e Chambre Civile, 14 November 2006, [1980] *Dalloz*, p. 365.

material to determine the matter. Articles 148 and 149 empower the judge to modify the measures that he has ordered during the proceedings.[54]

The powers of the judge seem to be limited by Article 146 which provides that:

> A preparatory inquiry on a fact may be ordered only if the party who pleads it does not have sufficient material to prove it. In no case, a preparatory inquiry may be ordered for the sake of making up a party's deficiency to produce evidence.

However, the judge will be able to order a preparatory inquiry in most cases in which the victim does not have access to the needed information and documents. Indeed, if a document is held by either the author perpetrator of the anticompetitive actions or a third party, the plaintiff will not have the sufficient material to prove it.

The judge may also carry out personal verifications, including inspection of the premises,[55] and, during the process of verification, at trial or at any other venue, be assisted by an expert, or hear the parties or such other person whose testimony is useful to establishing the truth.[56]

Furthermore, a judge may order the parties, either individually or collectively or one of them, to appear in person.[57] This type of inquiry is relatively rare in civil procedures. The judge who orders this determines the venue, date and time of the personal appearance unless it has been done so in short order.[58]

The personal appearance may take place in a public hearing, but Article 188 provides that the hearing may always take place in the judge's council chamber; such a provision will be useful where matters relating to business secrecy may be mentioned.

Minutes will record the statements of the parties, their absence or refusal to answer questions of response.[59] The examined parties will sign the declaration after having verified or certified that it corresponds to their statements; in that case the minutes will refer to that. If necessary, the minutes declaration will state that the parties have refused either to sign or to certify it.[60] Article 198 further provides that the judge may draw any legal conclusion from the statements of the parties, from the absence or refusal to answer any of them and consider it as a

---

54. Article 148: The judge may combine several inquiries. He may at any time, even while they are being carried out, decide to add any other necessary inquiry to those that have been ordered. Article 149: The judge may at any time extend or restrict the scope of the prescribed inquiries.
55. Article 179 of the Code of Civil Procedure: 'The judge may, in order to check them himself, in any matter, carry out a personal inspection of the facts in dispute and the parties either be present or be summoned to attend'. He will undertake his own findings, evaluations, appraisals or reconstitutions that he considers necessary, by being present, if need be, on the spot'. Article 180: 'If he does not do it immediately, the judge will set the venue, date and time for the verification; if necessary, he will appoint a member of the trial bench'.
56. Article 183.
57. Article 184.
58. Article 187.
59. Article 194.
60. Article 195.

prima facie evidence in writing. This will be useful in order to reverse the burden of proof.[61]

It should finally be noted that even though good faith should prevail in the proceedings, the parties are not obliged to 'tell the truth to judge'.[62] Indeed, the Supreme Court ruled that the privilege against self-incrimination is a 'fundamental freedom'.[63] It is therefore not possible to require from the parties to the action to be entirely honest.

The French courts therefore have at their disposal means to enable them to overcome the difficulties mentioned by the Working Paper[64] concerning the access to the relevant evidence thus helping to make damages claims effective. The French judge's powers to order the production of evidence is not, however, as efficient as the common law 'discovery' rule, and is a source of delay in the conduct of the proceedings.[65]

However, the specialization of the courts, which will give jurisdiction for implementing French and EC competition law to a limited number of courts,[66] will certainly, or at least hopefully, have a positive effect on the involvement of the courts in damage actions for breach of EC competition law, and also on the understanding by the courts of the specificities of competition law cases.

The French courts may also ask the Commission for information and documents.

5.   THE RELATIONSHIPS OF THE FRENCH JUDGE WITH THE COMMISSION
           AND COMPETITION COUNCIL

a.   **The Transmission of Information and Documents
           to the Courts**

The judge may, under certain conditions, ask the Commission, acting as the '*amicus curiae*', for information and documents that it may have in its possession. Article 15 paragraph 1 Regulation 1/2003 provides that 'In proceedings for the application of Article 81 or Article 82 of the Treaty, courts of the Member States may ask the Commission to transmit to them information in its possession or its opinion on questions concerning the application of the Community competition rules'. The Commission emphasizes that its duty to communicate information it

---

61. *Ibid.*
62. S. Guinchard *et al*ii, *Droit et pratique de la procédure civile*, Dalloz, Dalloz Action, 2006-2007, No. 222.52.
63. Cour de Cassation, Chambre Sociale, 15 November 1990, *Bulletin Civil*, No. 560. On the case law of the European Court of Human Rights and of the European Court of Justice on the privilege against self-incrimination, see Chapter 4 'Disclosure – Access to information' *supra*.
64. Commission Staff Working Paper: Annexe to the Green Paper: Damages Actions for Breach of EC Anti-Trust Rules: (COM) (2005) 672 Final: SEC (2005) 1732 (19.12.2006).
65. J. Riffault-Silk, 'Les actions privées en droit de la concurrence: obstacles de procédure et de fond', [2006] *Revue Lamy de la Concurrence*, p. 89.
66. Article L.420-7 of the French Commercial Code as amended by the NER Law 2001-420 of 15 May 2001 and Decree 2005-1756. On the specialization of the courts, see *above*.

has in its possession extends to the communication of documents.[67] The Commission also states that it will try to respond to such a request within a month.[68]

A difficulty arises from the documents covered by the obligation of professional secrecy and that are in the Commission's possession. This mainly concerns business secrecy.

According to the Commission,[69] when communicating elements to the national courts, it will respect the guaranties set out in Article 287 EC which provides that 'The members of the institutions of the Community, the members of committees, and the officials and other servants of the Community shall be required, even after their duties have ceased, not to disclose information of the kind covered by the obligation of professional secrecy, in particular information about undertakings, their business relations or their cost components'. Moreover, it should be reminded that Regulation 1/2003 protects business secrecy.[70]

The Commission, in its Cooperation Notice of 2004,[71] explained that before transmitting information covered by professional secrecy to a national jurisdiction, it will remind the court of the obligation it has under EC law in relation to confidential information and will ask the court if it 'can' and 'wants' to guarantee the protection of confidential information and business secrecy. If the court cannot offer such a guarantee, the Commission will not communicate the confidential elements. The commission will not communicate the requested elements until the court guarantees that it will protect the confidential information and the business secrecy.

The Court of First Instance (CFI) had already developed the same solutions in *Postbank*.[72] The CFI ruled that Regulation 17/62 does not prohibit the communication of documents – whether confidential or covered by business secrecy – to the national courts, but that the Commission must take all necessary precautions to avoid undermining the rights of the corporations concerned. Regulation 1/2003 also provides for this possibility. The Commission must therefore, for instance, indicate to the judge the passages in the documents that contain secrets, and the court must then guarantee the protection non-disclosure of the information. The CFI also held that in certain 'exceptional' cases in which, despite the precautions

---

67. Notice on Cooperation between the Commission and the National Courts, [2004] *OJ*, C 101/04, point 21.
68. *Ibid*, point 22.
69. *Ibid*, point 25.
70. Article 28 provides that 'Without prejudice to the exchange and to the use of information foreseen in Articles 11, 12, 14, 15 and 27, the Commission and the competition authorities of the Member States, their officials, servants and other persons working under the supervision of these authorities as well as officials and civil servants of other authorities of the Member States shall not disclose information acquired or exchanged by them pursuant to this Regulation and of the kind covered by the obligation of professional secrecy. This obligation also applies to all representatives and experts of Member States attending meetings of the Advisory Committee pursuant to Article 14'.
71. Notice on Cooperation between the Commission and the National Courts, *Ibid*, point 25.
72. Case T-353/94, *Postbank*, 1996.

taken by the Commission, the protection of third parties would not be entirely guaranteed by the national court, the Commission must refuse to disclose communicate the documents. Since the French judge must guarantee that the adversarial principle will be respected in the framework of the proceedings, this obligation to guarantee the adversarial principle might well constitute an 'exceptional' case in the meaning of *Postbank*.[73] One may also wonder what a French judge must do when dealing with the passages that the Commission signalled as being confidential.[74]

Another difficulty is related to the way in which the French court will respect the adversarial system when asking for documents and information, especially where this is done sua sponte. Article 16 paragraph 2 of the Code of Civil Procedure provides that:

'In all circumstances, the judge must supervise the respect of, and he must himself respect, the adversarial principle.

In his decision, the judge may take into consideration grounds, explanations and documents relied upon or produced by the parties only if the parties had an opportunity to discuss them in an adversarial manner. He shall not base his decision on legal arguments that he has raised sua sponte without having first invited the parties to comment thereon'.

According to Article 16 paragraph 2, in his decision, the judge may only take into consideration documents communicated to all the parties and that were subject to an adversarial debate. Therefore, in the case where documents covered by secrecy are communicated, it does not seem appropriate for a judge to ask for and to obtain documents, where he cannot ensure that the adversarial system will be respected. Moreover, the Decree No. 2005-1668 of 27 December 2005[75] provides that when the judge envisages asking the Commission for information in application of Article 15 paragraph 1 Regulation 1/2003, he must notify the parties, and the Commission's answer must be notified disclosed to the parties, who can then present their observations.

It should be noted that in leniency procedures, an important consideration in determining whether to make an oral or written statement admission is the extent to which it may be subject to discovery procedures, in particular in cases involving a risk of civil damage actions. With regard to leniency procedures Carswell-Parmentier observes that:

With respect to the ability of third parties to obtain information from the Competition Council, notably a corporate statement, in the context of a civil action for damages, it should be kept in mind that the judge in a civil action can request communication of information and documents. According to Article 11 of the Code of Civil Procedure, a judge may order the production

73. G. Parléani, 'Actualité de la sanction judiciaire des pratiques anticoncurrentielles', *Petites Affiches*, 20 January 2006, No. 14, 3.
74. *Ibid.*
75. Decree No. 2005-1668, 27 December 2005 modifying Decree No. 2002-689 30 April 2002 *fixant les conditions de la liberté des prix et de la concurrence.*

of all documents held by third parties unless there is a legitimate reason preventing such communication. The Council has taken the position that if such a request occurred in the context of a leniency application, it would refuse to communicate the corporate statement as well as any information provided in support of a leniency application on the grounds that any such disclosure could damage the effectiveness of the leniency programme.[76]

Pursuant to Decree 2002-689 implementing the leniency rules, the French authorities will accept oral statements. As for the Commission, in its Cooperation Notice of 2004,[77] it indicated that it would abstain from communicating to the national courts information furnished by the author of a leniency claim without having obtained the author's prior consent.

**b.   The Opinions of the Commission and
            the Competition Council**

Pursuant to the Regulation 1/2003, Order No. 2004-1173 amended certain provisions of the Commercial Code to adapt French law in view of the application of EC competition law by the national courts.[78] Competition Authorities are viewed as experts whose opinion is asked for to enlighten the judge. This possibility is provided for under French and EC law.

Article L.462-3 of the Commercial Code, as amended, provides that:

> The courts may consult the council regarding the anti-competitive practises described in Articles L.420-1, L.420-2 and L.420-5 hereof and Articles 81 and 82 of the Founding Treaty of the European Community when they are raised in the cases referred to them. It may issue an opinion only after a procedure in which all parties were heard is concluded. If it already has information gathered during an earlier procedure, however, it may issue its opinion without implementing the procedure envisaged in the present text.

The limitation period is suspended, where applicable, when the council is consulted.

The Council's opinion may be published after the dismissal or judgment.

In accordance with Article L.462-3, the Competition Council may only transmit an opinion after an adversarial procedure has been respected, and may a priori only qualify facts, without making any recommendation on the possible

---

76. Lucie Carswell-Parmentier, 'Recent developments in French competition law – Commitments, leniency and settlement procedures – The French approach', in the process of being published.
77. Notice on Cooperation between the Commission and the National Courts, [2004] *OJ*, C 101/04, point 26.
78. Order No. 2004-1173 of 4 November 2004 Art. 4 *Official Journal* of 5 November 2004. See L. Idot, 'Adaptation du droit français au règlement 1/2003', [2004] *Europe*, 425; M. Malaurie-Vignal, 'Adaptation du droit français de la concurrence, [2005] *Concurrence, contr., consom.*, 178.

sanctions.[79] The opinion does not bind the court, but, as observed by the Ashurst Report for France, it is likely to be critical.[80]

Claudel observes that this procedure is oddly enough not very often implemented, and is actually used less and less often, which is paradoxical in regard to the development of cooperation between the national courts and the competition authorities.[81] The Competition Council's reports show that the number of requests for advice varies between zero and four a year. The specialization of the French courts for the application of competition law rules and the augured development of damages actions will hopefully change this trend.

Pursuant to Article 15 paragraph 1, the national courts may also ask the Commission for an opinion relating to the application of EC competition law;[82] the questions may concern economic, factual or legal matters.

In order to comply with the case law of the European Court of Human Rights and the general principles of French civil procedure, the opinions will have to be subject to discussion by the parties.[83]

According to the Decree No. 2005-1668,[84] the judge must notify the parties when he envisages asking the Commission, in application of the provisions of paragraph 1, Article 15 Regulation 1/2003, for an opinion. Unless the parties have already filed briefs on this opinion, the judge invites them to produce their observations in a delay that he fixes. As soon as he receives their observations or when the delay fixed expires, the judge can ask the Commission for an opinion by taking a ruling that is open to appeal. He postpones the proceedings until he receives the opinion or until the expiry of a delay that he fixed. The ruling, by which the judge asks for the opinion, and the possible observations, are transmitted to the Commission by the office of the clerk of the court. The ruling and the date of transmission of the file are notified to the parties. As soon as the court receives the opinion, the office of the clerk notifies the parties who can present their observations.

---

79. E. Claudel, 'La processualisation du droit de la concurrence', in *La modernisation du droit de la concurrence*, G. Canivet (ed.), [2006] *L.G.D.J.*, p. 306 and J.M. Mousseron and V. Selinsky, *Le nouveau droit de la concurrence*, [1987] Litec.

80. C. Momège and N. Bessot, op. cit., p. 30. The Report also notes that there is an example in which the Competition Council's opinion was not followed: Court of Appeal of Paris, 13 January 1998, *UGAP v. CAMIF*, [1998] JCP G, II, 10217.

81. E. Claudel, 'La processualisation du droit de la concurrence', in *La modernisation du droit de la concurrence*, G. Canivet (ed.), [2006] *L.G.D.J.*, p. 307.

82. Article 15 para. 1 Regulation 1/2003: 'In proceedings for the application of Article 81 or Article 82 of the Treaty, courts of the Member States may ask the Commission to transmit to them information in its possession or its opinion on questions concerning the application of the Community competition rules'.

83. B. Cheynel and C. Nourissat, 'Adaptation du droit français au droit communautaire: commentaire de l'ordonnance No. 2004-237 du 4 novembre 2004', [2005] *Revue Lamy de la Concurrence*, No. 2, p. 63.

84. Decree No. 2005-1668, 27 December 2005 modifying Decree No. 2002-689 30 April 2002 *fixant les conditions de la liberté des prix et de la concurrence*.

The system set out in the Decree No. 2005-1668 therefore seems to be in compliance with the French adversarial rules and with EC Art 6.1 of the ECHR.

c.   **The Intervention of the Commission and**
             the Competition Council

Article 15 paragraph 3 Regulation 1/2003 created a new procedure: 'Competition authorities of the Member States, acting on their own initiative, may submit written observations to the national courts of their Member State on issues relating to the application of Article 81 or Article 82 of the Treaty. With the permission of the court in question, they may also submit oral observations to the national courts of their Member State. Where the coherent application of Article 81 or Article 82 of the Treaty so requires, the Commission, acting on its own initiative, may submit written observations to courts of the Member States. With the permission of the court in question, it may also make oral observations'.

Article L.470-5 of the Commercial Code also allows the intervention of the administration in civil proceedings. According to Article L.470-5, the Minister for Economic Affairs or his representative may make submissions before the civil or criminal jurisdictions and develop these submissions orally during the hearing. Pursuant to the provisions of Article L.470-5, the Minister may also produce the inquiry reports and official records. Gavalda and Lucas de Leyssac consider that these provisions allow the administration to give the litigant help in establishing the anticompetitive practise.[85]

These interventions bring into the civil action an inquisitorial aspect, as the parties partially lose the control of the trial.[86] The 4 November 2004 Order, which is supposed to adapt French procedural law to EC law, strangely does not provide anything on the intervention of the Commission, and the Code of Civil Procedure does not contain any provision which could be used to this effect; the word 'observation' is not even utilized in the Code.[87]

With regard to the intervention of the French Minister in the proceedings in application of Article L.470-5, the Supreme Court held that the Minister is not a party:

> The Minister for Economic Affairs, when he files, before the Court of Appeal of Paris, briefs recommending measures exclusively based on the application of the Order of December 1, 1986, simply implements the powers he holds from Article 56 (today Article L.470-5 of the Commercial Code) and is not granted the qualification of a party to the proceedings.[88]

---

85. C. Gavalda and C. Lucas de Leyssac, [1988] ALD, 89, No. 176.
86. E. Claudel, 'La processualisation du droit de la concurrence', *ibid*, p. 308.
87. *Ibid*, p. 309.
88. Cour de Cassation, Chambre Commerciale, 6 November 2000, Bulletin IV, No. 266.

The Minister's mission to guarantee economic law and order therefore justifies his intervention. It is possible to consider that the Commission's intervention would be based on the same grounds.[89] In the same sense, the Commission states, in its Cooperation Notice, that its assistance to the courts is founded on its obligation to safeguard the public interest, and is therefore not aimed at serving the private interests of the parties in the cases.[90]

An important question however remains unanswered: namely as to whether the French judge have to submit the opinion to an adversarial procedure.[91] Academic legal opinion considers that the judge will have to respect the adversarial system,[92] but the rules governing the application of the law still remain to be set out.[93]

Finally, it should be noted that, in any event, the court remains independent, and is therefore not bound by the intervention of the Commission or of the Minister.[94] With regard to the intervention of the Commission, point 19 of the Cooperation Notice of 2004 states that whatever form the cooperation takes, the Commission will respect the independence of the national courts, and that the assistance of the Commission does not bind the courts.[95]

---

89. *Ibid.*
90. Notice on Cooperation between the Commission and the National Courts, op. cit., point 15.
91. J.M. Meffre and C. Guet, op. cit., 367.
92. See for instance G. Canivet, 'L'organisation des juridictions nationales pour l'application du droit communautaire de la concurrence', op. cit., p. 27.
93. E. Claudel, 'op. cit., p. 309.
94. Véronique Sélinsky, 'Quand les juges du commerce appliquent le droit de la concurrence...', *Revue Lamy de la Concurrence*, May/July 2005, 21.
95. Notice on Cooperation between the Commission and the National Courts, op. cit., point 19.

Chapter 10

French Procedure: Forms of Compensation and Costs of Action

A.   FORMS OF COMPENSATION

1.   THE DAMAGES AWARDED BY THE COURTS

Another consequence of the classical triptych of fault, damage and causal effect is that the damages awarded by the courts must compensate the loss actually suffered and not constitute punitive sanctions, unlike the damages which can be awarded in the US legal system.[1]

As the Ashurst Report for France[2] notes, provided that the claimant has suffered an injury that is direct and certain, any type of damage can be compensated: future injuries, material, moral, loss of amenities, loss of profits, etc.

In this respect, the French rules in terms of compensation of loss in competition cases seems to comply with the EC principles: in particular with *Brasserie du Pêcheur*, in which the ECJ held that 'National legislation which generally limits the damage for which reparation may be granted to damage done to certain, specifically protected individual interests not including loss of profit by individuals is not compatible with Community law'.[3]

---

1.   Jean-Louis Lesquins, 'La sanction judiciaire des pratiques anticoncurrentielles', *Decideurs Stratégie Finance Droit*, June 2004, n° 55, 79.
2.   C. Momège and N. Bessot, *Comparative Report - France*, p. 8, <www.ec.europa.eu>.
3.   Joined cases C- 46/93 and C-48/93 *Brasserie du Pêcheur v. Bundesrepublik Deutschland and The Queen v Secretary of State for Transport, ex parte: Factortame and others* ("Brasserie du Pêcheur") [1996] ECR I-1029, Para 90.

Moreover, a loss of chance may also be compensated. In *SA BMW France v SARL Rotative Typo*, for instance, the Versailles Court of Appeal held that by compelling its distributors to terminate their commercial relationships with their usual supplier, SA BMW France was the instigator of an illegal agreement, and therefore liable to pay damages to Rotative Typo for loss of chance to obtain a new supply contract.[4]

However, the courts may not, in principle, award damages by assessing the economic damages that have 'possibly' been suffered, nor by calculating the probable damage suffered using a standard multiplier. The variety of sources of damages for the victim makes it however difficult for the judge to comply with the principles of French law. Indeed, in competition law, the judge will find it difficult to assess with certainty the damages effectively incurred, since anti-competitive practices are extremely diverse: inventory of the markets directly and/or indirectly lost, consequences of the anti-competitive practices on available funds and on the self-financing capacity, irrecoverable investments, stocks that have become useless[5]. The courts will also have to take into account the damage in relation to the undermining of the competitive capacity, for instance loss of investment opportunities, difficulties to carry out research and development or commercial canvassing, and the moral prejudice.

In order to assess the amount of the damages to award, the judge may ask the Commission and the Competition Council to give an opinion.[6]

An evaluation may also be ordered by the judge or produced by the parties. The evaluation can be produced with the opinion of a specialist ('*sapiteur*') chosen by the expert for his specific knowledge in a particular field (a specific industrial sector for example), which will have important evidential value.[7] However, the intervention of a *sapiteur* entails additional costs and delays. An evaluation is not very often asked by the parties and is usually only ordered in important and/or complex cases.[8]

Furthermore, the French courts may not award punitive damages, since such a decision would conflict with general principles of French law. Moreover, the academic legal writing seems opposed to the introduction of punitive damages in France.[9]

The absence of punitive damages in French law could constitute an infringement of the doctrine of effectiveness, it being reminded that the Commission Staff Working Paper stated that 'disincentives created by restrictions on the amounts that can be awarded, such as the unavailability of punitive damages, can also constitute an obstacle to private actions'.[10]

---

4. Versailles Court of Appeal, September 11, 1997, *SA BMW France v SARL Rotative*, quoted by C. Momège and N. Bessot, op. cit., p. 43.
5. Jean-Louis Lesquins, 'La sanction judiciaire des pratiques anticoncurrentielles', op. cit., 79.
6. See above, (4), (v).
7. J. Riffault-Silk, 'Les actions privées en droit de la concurrence: obstacles de procédure et de fond', [2006] *Revue Lamy de la Concurrence*, p. 89.
8. *Ibid.*
9. C. Momège and N. Bessot, op. cit. 34.
10. Commission Staff Working Paper: Annexe to the Green Paper: Damages Actions for Breach of EC Anti-Trust Rules: (COM) (2005) 672 Final: SEC (2005) 1732 (19.12.2006).

The Green Paper on Damages Actions for breach of the EC antitrust rules suggests doubling the damages at the discretion of the court, either automatically or conditionally, for horizontal cartel infringement. This type of solution would constitute punitive damages, and would therefore require a modification of the French current rules through a modification of the French Civil Code.

In *Brasserie du Pêcheur*, the ECJ held that it is to the 'it must be possible to award specific damages, such as the exemplary damages provided for by English law, pursuant to claims for damages founded on Community law, if such damages may be awarded pursuant to similar claims or actions founded on domestic law'.[11]

On the contrary, it is submitted that nothing in EC case law leads to the doctrine of effectiveness requiring Member States to provide for punitive damages in private enforcement cases.

One can however ask whether the French law on liability should not be modified as regard competition law.[12] A possible solution would be for the judge to be allowed to use a multiplying coefficient, which would take into account the seriousness of the fault, where the damage assessed with certainty is probably inferior to the damage actually incurred. This would not, however, constitute punitive damages. Moreover, this would be in compliance with the obligation set out by the Court of Justice: the national law has to provide for effective and dissuasive sanctions.[13]

Even though the damages awarded may not be punitive, the victims must be able to recover entirely the damages suffered, not only because this will permit to have an 'economic justice'[14] in France, but also because the competition law policy of the EU is to facilitate claiming damages.[15] If the victims of anticompetitive practices find it difficult to recover the losses they have suffered, their legal actions will not be facilitated.

Finally, even though the Civil Code does not allow for a lowering in the standard of proof when damages are difficult to quantify, in practice the Civil and the Commercial Courts, and, in the case of an appeal, the Court of Appeal, have exclusive jurisdiction on the merits of the case and therefore have exclusive jurisdiction to quantify the damage.[16] This means that the courts do not have to

---

11. Joined cases C- 46/93 and C-48/93 *Brasserie du Pêcheur v. Bundesrepublik Deutschland and The Queen v Secretary of State for Transport, ex parte: Factortame and others,* [1996] ECR I-1029, Para 90.
12. G. Parléani, 'Actualité de la sanction judiciaire des pratiques anticoncurrentielles', *Petites Affiches,* 20 January 2006, n° 14, 3.
13. *Commission v Greece,* September 21, 1989, case C-68/88.
14. G. Parléani, op.cit., 3.
15. Green Paper, 'Damages actions for breach of the EC antitrust rules Damages actions for breach of the EC antitrust rules', COM (2005) 672 final: 'Facilitating damages claims for breach of antitrust law will not only make it easier for consumers and firms who have suffered damages arising from an infringement of antitrust rules to recover their losses from the infringer but also strengthen the enforcement of antitrust law'.
16. In France, the *Cour de Cassation* (Supreme Court for civil and criminal matters) only verifies if the judgement of the court of first instance or of the appeal court is in compliance will the applicable law.

explain precisely how they quantify the damage. The damages awarded by the courts are not, however, comparable to the damages awarded in the US.[17] Once again, the recent specialisation of the French courts may have a positive effect on the assessment of the damage in private enforcement cases.

2.   NULLITY

In order to hold that a clause or an agreement is null and void, the judge must decide whether a violation took place that in turn was not subject to an exemption, and therefore implement very complex legal and economic rules. It is for this reason that the competent courts are, in France, specialised courts[18] and why the courts may ask the Commission or the Council for an opinion.

Article 81(2) EC Treaty provides that 'any agreements or decisions prohibited (by Article 81(1)) shall be automatically void', which means that the courts will have to rule that such agreements are null and void. In case of nullity, any provision in violation of the EC Treaty disappears. This also allows one of the parties to ask the judge to rule on the nullity of a contractual requirement (such as the limitation

---

17.   These are a few examples of infringement findings on French and EC competition law cases:

   – *Parfumerie/Estée Lauder*, Court of Appeal of Paris (1995): cartel (Article 7 of the 1986 French Order) - 7.600 Euros;
   – *Eco-System/Peugeot*, Commercial Court of Paris (1996): cartel (Article 81 EC Treaty) - 240.000 Euros;
   – *BMW/Rotative Typo*, Court of Appeal of Versailles (1997): cartel (Article 7 of the 1986 French Order) - 11.000 Euros;
   – *Mors/Westland/Labinal*, Court of Appeal of Paris (1998): cartel and abuse of a dominant position (Articles 81 and 82 EC Treaty) - 5,2 million Euros;
   – *Bibliothèque de Limoges*, Court of Appeal of Paris (1998): cartel (Article 7 of the 1986 French Order) - 69.000 Euros;
   – *CAMIF/UGAP*, Supreme Court ('*Cour de cassation*') (2000): cartel and abuse of a dominant position (Articles 81 and 82 EC Treaty, and Articles L.420-1 and 420-2 of the Commercial Code) - 1,5 Euros;
   – *Speedy France*, Court of Appeal of Paris (2002): cartel and abuse of a dominant position (Articles L.420-1 and 420-2 of the Commercial Code) - 300.000 Euros;
   – *Editions Montparnasse/TF1*, Court of Appeal of Paris/Supreme Court (2003): cartel and abuse of a dominant position (Articles L.420-1 and 420-2 of the Commercial Code) - 1,5 million Euros;
   – *Vérimédia/Médiamétrie*, Court of Appeal of Versailles (2004): abuse of a dominant position (Article 8 of the 1986 French Order) - 100.000 Euros;
   – *Marbreries Lescarelles/OGF*, Court of Appeal of Paris (2004): cartel and abuse of a dominant position (Articles 7 and 8 of the 1986 French Order) - 1.8 million Euros.

   Taken from P. de Montalembert and M. Henry, 'Indemnisation du préjudice causé par des pratiques anticoncurrentielles: risques et opportunités', *Option Finance*, 6 June 2006, 45.
18.   Article L.420-7 of the French Commercial Code as amended by the NER Law 2001-420 of May 15, 2001 and Decree 2005-1756. On the specialisation of the courts, see above, (1).

of a distributor or a licensee's freedom).[19] The nullity is also necessary in order to obtain compensation in the form of damages.

Even though the applicable national laws determine the consequences of the nullity, the Court of Justice set out certain applicable principles. The nullity is absolute[20] and can be claimed by any person who may have an interest in having the concerned specific provisions nullified, irrespective of whether the person is a party to the agreement or an offender[21]. As for the consequences of the nullity, the Court of Justice ruled that a nullified agreement does not have any effect, whether between the parties or as regard third parties.[22] The Court of Justice has also ruled that the nullity has a retroactive effect.[23] The extent of the nullity will depend on the applicable national law: the national law will determine whether only the clause itself is null or if the entire agreement is null and void.

In compliance with the doctrine of effectiveness, any party to an agreement that violates the provisions of Article 81 EC Treaty has a right to action. This doctrine affects the French rule *'nemo auditur propriam turpitudinem allegans'*. This adage means that a judge may hear no one whose claim is based on his own legal wrong; it may be used by a judge in order to refuse any restitution or compensation where an agreement is annulled as a consequence of a violation of public law and order. However, pursuant to ECJ case law, and in particular *Courage*, the national methods of enforcement of the EC competition law must not render excessively difficult or almost impossible the enforcement of EC competition rules. The ECJ case law thus encourages companies to denounce anticompetitive behaviour, even where they have participated to an unlawful cartel.

Therefore, the French *'nemo auditur'* rule, which would lead to refusing *a priori* a right of action due to the participation in an unlawful cartel, is set aside in the case of application of EC competition law, but not necessarily in the case of application of French competition law. The EC doctrine of effectiveness does not however require that the company which participated in the cartel have an automatic right to damages: where damages are not excluded *a priori* in each individual case, the national judge will have to assess the involvement of each party in the anticompetitive consequences.[24] In particular, the judge must take into account the possible weakness of one of the parties who may have been deprived of its freedom of action.

---

19. R. Bout, *et alii*, *Lamy Droit Economique* (Lamy, Paris, 2006), 2245.
20. ECJ, November 25, 1971, *Béguelin Import Co*, case 22/71, *Rec.* 949, point 29.
21. ECJ, September 20, 2001, *Courage Ltd v Bernard Crehan*, Case C 435/99 (2001) ECR I-6297, point 28.
22. *Béguelin* (1971) case C-21/71.
23. *Brasserie de Haecht* (1973) Case C-48/72.
24. Bout R., *et alii*, *Lamy Droit Economique*, op. cit., 2241.

3.   Injections and Iterim Measures (Measures of
       Conservation)

According to the case law of the ECJ, the full effectiveness of directly applicable Community law requires that national courts have jurisdiction to grant interim measures as well as damages.[25] It should be noted that interim measures are defined, for the following purposes, as those measures which a plaintiff may request in emergency procedures (*'procédure de référé'*) from the president of the civil or commercial court, i.e. injunction procedures that take place in *prima facie* cases.[26]

These interim measures may be also necessary when the national court has the obligation to suspend judgement, in particular in the cases of a preliminary ruling, which, in certain situations, is compulsory.[27] Point 14 of the Cooperation Notice of 2004 specifies that when a national court postpones proceedings, it has the obligation, in application of *Masterfoods*, to examine the necessity of ordering interim measures in order to protect the interests of the parties.[28]

The Ashurst report for France observes 'such [emergency] proceedings are often used in competition matters, and especially in cases of a dominant position. Competition law may be the basis for the main action or invoked in defence. In such proceedings, the president of the court may order that behaviour amounting to unfair competition cease. He may also award injunctions, for example, to cease an anti-competitive practice, to communicate a given document, to perform a contract, etc., or interim payment, for example, partial payment in advance by the defendant, of the damages to be awarded, especially where injury results from a fault'.[29]

The French judge has the power when applying Articles 81 and 82 EC, to order injunctions and interim measures in the framework of summary orders. The powers of the Competition Council as regards the injunctions which can be ordered are broader than the powers of the judges. Pursuant to Article L.464-1, the Council may adopt the interim measures which seem necessary. These measures include the suspension of the practice concerned and an order to the parties to return the situation to the prior state, but this list is not exhaustive[30] and the Council may

---

25. See also Commission Staff Working Paper: Annexe to the Green Paper: Damages Actions for Breach of EC Anti-Trust Rules: (COM) (2005) 672 Final: SEC (2005) 1732 (19.12.2006), p. 10.
26. Therefore, we will not study the issues relating to the granting of injunctive interim relief such as developed in cases C-213/89 *The Queen v Secretary of State for Transport, ex parte: Factortame and others* ("Factortame I") [1990] ECR I-2433; joined cases C-143/88 and C-92/89 *Zuckerfabrik Süderdithmarschen* and *Zuckerfabrik Soest* [1991] ECR I-415; C-465/93 Atlanta Fruchthandelsgesellschaft and others (I) v. Bundesamt für Ernährung und Forstwirtschaft [1995] ECR I-3761.
27. Article 16 Para 1 Regulation 1/2003 and ECJ, *Masterfoods*, case C 344/98, *Rec. ECJ* I. 11369.
28. Notice on Cooperation between the Commission and the National Courts, [2004] *OJ*, C 101/04, point 15.
29. The Ashurst Report, op. cit., p. 17.
30. Court of Appeal of Paris, 21 May 2002.

impose specific conditions on the parties, such as the suppression or the modification of a clause, the revision of prices.

The French judge may order interim measures in the sole interest of a party, whereas the Commission has such powers only where the market is at stake. Indeed, the Regulation 1/2003 provides that 'In cases of urgency due to the risk of serious and irreparable damage to competition, the Commission, acting on its own initiative may by decision, on the basis of a prima facie finding of infringement, order interim measures'.[31]

The powers of the court to order injunctions at the request of a claimant are limited to the statutory situations set out in the Code of Civil Procedure which the plaintiff sets forth and substantiates in his writ of summons.

- Article 808 of the French Code of Civil Procedure provides that 'In all cases of urgency, the president of the High Court may order in a summary procedure all measures that do not encounter any serious challenge or which the existence of the dispute justifies'.[32]
- Article 809 provides that 'The president may always, even where confronted with a serious challenge, order in an interim application such protective measures or measures to return the parties to their status ante as is necessary in order either to prevent imminent damage or to abate a manifestly illegal nuisance.

In cases where the existence of the cause of action is not seriously challenged, the judge may award an interim payment to the creditor or order the performance of the duty even where there is a mandatory duty to act'.[33]

Therefore, in a case of emergency, the judge will have the power, pursuant to Article 808 (and 872) to order any measures which are not seriously challenged. However, where there a serious challenge of the claim of the plaintiff by the defendant, the judge may order any interim measure if damage is likely to occur imminently and may also order any measure the purpose of which is to restore a situation to its original state where a clear legal breach exists.

Consequently, even where there is a serious challenge, the president of the court may order interim precautionary measures or measures aimed at restoring a

---

31. Article 8, paragraph 1.
32. The provisions of Article 808, which concern the Civil Courts, and of 872, which concern the Commercial Courts, are practically identical. Article 872 provides that 'In all urgent cases, the president of the Commercial Court may, within the confines of the competence of the court, order in a summary procedure, all measures that do not encounter any serious challenge or which the existence of the dispute justifies'.
33. The provisions of Article 809, which concern the Civil Courts, and of 873, which concern the Commercial Courts, are practically identical. Article 873 provides that 'The president may, within the same confines and even where confronted with a serious challenge, provide for by way of a interim application such protective measures or rehabilitation measures that the case justifies, either to avoid imminent damage or to abate a manifestly illegal nuisance. In the cases where the existence of an obligation is not seriously challenged, he may award an interim payment to the creditor or order the mandatory performance of the obligation even where it is an obligation to do'.

situation to its original state in order to prevent the occurrence of imminent damage or to stop a manifestly illegal nuisance. He may also order injunctions with a financial penalty, i.e. a periodic penalty payment to the claimant until the defendant complies with the injunction ordered by the judge. It should be noted that the 'manifestly illegal' nuisance is assessed in a flexible way, as, pursuant to the case law,[34] such a nuisance is not a prerequisite: it is only necessary for the facts to be sufficiently clear and probative.[35]

In the absence of urgency, the judge may award an interim payment to the creditor or order the performance of a contractual obligation where the existence of the contractual duty is not seriously challenged. This provision will, however, certainly be difficult to use in competition law cases.[36]

The Regulation 1/2003 provides that paragraph 3 of Article 81 EC Treaty is directly applicable. Therefore, the analysis of Article 81 paragraph 1 might be considered as a serious challenge,[37] which would have the effect of limiting the interim measures ordered by the judge to cases of manifestly illegal nuisance and imminent damage.

Indeed, before the enactment of the Regulation 1/2003, the judge was obliged to dismiss the claim for a summary order in most of the situations detailed above, unless the claimant had proved the existence of imminent damage or a manifestly illegal nuisance. If the claimant did not succeed in proving this, the president would be obliged to rule that there was a serious defence with respect to the legality under competition law of the agreement the performance of which was sought.[38] Not being competent to determine whether the agreement the lawfulness of which was opposed by the defendant was valid under Article 81(3), the judge had no other alternative other than to decide that the remedy sought raised a serious defence.

Pursuant to Regulation 1/2003, the president of the court, in a interim proceeding, may now henceforth apply Article 81 in its entirety. It seems, however, that where the provisions of Article 81(1) are used as a defence, the judge will often consider that the claim is seriously challenged.[39] Indeed, according to the case law of the Supreme Court[40], there is a serious question to be tried, that is, when the judge must rule on an issue on its merits; in such a situation, the judge may not order measures, at least not on the grounds of Articles 808 and 872 of the Code of Civil Procedure. For instance, the judge may not appoint an expert to analyse

---

34. Cour de cassation, April 18, 2000, D. 2000, AJ 289, obs. Marmontel and RTD Com 2000, 636, obs. Claudel; Court of Appeal of Paris, May 21, 2002, *Numéricâble*, Court of Appeal of Paris, July 16, 2002, Pharmajet.
35. G. Parléani, 'Actualité de la sanction judiciaire des pratiques anticoncurrentielles', op. cit., 3.
36. Bout R., *et alii*, *Lamy Droit Economique*, op. cit., 2247.
37. J.-M. Meffre and C. Guet, 'Modernisation du droit communautaire de la concurrence– Le contrôle a posteriori de la licéité des accords par le juge national: question de procédure', [2005] Dalloz, n° 5, 367.
38. *Ibid.*
39. *Ibid.*
40. Cour de cassation, 1re Chambre Civile, April 26, 1978, [1979] *JCP G*, II, 19251.

the documents disclosed by a company[41], or even rule on the validity[42], the qualification[43] or the interpretation[44] of an act.[45] Nevertheless, there will certainly be cases that will lead the judge to consider that there is not a serious issue to be tried, e.g. certain agreements will evidently not allow the successful implementation of Article 81(3).

In any event, only the existence of an imminent damage or manifestly illegal nuisance enables the French judge to uphold a claim which seeks either the ordering of conservatory measures or the restoration of a situation to its previous state as provided for in Articles 809 and 873. The scope of the provisions set out in Articles 809 and 873 shows that the legislator intended to give the judge a broad choice of measures likely to prevent the occurrence of damage and to put the parties in the situation which existed before the occurrence of the unlawful act.

However, in competition law cases, as regards the assessment of the legality of agreements by the president, it should be noted that in practice the judge would only ascertain the existence of either imminent damage or manifestly illegal nuisance by assessing the validity of the agreement for which the performance is claimed in the interim proceedings.[46] For instance, in a case concerning the violation, by a third party of a prohibition to sell products outside a distribution network, the head of the distribution network will not be entitled to prohibit the sale outside the network unless it is proved that the agreement is lawful under the EC competition law rules.[47] The head of the network may therefore only act on the grounds of Articles 809 or 873 if he proves, without this being contested, that the agreement does not violate competition rules and that therefore, the vendors operating outside the network are those who have caused the manifestly illegal nuisance.[48] Meffre and Guet observe that only the companies beneficiaries of an individual exemption (as well as companies that have received a favourable decision by a competition authority) will fulfil this requirement.[49] It is to be noted that this situation will be increasingly rare by reason of EC Regulation 1/2003.

The legal conditions set out by the Code of Civil Procedure which must be complied with in order to obtain an order for interim measures are therefore very restrictive. Claudel observes that it may be necessary to consider modifying the conditions of the interim proceedings in the framework of economic litigation,

---

41. Cour de cassation, 2e Chambre Civile, December 19, 1973, [1974] *JCP G*, II, 17790.
42. Cour de cassation, 3e Chambre Civile, 7 January 1976, *Bulletin Civil*, III, n° 4.
43. Court of Appeal of Aix-en-Provence, June 4, 1987, [1988] *JCP G*, II, 20917.
44. Cour de cassation, 1e Chambre Civile, April 26, 1978, *Bulletin Civil*, I, n° 157.
45. Generally on this question, see Guinchard S. *et alii, Droit et pratique de la procédure civile* (5th edn, Dalloz, Paris, 2006), n° 124.141 *et seq.*
46. J.-M. Meffre and C. Guet, 'Modernisation du droit communautaire de la concurrence– Le contrôle a posteriori de la licéité des accords par le juge national: question de procédure', op. cit., 368.
47. *Ibid.*
48. Ibid.
49. Ibid.

which is characterised by urgency.[50] The availability of interim measures may also be incompatible with the principle of effectiveness.

It should however finally be noted that if the conditions for an emergency procedure are not met, the president of the court may permit the plaintiff, at his request, to summon the defendant for a judgement on the merits on a fixed date.[51] This emergency procedure permits a judgement to be rendered on the merits.

B.   COSTS OF ACTIONS

As observed by the Green Paper, cost rules play an important role in being an incentive or a disincentive for bringing an action.

According to Article 6 of the European Convention on Human Rights (ECHR), 'In the determination of his civil rights and obligations or of any criminal charge against him, everyone is entitled to a fair and public hearing'. As the Working Paper observes, according to the case law of the ECHR, the right to access guaranteed by Article 6 of the Convention is not an absolute one; the contracting parties to the Convention have the right to formulate rules of access to civil tribunals if these rules serve a legitimate purpose and are proportional to the attainment of the interest.[52]

Moreover, the ECJ, in *Clean Auto Service*[53] held that the EC principle of effectiveness applies to the national rules of procedure concerning costs. The Member States are therefore 'under legal obligation to design their cost rules in such a way that actions for damage claims can "effectively" be brought before the competent national courts'.[54] In other words, the cost of access to the courts must not constitute a barrier to an effective judicial system for the benefit of everyone.

Under French law, three series of rules may play an important role in bringing an action: the rules relating to the burden of court fees and lawyers' fees, to the legal aid, and, finally, to contingency fees.

1.   TAXABLE CHARGES

The 30 December 1977 Act[55] has as an objective to reduce, for the litigants, the general costs of law suits.[56] It establishes the principle of free access to the judicial

---

50. E. Claudel, 'La processualisation du droit de la concurrence', in Canivet G. (ed.), *La moder-nisation du droit de la concurrence* (L.G.D.J., Paris, 2006), p. 303.
51. Article 788 *et seq* Code of Civil Procedure.
52. Commission Staff Working Paper: Annexe to the Green Paper: Damages Actions for Breach of EC Anti-Trust Rules: (COM) (2005) 672 Final: SEC (2005) 1732 (19.12.2006), p. 57.
53. *Clean Car Autoservice v. Stadt Wien and Republik Österreich*, Case C-472/99 (2001) ECR – I 9687.
54. Commission Staff Working Paper, op. cit., p. 59.
55. Act No. 77-1468.
56. See J. Vincent and S. Guinchard, *Procédure Civile*, (27th edn, Dalloz, Paris, 2003), p. 1111 and 1112.

system.[57] Despite this principle, any civil proceedings entail a certain amount of costs for the litigants, such as those relating to the lawyers, the bailiffs, the lawyer authorized to practise before the courts of appeal (*'avoués'*), the translators, the appointed experts, etc.[58]

The French Code of Civil Procedure makes a distinction between the 'legal costs' or 'taxable charges' (*'dépens'*), which are in a large part regulated, and all the other sums expended by the parties that are not included in the 'taxable charges'.

Article 695 defines the legal costs pertaining to proceedings (*'dépens'*), processes and enforcement procedures as including: the fees, taxes, government royalties or emoluments levied by the clerk's offices of courts or by the tax administration with the exception of fees, taxes and penalties which may be due on documents and titles produced in support of the claims of the parties; cost of translation of documents where the latter is rendered necessary by the law or international engagement; allowance for witnesses; expert fees; fixed amount disbursements; emolument of public officers; cost of advocates to the extent that it is regulated including the closing speech dues; expenses paid due to the notification of a process abroad; the cost of interpreting and translation rendered necessary by the inquiry orders to be carried out abroad at the request of courts pursuant to Council Regulation (EC) No.1206/2001 of 28 May 2001 on cooperation between courts of the Member States in the taking of evidence in civil and commercial matters.

It should be noted that, in the French system, court fees are not paid at the commencement but rather at the termination of the proceedings.[59] However, when an expert is appointed, which is often the case in competition law cases, the court determines, either at the moment of his appointment or as soon as possible thereafter, the amount of the retainer fee to be placed on the accounts for the payment of the expert as near as possible to the foreseeable final payment. The judge determines that the party or parties must deposit the retainer fee at the clerk's office of the court within the time limit that he sets. The judge adjust, if necessary, the instalments indicated in the deposit order.[60] At the end of the expert's intervention, the judge determines the amount to be paid to the expert, taking to account the expenses actually incurred.

---

57. See the Decree No. 762 of 20 January 1978 for the regulatory precisions.
58. Guinchard S. *et al* ii, *Droit et pratique de la procédure civile* (5th edn, Dalloz, Paris, 2006), No. 60.11.
59. This is particular to France and Luxembourg. D. Waelbroek, D. Slater and G. Even-Shoshan observe that the other countries of the EU provide for court fees, if they are payable at all, to be paid up front. Some countries (Estonia, Hungary, Lithuania, and Poland) have systems which allow for derogation from this rules and in others (Greece, Slovenia and Portugal) the only part of the court fee has to be paid up front with the remainder being payable at a later stage (in 'Study on the conditions of claims in case of infringement of EC competition rules – Comparative Report', 31 August 2004, p. 92).
60. Article 269 Code of Civil Procedure.

The general principle, set out by Article 696, provides that the legal costs will be borne by the 'losing party', unless the judge, by a reasoned decision (i.e., the judge must provide the reasons of his decision) imposes the whole or part of it on another party.

A party is considered to be a losing party even when he loses the case in relation to only a part of his claims.[61] This will also be the case where several parties lose the case, and the court will have a discretionary power in deciding whether only one losing party shall bear the costs[62] or if the costs are to be shared between the losing parties.[63]

Pursuant to Article 696, the court may decide to order the winning party to pay the court fees or a part of the court fees. When the court decides to implement this 'exceptional power', it must give, in its judgment, the reasons of its decision.[64] The Supreme Court ruled that it suffices that the court gives the reasons of its decision, i.e., the Supreme Court does not control the validity of these reasons.[65] The decision of a court may, for instance, be simply based on equity.[66]

In any event, these 'court fees' are relatively low in France, in particular because they are mostly regulated. Unlike fees calculated as a percentage of the value of the claim, the fixed sum type fees, because of their limited level, are not viewed as constituting an appreciable obstacle to the bringing of damages actions.[67] The French civil procedure rules in terms of court fees therefore seem to be in compliance with the principles set by the European Court of Human Rights in *Kreuz v. Poland*,[68] as well as with the Community law principles: the rules relating to court fees indeed comply with the principles of equivalency and effectiveness.

2.   THE CHARGES NOT INCLUDED IN THE TAXABLE CHARGES

Pursuant to Article 700 of the French Code of Civil Procedure, in all proceedings, whether before the High Courts of First Instance ('Tribunaux de Grande Instance')

---

61. Cour de Cassation, Chambre Sociale, 12 February 1992, *JCP G* (1992), IV, 118.
62. Cour de Cassation, 2e Chambre Civile, 6 February 1972, *Bulletin Civil* II, No. 50.
63. Cour de Cassation, Sociale, 16 October 1983, *Bulletin Civil* V, No. 689.
64. Cour de Cassation, Chambre Sociale, 22 March 1983, *Bulletin Civil* V, No. 180; Cour de Cassation, 2e Chambre Civile, 15 February 1984, *JCP* 1984, IV, 128.
65. Cour de Cassation, 10 February 1993, *Bulletin Civil* II, No. 55.
66. Tribunal of First Instance (*Tribunal d'instance*) of Rodez, 29 June 2000, quoted by Guinchard S. *et al*ii, *Droit et pratique de la procédure civile* (5th edn, Dalloz, Paris, 2006), No. 612.32.
67. D. Waelbroek, D. Slater and G. Even-Shoshan, 'Study on the conditions of claims in case of infringement of EC competition rules – Comparative Report', 31 August 2004, p. 116.
68. ECHR, *Kreuz v. Poland*, (Application No. 28249/95), 19 June 2001, in which the Court ruled that the collection of court fees was not contrary to the Convention as such requirement was justified by a legitimate aim was proportionate and did not infringe the 'essence' of the right conferred by Article 6 (i.e., everyone is entitled to a fair hearing by a tribunal in the determination of his civil rights and obligations), but found that the amount of court fees demanded was excessive (the national court had demanded court fees of PLN 100,000,000, an amount equivalent to the average annual income in Poland at that time).

or the Commercial Courts ('Tribunaux de Commerce'), the judge will order the party obliged to pay for taxable charges or, in default, the losing party, to pay to the other party the amount which he will fix on the basis of the sums expended but not included in the 'legal costs' defined by Article 695. Article 700 further provides that 'The judge will take into consideration the rules of equity and the financial condition of the party ordered to pay. He may, even *sua sponte*, for reasons based on the same considerations, decide that there is no need for such order'.

These charges not included in the taxable charges can be very important. The order to pay costs based on Article 700 follows the mechanism set out for the taxable charges; Article 700 provides that the 'judge will order the party obliged to pay for taxable charges'. According to case law, only the party who has the burden of all or part of the taxable charges may be ordered to pay to the other party the costs not included in the taxable costs, i.e., in particular the lawyers' fees.[69]

Article 700 provides, however, for the same derogation as the one provided for in Article 696 relating to the taxable charges: the court that orders a party on the basis of Article 700, where the said party has not been ordered to pay the taxable charges, has to specifically give the reasons for its decision.[70]

The powers of the judge in fixing these costs are very broad as Article 700 provides that the judge shall take into consideration the rules of Equity and the financial condition of the party ordered to pay; i.e., it is not necessarily the losing party who will be ordered to pay the costs, and the judge may fix at his discretion, but based on the claims of the parties, the amount to be paid.

Moreover, pursuant to Article 700 the judge may, even *sua sponte*, for reasons based on the same considerations, decide that there is no need for such order. The parties will present their arguments both orally and in writing which relating to the request for the order for costs. It should be noted that an appeal judgment may reverse the decision of the court of first instance (whether of a Tribunal de Grande Instance or a Tribunal de Commerce) relating to these costs.

It should also be noted that, in practise, the winning party is never fully reimbursed.[71] This is clearly an obstacle to private enforcement, especially since competition-related damage claims are often as costly as they are time consuming[72] and require specific expertise from the lawyers in charge of the action.

The Green Paper on damages actions for breach of the EC antitrust rules underlined that 'the rules on cost recovery play an important role as incentives or disincentives for bringing an action. In view of the fact that Community law as well as the European Convention on Human Rights demand effective access to courts for civil claims, consideration should be given to how cost rules can

---

69. Cour de Cassation, Chambre Commerciale, 6 November 1985, *Bulletin Civil* IV, No. 205.
70. The Supreme Court ruled that this could be the case, for instance, where a creditor uses legal proceedings which are to heavy in consideration of a very low debt (Cour de Cassation, 2e Chambre Civile, 1 December 1982, *Dalloz* 1983, IR, p. 153).
71. Clearly & Gottlieb law firm, 'Damages, Incentives, Legal Action – Lessons from practical experience: France', Conference 9 March 2005.
72. Commission Staff Working Paper, op. cit., p. 57.

facilitate such access'.[73] It is indeed necessary to reduce the cost risk for the unsuccessful claimant. The Green Paper suggested establishing a rule that unsuccessful claimants will have to pay costs only if they acted in a manifestly unreasonable manner by bringing the case, and also considered giving the court the discretionary power to order at the beginning of a trial that the claimant not be exposed to any cost recovery even if the action were to be unsuccessful.

The comparative report on the conditions of claims for damages in case of infringement of EC competition law[74] sets out the difficulty for national procedure rules in striking a balance between the interests and consideration clearly in contradiction:

> The general rule that applies in Member States is that the loser pays the winner's legal costs. This rule is an obstacle since it creates a risk that the plaintiff will have to pay the defendant's legal costs. However, the rule equally creates the possibility that the plaintiff will not have to pay any legal costs at all. The obstacle which generally applies to all types of litigation, given the general complexity and long duration of competition litigation, such a risk may make competition-based damages claims particularly unattractive.

However, given that the indemnity rule coupled with a risk of an order to pay all costs is counterbalanced by the possibility of paying nothing, it is unclear whether this rule constitutes a greater obstacle than the alternative rule which provides that all parties bear their own costs. The latter option eliminates the risk inherent in the loser pays rules but at the same time creates another obstacle by making payment of ones own legal costs inevitable.

The rules provided for by Articles 696 (on court fees) and 700 (on lawyers' fees) of the French Code of Civil Procedure seem, as far as possible, to achieve a balance, as the judge takes into consideration the rules of equity, the reasonableness of the claims and the financial condition of the party ordered to pay. The judge also has discretionary power to rule that an unsuccessful claimant will not have to pay for the costs.

3.   LEGAL AID

In *Steel and Morris*,[77] the ECHR ruled that Article 6 of the Convention guarantees, in certain circumstances, a right to legal aid. According to the ECHR, there is no absolute right to legal aid in all proceedings, and the State was not obligated to guarantee a total equality of arms between the parties. The Court however considered that given the circumstances of the case, because of the radical difference in resources between the claimant and the defendants, 'the denial of

---

73. Commission Green Paper, 'Damages actions for breach of the EC antitrust rules Damages actions for breach of the EC antitrust rules', COM(2005) 672 final, p. 10.
74. D. Waelbroek, D. Slater and G. Even-Shoshan, op. cit., 2004, p. 116.
77. ECHR, *Steel and Morris v. United Kingdom*, (Application No. 68416/01), 15 February 2005.

legal aid to the applicants deprived them of the opportunity to present their case effectively before the court and contributed to an unacceptable inequality of arms with McDonald's. There has, therefore, been a violation of Article 6 § 1'.

According to the Commission Staff Working paper, 'Transposed to the field of competition law, this case might well indicate that there is an obligation to grant legal aid in those circumstances in which such a profound difference exists'.[78]

In France, the legal aid mechanism is intended for natural and legal persons whose financial resources are insufficient to enable them to assert their rights before a court. In order to be entitled to legal aid, it is necessary to demonstrate that one does not have sufficient resources. In order to be granted the entire aid, the resources must be lower than an upper limit.[79] On an exceptional basis, it is possible to grant the legal aid where the person fulfils the financial conditions but where the situation appears to be worthy of the aid in regard the object of the case and/or the foreseeable costs of the trial. Where the person is the plaintiff in the case, the action must not appear as being manifestly inadmissible or groundless. Because of this condition, that France was likely to be condemned for denying the right of access to the courts. However, the European Court ruled that:

> As regards the ground on which the (French) Legal Aid Office and the President of the Court of Cassation refused the applicant's application – namely, the lack of an arguable ground of appeal – it is a ground expressly laid down by Law no. 91-647 of 10 July 1991 and was undoubtedly explainable by the legitimate concern: namely, that public money should only be used for legal-aid purposes for appellants to the Court of Cassation whose appeals have a reasonable prospect of success. As the European Commission of Human Rights has stated, it is obvious that a legal-aid system can only operate if machinery is in place to enable a selection to be made of those cases qualifying for it.[80]

A safety valve[81] is, however, provided for by the law to correct by appeal a mistake of appreciation of the inadmissible or groundless character of the action: if the court rules in favour of the plaintiff whereas the legal aid was refused for this reason, his costs will be reimbursed up to the amount which he would have received.[82]

The method of calculation of the lawyer's fees is quite complex and rather basic in terms of amounts. This means, therefore, that it will be difficult for an impecunious claimant to convince a specialist competition law firm to accept his case for the amounts paid on the grounds of legal aid. Moreover, when a person receives the entire legal aid, the remuneration paid by the State is exclusive of any

---

78. Commission Staff Working Paper, op. cit., p. 58.
79. In particular determined by Articles 3 and 4 of Decree December 1991.
80. ECHR, *Gnahoré v. France* – 40031/98 [2000], 19 September 2000, (Application No. 40031/98).
81. J. Vincent and S. Guinchard, *Procédure Civile*, (27th edn, Dalloz, Paris, 2003), p. 1132.
82. Act No. 91-647, 10 July 1991 on the legal aid (*JORF*, 13 July 1991), Article 7, paragraph 4.

other form of complementary fee, except in the event the client's financial situation improves pursuant to the judgment.[83]

It should be noted that where the claimant is only partially entitled to the legal aid, the complementary retainer may be freely negotiated between the claimant and his lawyer.[84] However, the amount and the terms and conditions of the retainer must be fixed in a written agreement, taking into account the complexity of the case. Further, the retainer must be compatible with the resources of the client.[85] Moreover, if the lawyer is a member of a bar that provides for a method for the calculation of legal fees finally, the amount of the complementary retainer will have to be calculated using that method.[86] The '*bâtonnier*' (the elected head of the bar) verifies the legality of the agreement and of the amount of the complementary retainer.[87]

The claimant who qualifies for legal aid either wholly or partially, will certainly be unable to pay the fee of a specialist competition law firm. It should however be noted that the agreement can provide that the complementary retainer will take the form of a contingency fee, which may help the claimant in finding a specialized law firm.

4.   CONTINGENCY FEES: PROHIBITION OF '*QUOTA LITIS*' AGREEMENTS

The Commission Staff Working Paper observes that 'contingency fees are a strong incentive because the financial risk for bringing the action is borne not by the claimant but by private attorneys. The experience of US law suggests that the existence of contingency fees is a factor in the emergence of a claimant bar strongly associated with bringing actions for damages'.[89]

In France, a '*quota litis*' agreement ('success fee') is an agreement entered into by a lawyer and his client before the final judgment, in which it is provided that the entire fee is based on the judicial result of the case. Pursuant to Article 10 paragraph 3 of the 31 December 1971 Act, such agreements are illegal, i.e., any fee based exclusively on the judicial result of the case is prohibited.[90] However, the same paragraph specifies that the agreement that provides for the remuneration of the lawyer for the services performed as well as the determination of a complementary retainer based on the result obtained is legal.

It is therefore possible to circumvent the '*quota litis*' prohibition by stipulating in the agreement a low remuneration of the lawyer for the services performed coupled with a high 'success fee'.[91] The First President of the Appeal Court of

---

83. Article 36 of the 1991 Act.
84. Article 35, paragraph 1 of the 1991 Act.
85. Article 35, paragraph 2 of the 1991 Act.
86. Article 35, paragraph 4 of the 1991 Act.
87. Article 35, paragraph 3 of the 1991 Act.
89. Commission Staff Working Paper, op. cit., p. 62.
90. The harmonized internal regulation of French bars ('*Règlement intérieur harmonisé des barreaux de France*') provides for the same principle.

Lyon however condemned this practise by interpreting restrictively the terms 'complementary retainer'.[92] However, the Supreme Court (*'Cour de cassation'*) interpreted the principle very broadly and reversed the decision.[93] The Supreme Court considered that the Appeal Court had created a condition that did not exist in the law.[94]

It should be noted that an excessive percentage would however likely be refused by the Courts as being not justified because it would not correspond to the necessary 'complementary' nature of contingency fees.[95]

By allowing contingency fees, even though such fees must have a complementary nature, the French rules of procedure favour the actions for damages.

The French rules of civil procedure concerning costs of actions provide for the judge to take into consideration the following matters: the rules of equity, the reasonableness of the claims, the financial condition of the party ordered to pay, and the possibility of contingency fees. The rules of procedure do not, therefore, appear to constitute a serious obstacle to private enforcement.

However, it has been observed that in practice the winning party never fully recovers the sums outlayed for the trial. Nevertheless, it is very difficult to strike a perfect balance in terms of costs of action. For instance, the fact that the winning party recovers the sums outlayed may at the same time constitute an obstacle to private enforcement. Therefore, the rules set out in French Code of Civil Procedure seem, taken as a whole, to be consistent with the doctrine of effectiveness.

---

92. Order, 2 November 1993, not published, quoted by R. Martin, op. cit., p. 195.
93. Cour de cassation, 1re Chambre Civile, 10 July 1995, *Bulletin Civil* I, No. 311.
94. See also Cour de cassation, 1re Chambre Civile, 3 October 1995, *Juris-Data* No. 003171.
95. C. Momège and N. Bessot, op. cit. p. 28.

Chapter 11

German Procedure: Representative Actions and Binding Effect of Cartel Authorities' Decisions'

A. PRIVATE ENFORCEMENT OF COMPETITION RULES
FROM A GERMAN PERSPECTIVE

Private Enforcement of competition law in Germany has not played the significant role that the legislature originally envisaged,[1] even though the picture altogether is not as dim as presented by the Ashurst-Report.[2] Each year, the Federal Cartel Authority (Bundeskartellamt) is notified under § 90 Act against Restraints on Competition (*Gesetz gegen Wettbewerbsbeschränkungen* – GWB) of several hundred civil litigation cases involving competition rules. Data for the year 2004[3] shows 240 proceedings in which the infringement of competition law was alleged. In the majority of cases, the allegation of anti-competitive practises

---

1. W.H. Roth, 'Das Kartelldeliktsrecht in der 7. GWB-Novelle', in *Festschrift für Ulrich Huber*, T. Baums, J. Wertenbruch, M. Lutter, K. Schmidt (eds) (Mohr Siebeck, Tübingen, 2006), p. 1136 *et seq.*; R. Hempel, 'Privater Rechtsschutz im deutschen Kartellrecht nach der 7. GWB-Novelle', [2004] WuW 365.
2. The report mentions 159 civil proceedings in the years 1958 to 2004, 29 of which were actions for damages. In this period, damages were allegedly awarded in nine cases only and of these, one award was based, *inter alia*, on the infringement of EC competition rules, cf. K. Wach *et al.*, Ashurst Report Germany, p. 30 at J (vii) and Executive Summary Germany, p. 7 at J. (viii), <ec.europa.eu/comm/competition/antitrust/others/actions_for_damages/study.html>. For a thorough criticism of the report's methodical approach refer to Bundeskartellamt, *Private Kartellrechtsdurchsetzung. Stand, Probleme, Perspektiven.* (2005), <www.bundeskartellamt.de>, 1 October 2006, p. 5.
3. Bundeskartellamt, *Private Kartellrechtsdurchsetzung. Stand, Probleme, Perspektiven.* (2005), <www.bundeskartellamt.de>, 1 October 2006, p. 4 *et seq.*

was raised as a defence to prevent the enforcement of a contractual agreement, but in 68 cases, 38 of which constituted claims for damages, it was the plaintiff who submitted a breach of competition rules. Twelve proceedings in which antitrust claims were asserted 'offensively' were based on Community law. Of these, the plaintiff was successful in only three cases. Overall, the majority of disputes concerned vertical agreements as well as abusive practises and cases of discrimination against dependent companies by a dominant or powerful undertaking. Hardcore cartels were hardly ever the subject of civil litigation.

From a public interest perspective, private enforcement of competition law is inferior to public enforcement, because private parties who pursue their individual goals are able to control the proceedings. Of particular importance is the parties' freedom to terminate civil litigation, i.e., by way of settlement. In such instances, the dispute is terminated whilst the legal questions remain unresolved, which is not a positive outcome from a public interest perspective. Indeed, in the last years a couple of cases seem to have been 'bought off', before the *Bundesgerichtshof* (Federal Court of Justice) had a chance to clarify the law with respect to matters of general interest and significance.[4]

In an attempt to strengthen private enforcement of competition rules, the German Parliament enacted a number of changes in the course of a reform of the Act against Restraints of Competition (GWB) termed the '7th GWB-amendment', which entered into force on 1 July 2005. It is yet too early to assess whether the new provisions have proven of value. This section describes the obstacles, both in terms of substantive and procedural rules, which stood in the way of efficient private enforcement before the 7th GWB-amendment entered into force. Further, the changes made in the course of the reform will be explained.

1.   OBSTACLES TO PRIVATE ENFORCEMENT PRIOR TO
            THE 7TH GWB-AMENDMENT

The reasons given for the relatively small significance of private enforcement of both EC and German competition rules in Germany under the previous legal regime are multi-fold.

In terms of the substantive law, it was easy enough for the defendant to plead anti-competitive behaviour on the part of the Claimant if the parties were in dispute regarding the enforceability of a contract. Any breach of Art. 81, 82 EC would render the respective contractual clause invalid under §§ 134, 138, 242 BGB. In contrast, the sections providing for a right to damages for losses suffered, §§ 33 GWB, 823(2) BGB, were interpreted quite restrictively by the courts and did not encourage potential plaintiffs to raise a claim. § 33 GWB in its former wording required that the person who had suffered a loss as a consequence of a breach of

---

4.   J. Bornkamm, *Kommentar zum deutschen und europäischen Kartellrecht*, vol. 1: *Deutsches Kartellrecht*, E. Langen and H.J. B.unte (eds) (10th ed., Luchterhand, Neuwied, 2006), § 33 para. 9 cites the cases BGH KZR 26/01; BGH KZR 12/02; BGH KZR 11/04.

German competition rules belong to a group of persons covered by the protective purpose of this norm. The same was true for damages actions pertaining to an infringement of Community law which were based upon § 823(2) BGB.

There was substantial case law to suggest that damages would only be awarded if the plaintiff succeeded in proving that the infringement of competition law was directed specifically against it.[5] Needless to say, this led to the surreal consequence that the more comprehensive a cartel the less likely a successful damages claim.[6] Further, to the dismay of most academics,[7] the defence that direct purchasers had passed on their losses to their customers was accepted by some courts.[8] Other reasons for the limited extent of civil litigation in this field include the high cost risk and the difficulties in proving the prerequisites of a damages claim, in particular the infringement of competition law. The 7th GWB amendment addressed the former matter with a new cost rule in § 89a GWB, but left the latter unresolved. Both issues shall be dealt with subsequently.

2.   CHANGES IMPLEMENTED BY THE 7TH GWB-AMENDMENT

The GWB amendment contains a number of changes intended to enhance private enforcement of competition law. Damages claims for the infringement of EU competition law are now based upon § 33 GWB, a modification which is mainly technical in nature. The most important change would seem to be that a claim for damages or a request for injunctive relief no longer requires the plaintiff to belong to a group of persons encompassed by the 'protective purpose of the norm'. Instead, the revised text of § 33 GWB awards protection to any person 'affected' by the breach. The significance of the change is not encapsulated in the wording, but may instead be seen in the legislature's clarification which establishes that it is irrelevant whether the breach was directed specifically at the plaintiff, as most of the existing case law had suggested. Still, the debate continues as to which persons belong to the group or circle 'concerned' by the infringement; in particular,

---

5. BGH, NJW 1975, 1223, 1225 – *Krankenhaus-Zusatzversicherung*; BGH, NJW 1984, 2819, 2822 – *Familienzeitschrift*; OLG Düsseldorf, [1990] WuW/E OLG 4454 – *Ennepetal-Vertrag*; OLG Düsseldorf, [1990] WuW/E OLG 4454 – *Schmiedeeisenwaren*; LG Berlin, WuW/E DE-R 1325, 1326 f. – *Berliner Transportbeton II*; LG Mannheim, GRUR 2004, 183, 183 f. – *Vitaminpreise Mannheim*; LG Mainz, WuW De/R 1349, 1350 *et seq.* – *Vitaminpreise Mainz*; opposing view held by OLG Stuttgart, NJW-E WettbR, 1998, 260, 261 – *Carpartner II*; LG Dortmund WuW DE-R 1352, 1353 – *Vitaminpreise Dortmund*.

6. M. Lutz, 'Schwerpunkte der 7. GWB-Novelle', [2005] WuW, 727; G. Berrisch and M. Burianski, 'Kartellrechtliche Schadensersatzansprüche nach der 7. GWB-Novelle', [2005] WuW, 881.

7. G. Berrisch and M. Burianski, 'Kartellrechtliche Schadensersatzansprüche nach der 7. GWB-Novelle', [2005] WuW, 885 *et seq.*; H. Köhler, 'Kartellverbot und Schadensersatz', [2004] GRUR, 101 *et seq.*; T. Lettl, 'Der Schadensersatzanspruch gemäß § 823 Abs. 2 BGB i.V. mit Art. 81 Abs. 1 EG', (2003) 167 ZHR 487; opposing view held by J. Beninca, 'Schadensersatzansprüche von Kunden eines Kartells?', [2004] WuW 606 *et seq.*

8. LG Mannheim, GRUR 2004, 183, 183 f. – *Vitaminpreise Mannheim*, confirmed by OLG Karlsruhe, NJW 2004, 2243, 2244 *et seq.*

whether indirect customers are included.[9] Further, while § 33(3) GWB now states that a passing-on of disadvantages does not exclude the onset of a loss suffered by a direct customer, the courts are free to find that such losses were later compensated by benefits when the undertaking affected passed them on to its own customers (*Vorteilsausgleich*).[10] The only matter which appears to be settled is that the burden of proof that the price increase was passed on rests with the cartel member.[11]

Further changes include a facilitation of the assessment of damages as courts will now be allowed to take into account the infringer's profit.[12] Interest on damages will accrue from the moment the loss was suffered, and the effluction of time will be halted when public authorities institute proceedings for a violation of competition law.[13] Moreover, certain decisions of the Commission and the NCAs now bind the civil courts.[14] Organizations for the promotion of commercial interests, which had hitherto solely been allowed to request injunctive relief, may raise an action to recover the infringer's profits under § 34a GWB, although the proceeds will be awarded to the Federal budget. Finally, a specific costs rule was introduced to make allowances for parties with a poor economic standing.[15]

a.   Competition Cases' Allocation

§§ 87, 95 GWB refer the exclusive competence to adjudicate any civil litigation involving matters governed by rules of the GWB, Art. 81, 82 EC or Art. 53, 54 EEA to the district courts (*Landgericht*), irrespective of the amount in dispute. An exception is made for actions concerning compulsory health insurance as well as compulsory and private long-term care insurance, which are assigned to the Social Courts even if third parties are affected, cf. §§ 51(2) Code of Social

---

9.   Favouring the compensation of indirect customers: U. Böge and K. Ost, 'Up and Running, or is it? Private enforcement – the Situation in Germany and Policy Perspectives', [2006] ECLR, 201; T. Lettl, 'Die Auswirkungen der 7. GWB-Novelle auf die Kreditwirtschaft', [2005] WM 1591; Kessler, 'Private Enforcement – Zur deliktsrechtlichen Aktualisierung des deutschen und europäischen Kartellrechts im Lichte des Verbraucherschutzes', [2006] WRP, 1067 *et seq.*; W.H. Roth, 'Das Kartelldeliktsrecht in der 7. GWB-Novelle', in *Festschrift für Ulrich Huber*, T. Baums, J. Wertenbruch, M. Lutter, K. Schmidt (eds) (Mohr Siebeck, Tübingen, 2006), p. 1140 *et seq.*, 1154 *et seq.*; opposing view held by G. Berrisch and M. Burianski, 'Kartellrechtliche Schadensersatzansprüche nach der 7. GWB-Novelle', [2005] WuW, 886 *et seq*; H. Köhler, 'Kartellverbot und Schadensersatz', [2004] GRUR, 101.

10.   W.H. Roth, 'Das Kartelldeliktsrecht in der 7. GWB-Novelle', in *Festschrift für Ulrich Huber*, T. Baums, J. Wertenbruch, M. Lutter, K. Schmidt (eds) (Mohr Siebeck, Tübingen, 2006), p. 1162 with further references.

11.   W.H. Roth, 'Das Kartelldeliktsrecht in der 7. GWB-Novelle', in *Festschrift für Ulrich Huber*, T. Baums, J. Wertenbruch, M. Lutter, K. Schmidt (eds) (Mohr Siebeck, Tübingen, 2006), p. 1152, 1165 *et seq.*; U. Böge and K. Ost, 'Up and Running, or is it? Private enforcement – the Situation in Germany and Policy Perspectives', [2006] ECLR, 200.

12.   § 33(3) sent. 3 GWB.

13.   § 33(3) sent. 4 GWB.

14.   § 90 GWB.

15.   § 89a GWB.

Procedure (*Sozialgesetzbuch* – SGG), § 87(1) sent. 3 GWB. The said exemption is particularly relevant for claims raised by suppliers of goods and services against insurers providing compulsory health insurance or long-term care insurance.[16]

For the purposes of § 87 GWB, an action is considered to involve EC or national competition law not only in obvious cases, but also if a there exists a certain degree of probability that the dispute concerns competition rules.[17] This clearly includes not only actions asserting the infringement of competition provisions, but also 'defensive' strategies, i.e., if the defendant challenges the validity of an agreement and this preliminary question needs to be decided on the basis of competition law.[18] However, to avoid an overload of the cartel courts due to spurious allegations of competition infringements, § 87 GWB should not come into play if the answer to the preliminary question is fairly obvious.[19]

While the GWB does not provide for specialized competition courts, the panels which hear such disputes generally possess expertise in competition law. This is for two reasons: firstly, § 89 GWB entitles the State governments to concentrate jurisdiction in civil competition cases on one or more district courts within that state. All governments of the *Bundesländer* (states) except for one have made use of that provision – if one leaves aside the city-states which possess only one district court in the first place. Secondly, many courts allocate competition-related cases to one or two panels only, allowing them to develop the required specialization. The specialized courts and panels are listed in the Appendix. Finally, it should be noted that the dispute will be conferred to a commercial chamber upon request of one of the parties, §§ 87(2) GWB, 96(1), 98(1) GVG. However, as two of the three judges in commercial chambers are lay persons, parties oftentimes prefer to have their case decided by a civil chamber.[20]

Appeals against civil disputes under § 87 GWB are heard by specialized cartel panels within the Higher Regional Courts (*Oberlandesgericht* – OLG) following § 91 GWB. Again, it is up to state governments to concentrate appeals with one Higher Regional Court for the entire state.[21] Further appeals based on questions of

---

16. Cf. BGH, WRP 2000, 636 at 637 – *Hörgeräteakkustik*.
17. J. Bornkamm, *Kommentar zum deutschen und europäischen Kartellrecht*, vol. 1: *Deutsches Kartellrecht*, E. Langen and H.J. Bunte (eds) (10th ed., Luchterhand, Neuwied, 2006), § 87 para. 18 *et seq.*; U. Bumiller, *Handbuch des Kartellrechts*, G. Wiedemann (ed.) (C.H. Beck, München, 1999), § 60 para. 3 *et seq.*
18. K. Schmidt, *GWB*, U. Immenga and E.J. Mestmäcker (eds) (3rd edn, C.H. Beck, München, 2001), § 87 para. 27; U. Bumiller, *Handbuch des Kartellrechts*, G. Wiedemann (ed.) (C.H. Beck, München, 1999), § 60 para. 5 *et seq.*
19. J. Bornkamm, *Kommentar zum deutschen und europäischen Kartellrecht*, vol. 1: *Deutsches Kartellrecht*, E. Langen and H.J. Bunte (eds) (10th ed., Luchterhand, Neuwied, 2006), § 87 para. 24 *et seq.*; opposing view held by K. Schmidt, *GWB*, U. Immenga and E.J. Mestmäcker (eds) (3rd edn, C.H. Beck, München, 2001), § 87 para. 33.
20. J. Bornkamm, *Kommentar zum deutschen und europäischen Kartellrecht*, vol. 1: *Deutsches Kartellrecht*, E. Langen and H.J. Bunte (eds) (10th ed., Luchterhand, Neuwied, 2006), § 87 para. 41.
21. § 93 GWB.

law only (Revision) are heard by the cartel panel of the Federal Court of Justice (*Bundesgerichtshof*).[22]

b.   Locus Standi

There is no limitation on standing under German procedural law, apart from the prerequisite that a party base the action on an alleged existence of a right of its own (*Prozessführungsbefugnis*).

Any further restrictions are a matter of substantive law. Up until the 7th GWB-amendment private actions for competition infringements were considered to be unfounded, unless the plaintiff demonstrated that it belonged to a circle of persons whose protection was intended by the competition provision infringed. According to case law the plaintiff, moreover, had to prove that the cartel members deliberately intended to worsen its position in the market.[23] The revised § 33(1) GWB facilitates the obtaining of injunctions and the bringing of claims for damages by granting the right to claim damages or request injunctions to any person 'concerned', and specifying that any competitor or other market participant affected by the infringement is to be regarded as 'concerned'. Plaintiffs are consequently no longer required to prove that the breach was directed specifically towards them.[24] Apart from this laudable clarification, the reformulation of § 33(1) GWB has failed to yield much in the way of legal clarity and certainty.[25] As has already been noted, there is a lively academic debate as to whether indirect customers should be allowed to claim their losses.[26] As this is clearly a matter of substantive law, it shall not receive any further examination in this context.

22. § 94 GWB.
23. OLG Düsseldorf, [1990] WuW/E OLG 4454 – *Ennepetal-Vertrag*; OLG Düsseldorf, [1990] WuW/E OLG 4454 – *Schmiedeeisenwaren*; LG Berlin, WuW/E DE-R 1325, 1326 f. – *Berliner Transportbeton II*; LG Mannheim, GRUR 2004, 183, 183 f. – *Vitaminpreise Mannheim*; LG Mainz, WuW De/R 1349, 1350 *et seq.* – *Vitaminpreise Mainz*; opposing view held by OLG Stuttgart, NJW-E WettbR, 1998, 260, 261 – *Carpartner II*; LG Dortmund WuW DE-R 1352, 1353 – *Vitaminpreise Dortmund*.
24. Reasoning of the Government Draft, BT-Drucks. 15/3640, 35, 53.
25. A. Fuchs, 'Die 7. GWB-Novelle – Grundkonzeption und praktische Konsequenzen', [2005] WRP, 1394 *et seq.*
26. Favouring the compensation of indirect customers: U. Böge and K. Ost, 'Up and Running, or is it? Private enforcement – the Situation in Germany and Policy Perspectives', [2006] ECLR, 201; T. Lettl, 'Die Auswirkungen der 7. GWB-Novelle auf die Kreditwirtschaft', [2005] WM 1591; Kessler, 'Private Enforcement – Zur deliktsrechtlichen Aktualisierung des deutschen und europäischen Kartellrechts im Lichte des Verbraucherschutzes', [2006] WRP, 1067 *et seq.*; W.H. Roth, 'Das Kartelldeliktsrecht in der 7. GWB-Novelle', in *Festschrift für Ulrich Huber*, T. Baums, J. Wertenbruch, M. Lutter, K. Schmidt (eds) (Mohr Siebeck, Tübingen, 2006), p. 1140 *et seq.*, 1154 *et seq.*; opposing view held by G. Berrisch and M. Burianski, 'Kartellrechtliche Schadensersatzansprüche nach der 7. GWB-Novelle', [2005] WuW, 886 *et seq.*

3.   REPRESENTATIVE ACTIONS

a.   **Organizations for the Promotion of Commercial Interests**

While under the general rules of the German civil procedure there is no room for class actions or collective actions, § 33(2), 34a GWB do provide for certain types of representative actions in competitive disputes. Entities for the promotion of commercial interests are entitled to injunctive relief under § 33(2) and an action for account of the profits gained through the infringement, the proceeds of which will benefit the federal budget. As a safeguard to prevent spurious claims, such organizations have to meet a number of qualifications, which the courts treat as a matter of standing.[27] The requirements are as follows:

– Legal capacity of the organization;
– The organization's statutes define the promotion of commercial interests as its explicit purpose;
– The entity possesses a significant number of members who are undertakings present on the same market as the alleged infringer, whereas markets are defined generously for this purpose;
– The entity is sufficiently endowed both financially and with staff to promote the commercial interests of its members, i.e., by observing the market and bringing actions. Following case law, this includes the pursuit of legal disputes with a value of 30,000 to 50,000 EUR through all three instances.[28]

Whereas collective actions are prevalent in actions for unfair competitions under § 8(3) UWG, injunctive relief requested by entities for the promotion of commercial interests has so far led a shadowy existence in cartel law.[29] Presumably, this can be accounted for by public enforcement on the one hand and the difficulties in proving anti-competitive practises on the other hand, both elements which are not encountered similarly in the law of unfair competition. Finally, for a number of reasons founded in the substantive law, the new provision arranging for an account of profits, § 34a GWB, is considered ill equipped to yield any positive results.[30]

---

27. BGH, GRUR 1998, 953, 954 – *Altunterwerfung III*; BGH GRUR 2005, 689 *et seq.* – *Sammel-mitgliedschaft III*.
28. BGH NJW-RR 1998, 1421, 1422; OLGR Stuttgart 1999, 393 (396).
29. J. Bornkamm, *Kommentar zum deutschen und europäischen Kartellrecht*, vol. 1: *Deutsches Kartellrecht*, E. Langen and H.J. Bunte (eds) (10th ed., Luchterhand, Neuwied, 2006), § 33 para. 74, § 34a para. 3.
30. A. Fuchs, 'Die 7. GWB-Novelle – Grundkonzeption und praktische Konsequenzen', [2005] WRP, 1391; J. Bornkamm, *Kommentar zum deutschen und europäischen Kartellrecht*, vol. 1: *Deutsches Kartellrecht*, E. Langen and H.J. Bunte (eds) (10th ed., Luchterhand, Neuwied, 2006), § 33 para. 74, § 34a para. 1 *et seq.*

b. CONSUMER ORGANIZATIONS

The Federal Government's draft of the 7th GWB-amendment included a provision which enabled consumer organizations to raise representative actions requesting both injunctive relief and an account of profits. In doing so, the Government argued that it was 'taking account of the fact that the Competition Act protects the interests of consumers through securing effective competition'.[31] At virtually the last second, the intended changes were abandoned for unidentified reasons, much to the criticism of most academics.[32] As a result, §§ 33(2), and 34a GWB allow, exclusively, entities with commercial interests to raise representative claims.

Interestingly enough, requests for injunctive relief and an account of profits by consumer organizations remain possible under §§ 8(3), and § 10(1) of The Unfair Competition Act (*Gesetz gegen den unlauteren Wettbewerb* – UWG) in cases of unfair trade practises which are likely to impair effective competition. Such acts are exemplified in § 4 UWG, no. 11 of which stipulates:

> A person is engaging in unfair practises in particular, if [. . .] it acts contrary to a statutory provision that is designed to regulate market behaviour in the interest of members of the market.

It goes without saying that cartel provisions are as a matter of course designed to regulate market behaviour in the interest of market members. Consequently, following older case law of the Federal Court of Justice, a breach of cartel law regularly entailed an unfair trade practise.[33] Arguably, consumer organizations are able to make requests both for injunctive relief and an account of profits by taking a detour via the law of unfair competition. The counter-argument is obvious: since the legislature opted against introducing representative claims by consumer organizations through a revised § 33(2) GWB, to allow consumer organizations to raise such claims under § 8(3), and § 10(1) UWG would constitute a contravention of parliamentary intentions.[34]

---

31. Reasoning of the government draft, BT-Drucks. 15/3640, 53.
32. J. Kessler, 'Private Enforcement – Zur deliktsrechtlichen Aktualisierung des deutschen und europäischen Kartellrechts im Lichte des Verbraucherschutzes', [2006] WRP, 1068; J. Bornkamm, *Kommentar zum deutschen und europäischen Kartellrecht*, vol. 1: *Deutsches Kartellrecht*, E. Langen and H.J. Bunte (eds) (10th ed., Luchterhand, Neuwied, 2006), § 33 para. 75; J. Hartog and B. Noack, 'Die 7. GWB-Novelle', [2005] WRP, 1405; M. Lutz, 'Schwerpunkte der 7. GWB-Novelle', [2005] WuW 2005, 729 *et seq.*; W.H. Roth, 'Das Kartelldeliktsrecht in der 7. GWB-Novelle', in *Festschrift für Ulrich Huber*, T. Baums, J. Wertenbruch, M. Lutter, K. Schmidt (eds) (Mohr Siebeck, Tübingen, 2006), p. 1170.
33. BGH, NJW 1958, 1868 *et seq. – Zulässigkeit vertikaler Preisempfehlungen*; BGH, GRUR 1978, 445, 446 – *3 zum Preis von 4*; BGH, GRUR 1993, 137 (139) – *Zinssubvention*.
34. H. Köhler, *Wettbewerbsrecht*, W. Hefermehl, H. Köhler and J. Bornkamm (eds) (24th edn, C.H. Beck, München, 2006), § 4 para. 11.12; J. Bornkamm, *Kommentar zum deutschen und europäischen Kartellrecht*, vol. 1: *Deutsches Kartellrecht*, E. Langen and H.J. Bunte (eds) (10th ed., Luchterhand, Neuwied, 2006), § 33 para. 126; H.P. Götting, Lauterkeitsrecht, K.H. Fezer (ed.) (C.H. Beck, München, 2005), § 4–11 para. 112.

Nonetheless, the question arises whether the principle of effectiveness requires that consumer interests in competition disputes be procedurally secured via collective claims or class actions. If this were the case, the principle of effectiveness might require that preference be given to an interpretation of §§ 8(3), 4 no. 11 UWG which allowed consumer organizations to take collective action.

In *Courage v. Crehan*, the ECJ held[35] that the full effectiveness of Article 85 of the Treaty and, in particular, the practical effect of the prohibition laid down in Article 85(1) would be put at risk if it were not open to any individual to claim damages for loss caused to him by a contract or by conduct liable to restrict or distort competition.

The Court's remarks are limited to the right of 'any individual' to raise an action and unsurprisingly so, as this was the ambit of the questions referred to the ECJ by the Court of Appeal. There is nothing in the ECJ's case law to suggest that the principle of effectiveness requires the procedural law of the Member States to provide for actions securing the collective interests of consumers in competition cases. Moreover, it might be possible to draw an inference from the Directive 98/27/EC on Injunctions for the Protection of Consumers' interests[36] that a right for collective bodies to sue in the interest of consumers is not implied by the principle of effectiveness,[37] but exists only if specifically provided for, as is the case for the rules and regulations named in the annex of the Injunctions Directive.

4.   THE BINDING EFFECT OF A DECISION TAKEN IN PUBLIC ENFORCEMENT ON THE CIVIL LITIGATION ISSUES

a.   **Binding Effect of the Commission's and NCA's Decisions**

One of the major obstacles to private actions based upon EU antitrust law rests in the difficulty of proving the infringement, the damage and a causal relationship between the two. These concerns are alleviated if the Commission or an NCA has already rendered a decision finding an undertaking to have violated the competition rules. Follow-on claims which are raised in the slipstream of public enforcement therefore possess particular practical importance,[38] at least with respect to hard core cartels. § 33(4) GWB stipulates:

Regarding actions for damages based upon the infringement of any section of this statute or Article 81 or 82 of the Treaty establishing the European

---

35. ECJ, *Courage v. Crehan*, Case no. C-453/99, [2001] ECR I-6297, para. 26.
36. Directive 98/27/EC of the European Parliament and of the Council of 19 May 1998 on injunctions for the protection of consumers' interests, OJ No. L 352, 11 June 1998, p. 51.
37. Opposing view held by G. Cumming, *supra* p. 172 *et seq.*
38. F. Montag and A. Rosenfeld, 'A Solution to the Problems? Regulation 1/2003 and the modernization of competition procedure', [2003] ZWeR, 121.

Community, the court is bound by a definite decision establishing an infringement rendered by the Cartel Authority, the European Commission or the Competition Authority, or a court acting as such, of any other Member State of the European Union. The same applies for corresponding findings in final court rulings handed down as a result of a challenge to decisions in the meaning of sentence 1. Corresponding to Article 16(1) sentence 4 of Regulation (EC) 1/2003, this obligation is without prejudice to the rights and obligations under Art. 234 of the Treaty establishing the European Community.

Up until the 7th GWB-amendment, decisions of the German Cartel Office did not have a binding effect on German courts,[39] while the decisions of the European Commission were arguably binding[40] following the ECJ's decision in the *Masterfoods* case.[41] Henceforth, with regard to damages claims,[42] § 33(4) GWB provides for the binding effect of a decision establishing an infringement issued by the European Commission or any of the national competition authorities of the Member States,[43] provided the decision is no longer subject to appeal. Court judgments affirming the findings of Cartel Offices are also given binding effect. It needs to be emphasized that civil courts are only bound only with respect to the establishment of the infringement, whereas all other matters, in particular the amount of damages and causation, are to be weighed by the courts themselves.[44]

Interestingly, § 33(4) GWB does not entirely correspond to Art. 16(1) Reg. (EC) 1/2003, which possesses a broader ambit in that it applies to any action, not only claims for damages (without prejudice to stricter national laws which prohibit or sanction unilateral conduct, *cf.* Art. 3(2) Reg. (EC) 1/2003). Art. 16(1) Reg. (EC) 1/2003 remains particularly relevant regarding injunctions, a defensive use of

---

39.   V. Emmerich, *GWB*, U. Immenga and E.J. Mestmäcker (eds) (3rd edn, C.H. Beck, München, 2001), § 32 para. 13; R. Hempel, 'Private Follow-on Klagen im Kartellrecht', [2005] WuW, 140; opposing opinion held by J. Bornkamm and M. Becker, 'Die privatrechtliche Durchsetzung des Kartellverbots nach der Modernisierung des EG-Kartellrechts', [2005] ZWeR, 219. The courts did have the option of requesting the Cartel Office's files of the enquiry under § 273 (2) sent. 2 ZPO.
40.   A binding effect was generally presumed amongst practitioners and academics, cf. i.e., U. Böge and K. Ost, 'Up and Running, or is it? Private enforcement – the Situation in Germany and Policy Perspectives', [2006] ECLR, 199, but questioned by J. Bornkamm and M. Becker, 'Die privatrechtliche Durchsetzung des Kartellverbots nach der Modernisierung des EG-Kartellrechts', [2005] ZWeR, 220.
41.   ECJ, *Masterfoods v. HB*, Case no. C-344/98, [2000] ECR I-II369, para. 52.
42.   The restriction on damages claims was criticized by Monopolkommission, *Fünfzehntes Hauptgutachten der Monopolkommission 2002/2003*, BT-Drucks. 15/3610, para. 58; A. Fuchs, 'Die 7. GWB-Novelle – Grundkonzeption und praktische Konsequenzen', [2005] WRP, 1395.
43.   The fact that § 33(4) GWB accords binding effect to decisions of the NCAs of other Member States was heavily criticized, cf. the overview provided by W.H. Roth, 'Das Kartelldeliktsrecht in der 7. GWB-Novelle', in *Festschrift für Ulrich Huber*, T. Baums, J. Wertenbruch, M. Lutter, K. Schmidt (eds) (Mohr Siebeck, Tübingen, 2006), p. 1153 *et seq.*
44.   Gesetzesentwurf der Bundesregierung, BT-Drucks. 15/3640, 54; J. Hartog and B. Noack, 'Die 7. GWB-Novelle', [2005] WRP, 1404.

competition rules and Commission decisions under appeal.[45] In interpreting Art. 16(1) Reg. (EC) 1/2003, it has been doubted whether a judgment by a national court that a party failed to make a sufficiently detailed submission and to prove its allegation that an infringement of competition rules would really run counter to a decision by the Commission ordering an undertaking to abstain from infringing practises.[46] However, it would certainly go against the spirit of Art. 16(1) regulation 1/2003 and the principle of effectiveness if a party lost a dispute solely for its purported inability to prove an infringement which has in fact already been established by the Commission. Commission findings are therefore principally binding in all civil competition proceedings before the German Courts.

Art. 16(1) was modelled after the ECJ's decision in *Masterfoods*.[47] The rule is based upon the idea that Art. 10 EC requires courts of the Member States to abstain from any measure which could jeopardize the attainment of the objective of the EC treaty, and cannot take decisions running counter to that of the Commission. There is considerable argument to be had that this imperative is subject to limitations. A commission finding can only attain binding effect if and to the extent that the party disadvantaged by that decision was involved in the proceedings before the Commission.[48] This is particularly relevant with respect to findings of inapplicability under Art. 10 of Reg. (EC) 1/2003,[49] since the party pleading a breach of Articles 81 or 82 EC in civil litigation will not have been involved in the proceedings before the Commission – its only option insofar being the submission of an observation under Art. 27(4) of Reg. (EC) 1/2003.[50] Case law of the ECJ underlines the observance of the right to a fair hearing as a fundamental principle of Community law.[51] It would seem, therefore, that any party to the dispute must be

45. J. Bornkamm, *Kommentar zum deutschen und europäischen Kartellrecht*, vol. 1: *Deutsches Kartellrecht*, E. Langen and H.J. Bunte (eds) (10th ed., Luchterhand, Neuwied, 2006), § 33 para. 119.
46. J. Bornkamm, *Kommentar zum deutschen und europäischen Kartellrecht*, vol. 1: *Deutsches Kartellrecht*, E. Langen and H.J. Bunte (eds) (10th ed., Luchterhand, Neuwied, 2006), § 33 para. 117; J. Bornkamm and M. Becker, 'Die privatrechtliche Durchsetzung des Kartellverbots nach der Modernisierung des EG-Kartellrechts', [2005] ZWeR, 220.
47. ECJ, *Masterfoods v. HB*, Case no. C-344/98, [2000] ECR I-II369, para. 52.
48. Monopolkommission, *Das Allgemeine Wettbewerbsrecht in der Siebten GWB-Novelle. Sondergutachten 41*, <www.monopolkommission.de/sg_41/text_s41.pdf> (Bonn, 2004), para. 44; A. Fuchs, 'Die 7. GWB-Novelle – Grundkonzeption und praktische Konsequenzen', [2005] WRP, 1395 with Fn. 140; J. Bornkamm and M. Becker, 'Die privatrechtliche Durchsetzung des Kartellverbots nach der Modernisierung des EG-Kartellrechts', [2005] ZWeR, 222.
49. There is some debate whether findings under Art. 10 Reg. (EC) 1/2003 are binding in nature, cf. R. Bechtold, I. Brinker, W. Bosch, S. Hirsbrunner, *EG-Kartellrecht* (C.H.Beck, München 2005), Art. 16 VO 1/2003 para. 5 with further references.
50. J. Bornkamm and M. Becker, 'Die privatrechtliche Durchsetzung des Kartellverbots nach der Modernisierung des EG-Kartellrechts', [2005] ZWeR, 222.
51. ECJ, *Krombach v. Bamberski*, Case No. C-7/98 [2000] ECR I-1935, para. 38 *et seq.* with further references.

given the chance to submit and prove its legal position at some point in time, either in the official or the civil proceedings.[52]

Concerns have also been raised that the independence of the judges, which is guaranteed under Art. 97(1) of the Basic Law (Grundgesetz – GG) might be impaired if judges are bound by the findings of cartel authorities.[53] These concerns are unwarranted, as the privilege of Art. 97(1) GG extends to those matters only which are up for the decision of the requisite judge.[54] The binding effect is furthermore reconcilable with the separation of powers,[55] as any decision taken by the Commission or NCAs may be challenged in Community courts or the courts of the Member States. With respect to the right to be heard under Art. 103 GG, it suffices if a party has been heard by competition authorities and has had the opportunity to seek judicial redress against the cartel office's decision.[56]

b.   Relevance of Competition Authorities' Decisions in Other Instances

It has been outlined above that in some instances the decisions of either the Commission or a NCA may not possess a binding effect, namely findings of inapplicability rendered by the Commission as well as NCA decisions if the plaintiff is pursuing other goals than a compensation of its losses. In such a case, both the doctrine of effectiveness and the imperative derived from Art. 10 EC would require a court to make an inquiry under Art. 15 Reg. (EC) 1/2003, § 90a GWB, allowing an interested party to rely on the factual basis of the decision rendered by the

---

52. Monopolkommission, *Das Allgemeine Wettbewerbsrecht in der Siebten GWB-Novelle. Sondergutachten 41*, <www.monopolkommission.de/sg_41/text_s41.pdf> (Bonn, 2004), para. 44; J. Bornkamm, *Kommentar zum deutschen und europäischen Kartellrecht*, vol. 1: *Deutsches Kartellrecht*, E. Langen and H.J. Bunte (eds) (10th ed., Luchterhand, Neuwied, 2006), § 33 para. 122; G. Berrisch and M. Burianski, *Kartellrechtliche Schadensersatzansprüche nach der 7. GWB-Novelle*, [2005] *WuW*, 883; cf. further R. Bechtold, 'Grundlegende Umgestaltung des Kartellrechts: Zum Referentenentwurf der 7. GWB-Novelle', [2004], DB 239.
53. M. Meyer, 'Die Bindung der Zivilgerichte an Entscheidungen im Kartellverwaltungrechtsweg – der neue § 33 IV GWB auf dem Prüfstand', [2006] GRUR, 29; J. Gröning, 'Die dezentrale Anwendung des EG-Kartellrechts gemäß dem Vorschlag der Kommission zur Ersetzung der VO 17/62', [2001] WRP, 89; T. Lübbig, 'Die Reform des Zivilprozesses in Kartellsachen', [2006] WRP, 1212; J. Schwarze and A. Weitbrecht, *Grundzüge des europäischen Kartellverfahrensrechts* (Nomos, Baden-Baden, 2004), § 11 para. 60.
54. C. Classen, *Kommentar zum Grundgesetz*, H. Mangoldt and F. Klein (eds) (Franz Vahlen, 5th edn, München), Art. 97 para. 22.
55. M. Sura, *Kommentar zum deutschen und europäischen Kartellrecht*, vol. 2: *Europäisches Kartellrecht*, E. Langen and H.J. Bunte (eds) (10th ed., Luchterhand, Neuwied 2006), Art. 16 VO Nr. 1/2003 para. 4; Lampert T., N. Niejahr, J. Kübler and G. Weidenbach, *EG-KartellVO* (Recht und Wirtschaft, Heidelberg, 2004); with doubts J. Schwarze and A. Weitbrecht, *Grundzüge des europäischen Kartellverfahrensrechts* (Nomos, Baden-Baden, 2004), § 11 para. 60.
56. J. Bornkamm, *Kommentar zum deutschen und europäischen Kartellrecht*, vol. 1: *Deutsches Kartellrecht*, E. Langen and H.J. Bunte (eds) (10th ed., Luchterhand, Neuwied, 2006), § 33 para. 4.

Commission or NCA and the legal opinions voiced therein. This scenario shall be dealt with below, *infra* p. 247 *et seq.* It is to be expected that a deviation from the Commission's or NCA's decision by the civil courts will constitute the rare exception.[57]

c.   Persuasive Value of Decisions Rendered by the Competition Authorities

While the courts of the Member States must refrain from handing down judgments which run counter to decisions rendered by the European Commission or the NCAs under Art. 16(1) Reg. (EC) 1/2003 and § 33(4) GWB in the identical case, it needs to be emphasized that a court is not bound by decisions of either the Commission or the NCAs with respect to similar cases.[58]

> Art. 97(1) GG (Basic Law) stipulates:
> Judges are independent and subject to the law only.

The constitutional guarantee of the independence of judges implies that, under German law, there is no such concept as a binding precedent. Certainly, if a case has been referred back to a lower court by a higher instance due to a breach of the law, the higher instance's decision has a binding effect upon the lower court with respect to this individual case. Furthermore, courts will often concur with the decisions of higher instances in order to avoid excessive litigation costs and to establish legal certainty. Finally, Art. 97(1) GG does not pertain to specific matters of a dispute that are not for the requisite judge to decide, i.e., the definite interpretation of Community law which has been conferred to the European Court of Justice by virtue of Art. 234 EC.[59] However, to paraphrase Lord Hoffmann's words in *Crehan*, 'the decision making power on whether Art. 81(1) [EC] applies plainly belong to the [national] court',[60] unless the matter is covered by Art. 16(1) Reg. (EC) 1/2003. Thus, Art. 97(1) GG requires that the court form its own opinion both regarding the facts of the case as they appear from the evidence before the court and regarding the application of the law.

---

57. M. Meyer, 'Die Bindung der Zivilgerichte an Entscheidungen im Kartellverwaltungrechtsweg – der neue § 33 IV GWB auf dem Prüfstand', [2006] GRUR, 28.
58. A. Klees, *Europäisches Kartellverfahrensrecht* (Carl Heymanns, Köln, 2005), § 8 para. 112; M. Sura, *Kommentar zum deutschen und europäischen Kartellrecht*, vol. 2: *Europäisches Kartellrecht*, E. Langen and H.J. Bunte (eds) (10th ed., Luchterhand, Neuwied 2006), Art. 16 VO Nr. 1/2003 para. 9; J. Bornkamm and M. Becker, 'Die privatrechtliche Durchsetzung des Kartellverbots nach der Modernisierung des EG-Kartellrechts', [2005] ZWeR, 220; G. Hirsch, 'Anwendung der Kartellverfahrensordnung (EG) Nr. 1/2003 durch nationale Gerichte', [2003] ZWeR, 248.
59. BVerfGE 73, 339 (373); C. Classen, *Kommentar zum Grundgesetz*, H. Mangoldt and F. Klein (eds) (Franz Vahlen, 5th edn, München), Art. 97 para. 22.
60. *Inntrepreneur Pub Co (CPC) & others v. Crehan* (2006) UKHL 38 on appeal form (2004) EWCA Civ 637 per Lord Hoffmann at 69.

There is no contradiction between the guarantee of judicial independence under Art. 97(1) GG and the ECJ's argument in *Foto Frost*.[61] To reject the concept of a doctrine of consistency[62] with the acts of the Commission in similar cases does not in any way invalidate or render void the Commission's original decision, as the enforceability and declarative effect of the Commission decision with respect to the parties of the original proceeding will not be lessened by a court's failure to accept its argumentative power in a similar case. Moreover, as the parties to the 'similar' case did not possess an option to challenge the Commission's decision in the courts, to award a binding effect to Commission decisions in similar cases would raise serious questions of the right to a fair hearing and the separation of powers. This interpretation is reinforced by the Commission Notice on the co-operation between the Commission and the courts of the EU Member States, which clarifies that 'unlike the authoritative interpretation of Community law by the Community courts, the opinion of the Commission does not legally bind the national court'.[63]

Nonetheless, a decision rendered by the Commission in a similar case may be of relevance in two respects. First, under the *acte clair*-doctrine,[64] a court may be held to refer that case to the European Court of Justice if it disagrees with the legal observations given by the Commission.[65] Second, following Art. 16(1) of Reg. EC 1/2003, courts of the Member States must avoid giving decisions which would conflict with a decision contemplated by the Commission in proceedings it has initiated and may to that effect assess whether a stay of the proceedings seems appropriate.

§ 148 ZPO provides:

The court may stay the proceedings in case the decision is wholly or partially dependant upon the existence of a legal relationship which is the object of another pending lawsuit or which is to be established by an administrative authority, until the other lawsuit has ended or the administrative authority has rendered its decision.

---

61. ECJ, *Foto Frost v. Hauptzollamt Lübeck Ost*, Case no. C-314/85, [1987] ECR 4199, para. 15 *et seq.*
62. As suggested by the English Court of Appeal in *Bernard Crehan v. Inntrepreneur Pub Co. (CPC)*, Case A3/2003/1725, [2004] EWCA 637; cf. G. Cumming, *supra* p. 42 *et seq.*
63. Commission Notice on the co-operation between the Commission and the courts of the EU Member States, OJ No. C 101 17 April 2004, p. 54 *et seq.*, no. 29.
64. ECJ, *CILFIT*, Case no. 283/81, [1982] ECR 3415, para. 16. Following the *acte clair* doctrine, national courts may refrain from their duty to submit a question to the ECJ referred for a preliminary ruling, if the disputed provision of EU law has already been interpreted by the ECJ or if the correct application of EU law is so obvious as to leave no scope for any reasonable doubt.
65. J. Bornkamm and M. Becker, 'Die privatrechtliche Durchsetzung des Kartellverbots nach der Modernisierung des EG-Kartellrechts', [2005] ZWeR, 221.

The court's discretion regarding a stay of the proceedings under § 148 ZPO would necessarily need to be based upon an analysis of earlier Commission decisions. In view of Art. 10 EC, the court's intent to diverge from Commission decisions in comparable cases necessitates either a stay of the proceedings or a reference to the ECJ.[66] Likewise, if the Commission has indicated its intention to render a decision[67] and there is no guidance as to its outcome, it would generally be adequate to stay the proceedings.[68]

66. A. Klees, *Europäisches Kartellverfahrensrecht* (Carl Heymanns, Köln, 2005), § 8 para. 128 *et seq.*; M. Sura, *Kommentar zum deutschen und europäischen Kartellrecht*, vol. 2: *Europäisches Kartellrecht*, E. Langen and H.J. Bunte (eds) (10th ed., Luchterhand, Neuwied 2006), Art. 16 VO Nr. 1/2003 para. 13; R. Bechtold, I. Brinker, W. Bosch, S. Hirsbrunner, *EG-Kartellrecht* (C.H.Beck, München 2005), Art. 16 VO 1/2003 para. 7.
67. According to the Court of Justice, the initiation of proceedings implies an authoritative act of the Commission, evidencing its intention of taking a decision, cf. ECJ, *Brasserie de Haecht* Case no. 48/72, [1973] ECR 77, para. 16. To determine the intentions of the Commission, the court may seek information from the Commission on the state of any procedure which the Commission may have set in motion, cf. ECJ, *Delimitis v. Henninger Bräu AG*, Case no. C-234/89, [1991] ECR I-935, para. 53; Commission Notice on the co-operation between the Commission and the courts of the EU Member States, OJ No. C 101 17 April 2004, p. 54 *et seq.*, no. 12.
68. *Commission Notice on the co-operation between the Commission and the courts of the EU Member States*, OJ No. C 101 17 April 2004, p. 56, no. 12; cf. A. Zuber, *Die EG-Kommission als amicus curiae* (Carl Heymanns, Köln, 2001), p. 36 *et seq.* regarding the prognosis of whether the proceedings before the Commission will come to an official closing.

APPENDIX

COMPETITION CASE ALLOCATION IN GERMANY (1ST INSTANCE)

State	Circuit	District Court	Panel	Higher Regional Court
Baden-Württemberg	OLG Karlsruhe	LG Mannheim	7th civil 2nd commercial	OLG Karlsruhe
	OLG Stuttgart	LG Stuttgart	17th civil 41st commercial	OLG Stuttgart
Bayern	OLG München	LG München I	33rd civil 4th commercial	OLG München
	OLG Bamberg and Nürnberg	LG Nürnberg-Fürth		OLG München
Berlin	Entire state	LG Berlin		Kammergericht
Bremen	Entire state	LG Bremen		OLG Bremen
Brandenburg	Entire state	LG Potsdam	2nd civil	OLG Potsdam
Hamburg	Entire state	LG Hamburg		OLG Hamburg
Hessen	LG Darmstadt, Frankfurt, Gieβen, Hanau, Limburg, Wiesbaden	LG Frankfurt	3rd civil8th commercial	OLG Frankfurt
	LG Fulda, Kassel, Marburg	LG Kassel	2nd commercial	OLG Frankfurt
Mecklenburg-Vorpommern	Entire state	LG Rostock		OLG Rostock
Niedersachsen	Entire state	LG Hannover	8th civil 6th commercial	OLG Celle
Nordrhein-Westfalen	OLG Düsseldorf	LG Düsseldorf		OLG Düsseldorf
	OLG Hamm	LG Dortmund	13th civil 2nd commercial	OLG Düsseldorf
	OLG Köln	LG Köln	28th civil 1st and 4th commercial	OLG Düsseldorf
Rheinland-Pfalz	Entire state	LG Mainz	10th, 12th commercial	OLG Koblenz
Saarland	Entire state	LG Saarbrücken		OLG Saarbrücken
Sachsen	Entire state	LG Leipzig	5th civil 1st, 2nd, 6th commercial	OLG Dresden
Sachsen-Anhalt	Entire state	LG Magdeburg	7th civil	OLG Naumburg
Schleswig-Holstein	Entire state	LG Kiel	1st commercial	OLG Schleswig
Thüringen		Any district court		OLG Jena

Chapter 12

German Procedure: Evidence and Burden of Proof

A. DIFFICULTIES ENTAILED BY THE NON-
    INQUISITORIAL NATURE OF CIVIL LITIGATION

Private enforcement of competition law cannot adequately serve the function of an expedient which complements the – necessarily fragmentary – enforcement activities of public enforcement authorities, unless the realm of follow-on actions is left and stand-alone actions become more common. Actions raised by plaintiffs independently of public enforcement activities may play an important role in the development of the law and the establishment of legal certainty, while also utilizing the specific expertise of undertakings in the market.[1] Plaintiffs raising stand alone-actions before the German Courts face major problems in proving an infringement of competition law, the ensuing damage and the causal link between the two.[2] To a lesser extent, these difficulties are also experienced by parties raising the allegation of anti-competitive behaviour as a defensive shield. Both

---

1. R. Hempel, 'Private Follow-on-Klagen im Kartellrecht', [2005] WuW, 144; U. Böge and K. Ost, 'Up and Running, or is it? Private enforcement – the Situation in Germany and Policy Perspectives', [2006] ECLR, 197.
2. Monopolkommission, *Folgeprobleme der europäischen Kartellverfahrensreform. Sondergutachten 32* (Bonn, 2001), <www.monopolkommission.de/sg_32/text_s32_d.pdf>, para. 47; G. Berrisch and M. Burianski, 'Kartellrechtliche Schadensersatzansprüche nach der 7. GWB-Novelle', [2005] WuW, 881 *et seq.*; R. Hempel, 'Privater Rechtsschutz im deutschen Kartellrecht nach der 7. GWB-Novelle', [2004] WuW 374; J. Hartog and B. Noack, 'Die 7. GWB-Novelle', [2005] WRP, 1405.

the Green Paper and the Commission Staff Working Paper[3] identify the limited access to documents as a possible set-back for stand-alone claims. The Green Paper states:[4]

> Actions for damages in antitrust cases regularly require the investigation of a broad set of facts. The particular difficulty with this kind of litigation is that often the relevant evidence is not easily available and is held by the party committing the anti-competitive behaviour. Access by claimants to such evidence is the key to making damages claims effective. It must therefore be considered whether obligations to turn over documents or otherwise provide access to evidence should be introduced.

The Commission's concerns are of particular relevance for civil litigation in Germany. The difficulties facing a party pleading a breach of competition rules are two-fold:

(1) Lack of market information

In contrast to the European Commission and national cartel authorities, civil courts and parties to a civil proceeding do not possess wide-ranging investigative powers enabling them to collect the necessary information to analyse the respective market.[5] This is an obstacle both regarding the establishment of an infringement under Art. 81(1), 82 EC[6] and the inapplicability under Art. 81(3) EC.[7]

(2) Information held by the opposing party

Unless the party submitting anti-competitive behaviour is party to an infringing agreement, as was the case, i.e., in *Courage v. Crehan*, it regularly does not have access to evidence elemental to proving the infringement. Any such documents or witnesses will be in the sphere of the defendant.

---

3. Commission Staff Working Paper, COM (2005) 672 final, no. 54 *et seq.*
4. Green Paper – Damages actions for breach of the EC antitrust rules, COM (2005) 672 final, p. 5 at 2.1.
5. Monopolkommission, *Folgeprobleme der europäischen Kartellverfahrensreform. Sondergutachten 32*, <www.monopolkommission.de/sg_32/text_s32_d.pdf> (Bonn, 2001), 46; J. Topel, *Kohärenz der dezentralen Anwendung im System paralleler Kompetenzen*, <www.ec.europa.eu/comm/competition/conferences/2000/freiburg/speeches/topel_de.pdf>, p. 4; R. Hempel, *Privater Rechtsschutz im Kartellrecht* (Nomos, Baden-Baden, 2002), p. 69; A. Klees, *Europäisches Kartellverfahrensrecht* (Carl Heymanns, Köln, 2005), § 8 para. 25.
6. F. Montag and A. Rosenfeld, 'A Solution to the Problems? Regulation 1/2003 and the modernization of competition procedure', [2003] ZWeR, 121; R. Bechtold, I. Brinker, W. Bosch, S. Hirsbrunner, *EG-Kartellrecht* (C.H. Beck, München 2005), Art. 2 VO 1/2003 para. 10; partially dissenting G. Weidenbach and J.M. Schultze, 'Das Grünbuch zu Schadensersatzklagen im EG-Kartellrecht', [2006] GPR, 135.
7. F. Montag and A. Rosenfeld, 'A Solution to the Problems? Regulation 1/2003 and the modernization of competition procedure', [2003] ZWeR, 121; G. Weidenbach and J.M. Schultze, 'Das Grünbuch zu Schadensersatzklagen im EG-Kartellrecht', [2006] GPR, 135; R. Bechtold, I. Brinker, W. Bosch, S. Hirsbrunner, *EG-Kartellrecht* (C.H. Beck, München 2005), Art. 2 VO 1/2003 para. 5; opposing view held by J. Bornkamm and M. Becker, 'Die privatrechtliche Durchsetzung des Kartellverbots nach der Modernisierung des EG-Kartellrechts', [2005] ZWeR, 231.

This section sets out to expound the access to evidence under German procedural rules, the supportive role the Commission and NCAs may play in acting as an *amicus curiae* and finally the burden and standard of proof applied, in order to determine whether the doctrine of effectiveness might require changes to these rules.

B.   THE CONCEPT OF 'EXPLORATORY EVIDENCE'

Under the German principle of party presentation, a court may base its decision solely on information which has been introduced into the proceedings by the parties, and the taking of evidence is only considered admissible if it is required to prove the submitted facts (a corresponding provision i.e., to rule 19(3) CAT (Competition Appeal Tribunal) Rules does not exist). It constitutes a major obstacle to private enforcement that – contrary to the competition authorities – civil courts are restrained from undertaking their own inquiries, and potential claimants do not possess any investigative rights.[8] A motion that the court take so-called exploratory evidence (*Ausforschungsbeweis*) is principally not considered admissible.[9] The term exploratory evidence is used to describe a motion for the taking of evidence where there is no intention of proving facts already pleaded by the respective party, but rather an unfocused attempt to explore new facts or reveal as of yet unknown sources of information which would in turn enable the party to plead new facts.[10]

The concept of exploratory evidence seems much stricter than what might be deemed a 'fishing expedition' in Common Law terminology. At the same time, a clear-cut definition of the concept does not exist. The Federal Court of Justice tends to apply relatively lenient standards if the party bearing the onus of submission and proof is legitimately in the dark regarding factual matters resting within the sphere of the opposing party:[11] i.e., if a party does not possess immediate knowledge of arrangements between other undertakings, it may submit facts merely assumed and offer corresponding proof provided there are ample grounds for the correctness of its submissions. Such conduct is to be regarded as inadmissible exploratory evidence solely if it is arbitrary or constitutes an abuse of rights.[12]

---

8. Monopolkommission, *Folgeprobleme der europäischen Kartellverfahrensreform. Sondergutachten 32* (Bonn, 2001), <www.monopolkommission.de/sg_32/text_s32_d.pdf>, para. 46; J. Bornkamm, *Kommentar zum deutschen und europäischen Kartellrecht*, Langen E. and H.J. Bunte (eds) (10th ed., München, Luchterhand, 2006), § 33 para. 8; U. Böge and K. Ost, 'Up and Running, or is it? Private enforcement – the Situation in Germany and Policy Perspectives', [2006] ECLR, 198.
9. BGH, NJW 1998, 2100, 2101; BGH, NJW 1996, 3150.
10. *Greger*, Zivilprozessordnung, Zöller (ed.) (25th edn, Otto Schmidt, Köln, 2005), vor § 284 para. 5 *et seq.* with further references.
11. Cf. the case law cited by U. Foerste, *Kommentar zur Zivilprozessordnung*, H.J. Musielack (ed.) (4th edn, Franz Vahlen, München, 2005), § 284 para. 17 and L. Rosenberg, K. H. Schwab and P. Gottwald, *Zivilprozessrecht* (16th ed, C.H. Beck, München 2004), § 115 para. 15 *et seq.*
12. BGH, NJW 2001, 2327, 2328; BGH, NJW 1996, 3147, 3150; BGH, NJW-RR 1987, 335.

While mere speculations are insufficient to allow the taking of evidence, case law suggests that the courts need to be cautious in finding a request for the taking of evidence to be arbitrary.[13]

It is often pointed out that parties trying to prove an infringement in competition cases will possess little to no knowledge both regarding the cartel agreements as well as the market structure, and the threshold for a motion for exploratory evidence may easily be crossed.[14] However, in light of the above-mentioned case law of the Federal Court of Justice, it would seem that the principle of party presentation allows for sufficient flexibility to accommodate a party's difficulties, as long as circumstantial evidence provides sufficient grounds for an assumption of the existence of infringing practises. This is particularly true if the evidence sought does not concern documents within the sphere of the opposing party, but consists in the appointment of an assessor.[15]

In 2003, the President of the Federal Court of Justice, Günter Hirsch, pointed out:[16]

In view of the difficult economic facts that form the basis of proceedings concerning Art. 81(3) EC, the civil courts are held not to overdo requirements that the parties substantiate their submissions of fact. On the one hand, the German civil courts will need to apply a reinforced use to their obligation to direct and promote the proceedings under § 139 ZPO. On the other hand, there will be a need for expert evidence, in particular regarding the two positive prognosis factors under Art. 81(3) EC, as the parties will lack the requisite knowledge, whereas the courts currently lack sufficient experience. The threshold towards inadmissible exploratory evidence will thus need to be lifted, at least for the time being.

C.   ACCESS TO EVIDENCE IN THE SPHERE
            OF THE OPPOSING PARTY

Even if the concept of exploratory evidence is handled flexibly, a party's access to evidence lying within the sphere of the opposing party remains a tricky matter

---

13. BGH, NJW-RR 2002, 1433, 1435; an overview of the existing case law is provided by L. Rosenberg, K. H. Schwab and P. Gottwald, *Zivilprozessrecht* (16th ed, C.H. Beck, München 2004), § 115 para. 15 *et seq.*
14. OLG Stuttgart, [1988] WuW/E OLG 4214, 4215 – *City-Reisebüro*: a request that the court inquire with the Federal Cartel Authority about the alleged dominant position of the defendant was struck down because the plaintiff did not submit any facts, but solely issued a blanket allegation regarding the defendant's market position. See further A. Klees, *Europäisches Kartellverfahrensrecht* (Carl Heymanns, Köln, 2005), § 8 para. 32; R. Hempel, *Privater Rechtsschutz im Kartellrecht*, (Nomos, Baden-Baden, 2002), 75; G. Hirsch, 'Anwendung der Kartellverfahrensordnung (EG) Nr. 1/2003 durch nationale Gerichte', [2003] ZWeR, 240.
15. L. Rosenberg, K. H. Schwab and P. Gottwald, *Zivilprozessrecht* (16th ed, C.H. Beck, München 2004), § 115 para. 19.
16. G. Hirsch, 'Anwendung der Kartellverfahrensordnung (EG) Nr. 1/2003 durch nationale Gerichte', [2003] ZWeR, 240.

under German procedural rules. According to the prevailing opinion, the principle of party presentation implies that while a party is obliged to make complete and truthful submissions under § 138 ZPO, no one is held to contribute to the production of evidence against his or her own cause.[17]

Nonetheless, the ZPO in combination with the Civil Code (*Bürgerliches Gesetzbuch* – BGB) allow for a certain, albeit limited, degree of disclosure. While §§ 142, 144 ZPO enable the court to order a party to produce specific documents, § 242 BGB may provide a party with a substantive right to information against the opposing side, which would prompt the production of documents under § 422 ZPO. These options, as well as the hearing of the opposing party, witnesses and experts, will be examined below.

1.   DISCLOSURE UNDER §§ 142, 144 CODE OF CIVIL PROCEDURE
            (*ZIVILPROZESSORDNUNG* – ZPO)

Both § 142 and § 144 ZPO contain modifications of the principle of party presentation insofar as they allow the court to take evidence upon its own initiative without a corresponding request made by one of the parties. The scope of these provisions was substantially enlarged in the course of the comprehensive ZPO-reform implemented on 1 January 2002. Whereas under the former provisions a court was only able to order a party to present documents in its possession if the party itself had referred to them, it is now possible to order a party to produce material that the opponent has relied upon. However, a recent evaluation of the ZPO-reform has shown that while judges tend to hold a favourable view of their amplified powers under §§ 142, 144 ZPO, they are more than reluctant to exercise their discretion and issue orders under these provisions.[18] Possibly, the appeal of the said rules will grow over time.

§ 142 ZPO provides:

(1) The court may order a party or a third person to produce certificates or other documents in their possession, in case one of the parties has referred to them. The court may set a time limit for the production and may order the documents to remain in the court office for a stipulated period of time.

(2) Third parties are not obliged to present documents if such production cannot be expected of them or in case they are entitled to refuse testimony under §§ 383 to 385. §§ 386 to 390 apply accordingly.

---

17. BGH, NJW 1990, 3151; A. Baumbach, W. Lauterbach, J. Albers, P. Hartmann, Zivilprozessordnung (64th edn, C.H. Beck, München, 2006), § 284 ZPO n. 29.
18. C. Hommerich, H. Prütting *et al.*, *Rechtstatsächliche Untersuchung zu den Auswirkungen der Reform des Zivilprozessrechts auf die gerichtliche Praxis – Evaluation ZPO-Reform*, <www.bmj.bund.de/media/archive/1216.pdf>, p. 4.

§ 144 ZPO stipulates:

(1) The court may order an inspection by the court or a survey by an expert. For this purpose, it may order a party or a third person to produce a specific item and set a corresponding time limit. The court may also order a party to tolerate a measure taken under sentence 1, unless a residence is involved.

(2) Third parties are not obliged to present or tolerate said measures if this cannot be expected of them or in case they are entitled to refuse testimony under §§ 383 to 385. §§ 386 to 390 apply accordingly.

Unfortunately, §§ 142, 144 ZPO are only of limited help to a party seeking information from its opponent or third parties in order to prove an infringement of competition law.[19] This is for four reasons. First, cartel agreements tend to be oral and not fixed in documents.[20] Second, § 142 ZPO requires that one of the parties refer specifically to the document in question. The motive behind this prerequisite is to prevent the taking of exploratory evidence,[21] and the rule is consequently of little help if a party is unsure which the relevant documents are.[22] Third, the court has discretion as to whether to order disclosure. In exercising its discretion, the court may take various factors into account, i.e., the difficulty in proving an infringement via other means or the confidentiality of business information. According to the prevailing opinion, sensitive data cannot be protected by means of a limited disclosure to a neutral person under the proviso of confidentiality (*Wirtschaftsprüfervorbehalt*).[23] Appeals claiming an incorrect exercise of the court's discretion have so far proven unsuccessful.[24] Finally, there is one sanction, and one sanction only, in case a party refuses production of a document or an inspection by the court or expert: When the court forms its opinion as to whether the facts submitted by the parties are true, it may take the refusal to produce the evidence into account (§§ 286, 371(3), as well as an analogy to § 422 ZPO).[25]

---

19. G. Berrisch and M. Burianski, 'Kartellrechtliche Schadensersatzansprüche nach der 7. GWB-Novelle', [2005] WuW, 883.
20. G. Berrisch and M. Burianski, 'Kartellrechtliche Schadensersatzansprüche nach der 7. GWB-Novelle', [2005] WuW, 883; R. Hempel, 'Privater Rechtsschutz nach der 7. GWB-Novelle', [2004] WuW, 364.
21. LG Düsseldorf, InstGE 2, 231 *et seq.*; Law Commission Recommendation, BT-Drucks. 14/6036, 120 f.; L. Rosenberg, K. H. Schwab and P. Gottwald, *Zivilprozessrecht* (16th ed, C.H. Beck, München 2004), § 118 para. 45.
22. R. Hempel, *Privater Rechtsschutz im Kartellrecht* (Nomos, Baden-Baden, 2002), p. 306; R. Greger, 'Zweifelsfragen und erste Entscheidungen zur neuen ZPO', [2002] NJW, 3050; G. Berrisch and M. Burianski, 'Kartellrechtliche Schadensersatzansprüche nach der 7. GWB-Novelle', [2005] WuW, 883; J. Zekoll and J. Bolt, 'Die Pflicht zur Vorlage im Zivilprozess – Amerikanische Verhältnisse in Deutschland?', [2002] NJW, 3130.
23. *Cf.* the refererences provided by L. Rosenberg, K. H. Schwab and P. Gottwald, *Zivilprozessrecht* (16th ed, C.H. Beck, München 2004), § 115 para. 43 *et seq.*
24. OLGR Karlsruhe 2005, 484 (485); OLGR Frankfurt 2005, 594 (595).
25. *Greger*, Zivilprozessordnung, Zöller (ed.) (25th edn, Otto Schmidt, Köln, 2005), vor § 142 para. 4; L. Rosenberg, K. H. Schwab and P. Gottwald, *Zivilprozessrecht* (16th ed, C.H. Beck, München 2004), § 118 para. 45; Baumbach A., W. Lauterbach, J. Albers, P. Hartmann, Zivilprozessordnung (C.H. Beck, 64th edn, München, 2006), § 142 para. 27.

The quest to obtain documents from third parties, be it to establish the infringement or to provide material for a market analysis, is equally challenging. §§ 142(2), 144(2) ZPO refer to the privileges under §§ 383 *et seq.* ZPO. In particular, the third person may refuse the production of evidence if the revelation were to put the witness or a close relation at the risk of dishonour, criminal proceedings, direct financial losses or the revelation of business secrets (§ 384 ZPO). Even if the third party is not privileged following §§ 383 *et seq.* ZPO, the court may refrain from issuing an order if enlisting the third person would seem unreasonable, i.e., because of an unreasonable expenditure of time and money. It is of little consolation that the sanctions against a third party refusing to cooperate are much sharper than those available against parties, and include fines and imprisonment, cf. §§ 142(2), 144(2), 390 ZPO.

2.   Disclosure of Information under §§ 242, 259 BGB

While German procedural rules do not provide for general disclosure, the substantive law may be of help to a person seeking information from the opposing party. In theory, the information may be sought independently from a civil proceeding, but in practise, such claims are used in the context of and in order to facilitate litigation.[26] A right to information and an entitlement to the rendering of accounts is contained in various specific provisions, but may also be based upon the principle of good faith under § 242 Civil Code (*Bürgerliches Gesetzbuch* – BGB), if none of the specific rules apply. The duty to disclose information must be complied with in written form, but entails an obligation to produce documents only in exceptional cases.[27] In contrast, if a party is entitled to a rendering of accounts, supporting documents must be provided under § 259(1) BGB. Doubts as to the correctness and completeness of information may warrant the submission of an affidavit.[28] In the event that a party fails to comply with an order to disclose information or render accounts, it is subject to fines and imprisonment under § 888 ZPO.

Further, § 422 ZPO stipulates:
The opposing party is obliged to present a document if the party relying on the evidence is entitled to demand delivery or production of the document under civil law.

A failure to comply with this procedural obligation enables the court to find the other party's submissions regarding the content of the document to be true, if the circumstances described by §§ 426 *et seq.* ZPO are met.

---

26. P. Schlosser, 'Wirtschaftsprüfervorbehalt und prozessuales Vertraulichkeitsinteresse der nicht primär beweisbelasteten Prozeßpartei' in *Festschrift für Bernhard Großfeld*, U. Hübner and W. Ebke (eds) (Recht und Wirtschaft, Heidelberg, 1999), p. 998.

27. BGH, GRUR 2001, 841, 845 – *Entfernung der Herstellungsnummer II;* BGH, GRUR 2002, 709, 712 – *Entfernung der Herstellungsnummer III.*

28. § 259(2) BGB, cf. BGH, NJW 1994, 1958, 1959 – *Cartier-Armreif*; BGH, GRUR 2001, 841, 845 – *Entfernung der Herstellungsnummer II.*

None of the specific disclosure obligations are of particular relevance to competition cases, thus, any request for information must be based upon § 242 BGB. Following case law, a duty to provide information and render accounts under § 242 BGB may arise if (a) the plaintiff is justifiably in the dark about the existence or the extent of his rights, (b) the plaintiff is unable to obtain the lacking information necessary to prepare for and enforce his claim in a reasonable way and (c) the opposing party is easily able to provide the information.[29] These obligations, however, are subject to one major limitation: they require the existence of a special legal relationship (*rechtliche Sonderverbindung*) between the parties. The specific link may i.e., arise out of contract or tort, but it is certainly not considered sufficient if the plaintiff solely alleges that a legal connection in the form of a competition infringement exists.[30]

In competition cases, a disclosure obligation based upon § 242 BGB may arise in two instances. First, if a contractual relationship between the parties exists. For example, if the defendant is arguing the non-enforceability of a vertical agreement, it may require the plaintiff to reveal information which might help to establish an infringement of competition law.[31] Also, § 242 BGB will be of help to a plaintiff who has succeeded in establishing an infringement of competition law and an ensuing right to claim compensation, as the identification of a tort under § 33(3) GWB connotes a 'special legal connection'. Disclosure would then be sought to ascertain the amount of damages owed. In establishing the amount of loss suffered by the plaintiff, information by the party in breach will often be relevant, i.e., the time length of the cartel, singular price agreements, etc.[32] Furthermore, as § 33(3) sent 3 GWB allows the court to estimate damages on the basis of the infringer's profits, § 242 BGB may i.e., be used to determine delivery quantities, contract prices, delivery times, manufacturing and labour costs.[33]

Since the rights to information and to a rendering of accounts are anchored in the principle of good faith, they are subject to a process of balancing the interests of both parties, which is discussed under the terms necessity and reasonableness. In principle, the party underlying the disclosure obligation is not held to impart with information unnecessary to prove the other's allegations (necessity). However, so-called *Kontrolltatsachen*, namely surrounding facts required to monitor the completeness and correctness of the information may need to be revealed.[34] In determining the reasonableness of an information request, the courts will ponder the gravity of the infringement, the expenditure of parting with the information and

---

29.   BGH GRUR 1994, 630, 631 – *Cartier-Armreif*; BGH GRUR 2001, 841, 842 – *Entfernung der Herstellungsnummer II* with further references.
30.   BGH, GRUR 1980, 1105, 1111 – *Das Medizinsyndikat III*; GRUR 1986, 62, 64 – *GEMA-Vermutung I*; BGH, NJW 1990, 3151, 3152; OLG Köln, Magazindienst 1998, 945.
31.   *Cf.* OLG München, [2001] WuW/E DE-R 968.
32.   G. Berrisch and M. Burianski, 'Kartellrechtliche Schadensersatzansprüche nach der 7. GWB-Novelle', [2005] WuW, 884; regarding acts of unfair competition cf. BGH, GRUR 1961, 288, 293 – *Zahnbürsten*; BGH, GRUR 1987, 364, 365 – *Vier-Streifen-Schuh*.
33.   BGH, GRUR 1980, 227, 233 – *Monumenta Germaniae Historica*.
34.   BGH, GRUR 1978, 52, 53 – *Fernschreibverzeichnisse*; BGH GRUR 1980, 227, 233 – *Monumenta Germanae Historica*.

the rendering of accounts as well as the party's interest in protecting its business secrets[35] and finally the value of the information to the claimant.[36] In its decision *Entfernung der Herstellungsnummer II*, the Federal Court of Justice further held that higher-ranking public interests, such as public health, may play a role in the granting of an information request.[37] Since private enforcement of competition rules serves a supplementary function to public enforcement, it would seem that the public interest in disposing of anti-competitive behaviour could tip the balance in favour of a wide information obligation.

Insofar as the information given or the accounts to be rendered include business secrets, the order to disclose information may contain a proviso that the documents be handed over to a neutral certified accountant named by the plaintiff and paid for by the defendant (*Wirtschaftsprüfervorbehalt*). Again, the court needs to balance the interests of the parties under particular regard for the fact that this reservation impedes the procedural options of the claimant, who remains partly in the dark regarding the circumstances of the case and needs to rely on the monitoring abilities of the accountant, despite the fact that the latter lacks a comparable overview of the dispute.[38] Thus, such a proviso is only indicated in case of a significant preponderance of the interests of the defendant.[39] Finally, it should be noted that legal questions, i.e., which costs may be deducted in determining the illegal gain under § 33(3) GWB, are not suitable for appraisal by an accountant, which obviously limits the effectiveness of the use of such a neutral person.[40] Revealing such material exclusively to the attorneys is not an option, as German law does not contain any provisions debarring attorneys from disclosing information to their clients.[41] Rather, attorneys are obliged to inform their clients immediately under § 11 of the Federal Attorneys' Professional Code of Conduct (*Berufsordnung der Rechtsanwälte in der Bundesrepublik Deutschland* – BRAO).

3.   HEARING OF THE OPPOSING PARTY

The German Code of Civil Procedure (ZPO) also allows for a party to be heard in court, either upon the request of the opposing party (§ 445 ZPO) or by order of the court (§ 448 ZPO). However, such a measure is of subsidiary nature and may not be taken unless the existing evidence is insufficient to prove the facts submitted by the

---

35. U. Loewenheim, *Der Wettbewerbsprozeß*, H.J. Ahrens (ed.) (5th edn, Carl Heymanns, Köln, 2005), Ch. 72 para. 8 *et seq.*
36. BGH GRUR 1965, 313, 314 *et seq.– Umsatzauskunft*; U. Loewenheim, *Der Wettbewerbsprozeß*, H.J. Ahrens (ed.) (5th edn, Carl Heymanns, Köln, 2005), Chapt. 72 para. 10.
37. BGH, GRUR 2001, 841, 843 – *Entfernung der Herstellungsnummer II.*
38. BGH, GRUR 1999, 1025, 1031 – *Preisbindung durch Franchisegeber.*
39. BGH, GRUR 1999, 1025, 1031 – *Preisbindung durch Franchisegeber.*
40. J. Bornkamm, *Kommentar zum deutschen und europäischen Kartellrecht*, vol. 1: *Deutsches Kartellrecht*, E. Langen and H.J. Bunte (eds) (10th ed., Luchterhand, Neuwied, 2006), § 33 para. 110.
41. P. Schlosser, 'Wirtschaftsprüfervorbehalt und prozessuales Vertraulichkeitsinteresse der nicht primär beweisbelasteten Prozeßpartei' in *Festschrift für Bernhard Großfeld*, U. Hübner and W. Ebke (eds) (Recht und Wirtschaft, Heidelberg, 1999), p. 1010.

opposing party. Again, an unfocused hearing of the party, conducted solely to shed light on general circumstances of the case and in the hope of revealing new facts or sources of information is considered exploratory evidence. Parties are not under a statutory duty to speak in court and cannot be forced to do so. Instead, the refusal and its purported justification may be taken into account only when the court is considering the evidence, *cf.* § 446 ZPO.

4.   PRIVILEGE AGAINST SELF-INCRIMINATION

Requests for information made by cartel authorities under § 59 GWB are subject to a privilege against self-incrimination. Persons required to answer in public enforcement proceedings do not have to submit themselves or their relatives to the risk of criminal proceedings or a proceeding for regulatory offences following § 59(5) GWB. In civil litigation, this privilege may not be invoked by the parties of the dispute, irrespective of whether the obligation to provide the other party with information or documents is based upon §§ 142, 144 ZPO or §§ 242 BGB, 422 ZPO. This can be deduced from a judgment of the Federal Constitutional Court (*Bundesverfassungsgericht*) of 13 January 1981 with respect to the privilege against self-incrimination as it pertains to freedom of action (*Allgemeine Handlungsfreiheit*) under Art. 2(1) of the German Basic Law (GG) in the context of disclosure obligations under insolvency law.[42]

> The privilege against self-incrimination is not limited to criminal and similar proceedings. It has also been established for civil and similar proceedings that a party's duty to remain truthful is limited if the party was forced to reveal a dishonourable fact or a criminal deed committed. [...] While the law consistently grants witnesses, parties and the accused a right to be silent in case of self-incrimination, this principle does not hold up in the same way for such persons who are – be it by virtue of a contract or a statute – under a specific legal obligation to provide another person or an authority with information. [...] [The freedom of action] does not provide a complete guarantee from self-incrimination irrespective of whether interests worthy of protection belonging to third parties are affected. As this court has emphasized time and again regarding the freedom of action, the Basic Law resolves the tension between individual and society at large in favour of a concept of the individual as standing in reference to and being restricted by the community. An individual is thus bound by such restrictions on its freedom of action which the legislature has set, in order to foster and promote social interaction within the boundaries of general reasonability, provided that the autonomy of the individual is safeguarded. It would be unreasonable and incompatible with human dignity to force a person to provide the facts for its own criminal conviction or corresponding sanctions. Corresponding to well-established

---

42. BVerfG, NJW 1981, 1431, 1432 *et seq.*

legal traditions, Art. 2(1) GG insofar acts as a defensive right providing protection against public intrusions. However, if the information is sought to meet a justified need for information, the legislature is entitled to balance the interest of the various individuals involved.

The Federal Constitutional Court emphasizes that in enacting disclosure obligations and balancing the diverging interests, Parliament may consider whether disclosure is sought in the public interest or whether it also serves to protect the interests of third parties whose rights have been infringed. This is decisive in terms of private enforcement of competition rules: While § 59(5) GWB grants a privilege against self-incrimination in public enforcement, there is no such privilege for civil litigation, and an analogy to § 59(5) would 'unjustifiably favour those persons who acted in a particularly reprehensible manner to the disadvantage of their creditors'.[43] To safeguard the general privilege against self-incrimination, it is sufficient that any information a party is compelled to reveal in the course of civil litigation will be barred from being used in criminal or similar proceedings, which can be achieved by virtue of an analogy to § 136a(3) of the Criminal Procedural Code (*Strafprozeßordnung* – StPO).[44] The distinction between criminal proceedings and civil litigation ensures compatibility with ECtHR case law regarding the privilege against self-incrimination in decisions such as *Funke v. France* or *JB v. Switzerland*, as these concerned criminal charges.[45]

5.   WITNESSES

A party seeking to prove matters within the sphere of the opposing party or to establish market data may also resort to the calling of witnesses, i.e., employees of an undertaking in the market. Contrary to parties, witnesses are obliged to make an appearance and testify in court, if need be under oath.[46] However, the effectiveness of hearing witnesses to prove a competition infringement is hampered by three factors: first, a party does not necessarily know which persons on the opposing side possess the required knowledge[47] and the opponent is under no duty to submit the names of possible witnesses, i.e., his employees.[48] Second, the principle of party presentation requires that the party naming a witness submit the facts that are to be proved by the witness' testimony, as is clarified by § 373 ZPO. Finally, witnesses may rely on a number of relatively broad privileges, i.e., if they are closely related to one of the parties or subject to professional secrecy. Significantly, in terms of

---

43. BVerfG, NJW 1981, 1431, 1433.
44. BVerfG, NJW 1981, 1431, 1433; R. Stürner, 'Strafrechtliche Selbstbelastung und verfahrens-förmige Wahrheitsermittlung', [1981] NJW, 1760; U. Loewenheim, *Der Wettbewerbsprozeß*, H.J. Ahrens (ed.) (5th edn, Carl Heymanns, Köln, 2005), Ch. 72 para. 11.
45. ECtHR, *Funke v. France*, Case no. 82/1991/334/407, para. 44; ECtHR, *J.B. v. Switzerland*, Case no. *31827*/96, para. 44 *et seq.*, 63 *et seq.*
46. §§ 380, 390 ZPO.
47. R. Hempel, *Privater Rechtsschutz im Kartellrecht* (Nomos, Baden-Baden, 2002), p. 76.
48. R. Hempel, *Privater Rechtsschutz im Kartellrecht* (Nomos, Baden-Baden, 2002), p. 76.

competition cases,[49] a witness may refuse to answer questions following § 384 ZPO if the testimony would put the witness or its close relations at the risk of dishonour, criminal proceedings, direct financial losses or the revelation of business secrets. The term business secrets encompasses economic facts as well as working methods, business partners and sources of information, provided there is a substantial interest in not disclosing such facts.[50] Proving cartel agreements or even revealing relevant market information may thus fail on the basis of this broad privilege. For further discussion on whether the doctrine of effectiveness requires any changes with respect to the privilege, see section H infra (p. 263 *et seq*).

6.   EXPERT EVIDENCE

Finally, the commissioning of an expert report under §§ 402 *et seq.* ZPO to establish market data again raises the problem of how to protect sensitive data. The expert will need to base his or her assessment on business information supplied by the party allegedly engaging in anti-competitive behaviour. As the Federal Constitutional Court has established, the right to a fair hearing principally requires that the factual basis of expert evidence is revealed to the parties,[51] lest the evidence not be utilized.[52] The prevailing opinion in the ordinary judicature is that if the relevant data is not revealed to the parties, the court may not take the expertise into account when rendering its decision.[53] Again, refer to section H. as to changes required by the doctrine of effectiveness.

7.   THE HANDLING OF SENSITIVE DATA

Overall, the analysis of access to evidence under the German procedural rules has shown that there is an obvious conflict of interest between one party's need to obtain information resting within the sphere of other undertakings in order to prove an infringement and the legitimate interest of the opposing party or other players in the market to protect their sensitive business data. Only with respect to the disclosure obligation derived from the principle of good faith under § 242 BGB does the judicature accept a compromise between these conflicting interests in that it allows the information to be handed over to a neutral accountant. Interestingly, the courts do not accept such a balance of interests with respect to procedural

---

49. Lübbig T., 'Die Reform des Zivilprozesses in Kartellsachen', [2006] *WRP*, 1213.
50. *Greger*, Zivilprozessordnung, Zöller (ed.) (25th edn, Otto Schmidt, Köln, 2005), § 384 para. 7.
51. BVerfG NJW 1997, 1909, 1910; BVerfG, NJW 1995, 40, 41.
52. BGH NJW 1992, 1817, 1819 – *Amtsanzeiger*.
53. BGH NJW 1992, 1817, 1819 – *Amtsanzeiger*; OLG Köln, NJW-RR 1996, 1277; cf. the critique of P. Schlosser, 'Wirtschaftsprüfervorbehalt und prozessuales Vertraulichkeitsinteresse der nicht primär beweisbelasteten Prozeßpartei' in *Festschrift für Bernhard Großfeld*, U. Hübner and W. Ebke (eds) (Recht und Wirtschaft, Heidelberg, 1999), p. 1003 *et seq*.

disclosure obligations under § 142, 144 ZPO or witnesses statements regarding matters covered by a professional privilege. Employing an accountant will furthermore not serve the purpose if a legal assessment of the data released is necessary, and the German law does not contain any provisions which would allow an attorney to withhold information from its clients.

D.   THE COMMISSION AND THE FEDERAL CARTEL
            AUTHORITY ACTING AS *AMICUS CURIAE*

In view of the difficulties in proving anti-competitive behaviour and establishing a market analysis, the *amicus curiae* provisions in §§ 90, 90a GWB warrant a closer examination.

1.   PRINCIPLES

§ 90a GWB implements Art. 15(1) to (3) Reg. 1/2003, whereas § 90 GWB makes use of the scope granted to Member States under Art. 15(4) of the regulation. The said provisions guarantee the Commission and the Federal Cartel Authority a position as *amicus curiae* in order to protect the public interest, the main difference being that the Federal Cartel Authority is to be informed at the commencement of any judicial proceeding, whereas the Commission will be notified only after a decision has been rendered.

§ 90 Notification and Participation of the Cartel Authorities:

(1) The court informs the Federal Cartel Authority of all litigation under § 87(1). Upon request, the court forwards to the Federal Cartel Authority copies of any brief, record, decree and decision. Sentences 1 and 2 apply correspondingly to other disputes concerning Article 81 or 82 of the Treaty establishing the European Community.
        (2) The president of the Federal Cartel Authority may, in cases deemed appropriate to maintain public interest, appoint a representative from the members of the Federal Cartel Authority [. . .]. This representative is entitled to make submissions in writing to the Court, point out facts and means of proof and be present at hearings in which he or she may give oral submissions and pose questions to parties, witnesses and experts. Written submissions made by the representative are to be communicated to the parties.
[. . .]

§ 90a Co-operation of the courts with the European Commission and the Cartel Authorities:

(1) The court transmits to the European Commission via the Federal Cartel Authority a copy of any written judgment regarding the application of Articles

81 or 82 of the Treaty establishing the European Community, immediately after notification of the judgment to the parties. The Federal Cartel Authority may forward to the Commission documents received under § 90(1) sent. 2.

(2) The European Commission, acting upon its own initiative, may submit written observations to the courts of the Member States. The court transmits to the European Commission any document necessary for the assessment of the case, including copies of any brief, record, decree and decision, in case the Commission issues a corresponding request under Art. 15(3) sent. 3 of Regulation (EC) no. 1/2003. The European Commission may also make oral observations during the course of a hearing.

(3) In proceedings under section 1, the court may ask the Commission to transmit information in its possession or its opinion on questions concerning the application of Article 81 or 82 of the Treaty establishing the European Community. The court informs the parties about the request and forwards copies of the response to both the parties and the Federal Cartel Authority.

(4) Correspondence according to section 2 and 3 between the court and the European Commission may be conducted via the Federal Cartel Authority.

Past experience has shown that the Federal Cartel Authority rarely makes use of its right to act as *amicus curiae* under § 90(2) GWB before District and Higher Regional Courts, but regularly provides oral observations in hearings before the Federal Court of Justice.[54] Any factual submission by the Authority must be based upon information it already possesses, as the investigative powers under § 59 GWB are granted for the purpose of public enforcement only.[55] It would seem that the same applies to information forwarded by the Commission,[56] as no. 19 of Commission Notice on co-operation states:

> In fulfilling its duty under Art 10 EC, of assisting national courts in the application of EC competition law, the Commission is committed to remaining neutral and objective in its assistance.[. . .] As a consequence, the Commission will not hear any of the parties about its assistance to the national court.

---

54. J. Bornkamm, *Kommentar zum deutschen und europäischen Kartellrecht*, vol. 1: *Deutsches Kartellrecht*, E. Langen and H.J. Bunte (eds) (10th ed., Luchterhand, Neuwied, 2006), § 90 para. 1, 8.
55. KG, [1981] WuW/E OLG 2446, 2447 – *Heizölhandel*; R. Bechtold, *GWB* (3rd edn, C.H. Beck, München, 2002), § 90 para. 2; J. Bornkamm, *Kommentar zum deutschen und europäischen Kartellrecht*, vol. 1: *Deutsches Kartellrecht*, E. Langen and H.J. Bunte (eds) (10th ed., Luchterhand, Neuwied, 2006), § 33 para. 8.
56. Lampert T., N. Niejahr, J. Kübler and G. Weidenbach, *EG-KartellVO* (Recht und Wirtschaft, Heidelberg, 2004), Art. 15 para. 297 *et seq.*; J. Schwarze and A. Weitbrecht, *Grundzüge des europäischen Kartellverfahrensrechts* (Nomos, Baden-Baden, 2004), § 11 para. 46; M. Sura, *Kommentar zum deutschen und europäischen Kartellrecht*, vol. 2: *Europäisches Kartellrecht*, E. Langen and H.J. Bunte (eds) (10th ed, Luchterhand, Neuwied 2006), Art. 15 VO Nr. 1/2003 para. 7; Klees A., *Europäisches Kartellverfahrensrecht* (Carl Heymanns, Köln, 2005), § 8 para. 52; dissenting F. Montag and A. Rosenfeld, 'A Solution to the Problems? Regulation 1/2003 and the modernization of competition procedure', [2003] ZWeR, 132 *et seq.*

The wording of §§ 90, 90a GWB is clearly in line with Art. 15 Reg. 1/2003 and does, in itself, not raise concerns as regards the doctrine of effectiveness. Effectiveness is challenged, rather, by the German procedural principle of party presentation as well as the lack of provisions safeguarding confidentiality.

2.　　　　The Doctrine of Party Presentation

The principle of party presentation may be seen as a two-fold hindrance to the effectiveness of Art. 15 EC Reg. 1/2003. First, the prohibition of exploratory evidence suggests that a party has to submit the facts substantiating an alleged infringement of competition rules before evidence through the Commission or Federal Cartel Authority might be sought in order to prove the assertion.[57] Regularly however, information by public authorities will be necessary to make substantiated submissions in the first place.[58] Second, under the principle of party presentation a court is prevented from basing its decision on the information given or potential evidence pointed out by the Commission or Federal Cartel Authority, unless one of the parties subsequently relies on those facts or requests the evidence to be taken.[59] It is then up to the opposing party to counter these submissions with sufficiently substantiated pleadings[60] (which should regularly prove to be impossible).

This latter limitation does not raise serious concerns regarding the doctrine of effectiveness, even though an omission by the parties to refer to facts revealed through the participation of public enforcement authorities is suited to render Community Law less efficient. Nonetheless, it is for the parties to decide whether to privately enforce EC competition law and it is consequently their prerogative to decide how diligent their behaviour should be in arguing the case. This inference seems to be in line with para. 30 of the Commission Notice on co-operation between the Commission and the court of the EU Member States, which states: 'The [national court] will have to deal with the Commission's opinion in accordance with the relevant national procedural rules, which have to respect the general principles of Community law'.

---

57. Regarding an infringement of German competition law cf. OLG Stuttgart, [1988] WuW/E OLG 4214, 4213 – *City-Reisebüro*.
58. J. Bornkamm, *Kommentar zum deutschen und europäischen Kartellrecht*, vol. 1: *Deutsches Kartellrecht*, E. Langen and H.J. Bunte (eds) (10th ed., Luchterhand, Neuwied, 2006), § 90a para. 11.
59. T. Lampert, N. Niejahr, J. Kübler and G. Weidenbach, *EG-KartellVO* (Recht und Wirtschaft, Heidelberg, 2004), Art. 15 para. 295; A. Klees, *Europäisches Kartellverfahrensrecht mit Fusionskontrollverfahren* (Carl Heymanns, Köln, 2005), § 8 para. 62; J. Bornkamm, *Kommentar zum deutschen und europäischen Kartellrecht*, vol. 1: *Deutsches Kartellrecht*, E. Langen and H.J. Bunte (eds) (10th ed., Luchterhand, Neuwied, 2006), § 90 para. 9; M. Sura, *Kommentar zum deutschen und europäischen Kartellrecht*, vol. 2: *Europäisches Kartellrecht*, E. Langen and H.J. Bunte (eds) (10th ed, Luchterhand, Neuwied 2006), Art. 15 VO Nr. 1/2003 para. 6.
60. OLG Düsseldorf, OLGZ 1994, 80 *et seq.*; R. Hempel, 'Private Follow-on-Klagen im Kartellrecht', [2005] WuW, 140 *et seq.*

The former limitation, in contrast, warrants some examination. A court may make a request for information and the communication of observations to the Commission or the Federal Cartel Authority either by virtue of a preparatory request under § 273(2) no. 2 ZPO or an evidence decree following § 358a ZPO. Both options come into existence solely after the commencement of an action, which is of no particular concern as Reg. EC 1/2003 does not cover pre action enforcement.[61] However, following the principle of party presentation, the information to be provided by public enforcement authorities may only be sought and heard in order to shed light on facts submitted in some detail by one and disputed by the other party. Otherwise, such evidence would be deemed exploratory. Arguably, § 90a(3) GWB contains a deviation from the principle of party presentation, granting the court the power to address the Commission *ex officio*.[62]

In view of the imperative to interpret national provisions in the light of Community law, this question must be settled by analysing whether Art. 15(1) of EC Reg. 1/2003 requires the option of *ex officio* requests.[63] Recital 21 of the regulation points out that the Commission's observations 'should be submitted within the framework of national procedural rules and practises including those safeguarding the rights of the parties', which seems to imply that it is for to the procedural rules of the Member States to decide whether requests are made *ex officio* or upon application by the parties. On the other hand, while the wording of Art. 15(1) is non-conclusive, it does not rule out *ex officio* requests. Thus, it would seem that Commission Notice on co-operation no. 17 comes into play, which states 'to the extent that they are necessary to facilitate these forms of assistance, Member States must adopt the appropriate procedural rules to allow both the national courts and the Commission to make full use of the possibilities the regulation offers'. This interpretation is reinforced by no. 9 of the notice: 'Those Community law provisions may provide for the faculty of national courts to avail themselves of certain instruments, e.g. to ask for the Commission's opinion on questions concerning the application of EC competition rules [. . .]. These Community law provisions

---

61. Commission Notice on co-operation between the Commission and the courts of the EU Member States in the Application of Articles 81 and 82 EC, OJ No. C 101, 27 April 2002, p. 54 *et seq.*, no. 27: 'to a case pending before it'.

62. W. Wurmnest, 'Private Durchsetzung des EG-Kartellrechts nach der Reform der VO Nr. 17' in *Europäisches Wettbewerbsrecht im Umbruch*, P. Behrens, E. Braun and C. Nowak (eds) (Nomos, Baden-Baden, 2004), p. 235; of a different opinion J. Bornkamm, *Kommentar zum deutschen und europäischen Kartellrecht*, vol. 1: *Deutsches Kartellrecht*, E. Langen and H.J. Bunte (eds) (10th ed., Luchterhand, Neuwied, 2006), § 90a para. 11 *et seq.*

63. *Ex officio* request are envisaged by M. Sura, *Kommentar zum deutschen und europäischen Kartellrecht*, vol. 2: *Europäisches Kartellrecht*, E. Langen and H.J. Bunte (eds) (10th ed, Luchterhand, Neuwied 2006), Art. 15 VO Nr. 1/2003 para. 4; W. Wurmnest, 'Private Durchsetzung des EG-Kartellrechts nach der Reform der VO Nr. 17' in *Europäisches Wettbewerbsrecht* im Umbruch, P. Behrens, E. Braun and C. Nowak (eds) (Nomos, Baden-Baden, 2004), p. 235. The opposing opinion is held by J. Bornkamm, *Kommentar zum deutschen und europäischen Kartellrecht*, vol. 1: *Deutsches Kartellrecht*, E. Langen and H.J. Bunte (eds) (10th ed., Luchterhand, Neuwied, 2006), § 90a para. 11 *et seq*; A. Klees, *Europäisches Kartellverfahrensrecht mit Fusionskontrollverfahren* (Carl Heymanns, Köln, 2005), Art. 15 para. 64.

prevail over national rules. Therefore, national courts have to set aside national rules which, if applied, would conflict with these Community law provisions'.

Arguably, an inference may also be drawn from § 90a(3) sentence 2 GWB, since it might seem superfluous to inform the parties of an inquiry with the Commission, if the Commission was to be contacted only upon the request one of the parties. Further, the possibility of an *ex officio* request is in line with the ZPO-reform of 1 July 2002, which amplified the courts' *ex officio* powers under §§ 142, 144 ZPO.[64] Consequently, it would seem that the principle of party presentation and the prohibition of exploratory evidence requires relaxation regarding § 90a(3) GWB to guarantee the full effect of Community Law. It is hard to understand why the Commission or the Federal Cartel Authority, acting upon their own initiative, should be entitled to submit an economic and legal analysis of the facts underlying the case pending before a national court,[65] which would most certainly include market information, whereas a court may not request the transfer of such information unless one of the parties manages to submit facts which will regularly lie outside the sphere of its knowledge. Thus, the doctrine of effectiveness requires an interpretation of § 90a GWB that allows a court to address the Commission *ex officio* regarding such information and documents which are relevant to the case.[66]

The information and economic analysis transmitted by the Commission or the Federal Cartel Authority may, depending on their nature, be regarded as documentary (§§ 415 *et seq.* ZPO) or expert evidence (§§ 402 *et seq.* ZPO).[67] Their evidentiary value is to be determined by the court just like any other evidence.[68]

3.   CONFIDENTIAL INFORMATION AND BUSINESS SECRETS

Information transmitted by the European Commission may include facts concerning both the parties of the dispute and market analyses suited to shed light on other undertakings in the market. Regarding this information, Art. 287 EC obliges the members of the Commission to maintain professional secrecy, which is to be upheld in cooperation with the national courts. The Commission

---

64. Supra p. 239.
65. Cf. Commission Notice on co-operation between the Commission and the courts of the EU Member States in the Application of Articles 81 and 82 EC, OJ No. C 101, 27 April 2002, p. 54 *et seq.*, no. 32.
66. Cf. G. Cumming, supra p. 34.
67. ECJ, *van der Wal v. Commission*, Case no. C-174/98 P and C-189/98 P, 2000 [ECR] I-47, para. 25; A. Zuber, *Die EG-Kommission als amicus curiae* (Carl Heymanns, Köln, 2001), p. 118; W. Wurmnest, 'Private Durchsetzung des EG-Kartellrechts nach der Reform der VO Nr. 17' in *Europäisches Wettbewerbsrecht im Umbruch*, P. Behrens, E. Braun and C. Nowak (eds) (Nomos, Baden-Baden, 2004), p. 235.
68. W. Wurmnest, 'Private Durchsetzung des EG-Kartellrechts nach der Reform der VO Nr. 17' in *Europäisches Wettbewerbsrecht im Umbruch*, P. Behrens, E. Braun and C. Nowak (eds) (Nomos, Baden-Baden, 2004), p. 236.

Notice on co-operation between the Commission and the courts of the EU Member States declares that:

> Only when the national court has offered a guarantee that it will protect the confidential information and business secrets, will the Commission transmit the information requested, indicating those parts which are covered by professional secrecy and which parts are not and can therefore be disclosed.

Safeguarding the professional secrets of the Commission members is problematic under German procedural rules, as court hearings are open to the public and, more importantly, the constitutional right to a fair hearing in principle guarantees the parties access to any evidence taken by the court,[69] including the right to challenge the factual basis of any expertise submitted.[70]

a.   Exclusion of the Public

Under § 169 Court Constitution Code (*Gerichtsverfassungsgesetz* – GVG) any court hearing is in principle open to the public. §§ 170 *et seq.* GVG enable a court to exclude the public from proceedings in specific cases.

> § 172 GVG provides:
>
> The Court may exclude the public from the hearing or a part thereof, if
> [. . .]
>   2. an important business, trade or tax secret or a secret pertaining to an invention is being discussed and the public discussion would impair predominant interests under protection.

In view of Art. 10 EC it would seem that a Court requesting information from the Commission may make use of its discretion under § 172 no. 2 GVG in advance by issuing a guarantee that the public be excluded from hearings in which information described as confidential by the Commission is to be discussed.

b.   Excluding Parties from Evidence

Exclusion of the general public is of little value if the confidential information is distributed to the parties of the dispute, particularly since they are likely to be competitors. In this context, regard is to be had to § 357(1) ZPO.

> § 357(1) ZPO
> Parties are entitled to witness the hearing of evidence.

As Hartmann states: 'The so-called *Parteiöffentlichkeit* may be traced back to [the right to be heard under] Art. 103(1) GG; it is one of the most important rights of the

---

69. BGH NJW 1992, 1817, 1819 – *Amtsanzeiger*; OLG Köln, NJW-RR 1996, 1277.
70. BVerfG NJW 1995, 40 *et seq.*; BVerfG NJW 1997, 1909 *et seq.*

parties and a pillar of the law of evidence'.[71] The ZPO does not provide for an exception to the rule of § 357(1). There is some debate as to whether an analogy might be drawn in civil procedure to § 247 of the Criminal Procedural Code (*Strafprozeßordnung* – StPO).[72] Be that as it may, such an analogy would not safeguard the professional secrecy of the members of the Commission, as § 247 StPO only provides for the exclusion of a defendant to the testimony of a witness for fear that the witness may not tell the truth in his presence, and the court is to inform the defendant of the content of the testimony once he is readmitted to the proceeding. Further, § 117(2) ZPO establishes that applications for legal aid, which include confidential information regarding the applicant, can be accessed by the opposing party only with the consent of the applicant. Again, an analogy to this provision regarding information forwarded by the Commission is not feasible, as § 117(2) ZPO pertains to the application for legal aid only and does not concern evidence relevant for the substantive decision.

Any cooperation between the Commission and German courts is, therefore, thwarted if the information sought contains trade secrets not to be released to the parties of the dispute.[73] German Courts are free to issue the Commission a guarantee that they will protect the confidential information, but following the case law of the Federal Court of Justice, such information will be useless, as a court is not entitled to base its decision on information not disclosed to the parties.[74] This raises concerns as regards the doctrine of effectiveness, since factual information to be supplied by the Commission will most likely be of particular interest if it contains inferences drawn from insider information. A more adequate interpretation will be addressed in section H infra p. 263 *et seq.*

4. EFFECT OF LEGAL OPINIONS RENDERED BY
    THE COMMISSION OR NCA

Legal clarifications submitted by the Commission or by the Federal Cartel Authority do not in any way possess a binding effect on the court,[75] as is self-explanatory in view of the constitutionally guaranteed independence of the judicature and the

---

71. A. Baumbach, W. Lauterbach, J. Albers, P. Hartmann, Zivilprozessordnung (64th edn, C.H. Beck, München, 2006), § 357 para. 2; BSG MDR 77, 346.
72. Cf. A. Baumbach, W. Lauterbach, J. Albers, P. Hartmann, Zivilprozessordnung (64th edn, C.H. Beck, München, 2006), § 357 para. 2 with further references.
73. J. Bornkamm, *Kommentar zum deutschen und europäischen Kartellrecht*, vol. 1: *Deutsches Kartellrecht*, E. Langen and H.J. Bunte (eds) (10th ed., Luchterhand, Neuwied, 2006), § 90a para. 15; R. Bechtold, I. Brinker, W. Bosch, S. Hirsbrunner, *EG-Kartellrecht* (C.H. Beck, München 2005), Art. 15 VO 1/2003 para. 11.
74. BGH, NJW 1952, 305 *et seq.*; BGH NJW 1992, 1817, 1819 – *Amtsanzeiger*; OLG Köln, NJW-RR 1996, 1277.
75. Commission Notice on the co-operation between the Commission and the courts of the EU Member States, OJ No. C 101 17 April 2004, p. 54 *et seq.*, no. 29; M. Sura, *Kommentar zum deutschen und europäischen Kartellrecht*, vol. 2: *Europäisches Kartellrecht*, E. Langen and H.J. Bunte (eds) (10th ed, Luchterhand, Neuwied 2006), Art. 15 VO Nr. 1/2003 para. 4; cf.

separation of powers. However, under the *acte clair*-doctrine, an intention on the part of the Federal Court of Justice – acting as final instance – to deviate from the legal submissions of the Commission or even the Federal Cartel Authority will regularly trigger an obligation to refer the case to the European Court of Justice.[76]

5.   PRELIMINARY CONCLUSION REGARDING THE ACCESS TO EVIDENCE

This brief review of the parties' options to access information within the sphere of the opposing party or other market participants has shown that acquiring proof for anti-competitive practises may prove to be quite difficult. This is particularly true with respect to sensitive data, as German procedural rules do not provide for in camera proceedings. By the same token, the effect of the *amicus curiae* provisions is limited in view of the need to safeguard the Commission members' obligation of professional secrecy. Obviously, a party's difficulty in obtaining evidence may be alleviated by a favourable allocation of the burden and standard of proof. Before assessing whether the doctrine of effectiveness makes a change in law seem desirable, the said matters shall be examined in the following sections (even though they may partially be qualified as matters of substance, rather than procedural law).

E.   BURDEN OF PROOF

1.   ARTICLE 2 REG. (EC) 1/2003

The basic principle in civil litigation establishes that the burden of proof regarding all facts supporting the claim rests with the plaintiff, whereas it is upon the defendant to prove his defences to the claim.[77] Regardless of whether the assertion of anti-competitive practises is raised as a shield or a sword, it is consequently up to the party alleging the infringement to supply the supporting proof. Any attempt to shift this burden in view of the unfavourable access to evidence under German procedural rules is stopped in its tracks by Art. 2 Reg. 1/2003,[78] which establishes that 'the burden of proving an infringement of Articles 81(1) or 82 of the Treaty shall rest on the party or authority alleging the infringement'.[79] If the plaintiff

---

furthermore J. Schwarze and A. Weitbrecht, *Grundzüge des europäischen Kartellverfahrens-rechts* (Nomos, Baden-Baden, 2004), § 11 para. 47.

76. A. Klees, *Europäisches Kartellverfahrensrecht mit Fusionskontrollverfahren* (Carl Heymanns, Köln, 2005), § 8 para. 80; J. Bornkamm, *Kommentar zum deutschen und europäischen Kartellrecht*, vol. 1: *Deutsches Kartellrecht*, E. Langen and H.J. Bunte (eds) (10th ed., Luchterhand, Neuwied, 2006), § 90a para. 2 *et seq*.

77. L. Rosenberg, K. H. Schwab and P. Gottwald, *Zivilprozessrecht* (16th ed, C.H. Beck, München 2004), § 114 para. 10.

78. G. Berrisch and M. Burianski, 'Kartellrechtliche Schadensersatzansprüche nach der 7. GWB-Novelle', [2005] WuW, 883.

79. *Cf.* T. Eilmannsberger, 'Zum Vorschlag der Kommission für eine Reform des Kartellvollzugs', [2005] JZ, 372 with further references for criticism regarding the rule.

requests damages, it further needs to establish both the inflicted damage and the causal link between damage and infringement. Finally, Art. 2 Reg. 1/2003 clarifies that an 'undertaking or association of undertakings claiming the benefit of Article 81(3) of the Treaty shall bear the burden of proving that the conditions of that paragraph are fulfilled'.

2.   UNRESOLVED QUESTIONS

While the principle embedded in Art. 2 (EC) Reg. 1/2003 is clear enough, at least two matters remain unresolved: The application of the *de minimis* criteria in civil litigation and the line of demarcation between Art. 81(1) and Art. 81(3) EC.

a.   *De Minimis* **Criteria in Civil Proceedings**

Following the Commission's *de minimis* Notice,[80] agreements between undertakings which affect trade between Member States do not appreciably restrict competition within the meaning of Art. 81(1), if the aggregate market share held by the parties to the agreement does not exceed 10 per cent (horizontal agreements), respectively 15 per cent (vertical agreements). It is up to debate whether a party relying on an infringement of competition rules would have to prove that these thresholds have been crossed. Böge and Ost[81] suggest that:

> In such a case potential claimants would have to provide extensive statements on market definition, market shares and structures, even on the existence of cumulative foreclosure effects caused by parallel distribution networks. The *Bundeskartellamt's* [Federal Cartel Authority's] view is that '*de minimis*' rules should only regulate the respective authority's discretion to take up a case; even if, following to its *de minimis* Notice, the *Bundeskartellamt* does not intervene, this does not imply that there is no competition infringement.

The Commission's viewpoint on this matter is unclear. The *de minimis* Notice holds that 'in cases covered by this notice the Commission will not institute proceedings either upon application or on its own initiative',[82] which would seem to imply that private enforcement is not covered by the notice. However, the Commission goes on to state that 'Although not binding on them, this notice also intends

---

80. Commission Notice on agreements of minor importance which do not appreciably restrict competition under Art. 81(1) of the Treaty establishing the European Community (*de minimis*), OJ No. C 368, 22 December 2001, p. 13 *et seq.*, no. 7 *et seq.*; *cf.* further ECJ, *Cardillon v. Höss*, Case no. 1/71, [1971] ECR 351, para. 7 *et seq.*

81. U. Böge and K. Ost, 'Up and Running, or is it? Private enforcement – the Situation in Germany and Policy Perspectives', [2006] ECLR., 203.

82. Commission Notice on agreements of minor importance which do not appreciably restrict competition under Art. 81(1) of the Treaty establishing the European Community (*de minimis*), OJ No. C 368, p. 13 *et seq.*, no. 4.

to give guidance to the courts and authorities of the Member States in their application of Article 81'.[83]

As Lettl points out, an application of the *de minimis* rule in private enforcement would lead to an unequal treatment of identical matters which is difficult to justify: It is hard to conceive why a claim for compensation should be granted to one person who suffered a loss and denied to the other for the sole reason that the *de minimis* threshold was passed in the first case and not arrived at in the second.[84] It is therefore suggested that civil courts ought not to demand the plaintiff to prove that the *de minimis* requirements are fulfilled.

b.   Line of Demarcation between Articles 81(1) and 81(3) EC

The current debate concerning a 'more economic approach' with respect to Art. 81(1) EC is deemed to blur the lines between Art. 81(1) and 81(3) EC.[85] It would seem that there is some leeway for courts to define whether probable effects on the market are to be considered under Art. 81(1) or (3) EC and the onus of proof is to be allotted correspondingly. The effectiveness of Community antitrust provisions will be promoted if such questions are addressed under Art. 81(3) EC.[86]

F.   STANDARD OF PROOF AND LEGAL PRESUMPTIONS

Recital 5 of Reg. 1/2003 clarifies that the Regulation does not have an impact on the standard of proof applied in the Member States, 'provided that such rules and obligations are compatible with the general principles of Community law'. The standard of proof in German procedural law is set by § 286 ZPO, according to which the judge is to decide on the basis of his or her free conviction whether he or she finds the facts submitted by the parties to be true. This standard is decidedly stricter than a balance of probabilities test. Following case law of the Federal Court of Justice, § 286 ZPO does not require that the judge relinquish all possible doubts as to the correctness of the pleaded facts, but a mere or even predominant probability is insufficient.[87] The Federal Court of Justice generally uses the expression of a 'degree of certitude which is feasible in practical life'.[88] A deviation is provided in § 287 ZPO, which allows for an *ex aequo et bono* estimate regarding

83. Bornkamm and Becker suggest that the Commission intends for the *de minimis* Notice to apply to civil litigation, as its purpose of providing a 'safe harbour' might otherwise not be achieved, cf. J. Bornkamm and M. Becker, 'Die privatrechtliche Durchsetzung des Kartellverbots nach der Modernisierung des EG-Kartellrechts', [2005] ZWeR, 232.
84. T. Lettl, 'Der Schadensersatzanspruch gemäß § 823 Abs. 2 BGB i.V. mit Art. 81 Abs. 1 EG', (2003) 167 ZHR, 475.
85. J. Bornkamm and M. Becker, 'Die privatrechtliche Durchsetzung des Kartellverbots nach der Modernisierung des EG-Kartellrechts', [2005] ZWeR, 231 *et seq.*
86. J. Bornkamm and M. Becker, 'Die privatrechtliche Durchsetzung des Kartellverbots nach der Modernisierung des EG-Kartellrechts', [2005] ZWeR, 233.
87. BGH, NJW 1998, 1870; BGH, NJW 1970, 946, 948 – *Anastasia.*
88. BGH, NJW 1994, 801, 802; BGH NJW 1993, 935, 937; BGH, NJW 1970, 946, 948 – *Anastasia.*

the extent of loss suffered.[89] The prevailing opinion extends the power of the court to make such an estimate to the occurrence of a loss and the causal link between infringement and the damage suffered.[90]

1.   LEGAL PRESUMPTIONS UNDER THE GERMAN ACT AGAINST
        RESTRAINTS ON COMPETITION

German competition law provides for a number of legal presumptions which may be of help to a party alleging an infringement, but can be rebutted if the opposing party manages to prove that the presumption is wrong, namely §§ 19(3), 20(2), 20(4), 20(5) GWB.[91] These presumptions are restricted to alleged infringements of German cartel law,[92] and cannot be expanded under the principle of effectiveness[93] in view of the necessity of a uniform application and autonomous interpretation of Art. 81 and 82 EC.[94] However, Art. 3(2) sent. 2 of Reg. (EC) 1/2003 states that Member States shall not under this Regulation be precluded from adopting and applying on their territory stricter national laws which prohibit or sanction unilateral conduct engaged in by undertakings. It follows that a party may plead an infringement of §§ 19, 20 GWB, instead of relying on Art. 82 EC, and reap the benefit of the aforementioned legal presumptions.

2.   ALLEVIATING THE STANDARD OF PROOF

a.   **Proving the Infringement**

There is some discussion amongst academics as to whether the standard of proof in competition cases should be lowered in order to promote the effectiveness of Community competition rules.[95] In fact, the failure of Parliament to introduce a provision to that effect has been described as 'the fundamental deficiency' of the 7th GWB-amendment.[96]

---

89.   The court's estimate is to be made with reference to a factual basis and to life experience, cf. BGH, NJW-RR 1991, 470, 471; BGH NJW 1988, 3016, 3017.
90.   BGH, NJW 1995, 1023, 1024; BGH, NJW 1992, 3298 3299; BGH, NJW 1973, 1413, 1414.
91.   Whether these presumptions are applicable to civil proceedings is debated, cf. the overview given by R. Hempel, *Privater Rechtsschutz im Kartellrecht* (Nomos, Baden-Baden, 2002), p. 70 *et seq.*
92.   T. Lampert, N. Niejahr, J. Kübler and G. Weidenbach, *EG-KartellVO* (Recht und Wirtschaft, Heidelberg, 2004), Art. 2 para. 65 *et seq*, Fn. 113.
93.   Opposing view held by W. Wurmnest, 'Private Durchsetzung des EG-Kartellrechts nach der Reform der VO Nr. 17' in *Europäisches Wettbewerbsrecht im Umbruch*, P. Behrens, E. Braun and C. Nowak (eds) (Nomos, Baden-Baden, 2004), p. 233.
94.   ECJ, *Bollmann v. Hauptzollamt Hamburg*, Case no. 40/69, [1970] ECR 69, para. 9.
95.   A. Klees, *Europäisches Kartellverfahrensrecht mit Fusionskontrollverfahren* (Carl Heymanns, Köln, 2005), § 8 para. 26, 35.
96.   G. Berrisch and M. Burianski, 'Kartellrechtliche Schadensersatzansprüche nach der 7. GWB-Novelle', [2005] WuW, 888; W. Wurmnest, 'Private Durchsetzung des EG-Kartellrechts nach

The main suggestion is to introduce a so-called 'secondary burden of submission' for facts lying within the sphere of the undertaking accused of engaging in anti-competitive behaviour.[97] The term 'secondary burden of submission' (*sekundäre Darlegungslast / Behauptungslast*) is used to describe situations in which the party burdened with pleading and proving specific facts does not have any insight regarding the course of events, whereas the opposing party possesses the required knowledge and may reasonably be expected to part with such details.[98] The party which bears the onus of proof is in these instances only held to submit those facts which it reasonably presumes to be true and provide sufficient grounds for its assumption. The opposing party may not simply deny the proposed facts, but must substantiate the denial with a pleading of the actual course of events and an offer of the requisite proof. Any failure to do so may be regarded as a concession of the facts presumed by the party claiming the infringement under § 138(3) ZPO.

Accordingly, the president of the Federal Cartel Authority, Ulf Böge, suggested:

> In view of the information asymmetry which undisputedly exists between cartel members and claimants a legal provision (or judge made rule) would, however, be welcome to ensure a more generous acceptance of *prima facie* evidence concerning competition law infringements. Such a regulation would correspond to provisions in other areas of tort law and could be integrated quite easily into the existing legal system. This applies all the more since, in cases of information asymmetry, the Federal Supreme Court [= Federal Court of Justice] has been quite prepared to expect the party which does not bear the burden of proof to exercise a certain degree of co-operation in clarifying the facts.[99]

The development of the envisaged judge-made rule does not seem completely illusionary, as can be inferred from the following statement made by the president of the Federal Court of Justice, Günter Hirsch, in 2003.[100]

---

der Reform der VO Nr. 17' in *Europäisches Wettbewerbsrecht im Umbruch*, P. Behrens, E. Braun and C. Nowak (eds) (Nomos, Baden-Baden, 2004), p. 228.

97. Monopolkommission, *Fünfzehntes Hauptgutachten der Monopolkommission 2002/2003*, BT-Drucks. 15/3610, para. 114; T. Lübbig, 'Die Reform des Zivilprozesses in Kartellsachen', [2006] WRP, 1214; F. Schöler, *Die Reform des Europäischen Kartellverfahrensrechts durch die Verordnung (EG) Nr. 1/2003* (Peter Lang, Frankfurt, 2004), p. 112; W. Wurmnest, 'Private Durchsetzung des EG-Kartellrechts nach der Reform der VO Nr. 17' in *Europäisches Wettbewerbsrecht im Umbruch*, P. Behrens, E. Braun and C. Nowak (eds) (Nomos, Baden-Baden, 2004), p. 233; H. Köhler, 'Kartellverbot und Schadensersatz', [2004] GRUR, 103.

98. BGH, NJW 2005, 2614, 2615; BGH NJW-RR 2004, 989, 990; BGH GRUR 2004, 268, 269; BGH, NJW 1990, 3151, 3152; BGH NJW 1987, 1201; BGH NJW 1987, 2008, 2009; BGH NJW 1961, 826, 828.

99. U. Böge and K. Ost, 'Up and Running, or is it? Private enforcement – the Situation in Germany and Policy Perspectives', [2006] ECLR., 202.

100. G. Hirsch, 'Anwendung der Kartellverfahrensordnung (EG) Nr. 1/2003 durch nationale Gerichte', [2003] ZWeR, 242.

Whether the national civil courts will grant the plaintiffs alleviations regarding the required proof with respect to facts lying within the sphere of the opposing party, i.e., under the principles of the 'secondary burden of submission' (possibly including a reversal of the burden of proof), is a matter to be decided in light of each individual case. [. . .] It is up to the courts to shape the requirements for the submission and clarification of facts in each individual dispute. Even though the clarification of facts requires an economic analysis, it may be assumed that the national civil courts will be able to solve this task with economically sound decisions for the undertakings involved.

There is ample case law for alleviations of the standard of proof in medical and product liability cases,[101] but it would seem that competition cases are not generally comparable to these categories. First, in medical and product liability disputes it is initially up to the plaintiff as a minimum to prove the loss suffered. In competition cases, it is impossible to live up to this challenge before an infringement has been established, as the loss will be purely economic and dependent upon the infringement. Secondly, neither physicians nor producers are forced to reveal business secrets in the course of fulfilling the 'secondary burden of submission'. Quite the opposite is true for undertakings submitting facts to substantiate the legality of their actions under Articles 81 and 82 EC,[102] as they cannot reasonably be expected to reveal business details to an opposing party.[103] Exceptions obviously apply. If a plaintiff raised an action based upon its exclusion from a selective distribution system, its presumption that the respondent engaged in anticompetitive practises by applying other than qualitative criteria to its choice might be supported by proof of the plaintiff's own qualifications and comparisons drawn to the distributors affiliated to the system. In case the court finds the presumption to be well-founded, the respondent could be reasonably expected to explain and prove the qualitative criteria applied.[104]

Finally, the *prima facie*-proof (*Beweis des ersten Anscheins*) may be of help to a party seeking to establish a claim for compensation based upon anti-competitive behaviour. If the facts of the dispute correspond to a typical course of events which – based upon general life experience – allows inferences as to other facts, the court will presume that such other facts were also present in the said case. The onus then shifts to the opposing party to show that the circumstances of the case allow for a deviation of life experience. In other words, the opposing party must only seriously rebut the *prima facie* case; it is not held to provide full proof to the contrary. A *prima facie*-proof may be of particular relevance in establishing the

---

101. An overview is provided by H.W., Laumen 'Die Beweiserleichterung bis zur Beweislastumkehr – ein beweisrechtliches Phänomen', NJW 2002, 3739 *et seq.*

102. T. Lübbig, 'Die Reform des Zivilprozesses in Kartellsachen', [2006] WRP, 1214.

103. BGH, NJW 1992, 1817, 1819; BGH NJW 1961, 826, 828; T. Lübbig, 'Die Reform des Zivilprozesses in Kartellsachen', [2006] WRP, 1214.

104. Example provided by J. Bornkamm and M. Becker, 'Die privatrechtliche Durchsetzung des Kartellverbots nach der Modernisierung des EG-Kartellrechts', [2005] ZWeR, 234.

causal link between the infringement and a loss suffered by the plaintiff.[105] The obvious danger is that courts might jump to conclusions in drawing inferences from an alleged general 'life experience'.[106]

Arguably, the doctrine of effectiveness requires that the standard of proof applied by German civil courts be alleviated utilizing one of the schemes described above.[107] At the same time, it should be remembered that Art. 2 of Reg. (EC) 1/2003 determines the burden of proof, thus, a facilitation of the standard of proof to an extent which would amount to a reversal of proof, i.e., by applying a general presumption, is impossible.[108] Guidance may be sought from the ECJ decisions *GT-Link* and *Weber's Wine World*. In *GT-Link*,[109] the Court held that:

> In accordance with those principles, the Court has previously held, in connection with repayment of charges levied by a Member State in breach of Community law, that any requirement of proof which has the effect of making it virtually impossible or excessively difficult to secure that repayment is incompatible with Community law (Case 199/82 *Amministrazione delle Finanze dello Stato v. San Giorgio* [1983] ECR 3595, paragraph 14).
>
> The same principles apply where it is necessary to prove breach of a provision of Community law which, like Article 86 of the Treaty, is capable of having direct effect. Consequently, the reply to the fifth question must be that it is for the domestic legal order of each Member State to lay down the detailed procedural rules, including those relating to the burden of proof, governing actions for safeguarding rights which individuals derive from the direct effect of Article 86 of the Treaty, provided that such rules are not less favourable than those governing similar domestic actions and do not render virtually impossible or excessively difficult the exercise of rights conferred by Community law.

The consequence may be that if the burden of proof under Community law combined with a difficulty in obtaining evidence under the procedural rules of the Member States renders the exercise of rights conferred by Articles 81 and 82 EC excessively difficult, the doctrine of effectiveness obliges the courts of the Member States to adjust the standard of proof. As the ECJ clarified in *Weber's Wine World*, if proof of specific circumstances cannot be adduced without the co-operation of

---

105. W. Wurmnest, 'Private Durchsetzung des EG-Kartellrechts nach der Reform der VO Nr. 17' in *Europäisches Wettbewerbsrecht im Umbruch*, P. Behrens, E. Braun and C. Nowak (eds) (Nomos, Baden-Baden, 2004), p. 233.
106. Cf. OLG Karlsruhe, NJW 2004, 2243, 2244: It corresponds to general experience that distributors pass high prices on to their customers; opposing view held by LG Dortmund, [2004] WuW/E DE-R 1352.
107. G. Berrisch and M. Burianski, 'Kartellrechtliche Schadensersatzansprüche nach der 7. GWB-Novelle', [2005] *WuW*, 883 *et seq.*; W. Wurmnest, 'Private Durchsetzung des EG-Kartellrechts nach der Reform der VO Nr. 17' in *Europäisches Wettbewerbsrecht im Umbruch*, P. Behrens, E. Braun and C. Nowak (eds) (Nomos, Baden-Baden, 2004), p. 232 *et seq.*
108. R. Bechtold, I. Brinker, W. Bosch, S. Hirsbrunner, *EG-Kartellrecht* (C.H. Beck, München 2005), Art. 2 VO 1/2003 para. 34.
109. ECJ, *GT-Link v. DSB*, Case no. C-242/95, [1997] ECR I-4449, para. 23 *et seq.*

the opposing party, Community law does not debar the law of a Member State to require such co-operation.[110] This is reinforced by the Court's decision in *Aalborg Portland*,[111] where it held that:

> Although according to those principles the legal burden of proof is borne either by the Commission or by the undertaking or association concerned, the factual evidence on which a party relies may be of such a kind as to require the other party to provide an explanation or justification, failing which it is permissible to conclude that the burden of proof has been discharged.

b.   Proof of Inapplicability under Article 81(3) EC

While it has been argued that proving the applicability of Art. 81(1) EC may be excessively difficult for private parties, especially in scenarios such as *Delimitis v. Henninger Bräu*, it may prove equally difficult for a party defending its practises as legitimate to show that the requirements of Art. 81(3) are fulfilled. It is up to this party to show that an agreement promotes technical or economic progress, that consumers will obtain a fair share of the benefits of such agreement, and that the agreement does not afford the undertakings the possibility of eliminating competition in respect of a substantial part of the products in question. In its decision-making, the Commission addresses these matters with a standard of probability,[112] and indeed they are subject to an economic prognosis unable to yield any certitude. Any civil court deciding upon the prerequisites of inapplicability under Art. 81(3) EC will likely seek the help of an economic expert, but as Kirchhoff has pointed out:[113]

> We are not dealing here with the solid, or at least predominantly solid terrain of medical, scientific or technical expertises [...]. In terms of economic expertises, there are splendid debates to be had regarding the methodical approach and reliability of the data used. This is all the more true with respect to the inferences drawn by the economic experts.
>
> Such expertises may describe efficiency gains or a fair participation of the consumers in terms of the Commission's practise as probable, adequately probable or sufficiently probable. However, economic expertises are often-times, if not regularly, bound to fail in establishing certitude relating to the standard of proof required under the ZPO. The party denying that the pre-requisites for inapplicability under Art. 81(3) have been met will oftentimes

---

110. ECJ, *Weber's Wine World et al v. Abgabenberufungskommission Wien*, Case no. C-147/01, [2003] ECR I-11365, para. 115.
111. EJC, *Aalborg Portland*, Joined case no. C-204/00 P *et al.*, [2004] ECR I-123, para. 79.
112. Overview provided by W. Kirchhoff, 'Sachverhaltsaufklärung und Beweislage bei der Anwendung des Art. 81 EG-Vertrag', [2004] WuW, 745 *et seq.*
113. W. Kirchhoff, 'Sachverhaltsaufklärung und Beweislage bei der Anwendung des Art. 81 EG-Vertrag', [2004] WuW, 749.

easily shed doubts on the persuasiveness of an expertise, which a dedicated judge may find hard to silence.

In this context, it seems appropriate to recall Art. 3(2) of Reg. (EC) 1/2003, which holds that:

> The application of national competition law may not lead to the prohibition of agreements, decisions by associations of undertakings or concerted practises which may affect trade between Member States but which do not restrict competition within the meaning of Article 81(1)of the Treaty, or which fulfil the conditions of Article 81(3)of the Treaty or which are covered by a Regulation for the application of Article 81(3)of the Treaty.

In other words, the doctrine of effectiveness does not only apply to damages claims for anti-competitive behaviour, but also encompasses findings of inapplicability under Art. 81(3) EC.[114] This implies that in assessing the prognostic factors to be regarded under Art. 81(3), a standard of proof requiring the conviction of the judge may be too strict; instead, a standard of sufficient probability should be adopted.[115]

G.   CALCULATION OF LOSSES SUSTAINED

A Plaintiff claiming compensation for its losses will regularly experience difficulties not only in proving the infringement, but also in demonstrating the damage suffered. These difficulties are alleviated to some extent by two provisions of German substantive law (§ 252 BGB, 33(3) GWB) and one procedural rule (§ 287 ZPO). § 252 BGB provides a legal presumption that damages for lost profits amount to such profits as were to be expected in the normal course of business. Furthermore, as the exact amount of loss will be difficult to define, § 287 ZPO allows for an *ex aequo et bono* estimation. In doing so, the court may avail itself of the help of an assessor.[116] Finally, § 33(3) GWB allows the court to consider the defendant's illegal gain for the purposes of § 287 ZPO. The goal is to facilitate the estimation of damages in cases in which establishing a hypothetical market price proves to be difficult; therefore, the provision does not refer to the profit directly caused by the infringement, but to any profit resulting from the respective sales.[117]

---

114. W. Kirchhoff, 'Sachverhaltsaufklärung und Beweislage bei der Anwendung des Art. 81 EG-Vertrag', [2004] WuW, 749.
115. W. Kirchhoff, 'Sachverhaltsaufklärung und Beweislage bei der Anwendung des Art. 81 EG-Vertrag', [2004] WuW, 749 *et seq.*; F. Montag and A. Rosenfeld, 'A Solution to the Problems? Regulation 1/2003 and the modernization of competition procedure', [2003] ZWeR, 122; R. Bechtold, I. Brinker, W. Bosch, S. Hirsbrunner, *EG-Kartellrecht* (C.H. Beck, München 2005), Art. 2 VO 1/2003 para. 32.
116. R. Hempel, *Privater Rechtsschutz im Kartellrecht* (Nomos, Baden-Baden, 2002), p. 76.
117. The Government Draft holds that 'Profits are principally calculated by subtracting from the turnover the production costs of the goods or services rendered and the operating costs accrued. Overhead costs or other business expenditures, which would also have accumulated without the anti-competitive behaviour, cannot be subtracted', *cf.* BT-Drucks. 15/3650, p. 54;

H.   EVIDENCE AND THE DOCTRINE OF EFFECTIVENESS

Private enforcement of EC competition law presents civil courts with a number of challenges which are mainly due to the fact that civil litigation is not inquisitorial in nature, but based upon the principle of party presentation. Whilst considering the nature and operation of the relevant economic market or markets is a challenging task which the courts are willing and able to address with the help of economic experts and possibly an alleviation of the standard of proof, acquiring sufficient data in establishing an infringement or the prerequisites of inapplicability under Art. 83(1) EC constitutes a seemingly insurmountable obstacle for parties, unless the action is raised as a follow-up to an enforcement decision of the Commission or a NCA.

It would seem that improving the effectiveness of Community competition law from the perspective of German civil procedure might require an adaptation of the law in two aspects: firstly, improved access to evidence held by the opposing party, and secondly, a change in the law regarding the protection of sensitive data.

The former matter is frequently discussed with the bogey of an US-style pre-trial discovery in mind, which is perceived as expensive, time-consuming and prone to abuse.[118] As the above analysis of the 'secondary burden of submission' has shown, this need not be the case. In adapting the standard of proof, the courts do possess an instrument that allows for the revelation of information to the other party under the control of the court. Admittedly, this would require an increased use of the court's power to provide guidance and discuss matters with the parties under § 139 ZPO, and a decreased significance of the principle of party presentation. Nonetheless, if business secrets of the party under the disclosure obligation are protected such steps are seemingly justified in order to promote the effectiveness of Community competition rules, which, after all, are enacted in the public interest.[119]

Any discussion of an improved access to evidence is certain to raise concerns regarding the protection of sensitive data, business secrets in particular. Case law allows for material to be reviewed by a neutral certified accountant

---

G. Berrisch and M. Burianski, 'Kartellrechtliche Schadensersatzansprüche nach der 7. GWB-Novelle', [2005] WuW, 884; J. Bornkamm, *Kommentar zum deutschen und europäischen Kartellrecht*, vol. 1: *Deutsches Kartellrecht*, E. Langen and H.J. Bunte (eds) (10th ed., Luchterhand, Neuwied, 2006); W.H. Roth, 'Das Kartelldeliktsrecht in der 7. GWB-Novelle', in *Festschrift für Ulrich Huber*, T. Baums, J. Wertenbruch, M. Lutter, K. Schmidt (eds) (Mohr Siebeck, Tübingen, 2006), p. 1166.

118.   U. Böge and K. Ost, 'Up and Running, or is it? Private enforcement – the Situation in Germany and Policy Perspectives', [2006] ECLR, 202; T. Lübbig, 'Die Reform des Zivilprozesses in Kartellsachen', [2006] WRP, 1215; G. Weidenbach and J.M. Schultze, 'Das Grünbuch zu Schadensersatzklagen im EG-Kartellrecht', [2006] GPR, 137.

119.   W. Kirchhoff, 'Sachverhaltsaufklärung und Beweislage bei der Anwendung des Art. 81 EG-Vertrag', [2004] WuW, 751; G. Hirsch, 'Anwendung der Kartellverfahrensordnung (EG) Nr. 1/2003 durch nationale Gerichte', [2003] ZWeR, 250; F. Montag and A. Rosenfeld, 'A Solution to the Problems? Regulation 1/2003 and the modernization of competition procedure', [2003] ZWeR, 122.

(*Wirtschaftsprüfervorbehalt*), if the documents are submitted in the course of a discharge of an information obligation under § 242 BGB. On the other hand, the prevailing opinion does not allow for the intervention of a neutral person or for in camera proceedings when it comes to procedural disclosure obligations, i.e., under §§ 142, 144, 444, 448 ZPO, which is reinforced by the principle of § 357(1) ZPO. Furthermore, is deemed impermissible to base a judgment upon any information submitted by the Commission or a NCA in their position as *amicus curiae*, unless all the information is disseminated to the parties.

Schlosser[120] points out that:

> While [the proviso that documents are to be handed over to a neutral, certified accountant in cases of information obligations under substantive law] appears to be well balanced and plausible, it surprises that everything is supposed to be different in litigation. The principle of a fair hearing supposedly requires that everything which reaches the ears of the court and everything heard by an expert must also be revealed to the parties.

And indeed, the prevailing opinion is not convincing. Certainly, a party would in most instances prefer that specific information revealed by its opponent was handed over to a neutral, certified accountant only – or even solely be revealed to the court – rather than lose the case because the court is prevented from basing its decision upon the information.[121] A party trying to establish an infringement of competition law has nothing to lose – whilst its right to challenge the information may be restricted, at least the sensitive data will be accessible in some form. Thus, it should be up for this party to choose between the option of challenging any material presented, even if that means that not all information will be divulged, and access to more comprehensive information combined with a restriction on its right to a fair hearing. The choice between the right to a fair hearing and the effectiveness of justice would seem to be a simple one to make[122] and a restrictive interpretation of § 357(1) ZPO seems feasible in the light of these arguments.

The situation is more delicate with respect to the data underlying economic analyses provided by the Commission as *amicus curiae* or submitted by a court-appointed expert, as this data will regularly pertain to third parties. In such an instance, there will always be one party to the litigation whose overall case is disadvantaged by the expert opinion rendered and who will therefore be interested

120. P. Schlosser, 'Wirtschaftsprüfervorbehalt und prozessuales Vertraulichkeitsinteresse der nicht primär beweisbelasteten Prozeβpartei' in *Festschrift für Bernhard Großfeld*, U. Hübner and W. Ebke (eds) (Recht und Wirtschaft, Heidelberg, 1999), p. 1003; L. Rosenberg, K. H. Schwab and P. Gottwald, *Zivilprozessrecht* (16th ed, C.H. Beck, München 2004), § 115 para. 45.

121. P. Schlosser, 'Wirtschaftsprüfervorbehalt und prozessuales Vertraulichkeitsinteresse der nicht primär beweisbelasteten Prozeβpartei' in *Festschrift für Bernhard Großfeld*, U. Hübner and W. Ebke (eds) (Recht und Wirtschaft, Heidelberg, 1999), p. 1008 *et seq.*

122. P. Schlosser, 'Wirtschaftsprüfervorbehalt und prozessuales Vertraulichkeitsinteresse der nicht primär beweisbelasteten Prozeβpartei' in *Festschrift für Bernhard Großfeld*, U. Hübner and W. Ebke (eds) (Recht und Wirtschaft, Heidelberg, 1999), p. 1005 *et seq.*; L. Rosenberg, K. H. Schwab and P. Gottwald, *Zivilprozessrecht* (16th ed, C.H. Beck, München 2004), § 115 para. 45.

in challenging the underlying data. Nonetheless, the right to a fair hearing does not always require the information to be disclosed to the parties, as the case law of the Federal Court of Justice suggests. Guidance is provided by a decision of the Federal Constitutional Court regarding an expertise on average lease prices.[123] The Court held that:

> The question of whether and to which extent the court and the parties require an acknowledgement of the facts underlying the expert opinion for an appraisal of the expertise eludes an abstract determination. Any judge is held to render this decision with regard to the specific circumstances of the case before it. In general, the parties' demand to examine the facts underlying the expert opinion will be all the more justified, the more the expert's opinion is based upon singular factual findings and the less it is based upon the expert's general expertise. However, the more general and comprehensive the facts utilized by the expert are, the less the value which will be attached to a critical challenge of the knowledge of particular circumstances. In such an instance it may possibly suffice if the parties are granted the possibility of spot checks. Insofar as the expert bases his or her opinion upon statistical or generally available data, individual data is regularly not necessary for a critical appraisal. The same applies for know-how and scientific insights.
>
> The extent to which facts need to be revealed in order for an expert opinion to be used in the proceedings cannot be determined in an abstract way, but is subject to the circumstances of the particular case. On the one hand, the parties should principally be provided with an opportunity to pursue any doubts that suggest themselves as to the correctness of the expertise. However, this right may be subject to limitations, especially in order to protect the privacy of third parties, in case the party does not sufficiently specify its doubts or if, in view of the overall circumstances, it cannot reasonably be expected that the value of the expert opinion will be questioned in the light of the examination.
>
> However, a limitation to the parties' right to a revelation of the facts may be justified if the expert's silence is based on commendable grounds and the failure to make use of the expert opinion would equate a loss of one of the parties' substantive rights. Such may be the case, if the facts underlying the expertise possess a general nature of utmost secrecy and not only the particular expert is debarred from disclosing them. The court's duty to sufficiently examine the factual basis of an expert opinion with the co-operation of the parties is anchored in the right to a fair hearing and the principle of a constitutional state. However, this obligation may be restricted by virtue of the rights of third parties. In the interest of the party bearing the onus of proof, the court may thus require less facts to be revealed in case the reasons given by the expert carry sufficient weight. This may particularly be the case if data regarding matters of immediate privacy pertaining to third parties not involved

---

123.   BVerfG, NJW 1995, 40, 41 *et seq.*; concurring BVerfG, NJW 1997, 1909 *et seq.*

in the dispute are concerned. [...] Insofar as the expert refuses a complete revelation of the facts on tenable grounds, while predominant interests of the party under the onus of proof require that the court does not forego using the expert opinion, the court must try to establish how the expert obtained its data, i.e., by questioning the expert. This may suffice to establish the judges' conviction in individual cases.

It follows from these considerations of the Federal Constitutional Court that the right to a fair hearing does not necessarily call for full party access to the information considered by the court. Instead, the legitimate interest to protect confidential information pertaining to one of the parties or a third party may be recognized. Admittedly, the Constitutional Court referred to information of an intimate and private nature, but did not specifically include business secrets. Nonetheless, it would seem that the courts need to find a workable balance between the constitutional guarantees of right to a fair hearing, the principle of effectiveness of justice and the protection of business secrets.

While the present law does not provide the court with an option to hold in camera proceedings or to prevent an attorney from passing information on to its client, instituting such options de lege ferenda would seem to be compatible with the Basic Law, if limited to very specific circumstances. With respect to the privileges granted to witnesses under §§ 383, 384 ZPO, any proposed change would also need to be instituted by the legislature. In view of the fact that the said provisions aim to protect a witness against disproportionate consequences of its civic duty,[124] while at the same time not rendering the exercise of Community rights virtually impossible or excessively difficult, provided there are other means of accessing evidence, it would not seem that the doctrine of effectiveness requires a change to the statute.

However, in light of what has been said above, both the constitutional principle of effectiveness of justice and the Community doctrine of effectiveness may require the ordinary jurisdiction to relax their strict stance regarding the intervention of a neutral certified accountant. Further, economic opinion submitted by a court-appointed expert and observations rendered by the Commission under Art. 15(1) Reg. (EC) 1/2003 could be utilized by the court in forming its conviction, even if some of the underlying data is classified as confidential. It would be for the court to decide on the basis of the amount of data withheld and its significance in shaping the expert's or the Commission's opinion, whether and to what extent the expert opinion may be utilized.

---

124. A. Baumbach, W. Lauterbach, J. Albers, P. Hartmann, Zivilprozessordnung (64th edn, C.H. Beck, München, 2006), § 384 ZPO n. 2.

Chapter 13

German Procedure Costs and Limitation Periods

A.   COSTS

As is true for any kind of litigation, high costs may form a disincentive to the private enforcement of competition infringements. The jurisdictional amounts in competition cases can be unusually high, leading to correspondingly high court and attorney fees.[1] The Green Paper questions the legitimacy of the indemnity rule in competition litigation,[2] suggesting:

> Option 27: 'Establish a rule that unsuccessful claimants will have to pay costs only if they acted in a manifestly unreasonable manner by bringing the case. Consideration could also be given to giving the court the discretionary power to order at the beginning of a trial that the claimant not be exposed to any cost recovery even if the action were to be unsuccessful'.

As a consequence of this suggestion, the successful defendant would have to bear the court's as well as its own attorney fees, even though the plaintiff was unable to establish a breach of EC competition law. This would seem patently unfair, however reasonable and bona fide the claimant was acting in raising the action.

---

1. The submission of the Federal Council of Germany regarding the 7th GWB-amendment refers to hundreds of thousands EUR attorney fees in public enforcement cases, BT-Drucks. 15/3640, 84; cf. the estimate made by the *Ashurst report*, 28, which puts the financial risk of litigation at 45,000 EUR for the first instance and 60,000 EUR for the appellate decision if the value in dispute is 1,000,000 EUR.
2. Green Paper – Damages actions for breach of the EC antitrust rules, COM (2005) 672 final, p. 9 at 2.6.

German law provides for the indemnity principle in § 91 ZPO, according to which the losing party in principle bears the cost of the proceedings, i.e., court and out-of-court fees, specifically attorney fees. In cases of partial success, § 92 ZPO provides that the costs be allocated proportionally. The reimbursement of attorney fees is limited to the statutory rate stipulated by §§ 13 *et seq.* of the Attorney Fee Scheme (*Rechtsanwaltsvergütungsgesetz* – RVG) and to the representation of one attorney only, § 91(2) ZPO. While client and attorney may agree on higher fees under § 4 RVG, such fees are not recoverable from the opposing party. Lower fees than those provided for by the RVG as well as contingency and *quota litis* fees are considered inadmissible following § 49b(1), (2) Federal Attorney Regulation (*Bundesrechtsanwaltsordnung* – BRAO). Both court fees and statutory attorney fees are generally defined in a degressive relation to the sum in dispute, while the kind of procedural measures taken (i.e., the hearing of witnesses) are also accounted for.

In order to enhance private enforcement of competition claims, the 7th GWB-amendment saw the introduction of a competition-specific rule on jurisdictional costs in § 89a GWB.

§ 89a GWB:

If, with respect to an action under § 33 or § 34a, one of the parties plausibly submits that its economic standing would be endangered if it had to bear the costs of the proceedings, the court may order upon this party's request that this party's obligation to pay the court fees be fixed according to a jurisdictional value adapted to its economic situation. In exercising its discretion, the court may consider a credible submission by that party that the costs are not directly or indirectly assumed on its behalf by a third person. As a consequence, the party favoured by such an order is bound to pay attorney fees only in relation to the adapted jurisdictional value. If this party is ordered to bear the costs of the proceedings, the opposing party's court and attorney fees are also to be paid according to the adapted jurisdictional value. Insofar as the out-of-court costs are to be borne by the opposing party, the attorney of the party favoured by the order may claim his fees from the opposing party in relation to the full jurisdictional value.

(2) A request under paragraph 1 may be declared in writing before the court office. The request is to be made before the initiation of the main hearing. At a later point in time, the request is only admissible if the jurisdictional value has been raised. The opposing party needs to be heard before granting the request.

§ 89a GWB seems a viable scheme to reduce the cost risk associated with private enforcement of competition rules.[3] The financial risk taken by a party with poor

---

3. Applauding the provision i.e., M. Schütt, 'Individualrechtsschutz nach der 7. GWB-Novelle', [2004] WuW, 1133; R. Hempel, 'Privater Rechtsschutz im deutschen Kartellrecht nach der 7. GWB-Novelle', [2004] WuW 373.

economic standing is considerably reduced in that if it loses the case, both its own as well as the opposing parties' attorney and court fees are calculated on the basis of a reduced, fictional sum in dispute. The flip side of the coin is that the opposing party remains liable for fees calculated in relation to the full amount of jurisdictional value and it seems doubtful whether the privilege granted to persons of poor economic standing should be paid for by the opposing party. The fact that § 89a applies to 'David vs Goliath'-scenarios[4] hardly justifies burdening 'Goliath' not only with its own attorney costs despite having won the case, but also with court fees it possibly paid up front in relation to the actual sum in dispute. It is for this reason that § 89a GWB and similar provisions in other statutes[5] have undergone heavy criticism,[6] but according to the Federal Constitutional Court such rules do not contravene the principle of procedural equality of arms.[7]

Case law of the ECtHR consistently emphasizes that a party to a dispute must be 'afforded a reasonable opportunity to present his case under conditions that do not place him at a disadvantage vis-à-vis his opponent'.[8] This notwithstanding, it would seem that Art. 6 of the European Convention on Human Rights does not preclude a provision such as § 89a GWB. Assessing the denial of a request for legal aid in *Steel and Morris v. The United Kingdom*, the Court pointed out that 'Article 6 § 1 leaves to the State a free choice of the means to be used in guaranteeing litigants the above rights. The institution of a legal aid scheme constitutes one of those means but there are others, such as for example simplifying the applicable procedure'.[9] Further on they stated: 'moreover, it is not incumbent on the State to seek through the use of public funds to ensure total equality of arms between the assisted person and the opposing party, as long as each side is afforded a reasonable opportunity to present his or her case under conditions that do not place him or her at a substantial disadvantage vis-à-vis the adversary'.[10]

The Court's reasoning in *Steel and Morris v. The United Kingdom* would principally seem to imply that – in line with the rationale of the German Federal Constitutional Court referred to above – Contracting States to the Human Rights Convention are granted a wide scope in establishing fee schemes. This seems particularly true if the financial balance between the parties is skewed from the outset and the discrimination does not impede the economically stronger party from presenting its case.

---

4. J. Bornkamm, *Kommentar zum deutschen und europäischen Kartellrecht*, vol. 1: *Deutsches Kartellrecht*, E. Langen and H.J. Bunte (eds) (10th ed., Luchterhand, Neuwied, 2006), § 89a para. 6.
5. Cf. §§ 144 Patentgesetz, § 142 Markengesetz, § 16 Gebrauchsmustergesetz, § 54 Geschmacksmustergesetz as well as the former § 23b Gesetz gegen den unlauteren Wettbewerb.
6. J. Bornkamm, *Kommentar zum deutschen und europäischen Kartellrecht*, vol. 1: *Deutsches Kartellrecht*, E. Langen and H.J. Bunte (eds) (10th ed., Luchterhand, Neuwied, 2006), § 89a para. 3 with further references.
7. BVerfG NJW-RR 1991, 1134.
8. ECtHR, *Steel and Morris v. The United Kingdom*, Case no. 68416/01, para. 59; ECtHR, *Dombo Beheer B.V. v. The Netherlands*, Case no. 144488/88, para. 33 *et seq.*
9. ECtHR, *Steel and Morris v. The United Kingdom*, Case no. 68416/01, para. 60.
10. ECtHR, *Steel and Morris v. The United Kingdom*, Case no. 68416/01, para. 62.

While it would seem that § 89a GWB cannot be said to infringe basic procedural rights, it is suggested that in terms of fairness, § 12(4) UWG (which provides for a general reduction of the jurisdictional value) seems certainly more adequate.

Furthermore, in terms of its effectiveness, it needs to be considered that the scope of the application of § 89a GWB is likely to be quite narrow. The application of § 89a GWB was envisaged mainly for representative actions raised by organizations under § 33(2) GWB.[11] This seemed expedient in view of the fact that consumer organizations were originally supposed to achieve *locus standi* under § 33(2) GWB. In turn, those entities that do posses *locus standi* under §§ 33(2), 34a(1), i.e., organizations for the promotion of commercial interests, will most likely make any of their actions dependent on a respective interest voiced by at least one of their members who are willing to guarantee the reimbursement of costs. In such cases, an adaptation of the jurisdictional value is ruled out, as is clarified by § 33(1) sent. 2.[12] It should also be kept in mind that such organizations are only considered to possess *locus standi* if they are sufficiently endowed to lead a dispute with jurisdictional values of EUR 30.000 to 50.000 through all three instances.[13]

Overall, it would seem that the fixed fee scheme of the RVG is generally suited to keep costs at bay, and the indemnity rule should not be sacrificed in the quest of enhancing effectiveness. While attempts to reduce the cost risk associated with private enforcement of competitions rules are generally to be applauded, it should not be neglected that the highest risk factor is the legal and factual uncertainty connected with actions based on an infringement of competition law.[14] Only clear cut liability rules, i.e., certainty regarding the admissibility of the passing-on defence or the rights of indirect customers, and options for the plaintiff to clarify the factual basis before initiating costly proceedings will reduce the risk of an action and the implied cost risk.

B.   LIMITATION PERIODS

In German law, limitation periods are clearly treated as matters of substantive, not procedural law. Since this qualification is not unanimous amongst the Member

---

11. Monopolkommission, *Das Allgemeine Wettbewerbsrecht in der Siebten GWB-Novelle. Sondergutachten 41* (Bonn, 2004), <www.monopolkommission.de/sg_41/text_s41.pdf>, para. 97.
12. J. Bornkamm, *Kommentar zum deutschen und europäischen Kartellrecht*, vol. 1: *Deutsches Kartellrecht*, E. Langen and H.J. Bunte (eds) (10th ed., Luchterhand, Neuwied, 2006), § 89a para. 7.
13. BGH NJW-RR 1998, 1421, 1422; BGH, GRUR 1994, 385; OLGR Stuttgart 1999, 393.
14. R. Hempel, *Privater Rechtsschutz im Kartellrecht*, (Nomos, Baden-Baden, 2002), p. 156; J. Schwarze and A. Weitbrecht, *Grundzüge des europäischen Kartellverfahrensrechts* (Nomos, Baden-Baden, 2004), § 11 para. 25.

States of the EU, a brief digression regarding prescription will ensue. Damages claims based on the infringement of EU competition rules are subject to a limitation period of three-years that starts to run at the end of the year in which the damages claim arose and the person damaged received or should have received knowledge of the facts giving rise to the claim and the identity of the debtor (§§ 195, 199 BGB).[15] § 199(3) BGB provides for an absolute time limit irrespective of the knowledge of the person which suffered the loss (ten years from the time the claim arose) or the time the claim came into existence (30 years starting from the action which triggered the damage).

The Commission Staff Working Paper maintains that 'Limitation periods (prescriptions) can impose significant restrictions on the recovery of damages'.[16] For two reasons, the German provisions do not seem to raise particular concerns in that regard. First, prescription will be suspended not only during ongoing legal proceedings, but also for the length of settlement negotiations (§§ 204(1) no. 1, 203 BGB). There is consequently no pressure on the Claimant to rush into a settlement or litigation for fear of the claim being time-barred. Secondly, § 33(5) GWB effects a coordination between public and private enforcement.

> § 33(5) GWB:
> The prescription of a claim for damages under section 2 is suspended, if the Cartel Authority initiates a proceeding because of an infringement in the meaning of section 1, or if the Commission of the European Community or the cartel authority of an EU Member State initiates proceedings because of an infringement of Article 81 or 82 of the Treaty establishing the European Community. § 204(2) of the Civil Code finds corresponding application.

In line with the ECJ's decision in *Brasserie de Haecht II*, the term 'initiation of proceedings' in § 33(5) GWB should be regarded as the first authoritative act of the Commission or the NCAs evidencing its intention of taking a decision.[17] That being said, the German provisions regarding the period of limitation may be seen to interfere with the effectiveness of EU competition law only insofar as § 199(3) BGB stipulates a prescription of claims ten years after the damage occurred, irrespective of the knowledge of the person which suffered the loss.

---

15. T. Lettl, 'Die Auswirkungen der 7. GWB-Novelle auf die Kreditwirtschaft', [2005] WM 1592; J. Bornkamm, *Kommentar zum deutschen und europäischen Kartellrecht*, vol. 1: *Deutsches Kartellrecht*, E. Langen and H.J. Bunte (eds) (10th ed., Luchterhand, Neuwied, 2006), § 33 para. 123.
16. Commission Staff Working Paper, COM (2005) 672 final, no. 261.
17. ECJ, *Brasserie de Haecht II* Case no. 48/72, [1973] ECR 77, para. 16; regarding § 54 GWB cf. R. Bechtold, *GWB* (3rd edn, C.H. Beck, München, 2002), § 54 para. 1; K. Schmidt, *GWB*, U. Immenga and E.J. Mestmäcker (eds) (3rd edn, C.H. Beck, München, 2001) § 54 para. 6.

However, as the Commission Staff Notice correctly points out, 'limitation periods perform an important role in providing for legal certainty by ensuring that the legal position of the parties concerned becomes irreversible at a certain point in time'.[18] This is in line with the ECJ's finding in *Manfredi*[19] that:

> It is for the national court to determine whether a national rule which provides that the limitation period for seeking compensation for harm caused by an agreement or practise prohibited under Article 81 EC begins to run from the day on which that prohibited agreement or practise was adopted, particularly where it also imposes a short limitation period that cannot be suspended, renders it practically impossible or excessively difficult to exercise the right to seek compensation for the harm suffered.

§§ 195, 199 do certainly not render a claim for damages practically impossible or excessively difficult. The German rules on the period of limitation are therefore consistent with the doctrine of effectiveness.

---

18. Commission Staff Working Paper, COM (2005) 672 final, no. 261.
19. ECJ, *Manfredi*, Joined cases no. C-295/04 to C-298/04, para 82.

Chapter 14
Conclusion

This study has proceeded on the basis of an examination of certain rules of the civil procedure used by the ordinary English, French and German courts to enforce EC Articles 81 and 82 in terms of actions for damages. The specific rules of each of the three national systems of civil procedure were chosen on the basis of the areas of enforcement which were identified by the European Commission in its Green Paper and the Commission Staff Working Paper as being problematic for enforcement of EC competition law. In the case of the English procedure, the rules of the CAT, a specialist tribunal for the enforcement of monetary actions[1] based upon infringement findings of EC Articles 81 and 82 made by the Office of Fair Trading and the Commission.

The most significant part of the analysis consists in the application of the doctrine of effectiveness and non discrimination to those elements of the national procedure which impede in some manner the effective enforcement of EC Articles 81 and 82. ECJ case law such as *San Giorgio,*[2] *Factortame,*[3] *van Schjindel,*[4] *Peterbroeck*[5] and *Crehan*[6] appears to establish a type of minimum enforcement standard which is required in order to justify the intervention of the principles of effectiveness and non-discrimination: that is, the standard is basically that the national rule of procedure, following the above cases, neither render excessively difficult nor almost impossible the enforcement of EC law and this subject to

---

1. The competence of the CAT extends beyond monetary actions provided in S 47A CA (1998).
2. *Amministrazione delle Finanze dello Stato v. SpA San Giorgio* 199/82 [1983] ECR 3595.
3. *R v. Secretary of State for Transport exp Factortame Ltd (No 2)* Case C-213/89, (No 3) Case C-221/89, Case C-48/93.
4. *van Schijndel v. Stichting Pensionenfonds voor Fysiotherapeuthen* Case C-430/93, 431/93 [1995] ECR I-4705.
5. *Peterbroek van Campenhout SCS & Co. v. Belgium* Case C-312/93 (1995) ECR I -4599.
6. *Courage Ltd v. Crehan* Case C-453/99, [2001] ECR I-6297.

possible justification in terms of the national principles of procedure such as legal certainty or as the ECJ held in *Peterbroeck* and *van Schijndel.*

> For the purposes of applying those principles, each case which raises the question whether a national procedural provision renders application of Community law impossible or excessively difficult must be analysed by reference to the role of that provision in the procedure, its progress and its special feature, viewed as a whole, before the various national instance. In light of that analysis, the basic principles of the domestic judicial system, such as the protection of the rights of the defence, the principle of legal certain and the proper conduct of the procedure must where appropriate be taken into consideration.

However, it is submitted that implicit within the principles of effective enforcement as established in cases such as *San Giorgio* and particularly *Peterbroeck*[7] is the concept of optimal enforcement: specifically, that in the context of what might be termed competing procedural solutions neither of which renders impossible the enforcement of EC competition law, that the concept of effectiveness necessarily entails the following: namely, that the more or most effective method of procedural enforcement be chosen among those which exist and which do not render the enforcement of EC competition law but some of which can be said to render the enforcement thereof less effective than others. Further, as noted in the course of the analysis, the concept of developed by van Gerven[8] of adequately effective as opposed to minimally effective is preferred: it is by virtue of the adequately or arguably optimally effective enforcement that one is able in certain cases to effect a choice between what might be regarded as competing procedural solutions with respect to enforcement of EC Articles 81 and 82.

A.   NATIONAL PRINCIPLES

1.   ENGLISH CPR AND CAT RULES RELEVANT FOR THE
                      APPLICATION OF THE DOCTRINE OF EFFECTIVENESS

As noted in earlier chapters, the CPR contains explicit procedural principles within the Overriding Objective; it implicitly also contains the Common Law principles of a fair trial, the existence of which historically preceded the creation of the CPR. These principles have been considered on each occasion that the doctrine of effectiveness required a modification of the CPR in order to ensure effective enforcement. In the case of the CAT, the fundamental procedural principles are expressed particularly in S 19 of its rules. Indeed that section along with SS 3.1–3.3

---

7.   As noted in the Introduction, it may be that *Peterbroeck* itself constitutes a pro-example of more
     adequate enforcement as opposed to minimally effective enforcement.
8.   W. van Gerven, 'Of Rights, Remedies and Procedures', [2001] CMLR 501 op. cit.

of the Guidelines were considered to reflect the basic principles of the CAT Rules. It is recalled that S 19.1 sets for the principles within the body of the rule:

> The Tribunal may at any time on the request of a part or of its own initiative at a case management conference, pre-hearing review or otherwise, give such directions as are provided for in paragraph (2) below or such other directions as it thinks fit to secure the just expeditious and economic conduct of the proceedings.

Further, in the Guidelines:

> The rules are based on the same general philosophy of the CPR and pursue the same overriding objective of enabling the Tribunal to deal with cases justly in particular by ensuring that the parties are on an equal footing, that expenses are saved and that appeals are dealt with expeditiously and fairly.

To achieve this objective in the particular context of the 1998 Act, the Rules are modelled party on the CPR and partly on the Rules of the Court of First Instance of the European Communities (CFI) which deal with appeals in competition cases arising under Articles 81 and 82 of the Treaty. A central feature of both the CPR and the Rules of Procedure of the CFI is case management by the Court.

However it should be borne in mind that the Tribunal's Rules are different in various respects. Parties should not assume that the CPR or the Rules of Procedure of the CFI apply to a particular procedural issue.

It is submitted that in the spirit of S.3.1 of the Guidelines, the CAT also contains implicit principles concerning a fair trial. Once again these principles have been considered in the few instances where the doctrine of effectiveness may require changes to the CAT Rules. It was by applying the principle of effectiveness in relation to the aforementioned principles of the CPR and the CAT Rules that three categories of changes to the rules in both cases were constructed. These categories will be discussed later within the section dealing with the English procedure.

2.   French Principles Relevant for the Application of the Doctrine of Effectiveness

The Civil and Commercial Courts apply the rules set out in the Code of Civil Procedure ('Nouveau Code de Procédure Civile') when ensuring enforcement of Articles 81 and 82 EC Treaty. The courts may also have to apply certain specific rules contained in other Codes.[9]

International civil procedure principles of direct application (in particular the provisions set out in the European Convention on Human Rights), as well as

---

9. For instance Article L.420-7 of the commercial Code on the specialization of the courts in competition law matters.

constitutional principles, have been considered in order to assess whether rules that constitute an obstacle to private enforcement are justified in terms of the French fundamental principles underlying civil procedure rules. In particular, the right to an action, which is considered as being a personal right (freedom of the person),[10] justifies the restrictive rules in terms of collective actions. Further, the principle of the independence of the courts justifies claimants having the burden of proving the breach of EC Art 81 or 82 where the Competition Council has already made a ruling on agreements, decisions or practises under those articles (Articles 81 and/ or 82 EC Treaty.)

3.   GERMAN PRINCIPLES RELEVANT FOR THE APPLICATION OF
            THE DOCTRINE OF EFFECTIVENESS

The fundamental procedural principles of the Code of Civil Procedure (ZPO) apply in order to ensure enforcement of EC Articles 81 and 82 by reason of the absence of specific procedural rules for the private enforcement of competition law in Germany (if one leaves aside the matter of competition case allocation, §§ 87 *et seq* WB. In the course of this analysis, several of these principles have been considered in order to ascertain whether the principle of effectiveness may require changes to the ZPO or call for a different interpretation than the one proposed by the prevailing academic and judicial opinion. Of particular importance are the fundamental principles protected under the Basic Law, namely the right to effectiveness of justice, the right to a fair hearing and the right to be heard. Further, the constitutional guarantee of the independence of judges may play a role in limiting the binding effect of Commission decisions. On a number of occasions, the doctrine of party presentation has been examined as possibly limiting the effectiveness of Community law and, as a consequence, it was proposed to relax the standard pertaining to this doctrine in specific instances.

B.   ENGLISH CPR AND CAT RULES: CATEGORIES OF
            CHANGES REQUIRED BY THE APPLICATION OF
            THE DOCTRINE OF EFFECTIVENESS

The analysis of the English system has arguably led to the making of certain observations and establishing the following categories of possible changes within the CPR and the Rules of the CAT.

(1) Arguably, the EC doctrine of effectiveness applies primarily in terms of its limb which concerns effective enforcement rather than non discriminatory enforcement. This would seem to correspond to the observations made by

---

10. Constitutional Court (*'Conseil Constitutionnel'*), No. 257 DC, 25 July 1989, (1989) *Dr. Soc.*, p. 627.

Perchal[11] and *van Gerven*[12] concerning the frequency of the use of the doctrine of effectiveness as opposed to that of non-discrimination.

(2) That being said, there are at least two notable example of where the doctrine of non-discrimination applies: first with respect to representative actions whereby S 58 A CA (1998) monetary actions involving OFT and Tribunal infringement decisions of EC Articles 81 and or 82 would require the use of a representative action such as exists for actions under S47 A CA (1998) by the CAT in terms of similar in terms of the CPR in relation to the CAT Rules. The other possible example might be the CAT rules concerning the indemnity rule and conditional fees: it may that the principle of non-discrimination would require that the CAT apply the Scots rule as it pertains to the indemnity rule to proceedings in England on the assumption that the both enforcement systems exist within the same Member State, namely the UK. It would seem that in the case of both the representative actions and the conditional fees, the fundamental criterion necessary for the application of the doctrine of non-discrimination apply: firstly, that the category of action namely, the monetary actions and the conditional fees are the same both in terms of the CPR and the CAT Rules as they are applied in England to the representative actions and in respect of the CAT Rules England and Scotland as they apply to conditional fees, and the CAT Rules and the CPR as they apply to conditional fees in England. The next step is to consider whether the restrictions on the availability of the representative action in the CPR is reasonable; it would seem that at a minimum, the existence *ipso facto* of a representative cause of action in the CAT Rules would seem to demonstrate that the restriction in the CPR is not reasonable in so far as it pertains to the enforcement of the same monetary action. Second, it would appear that the restriction upon the availability of the representative cause of action for enforcement of certainly monetary claims and free standing actions brought under the CPR does not appear reasonable when balanced against the overall restriction on enforceability of EC Articles 81 and 82 which results: this deficit can be aggravated unless the representative action is extended not only to consumers but to small businesses as in *Bernard Crehan v. Intrprenneur Pub Co.*

With respect to the use of the indemnity rule to shift the entire costs to the loser of the litigation under the CPR constitutes an expansion of that rule which is not reasonable for the following reasons: first, the Scottish rules appear to demonstrate that the overall funding of litigation through the use of the conditional fee as applied among other things potentially to the enforcement of EC Articles 81 and or 82 appears to function without difficulty. Second, the existence of the Scots rule would appear to accentuate the unreasonableness of the CPR use of the indemnity rule in so far as the latter may well result in reducing the enforceability EC Articles 81 and 82: that is in those cases where the eventuality of a

---

11. S. Perchal 'Community Law in National Courts: the Lessons from *van Schiyndel*' (1998) CMLR 501 op. cit.
12. See *generally*, W. van Gerven, 'Of Rights, Remedies and Procedures' (2000) CMLR 501 op. cit.

negative costs order may dissuade a litigant from asserting his rights pursuant to EC Articles 81 and or 82.

(3) With respect to the doctrine of effectiveness at least in terms of the minimum enforcement criterion intervening where the national measure renders impossible or exceedingly difficult the following procedural categories would be affected: first, although subject to the application of the doctrine of non-discrimination, the matters of representative actions and the operation of the indemnity rule for conditional fees. Further, it would appear appropriate to include the privilege of self incrimination in terms of ensuring that the EC *Orkem* privilege against self incrimination is utilized notably in terms of CPR disclosure. It may be that the doctrine could apply notably in such cases where, which is not clear in light of the case of *SGL Carbon*, there exists a difference in scope between the ECJ *Orkem* privilege against self-incrimination and that of the ECtHR as exemplified in such cases as *J.B. v Switzerland*. It would appear that there is nothing in the underlying English principles of the Overriding Objective or the underlying principles of the common law fair trial that would justify the retention of either the restriction upon the representative actions, the use of the indemnity rule to shift legal costs the amount of which need not be proportional to the losing litigant and finally, were it the case, the use of the privilege against self incrimination which may be so wide as to prevent entirely enforcement of EC Articles 81 and or 82. Accordingly, the doctrine of effectiveness would intervene to affect the changes so as to ensure a minimum degree of effective enforcement of EC Articles 81 and 82 in terms of both monetary actions and stand alone actions.

The matter of legal costs considered independently of conditional fees arguably constitutes a slightly different problem of enforcement. The problem is one of the degree of difficulty of enforcement: that is the procedural disposition rather than preventing the enforcement of EC competition law renders it exceedingly difficult if not almost impossible. In this regard, it is submitted that the system of costs which are calculated exclusively on an hourly basis can render exceedingly difficult the enforcement of EC Articles 81 and or 82 both before the ordinary courts and before the CAT. However, in the case of both the CAT and the ordinary court, this difficulty is somewhat mitigated with respect to one type of action, namely, monetary claims: first, SS47A and 58 A CA (1998) provide for enforcement decisions which are termed monetary claims whereby the Tribunal is bound by the infringement finding of either the European Commission or the OFT upon the effluxion of the appeal period and ordinary court with respect to a decision of the OFT. These provisions overall potentially reduce the costs of enforcement of EC Articles 81 and 82; second, however, the CAT unlike the ordinary court does not regularly follow the cost shifting rule whereby the losing party pays the winning party's costs. With respect to the CPR the real problem of costs arises in terms of enforcement through stand alone damages actions. In such cases, the calculation of the legal costs on an hourly basis when coupled with a the regular use of the indemnity rule can together render the enforcement of EC competition law exceedingly difficult if not almost impossible in the economic sense, i.e., in terms of high legal costs.

The stage at which the enforcement of EC competition law becomes excessively difficult or virtually impossible arises when there is a combination of various sections of the CPR which in themselves may simply make the enforcement more difficult: it is submitted that this point can arrive when there is a combination of the hourly method of fees combined with the indemnity rule and the absence of a representative action: or, the hourly method of fee calculation coupled with the indemnity rule in the context of the conditional fees, the hourly method of the calculation of fees coupled with the indemnity rule and the current method of the allocation of the burden of proof particularly if one adds a conditional fee may well have the effect of impeding the enforcement of EC Articles 81 and 82 by private individuals. As noted, it is the cumulative effect of the various procedural dispositions of the CPR rather than the individual effect which causes a serious breach of the infringement of the doctrine of effectiveness arguably to the level of rendering enforcement impossible primarily in the financial sense. This is the primary procedural weakness of the CPR in terms of enforcement of EC Articles 81 and 82 which, for the most part does not have a parallel in the operation of the Rules of the CAT. In may be however, that in first instance these negative financial consequences will be restricted to the categories of individual private litigants and notably that sub category of private litigants including small business which do not possess litigation insurance. The conclusion may therefore that the CPR in particular is suited primarily for enforcement of litigation by corporate clients were it the case for whom legal costs may be a burden but not private individual litigants and small litigants. Notwithstanding, the example of the CAT rules and their operation indicate at least in the context of the monetary claims that apparently cheaper enforcement of EC Articles 81 and 82 is possible for all potential litigants. In that perspective, it would seem that the doctrine of effectiveness would overall require that the CPR be modified so as to ensure effective enforcement of EC Articles 81 and 82 by all potential litigants irrespective of financial resources.

(4) It has been submitted that the doctrine of effectiveness also applies to what might be termed a third category of procedural enforcement: namely those situations where there exists effectively a choice between what might be termed competing methods of effective enforcement. It is the case that neither of the two procedural elements of the CPR renders the enforcement of EC competition law impossible or exceedingly difficult. However, one of the two procedural elements produces a more effective method of enforcement in terms of corresponding not only to the CPR overriding objective and the objective of the fair trial but also more generally to effective enforcement of EC Articles 81 and 82. This would be the case of the granting of the interim injunction pursuant to CPR 25 on the basis of the merits of the case and the appointment of assessor pursuant to CPR 35.15 to assist the judge in his task of evaluation expert economic evidence. As noted earlier, the granting of the interim injunction on the basis of the 'merits of the case' has the advantage of assuring more legal certainty than is the case with the balance of convenience. Accordingly, the principles of the merits of the case are to be preferred over the balance of convenience when granting an interim injunction in so

far as the greater legal certainty assists in ensuring a more effective enforcement of EC competition law in damages actions. It is submitted that the appointment of an assessor pursuant to CPR 36 can similarly increase the legal certainty of the decision which the court renders when based upon expert evidence. Accordingly, the greater legal certainty which the assessor provides in the understanding of the expert evidence will contribute to more certain and therefore better enforcement of EC Articles 81 and 82. Further, it is submitted that the conjunction of the Chancery judge assisted in certain cases by an assessor may then approximate that the specialist expertise which is available in the CAT notably with respect to enforcement of monetary decisions which may involve the assessment of economic loss. Clearly in terms of enforcement of monetary actions pursuant to SS 47A and 58A it is possible to argue that the principle of effectiveness and non discrimination would require the use of an assessor in order to ensure that the EC Articles 81 and 82 can be enforced effectively by the ordinary court as by the specialist CAT. However, the principle of non-discrimination cannot obviously apply to the free standing actions for damages of which only the ordinary court can be seized. Accordingly, the doctrine of effectiveness alone must be relied upon in order to ensure that that the court in certain circumstances uses its discretion pursuant to CPR 35.15 in order to appoint an assessor and thereby ensure the most effective enforcement possible of EC Articles 81 and 82.

C.	FRENCH CIVIL PROCEDURE: CATEGORIES OF CHANGES REQUIRED BY THE APPLICATION OF THE DOCTRINE OF EFFECTIVENESS

The analysis of the French system has not lead to establishing many categories of possible changes within the Code of Civil Procedure. In the first place, there are no rules in French civil procedure that seem to infringe the non-discrimination doctrine. Second, the situations in which French civil procedure might breach the doctrine of effectiveness are limited, and it is far from certain that the identified rules are actually in breach of the doctrine of effectiveness. There are several reasons for this. The first is that in situations where the French rules constitute a possible obstacle to effective private enforcement, fundamental principles often underlie the identified procedure rules. Second, whether irrespective of the concept of minimal or adequately effective enforcement, there are no situations in which the French procedural rules seem to render the enforcement of EC competition law exceedingly difficult or almost impossible.

Where rules constituting an obstacle to private enforcement are identified, the minimal enforcement standard, coupled with the principle(s) underlying the said rules, lead to the conclusion that there is not a direct breach of the doctrine of effectiveness, even though it may be observed that the French rules should nevertheless be amended in order to comply with the spirit of EC law, in particular of Regulation 1/2003, that is to favour private enforcement. It is submitted that an optimal enforcement standard does not lead to a different analysis. According to this standard, one is able in certain cases to effect a choice between what might be termed as competing procedures solutions with respect to enforcement of Articles 81 and 82 EC Treaty. We have not identified situations in which competing procedure rules might confront the judge with a choice in terms of effectiveness.

There are a few examples of procedure rules that render the enforcement of EC competition law difficult. First with respect to collective actions: representative actions and actions by associations for the protection of the collective interest they represent are available under French law but subject to very strict conditions. These rules are however justified in terms of the French fundamental principles under-lying civil procedure rules, i.e., the Constitutional Court ruled that courts may only settle disputes concerning individual litigations and that the right to action is a freedom of the person.[13] In any event, the restrictive conditions of French civil procedure as regards collective actions do not seem to render the enforcement of EC competition law almost impossible nor exceedingly difficult. However, in the light of the spirit of Regulation 1/2003, the French legislator should probably rethink the current procedure rules, and loosen the conditions for bringing collective actions.

Second, the rule according to which the decisions rendered by the Competition Council do not bind the French judge theoretically renders the enforcement of EC competition law more difficult in follow-actions, as the plaintiff will have the burden of proving a fault. The burden of proof under French law could therefore constitute a procedural obstacle to the effective enforcement of competition law. However, in practise, the courts usually give a decision rendered by the Competition Council an automatic effect on the existence of a fault. Moreover, a strong justification underlies this potential obstacle to private enforcement: under French Constitutional law and Article 6§ 1 of the European Convention on Human Rights, the courts have to rule in complete independence in disputes between individuals and corporations.

D. GERMAN CIVIL PROCEDURE: CATEGORIES OF CHANGES BY THE APPLICATION OF THE DOCTRINE OF EFFECTIVENESS

The reform of German competition law on 1 July 2005 (7th GWB-amendment) comprised a number of changes which facilitate the private enforcement of competition rules. As the analysis has shown, there seem to be no instances in which the doctrine of non-discrimination would require changes to the law. German and EC competition rules are treated equally. In terms of the doctrine of effectiveness, it was proposed in a number of instances that a more adequate interpretation of the law be applied or that changes with respect to the access to evidence be instituted. First, it would seem that the concept of the inadmissibility of 'exploratory

---

13. Constitutional Court (*'Conseil Constitutionnel'*), No. 257 DC, 25 July 1989, (1989) *Dr. Soc.*, p. 627.

evidence' needs to be interpreted in a sense that allows the taking of evidence on the basis of reasonable presumptions regarding an infringement or a specific market structure. Further, § 90a GWB requires an interpretation allowing for *ex officio* requests of civil courts to the Commission. Second, access to evidence which is not in the possession of the party bearing the onus of proof must be facilitated. Finally, the risk that sensitive data, business secrets in particular, be revealed, must be accepted in specific circumstances in order to promote the effectiveness of Community law and the constitutional guarantee of effectiveness of justice.

It is generally presumed that the principle of party presentation allows for evidence to be admissible only in instances in which the party bearing the onus of proof was able to submit in sufficient detail the facts to be proven by the evidence, lest the evidence be deemed 'exploratory' and, as such, inadmissible. This may serve to hinder claims based upon competition rules, as a party will regularly possess little to no knowledge both regarding the cartel agreements as well as the market structure. The analysis of case law has shown that the concept of inadmissible 'exploratory evidence' is handled in quite a flexible way by the judicature, with the Federal Court of Justice finding that a party 'may submit facts merely assumed and offer corresponding proof provided there are ample grounds for the correctness of its submissions. Such conduct is to be regarded as inadmissible exploratory evidence solely if it is arbitrary or constitutes an abuse of rights'.[14] Consequently, it is argued that in competition cases the doctrine of effectiveness requires the application of a lenient standard, if the party relying on an infringement of EU competition law manages to submit circumstantial facts which render the presumption of an infringement plausible. By the same token, it is submitted that § 90a(3) GWB, Art. 15(1) of Reg. (EC) 1/2003 are to be interpreted as taking precedence over the principle of party presentation, allowing a court to make *ex officio* requests asking the Commission to provide information and observations.

With respect to evidence in the sphere of the opposing party or third parties, it was set forth that both the procedural disclosure provisions under §§ 142, 144 ZPO and the sections on disclosure contained in the substantive law, mainly §§ 242, 259 BGB, are not entirely satisfactory as regards the ability of a party to prove anti-competitive behaviour. However, when examining the standard of proof, there are sufficient examples of case law in which the introduction of a 'secondary burden of submission' aids a party burdened with pleading and proving specific circumstances where it does not have any insight in the course of events. In these instances, if the opposing party possesses the required knowledge and may reasonably be expected to part with such details, the party who bears the onus of proof is only held to submit those facts which it reasonably presumes to be true and provide sufficient grounds for its assumption. The opposing party may then not simply deny the proposed facts, but must substantiate the denial with a pleading of the actual course of events and an offer of the requisite proof. It is argued that the

---

14.   BGH, NJW 2001, 2327, 2328; BGH, NJW 1996, 3147, 3150; BGH, NJW-RR 1987, 335.

main difficulty in applying the 'secondary burden of submission' to competition cases is the difficulty in protecting sensitive business data of the opposing party under German procedural rules in their interpretation of the German courts.

Consequently, there is a particular need to find a workable balance between one party's right to effectiveness of justice and the other party's interest in protecting its sensitive data. In this context, the refusal of the ordinary courts to allow for the intervention of a neutral, certified accountant (unless the disclosure obligation is based upon substantive law), limits the effectiveness of Community law. The same applies to the prevailing view that observations transmitted by the Commission and evidence of court-appointed experts cannot be utilized if the underlying facts are not revealed to the parties to the proceedings. The ECJ accepts that in assessing whether a procedural rule of a Member State renders excessively difficult the application of Community law, the basic principles of the domestic judicial system, such as the protection of the rights of the defence, the principle of legal certain and the proper conduct of the procedure must where appropriate be taken into consideration. However, it is submitted that the fundamental German principles do not stand in the way of a facilitated access of the court to information pertaining to business secrets. On the one hand, where such information relates to the opposing party, a party may chose to relinquish its right to be heard regarding specific information as long as such information is revealed at all – if only to a neutral person. On the other hand, the Federal Constitutional Court has rightly pointed out that one party's right to effectiveness of justice may limit the other party's right to a fair hearing:

> The court's duty to sufficiently examine the factual basis of an expert opinion with the co-operation of the parties is anchored in the right to a fair hearing and the principle of a constitutional state. However, this obligation may be restricted by virtue of the rights of third parties. In the interest of the party bearing the onus of proof, the court may thus require less facts to be revealed in case the reasons given by the expert carry sufficient weight. This may particularly be the case if data regarding matters of immediate privacy pertaining to third parties not involved in the dispute are concerned.[15]

Thus, it would seem that – contrary to the prevailing view – a German court may indeed guarantee the Commission the confidentiality of particular information transmitted under Art. 15(1) Reg. (EC) 1/2003, § 90a(3) GWB, deciding on a case-by-case basis which of the confidential information it may base its decision upon, even if the parties did not obtain access to such evidence.

German procedural rules do not provide for in camera proceedings and grant witnesses a relatively broad privilege which allows them to refuse answering questions if the witness was held to reveal business secrets in the process. While it is conceded that the law may insofar limit the effectiveness of Community competition rules, it is suggested that these rules do not render the application of Community law impossible or excessively difficult, provided that the changes to

---

15. BVerfG, NJW 1995, 40, 41 *et seq.*

the access to evidence proposed above are accepted. Furthermore, both of the said limitations serve fundamental principles of German procedural law, namely the right to a fair hearing and the principle of a constitutional state. Thus, in conclusion, while it may seem desirable to hold in camera proceedings in some instances and limit witnesses' privileges in others, such a fundamental change to the general procedural rules of a Member State is uncalled for by the doctrine of effectiveness pertaining to EC Competition law.

Bibliography

Ahrens, H.J. (ed.), *Der Wettbewerbsprozess* (5th edn, Carl Heymanns, Köln, 2005).

Ashurst, *A Study on the Conditions of Claims for Damages in Cases of Infringement of EC Competition for the Competition DG.*

Ashurst, Waelbroeck, D., Slater, D. and Even-Shoshan, G., *Comparative Report* (31 August 2004).

Ashurst, Clough, Q.C.M. and McDougall A., *UK – Executive Report and National Report* (2004).

Ashurst, Momège, C. and Bessot, N., *France – Comparative Report* (2004).

Ashurst, Wach, K., Epping, M., Zinsmeister, U. and Bonacker, E. *Germany – Executive Report and National Report* (2004), <ec.europa.eu/comm/competition/antitrust/ others/actions_for_damages/study.html>, 1 October 2006.

Aubert, J.L., *Introduction au droit, Armand Colin*, (9th edn, Dalloz, Paris, 2005).

Baumbach, A., Lauterbach, W., Albers, J. and Hartmann, P., *Zivilprozessordnung* (64th edn, C.H. Beck, München, 2006).

Bechtold, R., Brinker, I., Bosch, W. and Hirsbrunner, S., *EG-Kartellrecht* (C.H.Beck, München, 2005).

Bechtold, R. and Kartellgesetz, G.W.B., *Gesetz gegen Wettbewerbsbeschränkungen* (3rd edn, C.H. Beck, München, 2002).

Behrens, P., Braun, E. and Nowak, C. (eds), *Europäisches Wettbewerbsrecht im Umbruch* (Nomos, Baden-Baden, 2004).

Bellamy and Child, *European Community Law of Competition* (ed. Roth, 5th edn, Sweet & Maxwell, London, 2000).

Bout, R., *et al., Lamy Droit Economique* (Lamy, Paris, 2006).

Brook, H. Sir (ed.), *The White Book Service 2006* (Sweet & Maxwell, London, 2006).

Bundeskartellamt, *Private Kartellrechtsdurchsetzung: Stand, Probleme, Perspektiven* (2005), <www.bundeskartellamt.de>.

Canivet, G. (ed.), *La modernisation du droit de la concurrence* (L.G.D.J., Paris, 2006).

European Commission, *Green Paper: Damages Actions for Breach of EC Anti-Trust Rules, COM* (2005) 672 Final, <eur-lex.europe.eu>, 1 October 2006.

European Commission, *Commisison Staff Working Paper: Annex to the Green Paper, Damages Actions for Breach of EC Anti-Trust Rule, SEC* (2005) 1732, <eur-lex. europe.eu>, 1 October 2006.

European Commission Communication, *Professional Services: Scope for More Reform, COM* (2005) 405 Final, <eur-lex.europe.eu>, 1 October 2006.

European Commission, *Stocktaking Exercise on Regulation of Professional Services, COMP/D3/MK/D* (2004).

Faull, J. and Nikpay A., *The EC Law of Competition* (Oxford University Press, Oxford, 1999).

Fezer, K.H. (ed.), *Lauterkeitsrecht: Kommentar zum Gesetz gegen den unlauteren Wettbewerb (UWG)* (C.H. Beck, München, 2005).

Furse, M., *Competition Law of the UK and EC* (4th edn, Oxford University Press, Oxford, 2003).

Guinchard, S., *et al.*, *Droit et pratique de la procédure civile* (5th edn, Dalloz, Paris, 2006).

Hempel, R., *Privater Rechtsschutz im Kartellrecht* (Nomos, Baden-Baden, 2002).

Hefermehl, W., Köhler, H. and Bornkamm, J. (eds), *Wettbewerbsrecht* (24th edn, C.H. Beck, München, 2006).

Hommerich, C., Prütting, H., *et al.*, *Rechtstatsächliche Untersuchung zu den Auswirkungen der Reform des Zivilprozessrechts auf die gerichtliche Praxis* – Evaluation ZPO-Reform, <www.bmj.bund.de/media/archive/1216.pdf>, 1 October 2006.

Immenga, U. and Mestmäcker, E.J. (eds), *GWB: Gesetz gegen Wettbewerbsbeschränkungen* (3rd edn, C.H. Beck, München, 2001).

Institut für Höhere Studien (IHS), Paterson, I., Fink, M. and Ogus, A. (eds), *Economic Impact of Regulation in the Field of the Liberal Professions in Different Member States: Study for the European Commission, DG Competition* (Vienna, 2003), <www.ec.europa.eu/comm/competition/liberalization/conference/prof_services_ihs_part_1.pdf>, 1 October 2006.

Jolowicz, A., *On Civil Litigation* (Cambridge University Press, Cambridge, 2000).

Keane, A., *The Modern Law of Evidence* (5th edn, Butterworths, London, 2000).

Klees, A., *Europäisches Kartellverfahrensrecht mit Fusionskontrollverfahren* (Carl Heymanns, Köln, 2005).

Korah, V., *An Introductory Guide to EC Competition Law and Practise* (8th edn, Hart Publishing, Oxford, 2003).

Lampert, T., Niejahr, N., Kübler, J. and Weidenbach, G., *EG-KartellVO: Praxiskommentar zur Verordnung (EG) Nr. 1/2003* (Recht und Wirtschaft, Heidelberg, 2004).

Langen, E. and Bunte, H.J. (eds), *Kommentar zum deutschen und europäischen Kartellrecht, vol. 1: Deutsches Kartellrecht, vol. 2: Europäisches Kartellrecht* (10th edn, Luchterhand, Neuwied, 2006).

Lonbay, J. and Biondi, A, *Remedies for Breach of EC Law* (Wiley, London, 1997).

Mangoldt, H. and Klein, F. (eds), *Kommentar zum Grundgesetz* (5th edn, Franz Vahlen, München).

Mail-Fouilleul, S., *Les sanctions de la violation du droit communautaire de la concurrence* (L.G.D.J., Paris, 2002).

Martin, R., *Déontologie de l'avocat* (7th edn, Litec-LexisNexis, Paris, 2002).

Mousseron, J.M. and Selinsky, V., *Le nouveau droit de la concurrence* (Litec, Paris, 1987).

Musielack, H.J. (ed.), *Kommentar zur Zivilprozessordnung* (4th ed, Franz Vahlen, München, 2005).

Prechal, S., *Directives in EC Law* (2nd edn, Oxford University Press, Oxford, 2005).

Ritter, L., Braun, W.D. and Rawlinson, F., *European Competition Law: A Practioner's Guide* (2nd edn, Kluwer Law International, The Hague, 2000).

Rodger, B.J. and MacCulloch, A., *Cases and Materials on UK and EC Competition Law* (2nd edn, Cavendish Publishing Ltd, London, 2001).

Robert, P. and Zuckerman, A.A.S., *Criminal Evidence* (Oxford University Press, Oxford, 2004).

Rose, R., Sime, S. and French, D., *Blackstone's Civil Practise* (Oxford University Press, Oxford, 2006).

Rosenberg, L., Schwab, K. H. and Gottwald, P., *Zivilprozessrecht* (16th ed, C.H. Beck, München, 2004).

Schöler, F., *Die Reform des Europäischen Kartellverfahrensrechts durch die Verordnung (EG) Nr. 1/2003* (Peter Lang, Frankfurt, 2004).

Schwarze, J. and Weitbrecht, A., *Grundzüge des europäischen Kartellverfahrensrechts: Die Verordnung (EG) Nr. 1/2003* (Nomos, Baden-Baden, 2004).

Scott, I.R., *International Perspectives in Civil Justice* (Sweet & Maxwell, London, 1990).

Sime, S., *A Practical Approach to Civil Procedure* (Oxford University Press, Oxford, 2006).

Tapper, C., *Tapper & Cross on Evidence* (7th edn, Blackstone Press, London, 2000).

Terré, F., Simler, P. and Lequette, Y., *Les obligations* (9th edn, Dalloz, Paris, 2005).

Vincent, J. and Guinchard, S., *Procédure Civile* (27th edn, Dalloz, Paris, 2003).

Walter, W., *Der Anspruch auf rechtliches Gehör* (2nd ed, Schmidt, Köln, 2000).

Ward, T. and Smith, K., *Competition Law in the UK* (Thomson – Sweet & Maxwell, 2005).

Wiedemann, G. (ed.), *Handbuch des Kartellrechts* (C.H. Beck, München, 1999).

Wils, W., *The Optimal Enforcement of EC Antitrust Law: A study in Law and Economics* (Kluwer Law International, The Hague, 2002).

Whish, R., *Competition Law* (5th edn, Lexis Nexis, London, 2005).

Zuber, A., *Die EG-Kommission als amicus curiae* (Carl Heymanns, Köln, 2001).

Zöller (ed.), *Zivilprozessordnung*, (25th edn, Otto Schmidt, Köln, 2005).

Zuckerman, A.A.S., *Civil Procedure* (Lexis Nexis, London, 2003).

Zuckerman, A.A.S., *Principles of Criminal Evidence* (Oxford University Press, Oxford, 1989).

SELECTED WEBSITES:

Adam Smith Institute <www.adamsmith.org>, 1 October 2006.

Bundeskartellamt <www.bundeskartellamt.de>, 1 October 2006.

Civil Justice Council <www.civiljusticecouncil.gov.uk>, 1 October 2006.

Competition Appeal Tribunal <www.cattribunal.gov.uk>, 1 October 2006.

Competition Council <www.conseil-concurrence.fr>, 1 October 2006.

Court Services – High Court and Court of Appeal Judgments – England <www.courtservice.gov.uk>, 1 October 2006.

David Hume Institute <www.davidhumeinstitute.org>, 1 October 2006.

Department of Constitutional Affairs <www.dca.gov.uk>, 1 October 2006.

Electronic Journal of Comparative Law <www.ejcl.com>, 1 October 2006.

European Commission <www.eu.int>, 1 October 2006.

European Court of Justice <www.curia.europa.eu>, 1 October 2006.

Federal Court of Justice <www.bundesgerichtshof.de>, 1 October 2006.

Legifrance–Service Public pour la Diffusion du Droit <www.legifrance.gouv.fr>, 1 October
    2006.
Ludwig von Mises Institute <www.mises.org>, 1 October 2006.
Monopolkommission <monopolkommission.de>, 1 October 2006.
Parliamentary Publications (Germany) <drucksachen.bundestag.de>, 1 October 2006.
Parliamentary Publications–House of Lords Judgments <www.publications.parliament.uk>,
    1 October 2006. <www.publications.parliament.uk/pa/ld/ldjudgmt.htm>, 1 October 2006.
Rand Corporation <www.rand.org>, 1 October 2006.

Index

295

INTERNATIONAL COMPETITION LAW SERIES

15. Tzong-Leh Hwang and Chiyuan Chen (Eds.), *The Future Development of Competition Framework* (2004)
    (ISBN 90-411-2305-9)
16. Phedon Nicolaides, Mihalis Kekelekis and Philip Buyskes, *State Aid Policy in the European Community, A Guide for Practitioners.* Second Edition (2005)
    (ISBN 90-411-2394-6)
17. Doris Hildebrand, *Economic Analyses of Vertical Agreements–A Self-Assessment* (2005)
    (ISBN 90-411-2328-8)
18. Frauke Henning-Bodewig, *Unfair Competition Law–European Union and Member States* (2005)
    (ISBN 90-411-2329-6)
19. Duarte Brito and Margarida Catalão-Lopes, *Mergers and Acquisitions: The Industrial Organization Perspective* (2006)
    (ISBN 90-411-2451-9)
20. Nikos Th. Nikolinakos, *EU Competition Law and Regulation in the Converging Telecommunication, Media and IT Sectors* (2006)
    (ISBN 90-411-2469-1)
21. Mihalis Kekelekis, *The EC Merger Control Regulation: Rights of Defence. A Critical Analysis of DG COMP Practice and Community Courts' Jurisprudence* (2006)
    (ISBN 90-411-2553-1)
22. Mark R. Joelson, *An International Antitrust Primer: A Guide to the Operation of United States, European Union and Other Key Competition Laws in the Global Economy,* 3rd edition (2006)
    (ISBN 90-411-2468-3)
23. Themistoklis K. Giannakopoulos, *A Concise Guide to the EU Anti-dumping/Anti-subsidies Procedures* (2006)
    (ISBN 90-411-2464-0)
24. George Cumming, Brad Spitz and Ruth Janal, *Civil Procedure Used for Enforcement of EC Competition Law by the English, French and German Civil Courts* (2007)
    (ISBN 978-90-411-2471-5)